BARBARIANS AND ROMANS

BARBARIANS AND ROMANS

The Birth Struggle of Europe, A.D. 400-700

BY

JUSTINE DAVIS RANDERS-PEHRSON

Photographs by the Author

University of Oklahoma Press : Norman and London

By Justine Davis Randers-Pehrson

The Surgeon's Glove (Springfield, Ill., 1960)
Barbarians and Romans: The Birth Struggle of Europe, A.D. 400–700 (Norman, 1983)

This book has been published with the aid of a grant from the Andrew W. Mellon Foundation.

Library of Congress Cataloging-in-Publication Data

Randers-Pehrson, Justine Davis, 1910–
    Barbarians and Romans.

    Bibliography: p. 363
    Includes index.
    1. Rome—History—Germanic Invasions, 3d–6th
centuries.   2. Europe—History—392–814.   I. Title.
DG319.R36   1983   940.1'2   82–20025
ISBN: 0–8061–2511–X (paper)

3   4   5   6   7   8   9   10

FOR MY GRANDCHILDREN

Catherine Boyer Smith
Tamara Pehrson Smith
Michael Nils Randers-Pehrson
Justine Davis Randers-Pehrson
Timothy Ralph Randers-Pehrson
Laura Mabel Randers-Pehrson
Emily Elizabeth Randers-Pehrson
Christopher Brady Randers-Pehrson

CONTENTS

ILLUSTRATIONS

MAPS

PREFACE

IF I had never looked into the blank eyes of a small rodent in a carved vine that graces a panel in the little museum of Jedburgh Abbey, in Scotland, this book would have remained unwritten.

There is a profusion of "inhabited scrolls" all around the Mediterranean, their graceful leafy tendrils lively with curious animals, but it seemed incongruous to me to find this small creature and his vine in surroundings that are associated with the ascetic "Celtic" monks from Iona. The panel is thought to have decorated the tomb or shrine of one of the most modest and unassuming of men, Prior Boisil, of the monastery of Old Melrose, in southern Scotland.[1] Surely his companions would have found a simple "pillow stone" more fitting.

Not long before the death of Boisil there was a great confrontation at Whitby (in A.D. 663 or 664), during which a pro-Roman party managed to expel the missionary Celtic monks who were followers of Columba of Iona. No doubt the handsome piece of sculpture reflects the change brought about by that event.

As I contemplated the vine, I thought of the first art critics who examined it: possibly a few of the remaining Celtic monks, some descendants of Romans who once manned Hadrian's Wall, Picts, Christianized Anglo-Saxons, perhaps even a Saxon king, or the Venerable Bede, and surely priests and prelates of the new era, comparing it sagely with wonders that they themselves had seen in the Eternal City.

After my first visit to Jedburgh, I set about the task of finding out what the world was like when rude barbarians and Roman citizens were struggling to mesh their cultures and their lives.

My naïve belief that a few weeks in a scholarly library and perhaps a trip or so abroad would yield the information I wanted proved to be unfounded. As time went by, the problem became more and more enthralling and complex. I began to toy with the idea of writing a little monograph, illustrated with

Plate 1. Inhabited scroll, seventh century, Jedburgh Abbey, Jedburgh, Scotland. A garland inhabited by animals, human figures, and so on, is a Mediterranean motif. This panel is thought to have been part of the sarcophagus or shrine of Prior Boisil, a monk of the early Iona establishment at Old Melrose. *Courtesy of Scottish Development Department.*

photographs taken in the course of my investigations. In the event, twenty trips abroad were needed. Means of locomotion as diverse as helicopters, fishing boats, fellucas, and donkeys took me to out-of-the way places in twenty-two countries, in an area bounded roughly by Shetland in the north, the little island of Skellig Michael in the Atlantic on the west, Nubia in the south, and the steppes of central Asia in the east. My own two feet carried me through no less than ninety museums in search of material.

My photographs show things that people built, used, admired, worshiped, wore, treasured, feared, or loved in those centuries long ago. I feel that they may have more immediacy than the conventional "primary sources," documents from the weighty pens of bishops or members of an emperor's entourage, enlightening though such documents often are.

Many persons have had a hand in this project. All deserve my warmest thanks. Two died before the work was completed. Jessie Bigelow Martin had implicit faith that the book could be written, long before I myself had arrived at such a conclusion. It was for her sake that I began to write. My dear companion John Stacy Colman shared many a strenuous journey in the British Isles: he slogged through soggy cow pastures, stumbled across trackless heather and bracken, and climbed brochs and cliffs with me, all with unflagging determination and enthusiasm.

My friend Margaret Hackforth-Jones (M. S. Drower, M.B.E., F.S.A.) volunteered to walk out onto the desert near Aswān with me to visit the Coptic monastery there. Her command of Arabic opened doors that might otherwise have been closed to me, and I am glad to record my recognition of her gracious assistance.

I am grateful to A. M. Cubbon, O.B.E., Director of the Manx Museum, for his sustained interest in my investigations. His detailed answers to my hesitant questions were packed with information. He was also kind enough to read a chapter of my manuscript and to comment on it.

Thanks are due to Cyril Aldred, B.A., F.R.S.E., formerly of the National Museum of Antiquities of Scotland, who took time in the midst of preparations for a trip to Egypt to respond carefully to a query of mine, and who helped me in various other ways.

J. Close-Brooks and R. B. K. Stevenson, of the National Museum of Antiquities of Scotland, offered thoughtful comments on a Pictish carving in the collection at Saint Vigeans.

W. O'Sullivan, Keeper of Manuscripts in the Library of Trinity College, Dublin, provided useful bibliographical references relating to monastic book satchels.

Charles Thomas, Director of the Institute of Cornish Studies, in replying to a query about holy wells, kindly supplied a pamphlet on the primitive baptistery at Madron, in Cornwall.

Pauline Beswick, Keeper of Antiquities in the city of Sheffield, sent valuable information about *têtes coupées* in Britain.

G. Lloyd Morgan, of the Grosvenor Museum, Chester, generously gave me her time in a personally conducted tour of the museum collection and offered a splendid little discourse on Celtic and Roman hand mirrors.

Priscilla Smith, Head Librarian in the Freer Gallery of Art, Washington, D.C., was more than generous with her time in assembling material referring to Sarmatian mirrors.

I want to thank my friends Philip and Hermia Lambie for their willingness to translate epigraphic material from the Roman Forum. Other willing translators were William A. Grimes, who efficiently helped me with Russian correspondence; and Dimiter Daphinoff, of the University of Fribourg, and my son-in-law Ronald Baker Smith, of Yale University, who also translated Russian material. As meteorologist, Ron assisted me by providing information about the mountain wind called the bora that figured in the Battle of the Frigidus.

My dear friend Sigmund Skard, Professor Emeritus of the University of Oslo, allowed me to impose on his good nature. He resolved the problem presented by an incomplete Swedish citation and also read two chapters of this book in typescript, to offer an opinion on the general readability of the work.

Francis Howard Coffin, of the Smithsonian Institution, Washington, D.C., was kind enough to lend me his study notes on the Celtic goddess Epona and on Jupiter columns of the Rhineland.

Many institutions offered invaluable assistance. In particular I want to mention the Victoria and Albert Museum, London, where I was allowed to handle and photograph electrotypes of Scythian gold, and the British Museum, where Vandal coins were brought out for examination. At the Textile Museum, in Washington, D.C., I was given the opportunity to look at Coptic roundels at close range.

I must also mention the British Library, Yale University Library, the library of the Virginia Theological Seminary, the library of the Catholic University of America, and the library of Dumbarton Oaks. My debt to the Library of Congress is enormous.

The meticulous efforts of the technicians of Image, in Washington, D.C., who worked up many of my photographs, is deeply appreciated.

Patricia J. Cunnington, of Crystal World Travel Service, Arlington, Virginia, made my journeys smooth by her efficient management of my curious itineraries.

My old friend Dorothy R. Jones (Mrs. Ernest van B. Jones) deserves special thanks for careful reading of a major part of the draft and for sharp attack on ungainly stylistic mannerisms.

I am much indebted to my friend Hollis W. Piatt, who contributed more than she realizes. Her frank comment relating to an introductory chapter forced me to rethink the organization of the entire book.

My daughter-in-law Nancy Little Randers-Pehrson and my sons, Glenn and Gerhard Randers-Pehrson, read various chapters while the work was in progress. They criticized photographs and generally encouraged me with their steady interest. Gerhard, who happened to be living with me while I was working on the Narbonne chapter, bore up manfully under a four-month barrage of hypotheses about Emperor Constantius. My daughter Sigrid Randers-Pehrson Smith deserves an affectionate hug for her patience in preparation of sketch maps for this book. Any inaccuracies in those maps are mine, not hers. Madeleine Holt Sharp's kind assistance in the preparation of the index is gratefully acknowledged.

JUSTINE DAVIS RANDERS-PEHRSON

Reston, Virginia

BARBARIANS AND ROMANS

Plate 2. Barbarian captive, detail of the Roman arch at Carpentras, Vaucluse, France. The fur-clad, chained barbarian stands beside a Roman trophy hung with sheathed swords and topped by a cuirass and an open quiver of javelins.

TRIER

THE period that we are going to examine runs roughly from the early fifth century through the late seventh century A.D., a time of turbulence but hardly one of decline and fall. It was essentially a time of adjustments and beginnings.

History is a slippery material at best. It deals with processes, and processes are alive, defying static analysis. If we chop up the living continuum and pin things down by reciting dates, tracing lines on maps, and inventing names for various "ages," we squeeze out the vital juice.

Here we are, poised on the brink of the fifth century. The Roman Empire is foundering: barbarians are pouring in. Right away we have a problem, because "barbarian" is a rigid term that encourages oversimplification. In spite of ourselves we conjure up pictures of fur-clad monsters with dripping blades, straight out of a low-budget horror film. These creatures burst into the noble cities of Gaul and Italy and Africa, brutishly burning libraries and trampling or carrying off anything that might remotely be thought of as a product of civilization and, of course, raping every woman in sight. The Roman people cower in the rubble while vultures glide overhead.

Writers like Salvian of Marseilles may have made the oversimplification inevitable. Salvian wrote his great treatise, *De gubernatione Dei*, around the year 450, when the memory would still have been fresh. His eyewitness account must therefore have a considerable core of truth. In his lifetime the city of Trier (Trèves), on the Moselle, which may have been his boyhood home, suffered a Vandal sack that sent people running for their lives to the protection of the thick walls of the amphitheater. Then there seem to have been three Frankish invasions between the years 411 and 439. Who has read Salvian's description of packs of dogs lacerating naked corpses in the streets and not kept it vividly in his own store of memories as a kind of set piece that typifies the end of the Roman world? Even today the impressionable tourist stares up at the great pile

3

of Trier's formidable "Black Gate" (Porta Nigra) seeing it as a suitable roost for carrion birds.

We ought to consider what actually went on in the city of Trier, in order to form some notion of the kinds of yeasty influences at work there before the actual calamity. Trier, "Rome of the West," became important very early because European geography is such that an enemy on the Rhine could pose a threat to the city of Rome. If an invader were to gain control of the Rhone Valley, there would be little to bar his progress into Italy. In the time-honored Roman program of aggression and conquest the guiding principle seems always to have been to take territory for defensive purposes. Overpopulation was never a problem, but defense was always a serious one, for the people on the far side of the Rhine and the Danube were land-hungry. Because of the need to protect Rome, for generations varied throngs had been passing in and out of Trier's huge black fortress gate. The fourth-century city was indeed a cosmopolitan place, teeming with life and energy. It was in fact just about as complex as any of the great urban centers of the Mediterranean.

By the fourth century Trier was already old according to our standards, though there is not much evidence to indicate that this place, so auspiciously sited on the Moselle, was ever a tribal capital or even a major Roman fort.[1] Its importance stemmed from its good backup position with respect to the Rhenish garrisons and its relationship to the empire as a whole.

The Moselle flows into the Rhine, and on the south its course passes close to the heart of Gaul. By the time of Emperor Claudius (41–54) military highways converged at Augusta Treverorum (as Trier was then called), including one that came up from Lyons and thus linked the north with the Mediterranean by way of the Rhone. It was possible to travel to Aquileia, at the head of the Adriatic, by skirting north of modern Switzerland and to reach the difficult transalpine passes used by emissaries shuttling to and from Milan. The road system also offered direct access to Britain by way of Boulogne.

In the fourth century the defense of Gaul was one of Rome's major concerns, but we must remember that in the time of Julius Caesar it was the Gauls who were the barbarians. The city of Trier was subsequently set down in Gallic territory, on land that belonged to the Treveri tribe, for the control of unruly Gauls as well as for defense against would-be Germanic invaders.

Galli, the Romans said. The peoples of Gaul referred to themselves as Keltoi. Gauls or Celts, it was this population that gradually became Romanized. It was they, as Gallo-Romans, who eventually had to withstand and cope with and adjust to the onslaught of the Germanic tribes and the Huns.

There seems to be little question that the core of the city of Trier was Celtic. There was some blurring in the minds of the Treveri themselves on this point. They rather thought that they might be German. They had a dim tribal memory of a past when the homeland had been on the right bank of the Rhine

Plate 3. Roman cavalrymen, ca. A.D. 60–70, found in the vicinity of Arlon, Belgium. The carving is probably a fragment of a corner pilaster, done in a transitional style that indicates a period after that of Emperor Claudius. *Courtesy of Musée luxembourgeois, Arlon, Belgium.*

instead of on the Moselle, but that would have been about four centuries before Caesar. The Rhine was never a true cultural frontier as Caesar thought of it; as Tacitus observed, "There was only a river between—a trifling obstacle." Celtic weapons and metalwork penetrated far into the north, and place-names indicate that the situation along the Rhine may have been in flux for some time. The Treveri leaders had Celtic names, in any case. Even as late as the fourth century Jerome commented that the language he heard in the streets of Trier was much like that of the biblical Galatians, a Celtic folk who had settled in Asia Minor after long wanderings. Although the allegiance of the Treveri to Rome admittedly had its ups and downs, it was more binding than any feeling of kinship with putative Teutonic cousins across the Rhine.

When Julius Caesar arrived in Gaul, the Celts were firmly installed there, having strayed in from the upper Danube region during the sixth century B.C. Caesar found them organized in distinct tribal territories with recognized tribal seats. He was able to describe a class structure and a system of government, and he thought that there was a correlation between Celtic and Roman gods. The web of Celtic civilization stretched from the Rhineland across most

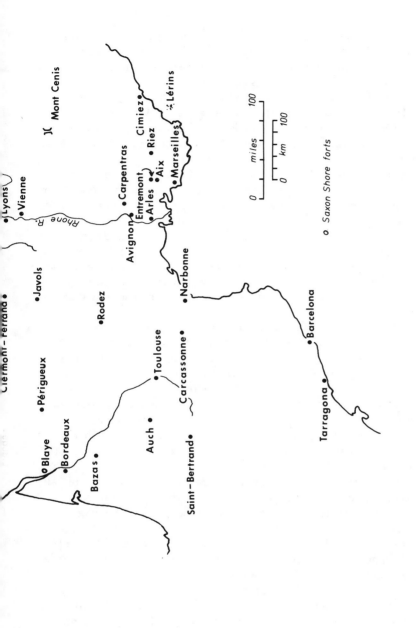

Gaul

of Gaul, over the Alps into northern Italy, and beyond the Channel into Britain. The term "La Tène culture" (which designates the culture of Continental Celts during the Iron Age in Europe) has an archaic sound, but it persisted in diluted form up to the time of Caesar's conquest.

We must not be misled by the absence of written documents or architectural splendors, nor must we let the Roman architect Vitruvius's remarks about simple Gaulish huts with roofs "made of earth mixed with straw" generate notions of a raw, primitive existence. A Celtic chieftain might preside in glory beneath such a roof.

The Celts were far from simple. Although the late La Tène Celts were still living more or less in the heroic age, they were keenly aware of the workings of the Roman system; indeed, in many ways they were ready to become a part of it. According to Caesar, the Gauls were "a most ingenious race, wonderful imitators, and very good at making practical use of ideas suggested to them by others," but that is not the whole story by any means. A peculiar intensity pervaded these people, who could be rash, impetuous, and innovative. They had enough self-assurance to be able to perform well in situations entirely new to them. Tacitus would have rejected this proposition; he thought that the Gauls were cowards.

Well, then, let us think of their heartbreaking struggle for freedom under Vercingetorix in 52 B.C. A cavalry charge may have come naturally to these horsemen from the hill forts, but they were embarking on something that in no way resembled the kind of guerrilla attacks that they knew how to manage. They were confronting the legions, on the legions' own terms. That would require steady, concerted action against the best-disciplined troops the world has ever known. As the war progressed, the Gauls met disheartening failures, especially at Bourges, where they handled a siege badly. Even in that crisis Vercingetorix was able to convince them that lack of experience had caused the disaster and win a vote of confidence.

We see the Gauls at close hand under severest stress during this bloody conflict, and at the same time we gain insights into their close-knit organization. Traditionally they elected a supreme commander only in time of crisis. The present chieftain, Vercingetorix, had a war council of elected tribal commanders. The council deliberated and made drastic decisions, for example, that all settlements and granaries along the Roman line of march should be burned. The council also received from Vercingetorix detailed instructions about when and where specific kinds of troops (cavalry, archers) were to assemble. Each tribe had its quota, and the numbers could be large. For the final battle Vercingetorix summoned to Alesia a total of 271,000 fighting men.

The Gauls had an efficient communications network. Caesar says that an event occurring in the morning would be known 150 miles away by nightfall. There were no riding couriers as we might imagine; news was shouted across the countryside.

In combat the Gauls showed extraordinary initiative and toughness, though in the end they were no match for the complex engineering of the Romans. Caesar says that they were not accustomed to working very hard, but they belied that statement by showing enormous strength and persistence, countermining tunnels, pulling down siege engines, setting fires in the night.

They could face the consequences of their actions without flinching. Caesar himself was impressed to see a succession of unhesitating warriors step up to an exposed position where a predecessor had fallen, where death was inevitable, and cast incendiary materials down upon the siege works. Vercingetorix was of the same mettle. When the final failure was upon him, this man submitted himself to the will of his people and went uncomplainingly forth to be Caesar's degraded captive for years and ultimately to be strangled at the conclusion of a Roman triumph.

All of this sounds so harsh that we wonder what kind of unrelenting gods such a people may have worshiped. That turns out to be a hard question. It seems safe to say in general that Caesar's confident assumption that the Gallic gods were the equivalents of Dis Pater, Mercury, Mars, Jupiter, and Minerva was not accurate. The Celtic gods remain largely enigmas.

In pre-Roman times many Celtic deities were clustered around springs and wells and river sources. Votive figures and human skulls were deposited at certain hallowed spots, such as the source of the Seine. War booty and treasure were also cast into bogs and lakes. Worship associated with water survived into the Christian Era. Gregory of Tours complained that people went in a body on certain days to the shore of a nearby lake, where they threw in pieces of flax and cloth or tufts of wool. [2] Even today, in Celt-tinged lands like Armenia, in the Soviet Union, there are vestiges of such practices: by ancient custom strips of cloth (in Cornwall they are called "clooties") are tied on bushes overhanging holy wells or springs (see plate 4). [3]

It is not at all clear that the Celts had distinct mental pictures of their gods. Possibly only priestly initiates looked at whatever images they had. Martin of Tours once mistakenly assumed that people in a funeral procession were carrying an idol because in his day "it was the custom of the Gallic rustics to carry round their fields the images of demons covered with white veils." [4]

Stone sculpture was not part of the La Tène tradition, though a few impressive pieces dating to the Hallstatt era (ca. 1500 B.C.) have come to light at sites known to have been Celtic. The "Hirschlanden man" from Württemberg (now in the Württembergisches Landesmuseum, Stuttgart) is a naked warrior with a torque around his neck, a bladed weapon at his waist, and a strange little round hat on his head. His bony-shouldered arm crosses his chest, and he stares at us with pinhole eyes. He may be mortal, but his size is certainly that of a superhuman being.

The meaning of other sculptured or cast figures has been hotly debated. We only need consider the conflicting opinions about the four heads of the

Plate 4. Strips of cloth as pilgrims' offerings. Above: In Armenian Soviet Socialist Republic. The scene was photographed not far from biblical Galatia, where Celts settled about 280 B.C. The people in the background brought a sheep to the local church for blessing. After that ceremony the sheep was slaughtered, and a picnic was prepared in the grounds adjoining the church. Right: Strips of cloth Madron holy well, Cornwall. The tearing of strips of cloth from one's own clothing is a survival of ancient Celtic practice. Here the "clooties" are tied to a bush above a well. Wells and springs were holy in Celtic lands.

Plate 5. Cernunnos, horned god of the Celts, one of the carved faces of an altar or pedestal found in the crypt beneath the choir of the Cathedral of Notre Dame, in Paris. The altar was dedicated in the time of Emperor Tiberius (A.D. 14–37) by the College of Nautae Parisiaci, an association of merchants and shipowners who moved their goods on the river (as opposed to Navicularii, who were overseas shippers). A pair of torques (metal collars characteristic of the Celts) is hung on the god's stag antlers. *Courtesy of Musée national des thermes et de l'Hôtel de Cluny, Paris.*

famous Saint Goar pillar (from Pfalzfeld, on the Rhine not far from Wiesbaden, ca. 300 B.C.) to understand just how slippery the footing is for anyone who wants to extract a cult significance accurately. These heads are ornamented with what writers variously describe as leaf crowns, swelling horns, drops, fish bladders, and even the headdress of the Egyptian goddess Hathor.[5] The noble helmeted heads on the Aylesford bucket in the British Museum seem to be wearing plumes. It is possible that the Saint Goar heads are also plumed. Again, what are we to make of a staring anthropomorphic statue with a torque around the neck and a highly realistic boar carved on the torso?

Another deity associated with animals appears frequently. He is Cernunnos, the horned one, the "most haunting figure of the Celtic pantheon" (see plate 5).[6] As he appears on the mysterious Gundestrup cauldron (which was found far off in Denmark, now in the Nationalmuseet, Copenhagen), he sits in a Buddhalike crouch, with a torque around his neck and another in his hand. His familiars are a ram-headed serpent and a rat.

The most distinctive and durable of all were the fertility goddesses known as the *matres* (see plate 6). The Celts were fond of triads: these women characteristically appear as triplets. Each has a puffed coiffure as though some patient hairdresser had worked on it for hours teasing it. In spite of this attention to personal appearance, they are unmistakably earthy little beings, because they frequently appear holding swaddled twin infants to their breasts.

Formal shrines were of the simplest sort, but they have been found in so many places that we are obliged to abandon the conventional notion that ritual was performed exclusively in sacred groves. There are similar squarish enclosures in the form of irregular earthworks ("Viereckschanzen"), each with a single entrance in such disparate places as Orne, in France; Holzhausen, in Bavaria; and Norfolk, in England.[7] Occasionally it has been found that there was once within the enclosure a tall post or an offering shaft for deposition of flesh-and-blood sacrifices.

We know about the sacred groves. Far off in Asia Minor the Galatians had a meeting place that they called Drunemeton (*nemeton* is the Celtic word for "grove"). It is too bad that we must lean on florid Lucan for the description of such a place (a modern translator uncharitably dubs him "the father of yellow journalism").[8] Every single tree in the grove was sprinkled with human blood, reported Lucan. "Sometimes serpents coiled around the oaks, which blazed with fire but did not burn." It was such a fearsome wood that Caesar was brash enough to destroy because he grew short of timber while laying siege to Marseilles.

The Romans made a point of being horrified by human sacrifice, relating with relish that the druids' victims were burned alive in huge wicker cages. They overlooked or forgot that they themselves had sacrificed human beings not so very long before, following the defeat at Cannae in 216 B.C., when the Sibylline Books were consulted, and it was revealed that there must be a ritual murder in the Forum. Perhaps the Celts similarly reserved the rite for situations of direst stress.

Our imaginations have always been teased by the idea of druids. The most sensible assessment of their role seems to be Nora Chadwick's. She concludes that they were not priests at all; there is no known connection between the druids and the Celtic gods and the sanctuaries, she says. They were already well past the crest of their power by the time the Romans conquered Gaul. Chadwick suggests that their vaunted learning was a diluted, rather barbarized version of Hellenic culture that spread up the Rhone at an early date from the ancient colonies around Marseilles.[9] It is tiresome to have such skimpy information about the druids, especially when we realize that they could have left written records about themselves if they had felt so inclined. They used the

Plate 6. Celtic mother goddess, place of origin and date unknown.
Gallo-Roman figurines were the last terra-cottas of antiquity. The production center was along the Allier Valley, in shops that also manufactured the Roman red pottery called *terra sigillata*. The fertility goddess
is shown nursing two infants as she sits in a wicker armchair. The
figurines, or *matrones*, were placed in household shrines, in sanctuaries
by springs and wells, in graves, and so on ("La Gaule romaine," *La
documentation photographique* 5–261 [January, 1966], sheet 7). *Courtesy of
Musée Rolin, Autun, France.*

Greek alphabet for keeping accounts but otherwise committed everything to memory and required that feat of the many students who flocked to them, Caesar says, to avoid military service.

Whatever their actual status may have been in Caesar's day, the druids were the intellectuals of Celtic society, those who knew the history and the law. It follows that Celtic society as a whole relied on verbal transmission of information. In short, with the exception of their druids, the Celts were illiterate—illiterate and crude.

The Celts had a primordial conviction that there was special power in the human head.[10] In Provence shrines had been found in which skulls are essential components of the general scheme.[11] Carved heads appear in many places in Celtic lands, indicating how widespread the cult must have been.[12] The carvings unmistakably represent severed heads (called by art historians *têtes coupées*). They never have necks, and usually they have no ears either. In a famous passage Strabo relates than an early traveler, Posidonius, had seen heads of enemies nailed to the doorways of Celtic houses and had been sickened by the sight, though he was candid enough to admit that he got used to them in time.

Those Celtic headhunters were elegant people. It is an unsettling experience to come all unprepared upon the statue of an imperious, slender-waisted nobleman in tight jerkin and elaborate jewelry, sitting cross-legged like the god Cernunnos, and to realize that the statue once held an enemy head poised on its knee. Even the severed heads have a look of power, with broad brows and thin, commanding mouths.

Metalwork from Celtic graves and sacred bogs is often exquisite, its workmanship eliciting our awed admiration and at the same time tending to falsify our mental picture of Celtic life (see plate 7). These were the possessions of the haughty few who could afford to import the very best and to attract skilled artisans from remote places. As usual, the humble belongings of the poor have rarely survived. Presumably the marvelous helmets, sword scabbards, horse trappings, torques and armlets, and superb flagons and drinking vessels of northern Gaul belonged to the warlords, with the exception of the treasure of Vix with its huge Etruscan *krater*, which was buried with a royal princess about five hundred years before the Christian Era. That the burial finds impress us so much today shows that the Celtic chieftain was on the right track with his conspicuous consumption. His message rings out across the centuries: this was a man of awesome authority. There is something else that strikes anyone who has ever stared in consternation at the gross displays of opulence in royal treasures (all those top-heavy crowns and overloaded scepters, gaudy porcelains, hideous saltcellars, and idiotic gilded coaches). What we contemplate here with deep respect suggests singularly refined aesthetic judgment and appreciation of line. Such work would never have been commissioned or ac-

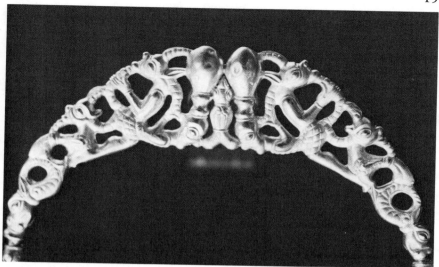

Plate 7. La Tène gold, fourth century B.C., found at Erstfeld, Canton Uri, Switzerland. The maker of this torque (collar) was no doubt influenced by Etruscan and Greek work, but he was no copier. The animal-headed figures are distinctively Celtic. Zurich, Schweizerisches Landesmuseum, permanent deposit, Kt. Uri, 3192. *Courtesy of Schweizerisches Landesmuseum, Zurich, Switzerland.*

cepted by an oaf who merely wanted his fame to be trumpeted about. There must have been a fineness in the Celtic mentality.

The Romans came to recognize and honor the eloquence of Gallic rhetors. Even polished Symmachus (prefect of Rome in the year 384) learned his technique from a Celtic teacher. It is worth noting that Gallic rhetors came into their own during the latter days of the empire, as court panegyrists. The Celts are said to have felt that eloquence had greater power than mere physical strength.[13] We would hardly expect to find such perceptiveness in a people still living in the heroic age, and we wonder how they might have turned out had they not been required to conform somehow to the ways of down-to-earth military Rome.

The Gauls' way of conforming had its original features. We see this as we return to the Trier region.

When Trier became the official seat of the procurator of Belgica in the middle of the first century, many opportunities opened up for landed Treveri to improve their lot in the Roman style (see color plate 3). It does not take much imagination to think of the variety of goods that the Rhine garrisons needed or to envision the streams of craftsmen and traders converging on the area. What is interesting is to see how the descendants of the Celtic headhunters managed to fit into the new scheme. An arresting piece of evidence is the funerary column in the little town of Igel, a few miles west of Trier. It was erected around the middle of the third century by a family of textile merchants presumed to have been of original Celtic stock who were still holding their ancestral lands.[14] The old Celtic idea of blowing one's horn with a display of wealth was readily carried over into an entirely different context. The Igel monument is not so much a work of piety as an enormous stone billboard proclaiming that the family honored by it had the kind of affluence and authority that any modern corporation executive would understand and appreciate.

Unfortunately the lovely Celtic line and proportion have disappeared. This immense construction would not look too strange on the desert at Palmyra or even in Punic North Africa, but here it towers gawkily above the domestic vineyard-covered banks of the Moselle. How these people would have loved our skyscrapers. Goethe, who visited Igel several times and admired the column extravagantly, called it an obelisk. It is much too chopped up for that. It has a rather broad base and continues upward as a four-sided shaft divided into panels of different sizes with protruding cornices between. There is a bewildering display of mythological material, all suggesting that these wealthy people had some kind of expectation of an afterlife in which prestige and acclaim would continue. There is nothing original about these elements, which a sculptor could have seen over and over again almost anywhere in lands influenced by the Romans. What rivets our attention is the set of scenes that illustrate the family's homelife and occupations—all presumably regarded as justification for coming immortality.

The stones have weathered severely since appreciative scholars made meticulous drawings of them several centuries ago. We are forced to rely on their work for detail, though well-preserved fragments of other monuments can be found in regional museums on which similar scenes can be examined, if we want to check on what those early admirers of the Igel monument actually saw. Miraculously, the column itself has survived through all the centuries without tumbling down or undergoing any serious deliberate defacement. Its metal clamps were removed in the early Middle Ages. That kind of "vandalism" was to be expected where peasants were in need of tools and Roman stonework was handy. The Igel monument received special protection from the church at a fairly early date, for a ridiculous reason, not because of any understanding of its historic worth. In spite of its inscription someone decided that the panel showing the family at dinner was meant to portray Saint Helena, the mother of Constantine the Great, and her husband. Judging by the general evidence of the flexibility and drive of the Igel merchants, we may assume that their shades were not disturbed to find themselves Christianized and sanctified.

We can bypass the formal family portrait on the front panel, where all are looking stern and wearing togas. They were Roman citizens by the terms of Emperor Caracalla's edict of the year 212, and they evidently wanted to emphasize that important fact. Let us rather go directly to the dining room, which is indeed grand enough for a royal saint. A Moselle villa could be spacious, to judge by the astounding dimensions of the excavated foundations not far away at Nennig (a 600-meter-long front is indicated there, counting the portico and two vast wings). The Igel dining room has carved columns to support its ceiling, and drawn curtains at the back suggest the existence of an atrium behind them. The furniture in this room is massive: a heavy cloth-draped table and a large sideboard laden with platters. Here the gentlemen wear the loose, comfortable sleeved garment of the Treveri but recline on couches in the Roman manner (their ancestors sat cross-legged on heaped grasses). They gallantly offer cups to their wives, who sit like Roman ladies in high-backed chairs.[15] If royal Saint Helena ever sat on such a wicker chair, it would have been eminently suitable because the *matres* perch primly on them.

The main source of the family fortune, as noted, was the manufacture of textiles, probably on contract basis for the Rhine garrison. The enterprise was managed rather like a cottage industry, though some experts contend that one of the Igel panels may show a shop in the villa itself. Whatever the arrangement, a very large number of people was involved.[16]

We might inquire how it happened that a single family could control the output, indeed, the lives, of so many. In pre-Roman times the Celtic warlords did not actually own the land, which belonged to the tribe as a whole, but the lowlier members were bound to them in a kind of patron-client relationship. Under the Romans these same clients seem to have drifted into the condition of land-tied peasants, obligated as before to the overlords, whose interest was in production and profit, no longer in combat and booty. The overlords became so intent on production that, as the years passed, they were inclined to withhold their tenants from military duty, either buying them out of the army or paying for the recruitment of Germans in their stead. The end effect of this drastic change of purpose by the overlords was that the Roman army became barbarized, with a percentage of Gallo-Romans much lower than what the population could have furnished. We must agree that the great Gallic merchants and landholders contributed in their own way to the changes that impended.[17]

Tenants were required to pay for whatever protection or assistance they received. These humble dependents, as the sculpture shows them, have a careworn, anxious look. We see them bringing in poultry, fish, pelts, baskets of fruit, and so on. They also empty sacks of small coins onto the accountant's table. In passing, we observe that coinage in itself was no novelty to the Gauls. Various tribes had their own curious money as early as the third century B.C.[18] Bookkeeping was certainly an innovation, however. Here sits the bookkeeper

Plate 8. "The Travelers," ca. A.D. 170–180, from Arlon, Belgium. The illustration shows one of the faces of a large block that is presumed to have been part of a monument like the column at Igel. The travelers are seated in a four-wheeled vehicle called a *reda*. The older man wears a thick cloak and has a scarf knotted around his neck. He is reading tablets that he holds (Lefèbvre, *Les sculptures gallo-romaines du Musée d'Arlon*, pp. 67–69). *Courtesy of Musée luxembourgeois, Arlon, Belgium.*

on a grand, thronelike chair, its arms carved with dolphins in the Mediterranean style.

The Igel monument shows us details of the business. At the villa were kept stocks of fabric, folded and placed on shelves. We see them in the scene in which tenants deliver heavy bolts for inspection and approval (see plate 9). In another panel a bound bale is conveyed on a wagon (see color plate 2). This package is of great size, filling the vehicle. Five half-naked youths struggle to tighten ropes lashed around another bale, and on the river "company boats" carry two bales each and are towed upstream by men on shore who strain against ropes, steadying themselves with staves. On land we see a pack animal ascending a rocky slope to pass a little tollhouse. We also see the director in a smart wicker cart with a whip-cracking driver. Perhaps he is a commuter, with offices in Trier.

All this candid celebration of the tradesman's status is the peculiar and charming hallmark of Gallo-Roman sculpture. Merchants, we know, were never high on the Roman social ladder, where maximum prestige went to the senators, who prided themselves on their idleness, using the wealth they accumulated as absentee landlords to further their political aims. The lively, confident approach to the everyday existence of a prosperous businessman that we see in the work on the Igel monument and at Trier and nearby Arlon has been commented on by many art historians, whose interpretations vary. It is a commonplace to observe that these pieces are remote ancestors of Flemish genre painting. That is all very well, but surely it is more interesting to try to understand why this particular form of art should crop up in this region. Alfons Dopsch said that it is highly individual because the native population was somehow isolated, but he came closer to the mark when he went on to observe that these scenes were "based on the ideas of the men who ordered them."[19] *Celtic* ideas, let us add. The descendants of the hill-fort warlords had found a new route to power, and they were just as proud of themselves and as eager to advertise their success as their ancestors had been. Perhaps it is no accident that even today Gallic countries are the homelands of people who feel that a merchant is every bit as good as a professional man. In other words, perhaps the Celts injected a new social attitude into their part of the Roman Empire. When we reflect that the first "meaningful others" whom the Celts would have encountered in pre-Roman times were traders from the East, we may well speculate that this confident assessment of the merchant's place in the world may have been reinforced all along by the so-called Syrians ("Syrian" being anyone from the Hellenized part of the Mediterranean world). They might have been accepted as role models by the energetic Gauls.[20]

We wonder what effect the church may have had in this connection. Adolf Harnack points out that in its beginnings the church "did not teach its votaries the dignity of labor or the noble pleasure invariably afforded by work."[21] Perhaps the inspiration lay in the Stoic concepts of the cultured classes in Rome.[22] Admittedly Roman religious ideas had filtered through. At this point let us consider what happened to the Celtic deities when Asiatic and Roman gods crowded into Trier in the wake of the soldiers.

Roman Trier had a temple precinct in the part of the city known as the Altbachtal. Here Gallic and Roman divinities, like the human population, jostled and intermingled.[23] One small altar preserved in the Landesmuseum shows that at least the memory of bloody ancient rites could survive and be respected in the new environment. Four severed human heads and a ram's head decorate the altar, honoring a god named Pisintos.[24]

The *matres* maintained their popularity, and so did the equestrienne Epona.[25] Epona's fame spread among the Roman troops: stables in far-distant places were decorated with roses in her honor. In these days of struggle for

Plate 9. Inspection of manufactured textiles, carved panel from Hirzweiler, Land-kreis Sankt Wendel, Rhineland, West Germany, second century A.D. Two youths, dressed in the loose-fitting garments characteristic of the Treveri, inspect cloth for quality in a stockroom. Fringed cloth was prized as booty by the Goths. Trier, Rheinisches Landesmuseum St. W. 120. *Courtesy of Rheinisches Landesmuseum, Trier.*

women's equality it is heartening to see that Epona kept her independence and never became the consort of a Roman god. For that matter, even though a number of Celtic goddesses were mated with the dominant Roman males, they retained their distinctive names.

Cernunnos, the horned one, kept his torque and his familiar serpents and rat, but he acquired Roman attributes as well. Sometimes he had a purse, and on one startling occasion he assumed the guise of a stag spewing coins. The explanation appears to be that he had become merged with Dis Pater, god of the underworld. Dis Pater in turn had become associated with money when a shrine to him in Rome was built near a cavern that was in the custody of the Roman treasury. [26]

Roman gods sometimes received symbols that properly belonged to Celtic deities. The typical "Jupiter column" depicts the god on horseback at the top of a complicated shaft that starts with a base showing two pairs of Roman gods, then an octagonal portion with figures representing various aspects of the passage of time, this in turn being surmounted by a decorated column with Jupiter dressed in Roman armor. His steed is trampling or resting its forefeet on the shoulders of a serpent-legged giant who seems to be struggling up out of the earth. It is thought that this strange tableau refers to Celtic Taranis as a solar god and a being who represents earth and the underworld. The idea is supported by the importance that the Celts assigned to the horse in a solar cult of great antiquity. Horses could make wells spring up beneath their feet. There may be some connection also with ancient coins that show a monster with upraised arms and a horse above him. [27]

Mercury was extremely popular, which is not astonishing in a mercantile-minded society. The Gauls married him to a lovely goddess named Rosmerta, who seems to have represented abundance (see plate 10).

Gradually the Celtic gods acquired formal temples. The most elaborate one, built in the second century across the river from Trier at a site where there had been simpler structures before, was dedicated to a god with a Celto-Roman name, Lenus Mars. He may have been the leading tribal deity. [28] His priests, men of the equestrian class, were also priests of Augustus and Rome; the cult was deliberately developed by the Romans to ensure the loyalty of conquered peoples. The temple of Lenus Mars seems to have had something of the character of a temple of healing. The "sacred way" to it was flanked by resting places for pilgrims and by altars dedicated not only to Lenus Mars but also to his Celtic consort, Ancamna. There are traces of a theater associated with this temple and grotesque masks, perhaps marking the combination of ritual drama and a formal priesthood, but by the third century the place had become a Mithraeum. The Mithraic cult, perhaps the greatest of the religions of personal salvation and mystery that rivaled Christianity, was strongly ritualistic, but it had no organized priesthood. Not only Mithras came to Trier but the more exotic Anatolian Cybèle and Attis, and Isis from Egypt as well. [29]

The third century was a period in which Rome and its emperors became "orientalized." It may have been a mere trick of fate, but the only emperors who were strong enough to stem the tide of northern barbarians were all from the East, not from Rome.

The Germanic tribes, as outsiders, reacted in their own way to the Roman presence, looking in with a certain amount of envy at the awesomely golden

Plate 10. Mercury and his Celtic consort, the goddess Rosmerta, from the vicinity of Strasbourg, France, third century (?). The sandstone slab was utilized again to make a Merovingian sarcophagus. The two deities wear peasant garb. Mercury has tight-fitting trousers and an upper garment that is belted and buckled. Rosmerta has a pleated skirt and a sleeved garment with a round collar. Mercury carries his caduceus, and both he and Rosmerta hold purses as symbols of prosperity. *Courtesy of Musée archéologique, Strasbourg.*

empire. In Caesar's day even those Teutons who lived nearest the Rhine were predominantly pastoral, though they had a limited, rather primitive form of agriculture. As Roman forces blocked their movements, they could no longer go on raiding parties or take new land to satisfy needs arising from population growth or crop failure. It may be for this reason that we find such a marked contrast between what Caesar described and what Tacitus had to say about the Germans a century and a half later. The Teutons had been a classless society with no private ownership of land, "letting each man see that he himself is just as well off as the most powerful of the tribe."[30] By Tacitus's time (he wrote in A.D. 98) they had shifted from a seminomadic way of existence to something rather like the land-tied condition of the Celts. In addition to this drastic change people were beginning to show signs of separation into classes, indicated specifically by the kind of property they owned. Tacitus refers to a "national custom for gifts of cattle or agricultural produce to be made to the chiefs," amplifying this statement with a comment on the "particular pleasure in gifts received from neighboring states, . . . choice horses, metal discs and collars."[31] This is impressively borne out all over German territory, where grave goods unearthed by the archaeologists are evidence of lavish and persistent Roman diplomatic bribery.[32]

Contemporary evidence also exists of shifting societal patterns. Maroboduus, in the time of Augustus, started out as the elected head of a war-band, but he later styled himself king of the Marcomanni. His "capital" in Bohemia even had a permanent resident community of Roman merchants, who must have found it profitable, despite all the risks, to import glass, silver, bronze, textiles, and wine into this remote, lonely spot.[33]

All over the north, it seems, aristocrats were emerging as a class: not only chieftains but also a body of elites with rather unclear authority and warriors who were coalescing into retinues around the chieftains. These warriors were not the poor freemen of the kind clustered around the former Celtic warlords, who made up the Gallo-Roman farming and industrial communities. The retinue was an institution of nobility, fighting as cavalry.[34] It is hardly astonishing that before long these people began crossing the Rhine to seek their fortunes as mercenaries in the service of Rome.

Describing themselves as pressed by other tribes behind them, some Germans asked to be allowed to settle in the empire. The Romans began using one set of barbarians against another, shifting tribal units here and there to act as buffers and bringing in groups of Germans as agricultural workers, assigning them to individual Gallo-Roman families.

From the time of Emperor Commodus (180–192 A.D.), the Goths—the eastern Germanic tribes, in other words—were in movement along the Danube, and the situation everywhere became highly unstable. On the death of Commodus murderous struggles for the throne convulsed the empire, throwing it into a state of anarchy. By now the army had a strong voice in the election of the emperor, though a new one usually went through the motions of paying his respects to the members of the Roman Senate, who must have grimly recognized the irony of their situation. The legions made and unmade emperors, and the purple usually went to the candidate of the larger Danubian forces.

The final reaction of the Rhine officers was to proclaim an emperor of their own. They chose their garrison commander, Latinius Postumus (see plate 11). An able leader, he made Trier his capital, pushed back the potential German invaders, and set up an "Empire of the Gauls." Since he did so with the approval and cooperation of the Gallic provincials who sat in his senate, we may infer that they saw themselves as protectors of *romanitas*, not as fiery separatists. Where once the Romans had been uneasy lest their Gallic subjects form an alliance with the Germans, now the line was clearly drawn, and the Gallo-Romans perceived the peoples on the north as the enemy, but at that time, as in subsequent centuries, it was apparent that the Gallo-Romans could be detached from Rome if it seemed to them that Rome had forgotten them.

The empire might have disintegrated in the days of Postumus. Britain and Spain joined him, and at one point he even controlled some parts of northern Italy. As it was, this Empire of the Gauls survived for nine years, counting the reigns of Postumus's successors, the last of whom, Tetricus, self-styled "pius felix invictus Augustus, pontifex maximus, pater patriae" in scarlet cloak and yellow tunic, had to shuffle along ignominiously with an assortment of elephants and fellow captives, including Queen Zenobia in her heavy golden chains, in Emperor Aurelian's fabled Roman triumph.[35]

The tactics used by Rome to survive this critical time when it was likely that not only Gaul but also Syria might have broken away foreshadowed still further integration of Germans into the fabric of the empire. Emperor Gallienus (253–68) set up mobile cavalry, and at that stage cavalry meant barbarians. One of his successors, Emperor Aurelian (270–75), deliberately evacuated the province of Dacia, which Trajan had taken so much trouble to conquer, thus stabilizing the frontier but making way on the far side of the Adriatic for the Visigoths, who were sifting down from the region of the Vistula.

Survival was the work of a series of competent and determined emperors, all from the East, as we have already observed. They were Claudius Gothicus (268–70), Aurelian, and Probus (276–82). As his agnomen implied, Claudius had, to his credit, a number of victories over the Goths, after which "the provinces were filled with slaves and German cultivators." Aurelian made a treaty with the Vandals, who stopped their forays and retired to the Danube, promising to furnish cavalry. Probus drove back the swarms of German invaders who had crossed the Rhine. He killed about 400,000 of them in the

Plate 11. Coin of the usurper Postumus, who ruled his "Gallic empire" from Trier, A.D. 259–69. His domain extended as far as Spain and Britain: a milestone bearing his name stands in the parish church at Breage, Cornwall. Here he is shown wearing a radiate diadem, in reference to the god Helios. *Courtesy of Colchester and Essex Museum, Colchester, England.*

process, so Vopiscus tells us in the *Augustan Histories*, but it is prudent to take figures given by ancient historians with a fair amount of salt. In any case, as a follow-up to his penetration into northern territory, Probus brought back *coloni*, not only reviving but expanding the use of imported barbarians as farmers.

We have no way of knowing how many imported barbarians may have been involved in the next crisis, which was an internal one in Gaul, but on the face of it we might almost see in it a general reversion to type by those Celts who were at the bottom of the social heap. There had been sporadic troubles with the peasants before, but during the reign of Carinus, in 283–84, there was an outburst that assumed frightful proportions. It has been pointed out that, since it was the propertied classes that were most threatened, we cannot expect to hear much about the threat because the landowners would have attempted to conceal or even deny the existence of any group that might endanger their own existence.[36] The panegyric honoring Emperor Maximian, who suppressed the peasants by drastic action in 286, is worded this way by its author: "I pass this by hurriedly, for I see that such is your *pietas* you would prefer that the victory were forgotten rather than glorified."

The paramilitary movement had enough cohesion to warrant a collective name for the individuals engaged in it. They called themselves Bacaudae, but even this name appears only fleetingly in contemporary writings. Everything that concerns the Bacaudae is uncertain. The consensus seems vaguely to be that the word comes from a Celtic expression meaning "bands" or "fighters." Edward Gibbon mentions *bagad*, a tumultuous assembly. The Bacaudae had reason enough to be tumultuous, from the sheer accumulation of wretchedness. The German incursions had followed on the heels of all those years of skirmishing among the contenders for the throne, when armies moved hither and yon, demanding grain and supplies that depleted the farmers' reserves. Then came the Germans, ravaging towns and countryside. On top of that was the plague. Landlords who had suffered hard losses during the upheavals tried to recover by pressing their unfortunate tenants and slaves beyond endurance. Freemen, army deserters, and runaway slaves responded by simply wandering off, gradually forming into roving bands armed with farm implements and riding stolen horses.[37]

The bands grew larger as desperate townspeople and others with "a native Gallic craving for adventure" joined them.[38] The story that they established themselves at the confluence of the Marne and the Seine in an old Celtic stronghold is fiction.[39] There is also some doubt that they struck their own coins, though the idea has its attractions. The Bacaudae did in fact have elected leaders whose names are said to have appeared on the coins. Some historians go so far as to refer to these men as emperors, but that is stretching things. Parenthetically it is said that the coins had the single word "Hope" on the reverse.[40] The Bacaudae were bound to lose in the end, when the military might of the empire was turned against them. They were suppressed by Maximian, who thereafter became Emperor Diocletian's co-Augustus in the West. "Suppressed" may be too strong a word. Bacaudae continued to plague the West off and on, to the extent that the movement has been described as endemic. It broke out again full force in the fifth century; we shall see that at that later time the reaction of imperial authority was complex, indicative of deep concern.

Recovery after the disturbances of the third century was painfully slow in the Gallic heartland, but Trier entered a period of magnificence and world prominence. Emperor Diocletian's grand reorganization of the empire brought a new role to the city as capital of Belgica Prima and of the great Gallic dioceses, from which even Britain and Spain were administered.

The plan of Diocletian was ultimately to be perceived as a beginning of the cleavage between East and West, though that was not the intention at all. He wanted to divide the central power, to check ambitious upstarts and prevent bloody wars of succession. In his view the chief threat came from Roman generals in the field, not from barbarians. The empire was still to be a unit, but it was to be administered in sections by tetrarchs. These four were two emperors of equal rank (the Augusti) and two Caesars who assisted them and presumably were in line to succeed the emperors in due time.

The empire may have remained a unit in Diocletian's mind, but his administrative arrangements were destined to survive only in the Greek-speaking East and to collapse in the Latin West. The West was thinly populated and still predominantly rural. A bureaucracy could take root much more effectively in the East, where there was a much larger population, genuinely urban to a considerable degree.

Trier's connection with the East was firmer than any tie with the city of Rome. It therefore inevitably became more and more oriental, like Diocletian's own court, where the emperor affected silken robes and required his courtiers to prostrate themselves at his jeweled feet.[41] He was surrounded by large numbers of barbarian officers; it is possible that court ceremonial was devised to provide smoothness in an awkward situation, where different origins and degrees of education might make difficulties.[42]

In a way Trier became an artificial city, a boomtown with all the dislocations and imbalances that show up in any world capital that has such a role arbitrarily thrust upon it. There was a great influx of people demanding office space, fine housing, sophisticated entertainment, and luxury goods. Needless to say, people streamed in from the East, where luxury was an old story.

Architects, of course. Who among the locals could have designed the handsomely majestic audience hall? The only other pre-Byzantine structure made of tile throughout, like the Trier "basilica," is to be found at Pergamum. The Trier architect may have come from Asia Minor or Syria.[43] They needed someone to make mosaics: some of the mosaics at Trier are signed with a Greek name. Silk weavers came from Syria, forming a little colony. Trier is one of the two places known in the empire where *gyneciarii* wove silk-and-gold fabrics for private consumption as well as for the court.[44] Furniture, ivories, jewelry, sumptuous glass for insatiable customers—all were supplied by people from the East.

Although the major centers for glass manufacture in the Roman world were Alexandria, Syria, and Campania, some of the most astonishing masterpieces, so-called *diatreta* glass, seem to have come from an atelier in the Rhine-

Plate 12. Emperor Diocletian, marble portrait head, A.D. 280–85, found in
Nicomedia (modern Izmit, Turkey). This striking example of late Roman-
Hellenistic work shows the alert-faced Augustus wearing the *corona civilis*.
Courtesy of Arkeoloji Müzeleri, Istanbul, Turkey.

Plate 13. *Diatreta* (reticulated) glass beaker, third–fourth century, found in a sarcophagus at Niederemmel, northeast of Trier. Fragments of similar work were discovered in the rubbish at the baths of Trier, and also at nearby Konz, the site of an imperial palace on the Moselle River southwest of Trier. This beaker appears to be true *diatreta* glass; that is, the body of the vessel and the outer network are integral, the whole being cut or ground from one piece (Kisa, *Das Glas im Altertume*, pp. 616–26). See also color plate 1. Trier, Rheinisches Landesmuseum 50.15. *Courtesy of Rheinisches Landesmuseum, Trier.*

land (see plate 13 and color plate 1). Not many have survived, but most were found in such places as Cologne, Trier, and Strasbourg, and it is unlikely that they were far from their place of origin. We have no way of knowing who the master *diatretarii* (diatreta cutters) were or whence they came.[45]

For about thirty years Trier was the residence of Constantine the Great (Caesar, 306–307; Augustus, 307–26). Most of the awesome monuments that we gaze at today date from that brilliant period. The edifices were celebrated in poetry and panegyric at the time, no doubt to the satisfaction of the gleaming oriental court. Barbarians were not the only people who were changing the look of the West.

Christianity supposedly came early to Trier, but there is no clear evidence of it until the fourth century. Simple little slabs in the Christian cemeteries were primitively cut, certainly not by the sculptors hired by wealthy merchants (see plate 14). Aside from some awkward outline designs (dove, chi-rho, cross, peacock) they bear little more than a brief biography of the deceased person, who may have come from Anatolia or Syria, though there are a few stones in honor of individuals with Celtic or Frankish names like Bonosa and Marabaudis. One frequently recurring motif is that of pillars supporting arches representing the triple sanctuary of a church—an Eastern church, where the liturgy required preparation of the eucharistic bread and wine out of sight of the congregation.

Constantine and his mother, Helena, were avid church builders in many parts of the empire. At Trier there are traces of huge twin churches near Constantine's palace. Between the churches, connecting them, stood a twelve-sided baptistery, glorious with porphyry columns. The arrangement is matched in a number of remains on the Adriatic and in northern Italy, but the original was the great church in Jerusalem.[46]

The feet of some of the most illustrious church fathers must have crossed the threshold of Constantine's magnificent building. Without belaboring the point, we may say that the reasons that brought the holy men to Trier are in themselves a sign of the far-reaching consequences of the official recognition of Christianity. With such famous visitors in town even the lowliest boatman or farmer must have sensed that his world was large and complicated.

The patriarch of Alexandria, splendid Athanasius, who was a legend in his own lifetime, came twice to Trier, trailing with him the tangled web of the Arian controversy.[47] One of the things most difficult to understand, as we look back across the centuries, is that in times of grave social crisis many of the best minds could be wholly caught up in the intricacies of theological disputation and that arguments about the nature of the Trinity could lead to riots, banishment, torture, disgrace, and death. The arguments were passionately felt: conscience could command a greater allegiance than emperors ever imagined. People were writing and talking violently then with more conviction than we

Plate 14. Funerary slab showing the triple apse of a church, first half of the fourth century (?), from the Hospital of Maximin, Trier. Three round arches are supported by columns, and the space behind the columns is marked off with knotted curtains. This space, in the apse of a church, was divided into compartments to meet requirements of Eastern liturgy. The eucharistic bread and wine were prepared in the *prothesis*, out of sight of the congregation, while sacred vessels and books were stored in the *diaconon*, on the other side of the main compartment in which the altar stood and mass was celebrated. Other indications of Eastern influence are the chi-rho with its open loop and the knotted curtains. *Courtesy of Rheinisches Landesmuseum, Trier.*

do today. They were grappling with a problem that we have not yet quite settled—the relationship of church and state. Constantine the Great had thought that the chances for a unified and stable empire would be enhanced by official Christianity, but he quickly discovered that he had stepped into a quagmire, an ecclesiastical morass where dissent was protean, especially in the East, where theologians traditionally enjoyed considerable freedom. In his determination to control the situation, Constantine found himself calling for and presiding over ecumenical councils, not caring what the adopted doctrine might be.

The emperor ran into trouble because Christianity was already highly organized by the time he saw fit to recognize it. He therefore had to contend not only with the fervor of belief but also with the turbulence of prelates who

Plate 15. The Hebrews in the fiery furnace, detail of a sarcophagus from the abbey church of Saint Maximin, Trier. The motif was popular in Gaul. The frontality of the figures, the upraised *orans* position of the arms, and the Phrygian dress are indicative of Eastern influence. Else Förster identifies the sarcophagus as that of Bishop Agritius (314–36), while Reinhard Schindler believes it to be that of Agritius's successor, Bishop Maximin (336–46) (Förster, "Katalog der frühchristlichen Abteilung des Rheinisches Landesmuseums Trier," in Reusch, *Frühchristliche Zeugnisse im Einzugsgebiet von Rhein und Mosel*, no. 3; Schindler, *Landesmuseum Trier: Führer durch die vorgeschichtliche und römische Abteilung*, 2d ed., pp. 18–19, no. 3). Trier, Rheinisches Landesmuseum 37.518. *Courtesy of Rheinisches Landesmuseum, Trier.*

were keenly jealous of the importance of their respective sees. Antioch, Ephesus, Constantinople, and Alexandria were all in the contest. Constantine also overlooked the potentials of men of Athanasius's stamp, thinking, perhaps, that he could bend them to his will. To Athanasius questions of doctrine were of paramount importance.[48]

Anyone fortunate enough to talk with Athanasius would be likely to hear about the asceticism of the Desert Fathers of Egypt, whom Athanasius knew and deeply admired. He was the author of a biography of the first Christian monk, Saint Antony, which has been described as one of the all-time bestsellers. The idea of a life of withdrawal from the world caught fire. At Trier some people retired beyond the city walls to form a tiny monastic community, and it was the story of these people and of the life of Antony that appears to have triggered the conversion of Augustine.[49] The shock-waves of that event have not yet entirely subsided. Clearly Trier was a dynamic place, as a great city should be.

As time went on, other saints came to Trier on difficult and painful errands. Down in the south Bishop Priscillian had run afoul of certain Spanish colleagues because, inspired by the severe asceticism of the Desert Fathers, he had initiated practices that had the look of sorcery. After a long, complicated history that included a council at Saragossa in October, 380, an attempt to present a petition to Pope Damasus in Rome, and a synod at Bordeaux, Priscillian's case was referred to the praetorian prefect in Trier. Decisions of ecclesiastical authorities were not, in theory, subject to appeal to a civil court. Constantine had seen the hazards inherent in such an overlap and had forbidden it, but the church-state relationship was still relatively fluid. The churchmen discovered that it might be helpful to appeal to civil authorities who could apply force, which they as churchmen could not. In Bishop Priscillian's time Trier was in the hands of a usurper, Emperor Maximus, who as a newcomer was only too happy to have a chance to make a public show of his sternly orthodox Christianity. His rival in Milan, young Emperor Valentinian II, was an Arian.

No less a personage than Martin of Tours came to the court to protest the intervention of a lay magistrate in church affairs. This action of Martin's drew fire from orthodox churchmen of Gaul; it seems ultimately to have led imperial authorities to view the monastic movement with considerable suspicion and to act accordingly.

Martin was joined in his protest by another churchman who happened to be in town. He was Bishop Ambrose of Milan, visiting Trier for political reasons. Ambrose was not one to mince matters; he also had a politician's long-range insight into the implications of precedent-setting action. He refused to communicate with the bishops who had come to Trier to lodge their complaints against Priscillian, in effect also excommunicating Emperor Maximus for allowing the proceedings. Defiance did no good. Priscillian and six of his followers were executed, on the order of the praetorian prefect.

Ambrose had been sent to Trier on a delicate peace-keeping mission. He was in fact the ambassador of Valentinian II and the regent, Empress Justina. It was a novel role for a bishop. If we take Ambrose's mission to Trier as a central point, with Ambrose as the pivot, we can move on to his city of Milan and examine there the increasingly complex, strained situation of the empire, seeing how locked into it the barbarians had become. First, however, we must push far eastward. It was the activity on the Asiatic steppe that thrust into prominence the extraordinary people with whom Ambrose had to deal.

THE STEPPES OF ASIA

YOUNG Emperor Valentinian II, on whose behalf Bishop Ambrose approached the court of the usurper Maximus at Trier, was not a descendant of Constantine the Great. The succession had not passed to Constantine's line with the smoothness that he may have anticipated. Constantine the Younger reigned in Gaul for only three years. He was killed by his brother Constans, the ruler of Thrace, who took over Gaul. Constans (see plate 16) incurred the enmity of his troops, who replaced him with a Frankish officer: Magnentius, originally brought to Gaul as a captive, proved to be a formidable adversary for the remaining legitimate emperor, Constantius (see plate 17). After an enormous struggle the upstart was put out of the way, but, although Constantius emerged as the victor, the Roman military forces had been dangerously drained. The furious battle at Mursa in 351 ended with thousands upon thousands of Constantius's men dead on the field; thereafter the Eastern forces would be unable to cope alone with hostile peoples along their frontier, especially the Persians.[1]

This battle had another portentous effect. The Arian bishop of Mursa made use of the critical situation to act as Constantius's spiritual comforter. Edward Gibbon says, "The grateful emperor ascribed his success to the merits and intercession of the bishop of Mursa whose faith had deserved the public and miraculous approbation of heaven."[2] In other words, the orthodox empire, shaky as it was, and in desperate need of unity, was controlled by an Arianizing emperor.

When this steely man became aware that the Rhine was once more threatened, he sent for the only other survivor of the line of Constantine the Great, young Julian, invested him at Milan with the insignia of a Caesar, and dispatched him to Gaul to take military action there. Scholarly Julian had lived more or less as a prisoner in Cappadocia. He had no military experience whatsoever, but he threw himself into this assignment—too aggressively, in the

34

Plate 16. Emperor Constans, solidus from the Trier mint, ca. 340. Trier, Rheinisches Landesmuseum 14.3. *Courtesy of Rheinisches Landesmuseum, Trier.*

eyes of suspicious Constantius. The emperor appears to have trusted Julian at first, though Julian said that his royal cousin wanted to destroy him, the last remnant of the family he had murdered, and that he was disappointed by the turn of events. Julian subdued Alamanni and Franks and was able to state that he had secured the return of 20,000 captives of the barbarians across the Rhine.

Julian's army was largely German. The barbarians were not always adversaries by any means. When Constantius ordered the transfer of four of Julian's

Plate 17. Emperor Constantius II, heroic bronze head, ca. 360. This powerful portrait has evoked many awed comments. According to Richard Delbrueck, the face gives the impression of the resolute force of a cultivated, controlled mind (Delbrueck, *Spätantike Kaiserporträts von Constantinus Magnus bis zum Ende des Westreichs*, p. 141). Hans Peter L'Orange observed that the eyes "stare into eternity" (L'Orange, *Romerske Kaiser in marmor og bronse*, p. 140). These reactions may have been produced by contemplation of the austere, stylized presentation of the emperor's face as seen directly from the front. In this side view Constantius looks like a brooding, lonely man. *Courtesy of Museo del Palazzo dei Conservatori, Rome.*

legions, plus infantry contingents to be taken from the rest of the army in Gaul to fight in Persia, Julian remonstrated on the grounds that his men had "left their homes across the Rhine" with the understanding that they would never be led to regions beyond the Alps.[3] They had their families with them too. A commitment had been made, and Julian no doubt rightly felt that if his mercenaries were to learn that he had acted in bad faith they might mutiny. In any case, no more troops would be forthcoming from Germany.

The army mutinied. According to Julian's own account and that of the historian Ammianus Marcellinus, the young Caesar assembled the troops that he so unwillingly would send to Constantius, and on the eve of their departure he invited his officers to dine with him. The officers left the party, Ammianus says, "anxious and filled with twofold sorrow: because an unkindly fortune was depriving them both of a mild ruler and of the lands of their birth." In the night they broke into open revolt. Soon Julian's palace was surrounded by a dangerous, shouting mob calling for Julian to come out and show himself as Augustus. Julian begged them: "Return to your homes. You shall see nothing beyond the Alps, . . . and this I will justify to Augustus to his entire satisfaction." The tumult continued. The troops ultimately gave him an improvised diadem and raised him on a shield in true barbarian style (Julian appears to have been the first Roman emperor to be elevated on a shield; according to his admirer, Libanius, the shield was more fitting than the usual dais). If Julian's version of the event is the true one, he submitted to the troops, but when various obscure sources are patched together, it appears that Julian incited them to riot and was all too delighted to accept the dignity and authority of an Augustus.[4]

Julian and his loyal army executed a brilliant dash down the Danube, but Emperor Constantius died of a fever in 361, before an actual clash. Julian thereby became the sole ruler.

Ironically, Arianizing but nonetheless Christian Constantius was deified by the Senate, where revived paganism encouraged the honoring of ancient custom. The dynasty of the first Christian emperor ended with Julian the Apostate, who seems not to have intended to be a persecutor of the Christians. As a reformer he wanted to reestablish the cult of Helios. Julian had little use for Christians, embittered as he was by the murderous events in his own family that he attributed to Constantius the Christian. He is known to have observed that "there are no wild beasts so hostile to mankind as are most Christians in their hatred of each other." He had a personal leaning toward Eastern mystery religions, those that offered dramatic and sometimes bloody initiation ceremonies.

We cannot even guess how Julian might have developed as a ruler or what effect he might have had on religious life or on the interaction of barbarians and

Romans because, inheriting Constantius's war with Persia, he died of battle wounds in 363, while discoursing loftily like Socrates.[5]

The imperial situation became deceptive in its general outlines. There were elements that suggested continuity, though from the time of Julian's death onward there was little equilibrium in the reeling empire. A new emperor ruled in the West, hailed as Augustus by his troops, Valentinian I (Augustus, 364–75). As usual, he was engaged in subduing Germanic tribes on the Rhine. As usual, forts were constructed along the river, and chieftains were captured and executed, all in a depressingly familiar pattern. Valentinian's work was so thorough that the empire gained a little strength, and his young son Gratian, who succeeded him, had a semblance of control.

The Eastern Augustus was Valentinian's brother Valens, whom Valentinian appointed to the office. In the Danube region Valens was engaged in a campaign against Visigoths in the former province of Dacia, where they had been living for about a century, on seemingly good terms with the remaining Dacio-Romans, but where they had recently shown poor judgment in supporting a pretender to the throne. As Roman federates the Visigoths had received annual subsidies in return for their defense of the frontier, and they had also enjoyed favorable trading arrangements with the empire. All of this had been in force without a break since the time of Constantine the Great, both Romans and Visigoths carefully observing the terms of their treaty.

Valens crossed the Danube on a punitive expedition in 367, and for the next two years there was war. One mysterious aspect of the conflict was that the Visigoths, who as farmers and herdsmen should have been able to take care of themselves, are said to have felt "an extreme lack of the necessities of life" when Valens cut off trading relationships with them. It was on this account that they sued for peace even before any decisive battle had been fought. A new treaty set the Danube as boundary between the empire and the Visigoths, who lost their status as federates.

The real trouble brewing behind this seemingly familiar façade was infinitely more serious, more sinister, more complex, and more relentless, and also it was out of reach. Nomads from the steppes of central Asia were on the move—no one seems to know precisely why—and they were coming into collision with the Ostrogoths, who were spread out beyond the Visigoths in a vague terrain between the Dniester and the Don.

We need to know something about the Goths, who were a weak, uncertain wall between the empire and the true barbarians.[6] Like the Germans along the Rhine, they had a history of southward migration. Indeed, they came from the same Teutonic stock. Unfortunately there is nothing available to compare with the wealth of material in Gaul to illustrate the life of the Goths at the time. There are accounts by Roman historians and by Jordanes, a sixth-century historian who was himself a Goth. There are graves, as well as a treasure trove here and there, but it is difficult to extract from them a picture of individuals going about their daily routines.

We can infer that the Visigoths had had enough contact with the empire to modify somewhat their traditional ways. For instance, although they were still inherently tribal, their system was beginning to show cracks. Wealth was gravitating toward a few individuals, who even had their own slaves. The hoary general assembly had given way to a smaller council of elites. In time of crisis the tribes banded temporarily under a leader whose title the Romans translated as *iudex* ("judge" or "magistrate"); since times of crisis were becoming the rule rather than the exception, the Visigoths were learning to act together under a vaguely monarchical figure.

Very little has been determined about their religion, a fact not particularly astonishing since it was based on the tribe and therefore secret. They were known to have certain cult objects that they carried about in wagons. It is just possible that the treasure of Pietroassa, in modern Romania, could have been something of this kind. It held no weapons, no household goods, nothing that could indicate the presence of women; everything could have been related to ritual.

From the critical situation in the matter of trade during Valens's campaign, we might guess that the Visigoths had learned to live beyond their means, making use of consumer goods that they were unable to produce. Roman and Syrian traders had access to regions in Dacia where sub-Roman settlements persisted after the withdrawal of the military, and there were also small Visigothic villages where traders could have brought whatever it was these people believed that they required. Luxury goods have their practical uses, as evidence of social status. Since some kind of stratification had developed, it may be that the "necessities" were in fact luxuries for the leaders. What could the Visigoths offer in return? Alas, slaves were the chief export.

All of this suggests a lack of vigor and resourcefulness, in contrast to what we find among the Celts, but there were other aspects of Visigothic life that merit attention. They had their own words for carpenters and smiths, for example. They had metalworkers too, who decorated golden jewelry with glittering stones. Such work was not original with them, but their imaginative use of cloisonné techniques, or the setting of cut gems in perforated plates, shows that these people in the Danubian shops had learned well from the Sarmatians and deserved to be called artists in their own right.

The Visigoths were at least limitedly literate before Ulfila devised a Gothic alphabet for his translation of the Bible. Their metalworkers, as craftsmen and sages, performed a dual function and produced on iron weapons runic inscriptions beautifully inlaid in silver. "*Tilarids*" ("attacker") reads one; the word presumably imparted potency to the spear. A golden annulus in the Pietroassa treasure had runes, though they may have been Ostrogothic. It is unlikely that

Plate 18. Scandinavian runes on a Manx cross, ninth century, Braddan Parish, Isle of Man. Scandinavian runes in their earliest forms are often associated with those known to have originated among the Goths in south Russia. Though at first they were magical symbols, they were elaborated as an alphabet that could be used for practical purposes. Braddan Parish, Isle of Man, 138 [110]. *Courtesy of Manx Museum and National Trust, Isle of Man.*

more than a handful of Visigoths were literate before Ulfila's day (the middle of the fourth century), but the rune-masters must have had a command not only of the goldsmith's craft but also of a complex lore that runic inscriptions imply (see plate 18).[7]

Farther out on the steppe the Ostrogoths meanwhile had abandoned tribal ways and joined together under a succession of rulers, the most formidable of whom, aged Ermanaric (fl. 350–376) had subjugated lesser peoples, to control an empire of sorts from the Black Sea to the Baltic. Such an arrangement must have been very loose and fragmented. Those Ostrogoths who migrated into south Russia had been farmers before, and so they remained, though their rolling land would have been better utilized in herding.

Into this vast domain of sedentary farmers and tiny scattered villages the Huns came riding, "like a tempest of snows from high mountains," says Ammianus.[8] These strangers personified horror: "Fiercer than ferocity itself," Jordanes wrote. They "flamed forth against the Goths," those spry riders on their rough horses. They were said to be descendants of outcast warlocks and unclean spirits of the wilderness; in a way there was a fleck of truth here. The Huns were mongrels.

In few fields do scholars refute and contradict each other as briskly as in Hunnic studies. There are good reasons for this. The Huns came from somewhere in the steppes of central Asia and beyond, and in the course of their nomadic life through the centuries they had at least brushing contacts with many cultures. Scholars advance toward each other across no-man's-land, scrambling through appalling linguistic barbed wire. To handle adequately the problem of the Huns, one would have to master Chinese, Persian, Turkish, Greek, modern Hungarian, and Russian. Obscure records, needless to say, are in far-flung places. Archaeological finds, too, are impossibly scattered. Some progress has been made even so, and the literature now accumulating is no longer made up exclusively of contradictions and retractions. Archaeology is beginning to help sort out some of the strange assertions culled from Greek and Roman sources.

Ammianus may not have seen many Huns. From his account we derive a picture of a dirty rabble dressed in a patchwork of scruffy fur—"the skins of field mice," he says. They "eat the roots of wild plants and the half-raw flesh of any kind of animal whatever, which they put between their thighs and the backs of their horses and thus warm it a little."[9] This presumably is the literary source of *bœuf tatar*. In actuality, the practice is supposed to have been a way of poulticing a horse's saddlesores.

E. A. Thompson expressed the opinion that the Huns were wretchedly poor and that they were at such a low stage of development that they did not even possess those basic civilized skills spinning and weaving, though his point does not hold up too well, in view of the many spinning whorls that have been found. Spinning can be an ambulatory process. Women in the Middle East today wander along after their flocks, teasing out yarn from fleece that is wrapped around the wrist like a cuff. As for weaving, Ammianus refers to Hunnic women "weaving hideous garments" in their wagons,[10] but J. Otto Maenchen-Helfen denies that the Huns used their wagons as living space. They carried their roomy felt or sheepskin tents in them, he says. Ammianus "turned into the ordinary way of Hunnic life what his informants told him about a Hun horde on the move."[11]

We should not think contemptuously of the Huns as rank savages living in filth and chaos. Theirs was perforce a highly organized society, from the point of view of logistics. Mounted nomadism is a specialized form of life, a specific way of handling the problem of stock raising in a region where the climate changes so drastically in a year that there must be two bases for grazing. Two fixed points of habitation are established, in other words, with regular movement between them according to the cycle of the seasons. In his discussion of

Hunnic cauldrons Maenchen-Helfen refers to studies indicating that the nomads may have performed rites on watercourses in the spring, stored the vessels near the water when they went to summer pasture, and used them again in the fall.[12] Transhumance can entail the negotiation of tremendous distances not only with the herds under control but also with provision for the wants of the entire tribe during the trek. In the year 376 when reports about the Huns first began trickling through, they were supposedly largely dependent on their herds.

The very circumstance of the kind of life they led made it out of the question for the Huns ever to act as a huge, coherent army. The "horde" must not have counted many more than five thousand individuals.[13] Such units, acting independently and not imbued with any particular feeling of kinship and solidarity, could easily turn out fighting on opposite sides. When Huns fell on the Ostrogoths led by Ermanaric's successor, Vithimiris, that was indeed the situation. Vithimiris had Hunnic mercenaries fighting for him on the Ostrogoth side.[14]

When the Huns arrived on the frontiers of the empire, they were an unknown quantity. Our modern chatter about little green men in flying saucers is not too different from the popular reaction in the fourth century to Huns mounted on wiry horses.[15] The Huns were indubitably frightening, not only because of their Mongoloid features, their wild clothing, and their language that practically no one understood. Also frightening was their ability to dart around with lightning speed which must have multiplied their actual numbers in the minds of their alarmed adversaries. Their tactics involved a pretense of scattered flight, with quick reassembling and renewed attack. Then there were those deadly bows that they used. The Hunnic bow was a formidable weapon, by anyone's standards. Only a skilled professional could make bows, taking months on end to produce just one. The bow was a composite construction, with a stave made of several carefully selected, cured, and worked materials such as wood, sinew, and horn.[16] The Huns handled them with terrifying precision. We know from ancient art how fierce a backward "Parthian shot" could look.

If they shot arrows like Parthians and spoke a Turkish language and looked like Mongols, who were the Huns, and whence did they come? One clue is an extremely unattractive practice of theirs. They deliberately deformed the heads of their infants, the end result being anything but charming in the adult Hun. As Sidonius Apollinaris describes them, "Their heads are great round masses rising to a narrow crown."[17] The rest of Sidonius's statement is couched in his usual tortured Latin, but scholars agree on the meaning: the Hunnic nose was flattened "to make room for the helmets." In recent years statistical analysis has revealed that the earliest specimens of deformed skulls come from along the Talas River in the Tien Shan; next in graves along the Volga; then in

Plate 19. Chinese "many mountains" incense burner, detail, late Chou or early Han period, fourth–third century B.C. The small trousered figure leading the oxcart is a steppe nomad. Washington, Freer Gallery of Art 47.15. *Courtesy of Smithsonian Institution, Freer Gallery of Art, Washington, D.C.*

the Ukraine, the northern Caucasus, and the Crimea; then in Transcaucasia; and finally in central Europe. This pattern reflects the movements of the Huns.[18]

Another indication is the characteristic Hunnic cauldron. This cast-bronze vessel is cylindrical, very deep, with rigid handles and often a kind of "mushroom" at the top. Its shape is such that it could be lashed onto a pack animal. Photographs of such cauldrons make one think of early Chinese bronzes.[19] Here again, as with the deformed skulls, there is a demonstrated progression from far east to west.

A small "many-mountains" incense burner, of the late Chou or early Han period, is an enchanting piece of evidence that the Chinese were aware of the steppe nomads and that on the far side of the wastes they had their own notion of the strange environment in which the wanderers lived (see plate 19). Among

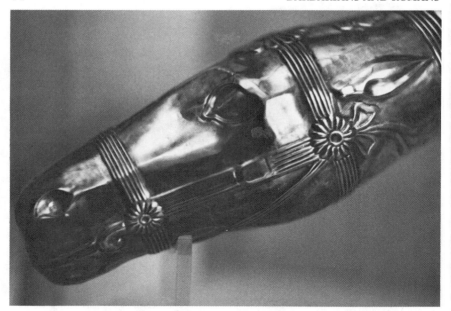

Plate 20. Sassanian rhyton (drinking horn) in the shape of a horse's head, sixth or seventh century A.D. The horn is silver, parcel-gilt, worked in repoussée. *Courtesy of Walters Art Gallery, Baltimore.*

the folds of tiny gold- and silver-inlaid mountain ranges toils a little trousered man with his oxcart—a rare illustration in the Orient of barbarian travel there. The combination of the burning of incense and an imagined barbarian world is instructive in itself, because incense was an import throughout China. There were two corridor routes for such trade across the steppe, encircling the Tien Shan region and splitting north and south around the Caspian Sea.[20] The Huns must have come into contact with a number of cultural streams flowing to and fro across their pasturelands.

If it is true, as some scholars think, that part of the heritage of the Huns comes from the Hsiung-Nu nomads, whose enormous domain in the Mongolian steppes rivaled that of the Han Dynasty for centuries, they had a complex, sophisticated background. Burials of peoples who must have been subject to the Hsiung-Nu are impressive. In the Baikal region, for instance, barrows have been opened to reveal a wealth of embroidered felts, silks, and fur garments.

Sarmatian influences reached as far east as northern China and the Gobi, and something of this extraordinary culture must also have touched the Huns.[21] The little pendant mirrors that the Huns carried are Sarmatian, in J. Otto Maenchen-Helfen's opinion.[22] Even in the fastnesses of Siberia the Huns must have acted as go-betweens. They appeared in the Minusinsk Basin in the early centuries of the Christian Era. Along with their advent a new "hybrid" mirror appeared there, in what was an ancient mirror-manufacturing center. The hybrid with its rimmed back subsequently spread all the way to Gaul, carried that far not by Huns but by other nomads, presumably Sarmatians.[23]

Other ancient nomadic peoples moving westward out of Asia settled near trade routes, whence ideas and art motifs were carried back to the steppe. The amazing animal art of the Scythians spread in that way. Once again the Huns must have played a part in the interchange. Many influences from distant places crossed and recrossed the wastes. In the High Altai are astounding frozen tombs that show the sophisticated use of complex materials from places as disparate as Siberia and Greece, China and Persia.[24]

The Huns had their own distinctive ornaments probably made for them by goldsmiths from the Pontic region around the Black Sea. Golden plates, for example, that were fitted onto the rigid parts of a bow are characteristically Hunnic. Other, smaller bows have been found that are entirely covered with plates. It is surmised that these were symbols of a chieftain's authority or that they may have been made especially to be placed with the dead.[25]

More utilitarian plates that are also typical of the Huns have been the subject of lively debate (see plate 21). They are flat, cut sometimes on a curve, sometimes triangular, and covered with a close repoussé "scale" pattern. The German word used to describe the scales is the same one that is applied to the tiny scales on a butterfly's wings, and indeed the effect is almost that delicate. There is little agreement among scholars about their function; once seen, however, they are instantly recognizable. It has been imagined that they were connected with kitchen utensils in some way. A set of them is displayed at the Musée Rohan, in Strasbourg, where they have been mounted on broad pieces of leather to indicate that they were quiver ornaments, on cases for a bow and arrows like those on the Kol Oba vase. Joachim Werner argues, convincingly, I believe, on the basis of an extended examination of a number of specimens, that they were saddle ornaments, probably made especially for burial. He calls attention to something that may or may not be coincidence. A Korean noble's grave from the same general period contained a saddle decorated with the scale pattern.[26] Hunnic saddles were made of wood, not leather. When Attila thought that he might be defeated in the Battle of the Catalaunian Fields, he had saddles stacked to make a funeral pyre onto which he could leap.

In one famous instance the Hunnic scales appear on a Roman shield, shown on a diptych at Monza. The personage represented in that ivory was

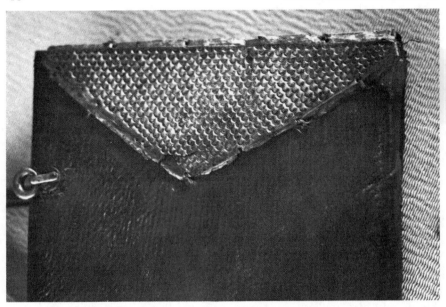

Plate 21. Hunnic saddle plate, ca. 450, from Mundolsheim, near Strasbourg. One of a pair of triangular pieces of gilded silver, here displayed as a quiver ornament. *Courtesy of Musée archéologique, Strasbourg.*

once thought to be Aëtius, the patrician who defeated Attila, but now he seems universally to be identified as Aëtius's predecessor, Stilicho. Either way a Hunnic design would have been appropriate. Aëtius was hostage to the Huns for years and was a friend of the Hunnic king Rua, while Stilicho had a loyal Hunnic bodyguard.

The Huns decked their women in beautiful jewelry. There are seven known "diadems," bandlike crowns made of gold sheet applied to bronze and profusely ornamented with almandines (see color plate 7). Almandines come from India, by the way. These diadems were worn over hoods or veils, and the women to whom they belonged went to their graves so dressed. Findspots for these crowns extend from Kazakhstan to Hungary.[27] There are also intricate paired pieces of gem-covered clips, thought to have been worn at the temples, perhaps on a hood. They are handsomely worked with filigrain. Again, this is the art of Pontic goldsmiths.

So here they come, those misshapen-headed people with their Chinese wagons and cauldrons, their Indian gemstones and Korean saddle ornaments,

Plate 22. Iranian gold lion appliqué. Archaemenid, sixth–fifth century B.C. Saint Louis, Saint Louis Art Museum 244:1955. Gift of J. Lionberger Davis. *Courtesy of Saint Louis Art Museum, Saint Louis, Missouri.*

their Pontic crowns and golden bows, and their Sarmatian mirrors, riding horses branded with Turkish *tamgas* (property marks; see plates 25 and 54.)

The first victims of their onslaught, in the year 374, were the Alans who lived in the Danube Basin. Next were the Ostrogoths, who fell after having tried to make a stand. Old Ermanaric died, of wounds, chagrin, or suicide— who is to say?—and his wobbly domain disintegrated into vassalage.

The changes that the conquest wrought were more drastic for the Huns than for the conquered peoples, whom they could now exploit. This must have been the first time that the Huns had continuous access to the products of agricultural settlements, as opposed to what they could snatch in sporadic raids. The new arrangement gradually altered their living patterns. By Attila's time, about a century and a half later, they were living in wooden houses built for them by Gothic carpenters and were wearing linen.

The Visigoths lost. Under their judge Athanaric they made an attempt at

Plate 23. Bronze girdle plate, eleventh–tenth century B.C., from Samtavro (Mtskheta), burial 276. Tbilisi, Georgian Museum of Anthropology and Ethnography, accession no. 12-54:7399. *Courtesy of the Georgian Museum of Anthropology and Ethnography, Tbilisi, Georgian Soviet Socialist Republic.*

defensive preparation behind a line of earthworks, anticipating an orderly, Roman kind of attack (they were forgetting how to be barbarians), but the untrustworthy nomads meanly forded the Dniester by moonlight and assaulted them from an entirely unorthodox angle.

Athanaric withdrew to the Carpathians, but most of his people set off with their families for safe Roman territory. They sent a panic-stricken plea to the emperor for admission, promising loyalty. While they waited for Valens's response, frightened and hungry, they stretched out their arms in woebegone appeal to anyone passing by on the opposite bank of the Danube.

Valens signified assent, and preparations were begun for the unprecedented migration of an entire people—some say as many as 200,000 individuals—as a unit onto Roman soil. They were to keep their personal gear but surrender their weapons; a terrible stipulation in the minds of the warriors.

Rome had never coped with anything like this before. It must be said that what followed was one of the most disheartening episodes in the whole history of the empire. It was contemptible. It was also a piece of gross miscalculation and mismanagement, at the very time when utmost skill was required if the empire was to survive. Men with "stained reputations": that is the expression that Ammianus used to describe the officials appointed by Valens to supervise the immigration.[28] These men, cruel and greedy, delayed ferrying the Visigoths across the river until they had taken from them all their cherished belongings and reduced them to the condition of selling their comrades-in-arms, their wives, and their children in exchange for dogs, which they were supposed to accept as food. When they finally reached the haven of empire, the Visigoths were starving and destitute. Their families were shattered, and they were bitter with a deep sense of betrayal. They were hardly the stalwart reinforcements that Valens needed. They managed to keep a few weapons, but not for the defense of predatory Romans.

The sequence of events at this point is one of growing anger and desperation among the Goths. At Marcianopolis in Lower Moesia, they again met with what looked to them like treachery. A brawl led to the massacre of the Gothic guards who had accompanied their leaders to a parley with Lupicinus, one of the "stained" men. Previously loyal Gothic mercenaries rebelled. Valens's forces pressed them up into the Thracian mountain passes, where they seemed to be hopelessly trapped, but somehow they managed to get messengers out through the Roman lines. These messengers approached the Alans and the Huns, promising dazzling booty, and an alliance was made. The Goths were able to extricate themselves from their trap. Deserters and slaves escaping from the mines flocked to swell the throng, who laid waste the countryside.

Outnumbered, Valens sent a call for help from the West. News could travel fast among the barbarians. The Western Augustus (Gratian, son of Valentinian I) had mercenaries in his command who passed the word along to Alamanni, across the Rhine, that the East was in trouble. This information triggered a huge breakthrough that forced Gratian and his Frankish generals to abandon their eastward march, defeat the Alamanni in a spectacular melée near Colmar, and chase the remnants back across the Rhine.

Valens attacked impatiently without waiting for Gratian, and the slaughter of Adrianople was on. Valens died in the battle, while the flower of the Roman army was mowed down by the barbarian cavalry. Alans are known to have fought along with the Goths, and it is even thought that Huns led the crushing assault.

Ostrogoths had joined Visigoths. We know the names of their chieftains: Alatheus and Saphrax. There is much scholarly argument about Saphrax, whose name may be Hunnic. At one time this same Alatheus and Saphrax shared the command of the Ostrogothic army; if Saphrax actually was a Hun, the Hunnic mercenaries would appear to have done well for themselves.[29]

Insofar as the empire was concerned, it did not matter who had administered this terrible blow. There was not much possibility for the resilient recovery that followed Hannibal's tremendous victory at Cannae: it was A.D. 378, not 216 B.C.

Plate 24. Wall painting, seventh century A.D., Afrasiab, Uzbek Soviet Socialist Republic. If we require evidence that the Asiatic steppe was a crossroads, we have it here. The silks and headdresses are clearly oriental. The campaign to uncover the wall paintings in the ruins of Afrasiab, the city that preceded Samarkand, was begun by Soviet archaeologists in 1965. *Courtesy of A. R. Muhamedjanov, director of the Institute of Archaeology, Samarkand, Uzbek Soviet Socialist Republic.*

The Goths were unable to follow through. Their attack on Constantinople came to nothing. The barbarians seem never to have mastered the art of taking a walled city. It may be because of this circumstance that they gained such a reputation for wanton destructiveness; over and over they abandoned a siege, to roam around scorching the fields. Unless a traitor inside opened the city gates or an engineer showed them how to crawl in through an aqueduct, they usually turned away. "I wage no war on stone walls," one Gothic commander said in disdain.

There is another side to this coin. In our own day we are all too aware of the endlessness of guerrilla warfare. It was that kind of hit-and-run combat that the Goths engaged in.

The surviving Augustus, Gratian, selected an extremely able man to replace the dead Valens. He was the Spaniard whom we know as Theodosius the

Great. It was part of his genius that Theodosius was able to focus his attention on the basic problem, the utter demoralization of the Roman army after Adrianople. He had to make the troops demonstrate to themselves that there was no need to be paralyzed by fear of invincible supermen. He did this by gradually subduing the Goths through application of their own tactics. In a series of tiny engagements in which he knew at the start that he occupied the favored position, he coaxed confidence back into his men and at the same time whittled down the adversary.

Theodosius had a talent for dealing with his enemies. After a victory he could be conciliatory, even gracious. In the year after the disaster of Adrianople he turned the situation around well enough to be able to enlist Goths among his own forces. By 381 his position was so secure that he could welcome aging Athanaric, the Visigothic judge, into his royal city. Old Athanaric died within a week or two, possibly overwhelmed by the splendor of it all, and Theodosius dramatically provided a grand funeral procession to escort the barbarian to the tomb, a gesture that must have won over many a hardened Goth.

By the terms of the treaty drawn in 382, something entirely new in the relationship between the empire and the barbarians was introduced. The Goths received land between the Danube and the Balkan range (in modern Bulgaria), where they were to live according to their own laws, under their own rulers. They had the status of federates and agreed to supply mounted archers in return for a subsidy. This was the first time that federates had lived inside the boundaries of the empire. It was also the first time that a tribal unit had been allowed to remain intact. Theodosius went on to place Goths in positions of high authority and even to make these men his personal friends. Thomas Hodgkin observed that there was something in Theodosius's character that harmonized all too well with the nature of the barbarians. He was cruel, impetuous, and undisciplined in a way that was to play right into the hands of Bishop Ambrose of Milan. He had the Gothic love of display and spectacle, and "he might have become an emperor of the barbarians instead of an emperor of the civilized commonwealth of Rome." [30]

At a somewhat later time Theodosius was able to make good use of his new friends and federates against the usurper Maximus, who had been acclaimed by the restive legions in Britain, but in the long run he did considerable damage by introducing such people into the Roman army. By and large he was able to handle them. Nevertheless, just before the confrontation with Maximus some Goths broke away and disappeared into the mountains of Macedonia, where they became brigands. [31]

Gratian had started off promisingly. Soon after his accession to the leadership of the West, he had been confronted with a disconcerting fait accompli. When his father, Valentinian I, died, that emperor's Frankish general Merobaudes and other influential commanders hurriedly invested Gratian's young

Plate 25. *Tamga*, ca. eighth century A.D., from Martinovka, Ukraine. This piece may have belonged to a ruling family of slavicized descendants of the Alans. See also plate 54. *Courtesy of British Museum, London.*

half brother with the purple, hailing him as the Augustus Valentinian II. They explained blandly that they had wanted to head off a dangerously ambitious commander named Sebastianus and that there had been no time to alert Gratian.[32] With considerable aplomb Gratian recognized the little co-Augustus and his mother, Empress Justina, the regent, so that for all intents and purposes the prefectures of Gaul and Italy received separate rulers. Gratian followed this pacific response in due time with his great military exploit at Colmar and his loyal effort to assist his uncle Valens when the East was in dire straits. After that, Gratian began to stumble.

The first misstep was a decision to abandon his traditional pagan title and office of pontifex maximus as unbecoming to a Christian emperor. That must have dismayed the pagan faction of the Roman Senate because it trained a spotlight on the nonofficial status of the still-existing cult of Rome. A few years later, in 382; Gratian issued a series of harsh decrees removing the revered Altar of Victory from the Curia, depriving the Vestals of their traditional privileges, and confiscating the sources of temple revenues. This action won applause from the Christians, and Bishop Ambrose no doubt congratulated himself on the evidence of his influence, but the pagans subtly began organizing in opposition.

The second misstep was the one that proved fatal to Gratian. Perhaps it was a clumsy, ill-conceived imitation of Theodosius's fraternization with the barbarians. Whatever the motive, it was deeply distasteful to the military careerists around Gratian, to see their emperor surrounded by an Alan bodyguard, wearing fur, and carrying a longbow in public. He overlooked the fact that his army, especially the commanders, were Franks of the old school, conservative pagans with a stern mental image of *romanitas*.[33] Gratian made a practice of promoting these Frankish nobles in his service to the highest rank, but their indignation was not softened.

The first to desert Gratian in favor of the usurper Maximus were not the Franks, however. He had some spectacular Moorish cavalry; these defected in a body, possibly because they had happy memories of days when they served under Maximus in Africa. Their desertion was followed rapidly by that of the rest of the troops, under the Frankish general Merobaudes.

Gratian may have been bold, playfully shooting lions in his hunting park,[34] but he fled at this point, to be brutally murdered, probably on Maximus's order.

Now the government of the West rested in the grip of Maximus in Trier and in the uncertain grasp of young Valentinian II and his mother, Justina, the headstrong Arian, in Milan. At last we are ready to move on to that great city, to observe the actions of Bishop Ambrose on his home ground.

MILAN

WHY was an orthodox bishop sent by an Arian regent to treat with an upstart like Emperor Maximus? The affairs of empire were muddled and full of oddities, and novelty was in the air.

We might begin by inquiring how it came about that Ambrose was a bishop in the first place. He had started out as a lawyer, obviously anticipating the kind of bright career that his father had had in Trier. Athough he was born in that Gallic city and was to become one of the most illustrious citizens of another Celtic city, Milan, Ambrose was no Gallo-Roman, nor was he a Celt. There were Greek names in his family—Soteris, Satyrus, even Ambrose, for that matter—but if that indicates a Greek strain, it must have come from a long way back. The Ambrosii were Roman. Ambrose's problem in coping with changing situations was that of the old, established aristocrats. He was wealthy and enjoyed prestige as a birthright. His father had been a highly placed official, possibly the praetorian prefect of Gaul. By 374, at the age of about forty, Ambrose was governor of Emilia and a member of the Senate. His responsibilities combined those of magistrate, overseer of public works, head of the postal service, and administrator of the civil services, with his head-quarters in Milan.[1]

Like Trier, Milan was an imperial city with origins that lay in a remote Celtic past. It had once belonged to the Etruscans but had early become a Roman *colonia*. By Ambrose's time provincial governors had been seated in Milan for about a century. Like Trier, Milan was the headquarters of a praetorian prefect under Diocletian. The Augustus of the West used it as his residence through most of the fourth century.

No great ruins remain at Milan to impress us as they do at Trier—only a forlorn row of columns survives—but Milan was once magnificent. The poet Ausonius, passing through in 379, wrote about it rhapsodically. This, he said, is a city that has absolutely everything. He reeled off a long catalog: a royal

Plate 26. Remains of a Roman palace, fourth century A.D. (?), Milan, Italy. The only other visible remains of Roman Mediolanum are the six Corinthian columns on the Corso Ticinese, which may have been part of the baths of Hercules mentioned by Ausonius.

palace, beautiful private residences, a thriving mint, the circus, the theater, statue-ornamented baths, and so on (see plate 26). Again like Trier, Milan was in a way a boomtown of businessmen and civil servants and military men and the hub of a highway system.

The social mix at Milan was different, however. The court was there, and the merchants, but there were also wealthy half-pagan intellectuals and a church that was a seat of controversy. Such a place was bound to attract the ambitious. It drew from faraway provinces not only young men who were frankly intending to move up to positions of influence and riches but also people who were firmly entrenched in the old order and intended to hold on.

We never have the impression at Trier that any earth-shaking philosophical debates were in progress or that the churchmen were in a central position. Trier was definitely not on the religious firing line as was Milan, where the whole population was aware of the tensions and even contributed to them. Consequently the position of bishop of Trier was not one that would attract the attention of a man bent on achieving personal power.

Milan's succession of bishops was long and honorable. The Christian community was already very much in being in 313, when Constantine the Great and Licinius had their summit meeting and agreed, in the "Edict of Milan," not only that persecution of the Christians should stop but also that confiscated church property should be restored. The orthodox Christians were still there in 355, when a council was held for the express purpose of condemning Athanasius. By that time the empire was hanging by a thread, its unity largely dependent on the kind of solidarity that united religious belief might impart, but the emperor was Constantine's Arianizing son Constantius II, who maintained his despotic court at Milan. At the council Bishop Dionysius of Milan was treated so insultingly that his flock became unruly, and the meeting had to be adjourned from public session to the quieter confines of Constantius's palace. "I myself am now appearing for the prosecution," the emperor announced. The upshot was that Bishop Dionysius was banished, probably to Cappadocia, and replaced by the Arian Auxentius, who was so much an oriental that he could not even speak Latin. Auxentius was a prime target of indignant orthodox leaders for years, but he held onto his see even under the most vitriolic attack until the year of his death, 374.

Election of a successor presented serious problems that would have to be resolved by the opposing factions themselves, because by 374 there was a new Augustus of the West, Valentinian I. Unlike his brother Valens in the East, who was an Arian, Valentinian was determined as a matter of principle not to take sides in religious matters. Ammianus tells us that the emperor never ordered anyone to reverence this or that.[2] When we consider that by this time many of the clergy and their congregations in Milan must have been in the Arian camp while the sees in the surrounding countryside remained orthodox, and when we further consider that the rules governing episcopal succession required that a bishop must be elected by the local clergy and consecrated by bishops from neighboring sees, we understand the difficulties. We are hardly astounded to learn that the electoral proceedings were in an uproar.

As provincial governor Ambrose was expected to keep the peace in Milan; he went to the church where the turmoil was. Legend is often a kind of shorthand. We are told that while Ambrose stood before the agitated throng a child's voice rang out in the church—"Ambrose Bishop!" The governor, an orthodox Christian though still unbaptized, was elected by popular acclaim.

What does this story mean? In the first place, it is not unique. Jerome complained that a man could be a catechumen one day and bishop the next. Evidently there was some justice in this remark, since it had been necessary to establish a canon specifically condemning the choice of a layman because of his wealth and prominence.[3] The Milanese congregation was able to overlook canon law, and so in fact were many other congregations in troubled times. In Gaul in the days of the great barbarian incursions, the man who confronted the barbarians in the name of the community was generally a bishop, chosen in some haste from the senatorial class.

In the second place, this story tells us something about social undercurrents. Episcopal elections assigned a highly significant role to the lower classes. [4] Ambrose was keenly and sympathetically aware of the humble and the poor; it may be for this reason that throughout his career he was able to sway crowds as he did. [5]

It seems plausible that Ambrose had come to see in the church a strong, highly integrated organization in a swiftly changing society and to regard it as an appropriate instrument for a power seeker. When his opportunity came, he grasped it with such consummate art that it is hard to believe that he had not thought out every step. He even honored the tradition that a newly elected bishop ought to "flee" from such elevation. [6] Gibbon as usual has the mots justes: "He cheerfully renounced the vain and splendid trappings of temporal greatness . . . and condescended for the good of the Church to direct the conscience of emperors and to control the administration of the Empire."

Even the most prescient of men, however, could hardly have foreseen the peculiar field of forces that was about to develop. As we know, Gratian became Augustus of the West in 375, when his father died. Almost immediately he had a co-Augustus forced upon him in the person of little Valentinian II. Gratian, only sixteen at the time, had not the skill to manage his general Merobaudes the Frank, who was responsible for Valentinian's promotion. When Valens, Augustus of the East, died in the Battle of Adrianople, Gratian appointed Theodosius to the vacant post. Since Theodosius was thus indebted to Gratian, we would look for quick supporting action when the latter's own territory was invaded by the usurper Maximus, who arrived from Britain at the head of an army. Theodosius did not respond. Furthermore, after the murder of Gratian he showed little or no inclination to defend Valentinian II against the intruder. Why?

No one has satisfactorily unraveled the mystery of the death of Theodosius's illustrious father, Theodosius the Elder, who was summarily executed in Africa for unknown reasons. Some scholars think that Valentinian I or Gratian was behind it, while others believe that the evidence points to Gratian's general Merobaudes. [7] Emperor Theodosius may have had dark suspicions. Add to this the circumstance that the usurper Maximus and Theodosius the Elder had served as brother officers in Africa. Theodosius's apathetic attitude toward Valentinian II may also have had a religious basis. Valentinian and his mother were Arians, while Maximus was an orthodox Christian. Theodosius was passionately devoted to the orthodox cause. It may be that for all these reasons the Eastern Augustus had little interest in taking up the cudgels for Justina and her son.

Those two were certainly in need of defenders. Maximus was intent on adding Italy to his domain, though he masked the threat with transparently friendly overtures. In this complicated trap Justina turned to the only public figure who would be able to treat with this orthodox "friend," Bishop Ambrose. She had not wavered in her religious convictions, but she appreciated the merit of having a respected Catholic speak to Maximus on behalf of Valentinian. Suppose Maximus were to try to inveigle Valentinian into moving to Trier; that maneuver had to be fended off at all costs, not only to assure the boy's physical safety but also to gain a little time. It was essential to keep Valentinian out of the clutches of Maximus and also to show that there was no need to cross the Alps in the name of orthodoxy. With a little extra time to think things over, perhaps Theodosius would see his way clear to come to the rescue.

It is odd to see Ambrose accepting such a charge. What advantage could he find in this ticklish assignment either for the church or for himself? He may have seen it as a way to the heart and mind of Valentinian, who would rule alone someday. Possibly Ambrose even hoped that Justina would become a milder Arian out of gratitude. If that was what he thought, he misjudged her badly. At any rate, off he went to Trier. Whatever time-saving he could effect by his good offices would be put to military use.

Justina and Valentinian had another champion to help them, Flavius Bauto, a powerful general, a new kind of personality in the evolving empire. A heathen Frank, Bauto came from the far side of the Rhine. He had risen through the ranks to become *magister militum* under Gratian. Since he had also seen service in the East when Gratian lent him to Theodosius during the struggle with the Goths after Adrianople, he was well known in both parts of the empire. Bauto was much more than a military commander. For a year or two, Ambrose thought that he was the most formidable man at Valentinian's court. Ambrose was uneasy about Bauto's great influence over Valentinian, and it must have been with some feeling of rivalry that he allied himself with Bauto in defense of the young emperor. Whatever their private thoughts may have been, the two acted as a team, Ambrose going to Trier for an audience with the enemy and Bauto marching troops into the Alpine passes in case worse came to worst.

Since Ambrose's route to Trier is recorded in his own writings, we can see what probably was regarded as the most expeditious way to travel through the Alps in those days. He went from Milan to Como, from there up to Chiavenna, through the Liro Valley, across the Splügen, down from the Splügen to Chur and the Rhine, and thence along the Rhine to Mainz and Trier. Just how long he and his retinue were on the road is not stated. He left Milan in late September or early October, 383, when the northern passes were not yet snow-blocked, and returned early the following year by a southern route (Lyons, Mont Cenis, Turin, and Milan). The passes were marked with stakes in winter, but they were especially treacherous in spring. Ammianus describes how wagons were lashed together and held back "by the powerful efforts of men or oxen at barely a snail's pace" through "chasms rendered perilous through the accumulation of ice."[8]

On the outward journey Ambrose met a messenger from Trier who was heading for Milan. Sure enough, the man was the bearer of a warm invitation to Valentinian to live with Maximus as a son.

Bishop Ambrose was as successful as anyone could have been in such a situation. He placatingly bore Maximus's somewhat arrogant treatment and stated that he had no authority to take up any question other than the important one of peace. Anyway, he commented with feeling, it is almost winter now, very rough travel for a tender lad and his widowed mother. He went on to paint a moving portrait of himself as protector of the orphaned and widowed.

Maximus did not care much for this. He told Ambrose to remain as "guest" of the court until his own ambassador, whom Ambrose had met on the road, returned with a definitive reply. The answer turned out to be cunningly vague. Not right now; later, perhaps.

Ambrose seems to have said more or less the same thing, and he was grudgingly allowed to leave. On his way back to Milan he met another delegation. This one had been instructed to express Valentinian's heartfelt joy over the prospect of peace. It was ominous, however, that on this same journey Ambrose saw Maximus's troops moving toward the Alpine passes.

Under an arrangement approved by Emperor Theodosius, Maximus was recognized as Augustus for Gaul, Spain, and Britain, while Valentinian kept Italy, Africa, and Illyricum. Ambrose had managed to gain time, Maximus had not crossed the Alps, Valentinian was still in Milan, and the way to that city was blocked by Bauto's army. When Ambrose went to Trier the second time, in 384, ostensibly to negotiate for the return of Gratian's body, Maximus raged that Bauto and the bishop had tricked him. The former senator and the Frankish general had managed to steer the empire past one more crisis—but at a price. Early in 384, Maximus had created a diversion by tacitly allowing the barbarian Juthungi to begin raiding Raetia, which was approximately in the region of modern Switzerland and the Tirol. Desperately Bauto had summoned Huns and Alans, who hurtled in from the Hungarian plains and drove out the Juthungi. Bauto then found that the only way to get rid of the Huns and the Alans was to buy them off with huge payments of gold.[9] That was but a foretaste of things to come.

The city populations of the empire always throve on excitement. How the Milanese must have relished the head-on clash between Empress Justina and their doughty little bishop, especially since they were able to take part. "Astonished and disturbed," as Augustine described them, the people seethed outside the palace while Ambrose held forth inside, refusing to surrender one of his churches for the use of an Arian congregation under an Arian bishop of Justina's choosing. On that occasion the near riot could be quelled only by Ambrose himself, at the request of the embarrassed court.

Ever since his consecration Ambrose had immersed himself in questions of doctrine and belief. He must have been an omnivorous reader all his life, to judge by the familiarity he shows with classic and philosophical writings (Augustine provides a vignette of the bishop absorbed in silent reading, escaping for a few minutes from the "crowds of busy men, to whose troubles he was a slave"). Ambrose never became a theologian in the intense way that Athanasius and the Eastern prelates did, but he knew what he believed and why, and he was ready to defend his convictions against all comers. He also knew that he had the trust of his flock and that they were just as ready for a fight as he was.

The events of Lent in 385 (or 386) seem oddly familiar to anyone who has participated in an action of civil disobedience. Ambrose and his fervent congregation engaged in a kind of sit-in for a considerable period, night and day, while their basilica was surrounded by Justina's troops (see plate 27). Ambrose, placed under sentence of banishment by the empress, refused to comply. Everyone, including Ambrose, thought that he was in physical danger. He doggedly preached sermon after sermon and helped relieve the tedium and keep up morale by teaching the congregation to sing Psalms antiphonally. These "freedom songs" were borrowed from the East. Antiphonal chanting was new to Milan, but it became a tradition there and ultimately spread throughout the West.

The deadlock at the basilica continued up to the Thursday before Easter, ending with Valentinian's abrupt removal of the soldiers, some of whom were much in sympathy with Ambrose.

A hard-riding courier could have covered the distance to Theodosius's court and back during the siege. It seems safe to guess that there had been a sharp admonition that this power struggle must cease. The withdrawal of the troops was certainly not a sudden impulsive act of goodwill. Those close to Justina and Valentinian were calling Ambrose a tyrant.

It is entirely correct to refer to him as the most powerful ecclesiastical prince of the West, but Ambrose must have been aware that a "tyrant" image would not serve him well in the long run. He was a canny man; he must have understood that unless he could coax the Arians into his fold there would always be conflict in Milan. It would not do much good to stand up in the pulpit expounding doctrine. Sixteen centuries ago the tortuous arguments of the contesting theologians may have been a little easier to grasp than they are at this distance, but it seems unlikely that at any time the man in the street, the pious matron, the ambitious courtier, or the gruff barbarian would have had much comprehension of it all. Most laymen probably lived in a state of

Plate 27. Basilica of San Lorenzo Maggiore, Milan. The core of this enormous structure dates from the days of Ambrose (340?–97). It may have been the site of the "sit-in" during the confrontation between Ambrose and the regent Justina's Arian court in 385 or 386.

suspended ignorance, accustomed to the notion that revealed religion was revealed only to bishops. If they were to live comfortably with a low-grade, superstitious kind of Christianity, they needed something to feed their faith, something at the level of sorcery and incantation. They were not far removed in time from paganism; they must have missed old familiar shrines where they could go in time of trouble.[10]

Confronting this problem, Ambrose had an inspiration. Accepting a revelation that was vouchsafed him, Ambrose "found" the skeletons of Gervasius and Protasius, two obscure martyrs, in a cemetery beyond the city walls, and these he boldly conveyed to his new basilica at the time of its consecration. The idea may have gone against the grain a bit for him, a true Roman reared in the Roman tradition. Romans never disturbed a dead body. It was only in the East that saints were dismembered for export and distributed far and wide among the faithful.[11] The action had more than a little bravado in it, following as it did by just four months a royal decree forbidding the translation of relics.[12]

By happy fortune, a blind man well known in Milan touched the fringes of

Plate 28. Portrait head, detail of the wooden doors of the basilica of Sant' Ambrogio, Milan, fourth century. The artist depicted a biblical scene, but he caught the credulous look of a true believer of any age, the kind of person who would have been swept along by the miracle that occurred when the relics of Gervasius and Protasius were brought into the city and a blind man recovered his sight.

the cloth that covered the holy remains during the solemn ceremonies and immediately was able to see. This splendid miracle and the general glory of the martyrs must have shaken many an Arian, in spite of the furious accusations of fraud that issued from the court. It is not quite clear who Gervasius and Protasius were or what deeds or virtues made saints of them, though many a church was dedicated to them after this excitement. The bones that Ambrose unearthed were covered with blood, he said. Red ochre, perhaps? If so, they are Paleolithic saints (see plate 28).

We smile and enjoy our superiority, siding with the irritated members of Justina's entourage. We are sixteen centuries away from the event, and it is only with a vigorous wrenching of our minds that we can even try to think along with Ambrose and his flock. In Ambrose's day the resurrection of the body was central to the Christian faith. That Jesus rose from the dead was the ultimate proof that he was divine. Along with that belief went the conviction that Jesus on earth was a healer. In the afterlife Jesus and the saints would manifest themselves by works of healing. From that position it is only a step to the belief that the presence of the body of a holy person or of some object associated with him would be miracle-working evidence of immortality. The miracle-working religion therefore was the true one. Let us not be too quick to label Bishop Ambrose a calculating cynic, ready to manipulate the people of Milan. [13]

Among the lowly participants in the stirring events was Augustine's long-suffering, possessive Berber mother, Monica. Some of the most moving things that Augustine ever wrote concern her. Theirs was a strong, intensely human bond. Augustine mentions a half-pagan custom of Monica's that she brought from her native Africa. She regularly took bread, pottage, and wine to the memorial shrines of the dead. She left the food at the shrines. The watery, tepid wine, as Augustine describes it, she took from shrine to shrine in a little cup, sharing it with other visitors. The church doorkeeper ordered her to stop this practice on the ground that Bishop Ambrose felt such tributes to the dead to be "too much like Gentile superstitions." Monica humbly obeyed, for love of the bishop, Augustine thought. [14]

Paganism was far from dead. Ambrose was perturbed whenever he saw evidence of it, even when it was harmless and charming, like Monica's little offerings. He was well aware that folk in the rural districts still took vows beside sacred trees and wells, a practice he disapproved of, but on the whole his thought was centered on paganism as it was manifested in the aristocratic families. Ambrose wanted a truly united church, undisturbed by heresy or pagan cults. He was making good headway against the Arians, and he wanted to deal an effective blow to paganism too.

Oddly enough—though admittedly the times themselves were odd—it is none other than Augustine who takes us into the pagan milieu and, by a strange extension, into the world of the heathen barbarians. When Augustine went to Milan, he was something of a social climber. His new appointment as court rhetorician was indeed a big step up for him. He would be called upon to deliver official panegyrics honoring the emperor and the consuls of the year. Naturally he would be expected to present the court and court policy in the most favorable light; in sum, the position was not much different from that of a minister of propaganda. [15] The striking thing about this situation is that the emperor was an Arian, and the ecclesiastical prince was orthodox Ambrose, whereas at that time Augustine was hardly a Christian at all. For whom was he supposed to be speaking, and whose propaganda was he supposed to spread?

Ever since his early youth Augustine had been an intellectual explorer. In the confusion of Carthage, replete as it was with strange spiritual undercurrents, Augustine had been drawn into the camp of the Manichees. For nine years he had been a member of that sect, whose dualist cosmology had something to offer to those who had difficulties with the inconsistency of Christian scriptures and wanted rational explanations. Augustine tired of the shallow "wisdom" of the Manichees, but though he was drifting from them when he first went to Rome to teach rhetoric, the ties were still close enough for members of the Manichee colony there to approach the prefect of the city, Quintus Aurelius Symmachus, on Augustine's behalf. Symmachus was the leading advocate of traditional Roman paganism.

When the Milanese court asked Symmachus to name a rhetor, he selected Augustine. This bald statement brings us a step toward the answer to our question, yet it involves a puzzle. Augustine would speak for the Roman pagans when he stepped forward in Milan to deliver a panegyric. We wonder, though, what connections Symmachus may have had at the court, inasmuch as he was the one who was asked to make the appointment.

The most powerful man at Valentinian's court in those days was the Frankish general Bauto. A powerful barbarian military commander no longer astonishes us, but it is a little confusing to find one who has a say in the choice of a panegyrist. It is frustrating that history tells us so little about Bauto the person. We gather that he was highly respected for bravery and competence, but we have no way of knowing anything about his education or the level of his sophistication. Bauto was a heathen, remaining loyal to the old religion of his youth beyond the Rhine. Was this loyalty to tradition enough to make a bond of sympathy between him and the highly sophisticated, fastidious Symmachus? The two men look like an improbable pair, but apparently their minds moved in the same channels.

It was Bauto who had been responsible for the appointment of two pagan aristocrats, Vettius Agorius Praetextatus and Bishop Ambrose's gentlemanly cousin Symmachus, as praetorian prefect and prefect of Rome, respectively. That paved the way for the introduction of an eloquent speaker at the Milanese court who presumably would not be averse to promoting pagan ideas. One of Augustine's very first assignments offered him a fine opportunity. He was to celebrate the elevation of Bauto to the rank of consul in 385. This piece of oratory unfortunately has not survived.

Even with a promising opening into court circles, these were difficult times for the supporters of the dignified, rather arid old religion that had been the mainstay of empire for so long. The Christians had their heresies and schisms, but pagans themselves were showing an alarming tendency to delve into extremist cults. What must have been the private thoughts of quiet, self-contained Symmachus when he contemplated the practices of colleagues in Rome and Ostia? A Roman of the old style, how could he converse comfortably with friends and associates, whether men or women, knowing that they had been able to bring themselves to stand in a pit to be baptized in the hot blood streaming down from the body of a slaughtered bull, even opening their mouths to receive this disgusting flow (see plate 29)? Friends and colleagues in Symmachus's own circle were associating themselves with the mystery religions in almost indiscriminate abandon, simultaneously becoming initiates in the cults of Magna Mater, Isis, and even Hecate, to name just a few.

No matter what bizarre pathways some senatorial families might be exploring, they shared one desire. They wanted the ancient Altar of Victory to be restored to the Curia. Following the Battle of Actium, Victoria romana had been set up in the Senate house, along with an altar, not so much to commemorate a spectacular naval victory as to celebrate the triumph of the Roman spirit (see plate 30 *a* and *b*).[16] Through the intervening centuries the statue and the altar had become symbols of the cult of Rome. It is therefore entirely understandable that, as the waves of Christianity beat more and more strongly, the traditionalists clung to those evocative monuments.

The attitude of Christian emperors had not shown much uniformity. Constantius, for instance, had the altar taken away (at least for the period of his presence in Rome) but allowed pagan cults to continue. Julian restored the altar. Valentinian I, with his hands-off policy, left the altar in the Curia but was somewhat uncertain: the pagans could have their confiscated temples back, but they must not perform any nocturnal ceremonies.[17] Bishop Ambrose pushed Gratian into renunciation of the imperial role of pontifex maximus and also persuaded him to turn over to the public treasury revenues from pagan priesthoods and confiscate the rich properties from which those revenues came. The pagan senators appealed these decisions through Symmachus, but Gratian's response was negative.

With Valentinian II as emperor and Bauto standing high, the pagans felt that their chances might be somewhat better than before. Once more they addressed an appeal through Symmachus to the court for restoration of confiscated property and return of the Altar of Victory. In all fairness it has to be said

Plate 29. Inscription recording initiation in 295 of Cornelius Scipio Orfitus into the cult of Attis, symbolized by a crook and a Phrygian cap. In the *taurobolium*, the initiate was "baptized" in the blood of a bull; a ram's blood was used in the *criobolium*. Symmachus's friends participated in such rites. *Courtesy of Museo capitolino, Rome.*

Plate 30. Above: Victoria romana, gold solidus, reverse. The emperor (Valentinian I?) stands facing right, holding the labarum and Victory on a globe. With his right foot he spurns a kneeling captive (Mattingly, Sutherland and Carson, eds., *The Roman Imperial Coinage* vol. 9; Pearce, *Valentinian I–Theodosius I*, p. 145). Mint mark SMSISC (Siscia). British Museum 1830, 6-1, 30. *Courtesy of British Museum, London.* Below: Victoria romana, gold solidus, reverse. Two emperors are enthroned. The one on the right holds the *mappa* (folded handkerchief), ready to signal the start of the consular games, while together they hold the orb. Behind them is the statue of Victory with her outspread wings (Mattingly, Sutherland and Carson, eds., *The Roman Imperial Coinage*, vol. 9; Pearce, *Valentinian I–Theodosius I*, p. 145). Siscia mint. British Museum 1860, 3–29, 101. *Courtesy of British Museum, London.*

that when property rights are involved religious conviction tends to take second place. A good many of the senators may have been more anxious about personal income than they were about their altar. Gratian's rulings had been severe to the point of being punitive; not only ancient Roman dignity was involved but also political and economic power that was tied with venerable priesthoods.

Modern historians have singled out Symmachus for hostile judgments.[18] His chief concern was the control of his African holdings. He was weak. He was timid. He did not really believe what he said. In his defense it may be said that, whereas he was at the very apex of the senatorial career and in theory his powers were impressive, in fact he held his exalted position only at the pleasure of the emperor. He was aware that he was being spied on. There may have been another reason behind the eirenic reserve of his noble third *Relatio*, which has been called "one of the most poignant documents of dying paganism."[19] The trouble was that Symmachus was simply out of touch with his times. He wanted to hold onto a Rome that had no more life in it. Exuberance and emotionalism were not for him, any more than the ostentation of the silver-ornamented official carriage that was his due as prefect of the city.[20] His tragedy was that pagans and Christians alike had moved on to something foreign.[21]

Bishop Ambrose, on the other hand, had the strength of conviction to sustain him, as well as the invigorating knowledge that Emperor Maximus was watching for a chance to hurry to the rescue of orthodox Christianity. Ambrose did not hesitate to make his own attitude clear, in a harsh personal letter to Valentinian. If the pagans receive their temples and altars again, he wrote, "you may come to the Church but you will either find no priest there, or one who opposes you."[22] This was an unadorned threat of excommunication.

After Ambrose had actually examined a copy of Symmachus's *Relatio*, he wrote another letter, packed with specious argument. "The Church has no possessions of her own," he wrote smugly, ignoring his handsome basilicas. The pagans require purple robes and grand litters and attendants for their vestals: "*Our* virgins subsist in poverty." If you want the dignified old faith so much, what are Cybèle and her orgiastic cult from Asia Minor doing in Rome? Without naming names, Ambrose remarked that the emperor should consult the military (that is, Bauto) on military matters, but for problems of religion he should direct his inquiries to the churchman. Valentinian rejected Symmachus's petition, and that would seem to be the end of the story, but paganism was going to have still one more chance, under extraordinary circumstances.

Meanwhile, the pagan aristocrats quietly banded together to perform a great service for all of us. We easily say that we owe our classic inheritance to the work of monastic copyists, but how was it to survive during the century and a half between the time of Valentinian II and that of Columba of Iona and his dedicated scribes? The preservation was the work of Symmachus and his coterie, done as an act of piety that was just as great, just as moving as the work of the monks who have received so much deserved honor for their silent labor. There was the same impulse: to make the manuscripts noble in appearance and worthy of the content. For the works of Vergil a special calligraphy was used.[23] It was because of Symmachus and his friends and their descendants who carried on the tradition that we have the *Aeneid*, Livy, and Juvenal in our hands today.

Throughout his minority Emperor Valentinian must have been pulled this way and that by Justina and Ambrose. His court remained strongly Arian throughout Justina's regency, making it impossible for him to call on his strongest potential ally to help him with Maximus in Trier, because Emperor Theodosius was such a militant guardian of the Trinity. When barbarians once more irrupted on the far side of the Adriatic, an embassy had to be sent to Maximus rather than to Theodosius. Ambrose was not the ambassador this time, which was a pity, because Ambrose was enough of a political animal to sniff out devious dealings, and the new emissary was not.

Maximus saw his opportunity: why, of course, he would be only too delighted to send troops to assist his young friend. What Valentinian's ambassador did not understand was that these helpful soldiers were to be the vanguard of Maximus's army, which negotiated the Alpine passes by this trick (Bauto was dead by that time).

Terrified, Valentinian and Justina fled, first to Aquileia and then on to Theodosius, in Thessalonica, whereupon Maximus triumphantly occupied Milan. His explanation to Theodosius indicated that harsh action had to be taken in defense of true Christianity.

Ambrose retreated discreetly from Milan, and Theodosius busied himself with the conversion of Valentinian. The story becomes even more tangled at this point. Somehow Justina managed to marry her beautiful daughter Galla to the infatuated Theodosius, whose wife had just died. As brother-in-law of Valentinian, Theodosius at last set to work, gathering an enormous army of Huns, Goths, and Alans and even contingents from as far away as Egypt.

In July, 388, battle was joined at Aquileia, where Maximus was resoundingly defeated (see color plate 6). With Maximus dead, Theodosius issued a general pardon and restored Valentinian to power as Augustus of the West, but in a way that was unfortunate for that perpetually unlucky young man. Perhaps subconsciously Theodosius did not really want to help him even then. His relationship with Gratian's half brother still had an aura of distrust. Theodosius delayed Valentinian's departure from Italy and dispatched Bauto's military successor, Arbogast, whom he regarded highly, to manage affairs in Gaul.

Arbogast, a heathen Frank, whose successful military career began under Gratian, won some spectacular victories over his own people in the Rhineland in 389. These successes opened for him the path to power. He seems to have had a faculty for impressing and drawing people to him. He is quoted as saying in response to a query: "Yes, I know Bishop Ambrose and have dined at his table. He loves me." Arbogast also drew and impressed members of the pagan faction, with whom he sympathized.

His first act in Gaul was the murder of Maximus's son. From then on he focused his attention on the administration of the country. He drew to himself a circle of Franks whose loyalty he secured by the customary route of promotion, whether military or civilian, as well as by his open character, his gener-

Plate 31. Theodosius I, Byzantine gold medallion, sixth century. Freer Gallery of Art 09.67. *Courtesy of Smithsonian Institution, Freer Gallery of Art, Washington, D.C.*

osity and indifference to personal gain, and the sheer force of his personality.[24]

When Valentinian arrived on the Gallic scene to set up his own independent regime at Vienne in the fall of 391, there was not much left for him to be independent about, but even Emperor Theodosius was no longer quite his own man. He had established himself at Milan, and there in his turn he came under the influence of Bishop Ambrose.

The bishop's hand was enormously strengthened when hot-tempered Theodosius committed an outrageous crime against the people of Thessalonica, ordering a wholesale massacre there as punishment for the killing of Botheric, the barbarian commander of the garrison. It is a measure of the general climate that the whole disgusting affair seems to have originated in a quarrel between Botheric and a popular charioteer over the favors of a beautiful boy. The charioteer had been thrown into jail for crimes against nature, and the angry circus fans murdered Botheric. The slaughter of 7,000 people was hardly the correct and temperate response of a Christian emperor, as Theodosius belatedly realized. He became fearful for the state of his soul.

Ambrose withdrew from Milan and wrote an earnest, confidential letter to the emperor, making it clear that public penance was necessary. It is not certain what actually happened. Theodosius hesitated, seemed almost to turn to the pagans, but may finally have gone through some kind of ritual admission of his fault. It is not at all likely that he was ever required to go through the humiliating performance of appearing at the symbolically barred church door to prostrate himself with groans and tears, but whatever his action was, Ambrose was satisfied. F. Homes Dudden thinks that Theodosius probably sat in the church without his imperial insignia and refrained from presenting himself for Communion, while Hans-Joachim Diesner suggests that he may have wept publicly and proclaimed himself a sinner.[25] "The motions of the royal animal will depend on the inclination and interest of the man who has acquired such dangerous authority over him," comments Gibbon drily.

Penance of this kind could be performed only once in a lifetime. Ambrose equated it with baptism in its solemnity. Absolved of his heavy guilt, Theodosius expressed his relief and gratitude by turning on the pagans, who heretofore had not been his targets. A series of repressive decrees was issued. Theodosius even went so far as to order the destruction of the Serapeum in Alexandria, one of the most famous sanctuaries of the ancient world. It housed the sacred Nilometer, a device for determining the flood flow of the Nile (see plate 33). Both the temple and the Nilometer were associated in the public mind with the well-being of the population of Rome and assurance of a steady supply of corn. Significantly, the cult statue in the Serapeum is said to have had a corn measure (a modius) as headdress.[26] Until that time (391) no one in the Christian empire had ever tampered with anything connected with Rome's vital food-supply line. Rites were still performed at Ostia to ensure the safe arrival of the grain ships. Theodosius's action was audacious, not only because of the risk of public tumult but also because it must have been in the backs of many minds that the corn crop might fail in retribution. If the truth be told, everyone was uneasy about the destruction of the Serapeum, in spite of the derisive report that mice scuttled out of the cult statue when it was hurled down.

The monks from Jerusalem who were supposed to purify the pagan site at Canopus by establishing a monastery on the site were so frightened by demonic apparitions that Egyptian monks had to be brought in instead.[27] As we

Plate 32. Monument to Porphyrius the charioteer, born about 480 and apparently a participant in the defeat of Vitalian in 515. This popular hero twice won the *diversium* in Constantinople. In the *diversium* the winner and loser of a first heat exchanged horses and raced again. Each attendant, wearing a short tunic, on the bottom panel below the quadriga (chariot drawn by four horses), holds the reins for the exchange. The horses were almost as celebrated as the charioteers. The names of Porphyrius's horses are carved in the small upper panel between the two *putti*: Aristides, Palaestiniarches, Purros, and Euthunikos (Alan Cameron, *Porphyrius the Charioteer*). *Courtesy of Arkeoloji Müzeleri, Istanbul, Turkey.*

Plate 33. Nilometer on Elephantine, in the Nile opposite Aswān. The level of rising flood waters could be determined by the flow that spilled through the slots.

shall see, demons were an accepted fact of monastic life in Egypt. The hardy Copts would be better equipped to cope with the scorpions, hippocentaurs, enormous roosters, bewitching maidens, lions, or whatever other forms the demons might select. Even a seventy-foot dragon would not terrify a Coptic athlete of God. [28] This sangfroid was not shared by the general population.

Now was the time for indignant pagans in the Senate to join forces and make contact with the formidable Frankish general Arbogast in Gaul. Barbarians in strategic positions are no novelty, but "barbarian" does not seem to describe Arbogast. He had been trained by Bauto, and like Bauto he was a friend of Symmachus. It is entirely possible that he thought of himself as an antique Roman.

At Vienne there had been unconcealed friction between Valentinian and Arbogast all along. They clashed when the Senate again asked for subsidies to maintain the pagan cult. Valentinian rejected the request, to Arbogast's deep disgust. Valentinian's weakness soon became apparent. The senators must have learned with interest that the emperor had been unable to shield one of his own men physically by throwing his sacred purple mantle about him; his henchman was killed, right at his feet. As Emperor Julian once remarked, unless the wearer held great power, imperial robes were insignificant rags. [29]

There is no way of knowing what actual threats may have been made, but it is a matter of record that Valentinian wrote a desperate letter to Bishop Ambrose, begging him to hasten to Vienne to baptize him, a sure indication that he felt himself in mortal danger. Even if Ambrose had acceded to the request, the good bishop would have been unable to reach him. Ambrose seemed inclined to believe that Valentinian was a suicide, though he also paradoxically appeared to think that Valentinian had been received in paradise.

Events now moved for "Roman reasons." [30] We shake our heads in wonderment, unable to believe that they were orchestrated by a barbarian general. Arbogast made no move to take the purple for himself. Instead, he championed an emperor who was not a military man but a scholar, a classicist, and a Christian in a halfhearted way. This was Eugenius, rhetor and friend of Symmachus. Eugenius was very much like Augustine, whom Symmachus himself once selected to be rhetor at the court of Milan. It has been suggested that Eugenius functioned as liaison between Arbogast and the senators. [31]

Symmachus had retired from public life shortly after the failure of his appeal for restoration of the Altar of Victory but continued to be an inveterate letter writer. The network joining his various correspondents is extremely interesting. It is not too astonishing to find Eugenius among Symmachus's correspondents. As head of a court secretariat, Eugenius was well up the social and political scale. Such a position, in fact, was equivalent in rank to the office of proconsul. In other words, Eugenius was higher up the ladder than Valentinian I or Valens or Theodosius at the time of their respective elevations.[32] Eugenius had been brought to Arbogast's attention by another Frankish general, Consul Richomer of Constantinople, who was Arbogast's uncle. On Richomer's recommendation Arbogast had appointed Eugenius to his high position. Symmachus was in correspondence with Richomer, and there is even a rather doubtful piece of evidence that in 385 he may have mentioned their shared friendship with Eugenius, though it is not proved that the subject of his letter was actually the rhetor and future usurper.[33] All the same, the sequence is striking: Symmachus's appeal for the Altar of Victory was rejected in 384, the year in which Richomer became consul, and the next year Symmachus mentioned someone named Eugenius in a letter to the great, powerful pagan Frank at Theodosius's court.

Richomer is another of those barbarian officers like Bauto about whom we know all too little. What we can deduce about his personality is tantalizing. It is tempting to speculate that he had seen enough of the old Roman aristocracy to have become an admirer of the gentlemanly restraint and detached approach to life that was so different from the harsh, bloody existence that he knew in the field. He was a man of action, with a spangled military record. He had even gone through the hell of Adrianople, sent there by Emperor Gratian to tell Valens that help was on the way. At one point during some negotiations Richomer stepped forward and volunteered to go to the enemy camp and was gathering his credentials together, "thinking this also to be a fine act and worthy of a brave man," when the proposed parley broke down.[34]

In the year 383, just before he became consul under Emperor Theodosius, Richomer passed through Antioch and there met one of Symmachus's most illustrious correspondents, the orator Libanius, who had been a friend and admirer of Emperor Julian. Libanius had a high regard for Hellenistic literary tradition and was convinced that Christianity was a threat to Greek civilization. He believed that Christians were at least indirectly the cause of the empire's troubles.[35]

Richomer and Libanius were extremely congenial. When Richomer returned to Constantinople and Emperor Theodosius inquired what had pleased him most at Antioch, "Libanius" was the prompt reply. The admired Libanius offered a panegyric in honor of Richomer as consul, and the two men exchanged letters over a period of years.

Thus we have four pagans maintaining contact with one another: Symmachus, the personification of ancient Roman *gravitas*; eloquent Libanius, whose web of personal relations throughout the polished aristocratic world was fantastic in its magnitude (twelve hundred letters from him exist, all composed in the brief period of Emperor Julian's reign); and two barbarian generals, Richomer at the court of Theodosius and his nephew Arbogast at the court of Valentinian. What was it that these four had in common? They do not look like members of a cabal, but we sense a personal bond. Pagans all, though Richomer and Arbogast were no sun worshipers, and not one of them had ever dabbled in mystery religions. Would it be too much to say that all four subscribed to some ancient code of honor, that they loved the dignity and restraint of the old, dying world?[36]

Arbogast managed the election of the rhetor Eugenius and his investiture with the purple, and therefore it is Arbogast who is generally called the first of the barbarian emperor makers.[37] The real activist, the most convinced of the pagan propagandists, was Symmachus's friend Nicomachus Flavianus. He spearheaded the whole effort, taking up where Symmachus's colleague Agorius Praetextatus had left off, though he was more aggressive in his way of furthering the cause of paganism.

The pagan Roman Praetextatus and his wife had made living symbols of themselves as initiates in many Eastern cults and restorers of the Porticus Deorum Consentium in the Forum. This appears to be the last pagan monument dedicated by an official of the city. The twelve deities of the Porticus presumably were thought to represent various aspects of the solar god. With his multiplicity of priesthoods there was no doubt in anyone's mind about Praetextatus's opinions, but he did not attempt to proselytize. Flavianus, on the other hand, was a determined man who defiantly paraded his beliefs, using "the whole organized activity of a *Herrschervolk*." Whereas the Eastern pagans complained, orated, and wrote, Flavianus applied pressure.[38] "The last Roman," Herbert Bloch calls him. Flavianus was rather too flamboyant for that title; perhaps it would paradoxically better describe his Frankish colleague Arbogast.

Virius Nicomachus Flavianus was related to Symmachus. His son Nicomachus Flavianus the Younger married Symmachus's daughter in 393 (this marriage was the occasion that inspired the charming ivory, now in the Victoria and Albert Museum, the one with the lovely priestess).

In the following year Flavianus the Elder accepted the office of consul under Eugenius and swung into action. Apparently he was able to encourage friends and associates to restore the temple of Hercules at Ostia.[39] In reaction to Theodosius's decree forbidding pagan rites of any kind, even in private, Flavianus defiantly led public processions in honor of Isis and Magna Mater. He even went so far as to consult the Sibylline Books. The message that Flavianus extracted was the consoling news that Christianity was about to disappear. He saw to it that this information was well publicized.

Emperor Theodosius was alarmed. By this time Eugenius and Arbogast were installed in Milan. Theodosius was deeply troubled by the thought of combat with the most brilliant general of the age. Devout and obedient Christian though he was, even he needed the kind of reassurance that his forebears would have sought from some famous oracle—at Didyma, perhaps. Bandy-

Plate 34. The god Bes, Dendera, Egypt. Originally a deity of subordinate rank, Bes enjoyed extraordinary popularity not only in Egypt but throughout the East, as patron of the home and childhood, of the toilet, music, and dance. He is always depicted frontally, an indication that he was not originally Egyptian. Ammianus Marcellinus (*Rerum gestarum* 19.12.3) described the oracle of Bes, where notables from all over the empire were incriminated by notes that they had left at the shrine. Even in the days of Theodosius I, Bes's image survived intact. Egyptian monks customarily hacked the faces of the ancient gods and carved or painted crosses on pagan structures.

legged Bes was flourishing at Abydos because his priests had a reputation for reliability as consultants, but the emperor could not approach a pagan source for comfort and enlightenment (see plate 34). He found a substitute in John of Lycopolis, a holy hermit of the Egyptian desert who was known to have the gift of prophecy. Theodosius's eunuch Eutropius was dispatched to the Nile to make inquiries on behalf of the emperor. While he waited for the answer, Theodosius fasted anxiously, prayed intensely, and advanced toward the reliquaries of the apostles and martyrs on all fours.[40]

John of Lycopolis had closed himself up long before in a triple-celled retreat on the eastern bank of the Nile, across from modern Asyūt. His fame was so great that monks had had to construct for him a kind of waiting room that could accommodate as many as one hundred people. Consultations were held two days a week.

The Egyptians deserve a chapter of their own, but for the moment we might at least pause to hear what John told one of his callers: "Forty years I have been in this cell, never beholding a woman's face or the sight of money. I have seen no one eating, nor has anyone seen me eating and drinking."[41] He seems to have been a kindly, rather witty man. From this unworldly recluse came words that were to sway the course of empire. Theodosius's messenger received "glad tidings about the tyrant," and the battle with Arbogast and Eugenius was joined.

This was surely one of the strangest confrontations in Roman history. If we still harbor any notion that a hard-and-fast line could be drawn between barbarian and Roman, we would do well to look at the people marching toward the bloody battlefield on the Frigidus (the site of this battle has never been located satisfactorily, but it was somewhere northeast of Aquileia, possibly in the Gorizia gap). On one side was Theodosius, the legitimate Christian emperor, a Spanish provincial by birth, with his Vandal general Stilicho, heading a force that included Iberians, Huns, Alans, and 20,000 Goths led by none other than Alaric. The Romans in this host must have been difficult to recognize because the soldiers wore hide breeches and heavy cloaks and shouted the blood-curdling Germanic war cry (the *baritus*),[42] while their officers, through long association with the barbarians, had massive ornaments on their breasts and weapons decorated with glittering cloisonné work.

Even Theodosius's heavenly supporters were hardly Roman. The apostles John and Philip came to him in a vision, on horseback like Gothic cavalrymen. Mounted saints were usually eastern (as, for example, Saint George of Merrie England), but they were also enormously popular among the Copts (see plate 36).[43]

Advancing to confront Theodosius and Stilicho came the rhetorician Eugenius, a Roman in spite of his name, and his two generals, the Roman consul Nicomachus Flavianus and Arbogast the Frank, at the head of an army of

Plate 35. Simeon Stylites, basalt monument (Syrian?). The best-known holy man of his day (389–459), Simeon was consulted by men of all stations in life, including Emperor Theodosius II. Simeon performed prodigies of self-denial, exemplifying the extremes of the ascetic idea. He lived on top of his sixty-foot pillar for thirty years. The basilica erected at his tomb at Qal'at Saman, in northwest Syria, still stands. Gregory of Tours (*History of the Franks* 8.15) relates the story of a Lombard deacon who tried to emulate Simeon in the Ardennes, but was forced to desist by order of his bishop (Delehaye, *Les saints stylites*, pp. i–xxxiv). *Courtesy of Musée du Louvre, Paris.*

Franks and Alamanni. They moved through mountain passes in which statues of Jupiter flashing golden thunderbolts had been set up as protection. The soldiers carried standards displaying images of Hercules. We see that Flavianus had selected the tutelary gods with care, since Jupiter traditionally represented the empire and Hercules the emperor. In other words, Flavianus made a patriotic reaffirmation of the idea of Rome.[44]

It was a religious war, with both sides feverishly invoking supernatural aid. At first the superior generalship of Arbogast, who made innovative tactical use of a difficult mountain pass, seemed about to bring victory to Hercules, because Theodosius's Goths were nearly wiped out. But then night fell, and Theodosius prayed until dawn. It is only fitting that the crisis of the Frigidus should have been resolved by a well-attested miracle. Theodosius displayed himself in the morning on a craggy cliff, high above both armies. There he prayed, publicly and conspicuously calling on heaven. He then made the sign of the cross as the signal to advance and stepped to the head of the column with a shout: "Where is the God of Theodosius?" A mighty wind roared from the mountains into the faces of Arbogast's men, blinding them with grit and dust, deflecting their weapons, jerking their shields this way and that. These soldiers were not on their home ground; they may never have heard of the Adriatic bora, let alone experienced anything like it. The psychological effect was more unnerving than the furious wind. The Roman gods met their match, and the last pagan army was shattered that day. Arbogast was the superior general, but Theodosius was luckier.

The emperor may have been alerted by some weather-wise local man in his entourage who recognized cloud formations characteristic of the high winds.[45] The forecasting of mountain winds is difficult even now, but a foehn wall (a bank of cumulus clouds barely showing over the mountain crests or lenticular clouds on the lee side of the mountains) is considered to be a fairly reliable indication that the wind will blow within the next hour or two.[46] The true miracle of the Frigidus may have been Theodosius's quick grasp of the possibilities of the situation.

Jupiter's golden thunderbolts were distributed among the jubilant troops, who joked that being struck by lightning was not so bad. Eugenius was beheaded; Flavianus and Arbogast turned their swords on themselves, like heroes of old.

It was a great day for the empire, people thought. The reason for rejoicing was the happy circumstance that Theodosius had managed to win a Roman victory. His Goths had spearheaded the attack on the first awful day, and thousands of them had fallen in the battle. That was highly satisfactory.[47]

Four months later, in January, 395, the great men of the empire assembled to hear Bishop Ambrose's funeral sermon for Emperor Theodosius, who died of a malady supposed to be related to dropsy. He left two young, not very intel-

Plate 36. Saint Victor, Coptic rider-saint, seventh–eighth century, limestone architrave from Sohâg, Upper Egypt. Saints on horseback were popular in Egypt and Syria; several of them were named Victor. British Museum 1276. *Courtesy of British Museum, London.*

ligent sons, Arcadius, emperor of the East, and Honorius, emperor of the West. On his deathbed Theodosius had placed Honorius under the guardianship of his trusted Vandal general Stilicho. Either the bishop concealed his misgivings or somehow he had lost his usual perceptiveness. Possibly he felt that in any case his own work was done: the pagans had been vanquished, and the church had effectively asserted its authority.[48] On that dreary occasion Ambrose seemed to feel that a new golden age of peace might be dawning. Yet there before him in the throng of mourners was Alaric, the man who was to lead the sack of Rome.

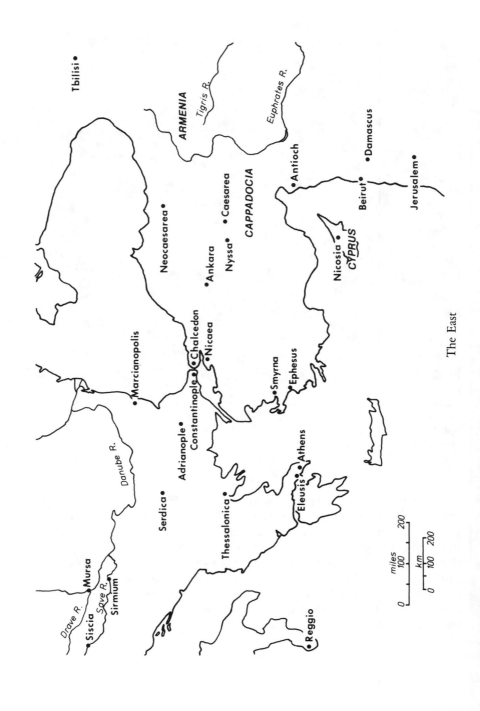

The East

CONSTANTINOPLE

Honorius and his brother, Arcadius, inherited a brittle empire that had a different look. The competent, Roman-minded Frankish generals and their aristocratic supporters were gone. In their place were clashing ministers who were acting in the name of the two bored young emperors, strong-minded women who were dangerously intent on advancing their own interests, and Gothic commanders who more often than not thought of themselves as leaders of their people rather than imperial officers.

If we were to select one year to mark the true crisis of the Roman Empire, we might not do badly in picking 395, the year in which Theodosius died, because from that time on cleavage between East and West became inevitable, with the barbarians acting as the wedge.

Even in Theodosius's time there was not much unity between the two parts of the empire. We need only remind ourselves of the long period of hesitation before Theodosius made up his mind to go to the rescue of Valentinian II when the latter was threatened by Maximus. Arianizing Milan had been unable to generate a feeling of partnership in the breast of orthodox Theodosius. His orthodoxy must have been a factor in the West too, where pagans and barbarian generals joined forces on behalf of Eugenius. The rise of Eugenius may have been largely the result of a reaction of outsiders to a growing clique of civil servants, who fitted too snugly into the rigid scheme of state religion that Theodosius had imposed.[1]

Further to complicate matters there was a struggle between the two parts of the empire concerning Illyricum, "the best nursery in the Empire for good fighting men,"[2] a territory that extended roughly over what is now northern Greece and the central Balkans. Probably in the time of Emperor Gratian, when Theodosius was summoned to become Augustus of the East, the part of Illyricum east of the river Save was placed under the administration of Constantinople. Under Theodosius it had not been important just how the diocese was managed, because in the final analysis it was the emperor who had control. When the West once more received its own Augustus, Honorius, the problem became more acute. Stilicho, as guardian for Honorius, promptly announced that Theodosius on his deathbed had told him that the whole of Illyricum henceforward should be part of the domain of the West. This unpalatable idea lead the East to try to make a tool of Alaric the Visigoth, for purposes of holding onto the territory, just as the West tried to use him in an effort to wrest it away.

East and West had a strange inability to realize that theirs was a common danger. They perceived the threats from barbarians on the frontiers and federates actually within the confines of the empire as purely localized phenomena. There was no longer any "central intelligence" to funnel accurate information back to the ruling authorities, and there were no recognizable diplomatic ties with powerful states beyond the Roman borders. In this piecemeal situation it would require extraordinary astuteness to comprehend that movements of barbarians in Numidia or on Britain's Saxon Shore or at the mouth of the Danube ought to evoke a total response from the imperial nerve centers. The use of barbarians as tools for on-the-spot operations continued, just as in the old days.[3] We have the considerable advantage of knowing how it all turned out, but it is curious to see that few persons in positions of authority were aware of the dangers inherent in such policies.

Although the central administration seems to have been either indifferent or lacking in caution, a current of public opinion, new in its strength, flowed directly from Theodosius's philobarbarian principles. Anti-Germanism was a growing force, especially in the East. Theodosius no doubt considered that he was merely extending a time-honored procedure when he deliberately courted former foes and made allies of them. Constantine the Great had relied heavily on Franks, as had Valentinian I and Gratian. For that matter there had been a Celtic legion as early as Caligula's day.[4] Why would it be wrong to entrust the empire to willing Goths?

We have seen how Roman in their attitudes some of the great Frankish officers like Bauto and Richomer could be. In the Goths, however, there was a formidable difference that Theodosius himself must have recognized to his chagrin. Even among those who remained at least outwardly willing to fit into the new scheme, the emperor had to deal with bloody strife originating in clashes between various Gothic factions intent on settling their own differences (the heathen Fravitta killed the Arian Eriulf right in the Great Palace at Constantinople, for instance). As early as 388, before the action against Maximus, in which Goths participated, some were discovered to be in treacherous negotiation with that usurper. These warriors fled to the swamps and mountains of Macedonia and sustained themselves there by raiding operations until

Theodosius was obliged to undertake a near-disastrous punitive expedition against them.

Inside the army the Goths were a demoralizingly disruptive force. Accustomed as they had always been to the most rigid discipline, what were Romans to make of a situation in which their comrades-in-arms came and went as they liked? Old-fashioned drill was abandoned, and the armed forces became less and less respectable every day.[5] Besides, the Goths were sometimes kept together as units under their own headstrong leaders. Within five years after the death of Theodosius these unruly bands were ravaging Asia Minor and Thrace, and for six bewildering months they even occupied Constantinople.

The East was extricated from this mess almost miraculously, by a combination of popular reaction and an organized antibarbarian movement in the court, plus assistance from the Huns, with the result that thereafter the West had to bear the brunt of the onrush of barbarian peoples. It might be said that Stilicho the Vandal, as guardian and later father-in-law and general of young Emperor Honorius, alone fell heir to the evils implicit in the policies of Emperor Theodosius.

It is almost impossible to determine just how or why this strange situation came about. We are at a loss in any attempt to discover the motives behind the actions of the most interesting protagonists. The historians of the period are even more contradictory than usual, and their writings are far more fragmented. We are thrown back on two unorthodox sources, neither of which offers much ground for confidence. The first, a set of overblown panegyrics, is Claudian, who was as much Stilicho's mouthpiece as a court poet.[6] In the words of Gibbon, "Some criticism will be requisite to translate the language of fiction or exaggeration into the truth and simplicity of historic prose." Claudian, incidentally, is an interesting phenomenon—the one poet of the times fit to rank with the poets of the classical age. So steeped was he in classical tradition and feeling that we would not even be aware of the existence of Christianity if his writings had happened to be the only ones to survive from his century.

Our second source of information is Synesius of Cyrene, a philosopher who went from his native Egypt to Constantinople on a political errand and became spokesman of the antibarbarian faction at court. Synesius perversely elected to present what he witnessed in the form of an elaborate roman à clef set in Egypt.

It is entertaining to watch reputable scholars earnestly poring over these literary creations, trying to derive firm data from them. Who are the *geminis tyrannis* of line 284 in Claudian's *De bello getico*? Reinold Pallman votes for Alaric and Radagaisus; J. Rosenstein, for Maximus and Eugenius, using that interpretation as foundation for a whole chronology of events in northern Italy.[7] The wolves in Synesius's *Egyptian Tale* were Huns, were they not?[8] And

Plate 37. Emperor Arcadius, ruler of the East after the death of his father, Theodosius I, marble portrait head, late fourth–early fifth century, found at Bayazit, Turkey. This is a much-idealized portrait of the somnolent emperor, who was putty in the hands of his wife and scheming courtiers. *Courtesy of Arkeoloji Müzeleri, Istanbul.*

who was Typhos, brother of Osiris, in the same story? Such questions as these are unsettling for the historian who wants events tidily under his control.

Antibarbarianism was explicit in Constantinople, and no wonder. We must have a look now at the period immediately following the death of Theodosius, to see what happened in the East.

We too readily assume that barbarians presented a united front. For the closing years of the fourth century we make an even more drastic error, picturing Alaric the Visigoth as the sole source of the empire's difficulties. The Visigoths split after the battle at the Frigidus. The pro-Roman general Gainas, who had outranked Alaric as commander of the Gothic contingent in the great victory over Eugenius, continued to head a large force, still taking his orders from Stilicho, though he and his troops properly belonged to Emperor Arcadius, in the East. Alaric, who had to content himself with a subordinate position under Gainas, led his more nationalist-minded people back to the far side of the Adriatic. He was still smarting from the humiliation of his inferior status and angry because of the exposed position that he and his men had had to occupy during the battle, as though they were cheap and expendable. He soon became the elected leader of the Visigoths. As the Gothic historian Jordanes explains it, "The contempt of the Goths for the Romans soon increased, and for fear their valor would be destroyed by long peace, they appointed Alaric king over them."[9] Election of a leader by the Goths implied a war footing.

There was no love lost between Alaric and Gainas, both proud, jealous men. Before long, it may fairly be said, Gainas, who originally supported Rome, embodied the barbarian problem as far as the East was concerned, whereas, ironically, anti-Roman Alaric was able to draw profit from this circumstance.

Gainas and his Goths might not have loomed so large if there had not been bitterness between Stilicho and his opposite number at the court of Arcadius, the clever, unscrupulous Rufinus, praetorian prefect of the East, who was bent on insinuating himself into a position of power equaling that of Stilicho at the court of Honorius.

At one time and another Rufinus entered into shady, complicated dealings with the barbarians, but there were some extenuating circumstances that the poems of Claudian neglect to mention. Rufinus had been left rather in the lurch when Theodosius marched off at the head of his gigantic army to do battle with Eugenius, and now Stilicho was holding that army, possibly with the intention of advancing on Constantinople to establish his authority in the East. Stilicho was letting it be known that Emperor Theodosius had made him the protector of both his sons. That may explain why Rufinus surrounded himself with a huge bodyguard, recruited from a splinter group of Huns who had been settled as federates in Thrace.[10] He is thought at that time to have entertained some notion of forming an alliance with the Huns against the

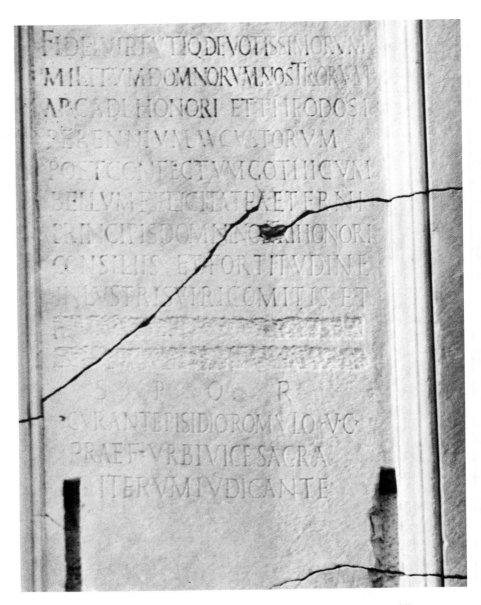

Plate 38. Defaced monument to Stilicho and others, Roman Forum. The monument was erected by the Senate and the people of Rome to celebrate the victory over the Goths at Pollenza in 402. The inscription praises the valor of the armies of Arcadius, Honorius, Theodosius, and "the renowned man, Count ———." The renowned man was Stilicho, whose name and titles were chipped away after his disgrace and execution in 408.

Goths.[11] Rufinus is supposed to have made use of the Visigoths also, inciting Alaric to lead his people out of Thrace into Greece. The only possible explanation of this outwardly preposterous move might be that he thought of Alaric as a decoy, intended to lure Stilicho into a position of weakness.

For what it is worth, it is true that Alaric did indeed break in, and it is likewise true that Stilicho reacted by moving not only the troops that belonged to the East but his own western forces as well. He reached Thessaly and outmaneuvered Alaric, penning the Goths in a narrow valley. At this point Rufinus played his risky trump card, causing his figurehead emperor to order Stilicho to quit his lands and leave the eastern forces behind, returning them to Constantinople. Stilicho obeyed, to the consternation of modern historians, who cannot see why he failed to push his advantage and settle the question of Illyricum right then. Stilicho's wife, Serena, and their child were in Constantinople at the time; perhaps he believed that hostile action by him would bring harm to them.

It is generally accepted that before Stilicho withdrew to Italy he and Gainas arrived at an agreement that Rufinus should be a target marked for destruction. Gainas, leading back the soldiers of Arcadius's reclaimed army, was met outside the walls of Constantinople by the emperor and his triumphant prefect. The murder of Rufinus before the eyes of his emperor was a grisly piece of work. Gainas's men literally tore Rufinus apart. It was not a military coup in the usual sense, for Gainas did not immediately step into an official position of power. Nevertheless, he was a feared presence from that time on.

All of this occurred late in 395, which was an eventful year in many other ways. In the spring of that year, even before the body of Theodosius had been returned to Constantinople, a beautiful young woman was escorted in a gorgeous procession to become the emperor's bride. She was consul Bauto's daughter Eudoxia. Since the death of her illustrious father she had been part of the household of Promotus, a friend of Stilicho's. The marriage was highly repugnant to Rufinus, who had cherished a dream of seeing his own daughter clothed in the dignity of an Augusta and himself the father-in-law of an emperor, to match Stilicho in power and prestige. Emperor Arcadius had not been adventurous enough to find a bride for himself. The eunuch Eutropius (the emperor's lord chamberlain), an enemy of Rufinus, had arranged the match on the sly. Inevitably, after Rufinus was murdered, Eutropius was able to move into a position of such influence that he could assume some of the administrative authority that properly belonged to the praetorian prefect,[12] to become the most feared man at the lamentably orientalized court, where the emperor lived in remote, unreal magnificence, out of touch, unaware, and indifferent. Offices could be bought and sold, and informers were everywhere.

At first Eutropius made a point of being friendly to Stilicho, though the amity was of short duration. It may be that he invited Stilicho to the East again for a confrontation with Alaric, who had been allowed to have his will in Greece after Stilicho's first abortive expedition. Stilicho, who seems to have been the only man of his time who was aware that the empire was only as strong as its weakest frontier, had just returned from a fast trip to the Rhine, where he had brought some order out of the various treaty relationships with the Franks and their jealous kinglets. Once again he pinned Alaric down, and once again the Visigoths went free. Stilicho turned back to Italy, this time because of the urgent need to deal with Gildo, the *comes* of Africa. Gildo was engaged in negotiations with Eutropius for the purpose of transferring his domain to the East.

Soon there was open enmity between Stilicho and Eutropius. Assassination attempts are said to have been made on both sides. Ultimately Emperor Arcadius was induced to declare Stilicho a public enemy and confiscate all his property in the East.[13]

Before his disengagement from the situation in Greece, Stilicho seems to have made an arrangement with Alaric whereby the Visigoths would occupy Illyricum for the benefit of the West, but Alaric kept his own eyes on the main chance and allowed Eutropius to give him a military title of some sort in the service of Arcadius. He may have become a dux, the title customarily given to barbarian chieftains responsible for guarding the frontier.[14] According to the *Notitia dignitatum*, the weapons factories of Illyricum were not under such an officer, yet we know that Alaric had control of them and used their output to arm his Visigoths in the Roman manner. The Eastern court may have suspected that Alaric would not be averse to an invasion of Italy. It would then make sense to ignore any overstepping of competence.[15] Alaric must have derived malignant amusement from the situation. Claudian puts these words into his mouth: "When legal authority was given me, I caused the Thracians to exert themselves prodigiously to produce missiles, swords and helmets. With legal authority, I compelled the Roman cities to deliver iron for my use."

Gainas, meanwhile, had not been idle. Evidently he managed to arouse Eutropius's suspicions, because the Theodosian Code for the year 397 contains legislation believed to have been framed with Gainas in mind. It prescribes the death penalty for anyone conspiring with soldiers or private persons, including barbarians, "against the lives of *illustres* who belong to our consistory."[16]

Eutropius was teetering on the razor edge of a disaster largely of his own making. His stupendous ill-gained wealth, his unsavory ways, his spies all combined to make him an object of hatred. The circumstance that he was a eunuch did not help him much. The fiercely patriotic antibarbarian party that coalesced around Aurelian, the aristocratic old-style prefect of the city, was so much attached to ancient tradition that its members felt disgraced when Eutropius the eunuch was made consul for the year 399.

There was a probarbarian party too, including even some Romans. One of these is assumed to have been the brother of the prefect Aurelian, though we know him only as "Typhos" in Synesius's Egyptian story. The fearsome Gothic commander Gainas had the support of this party. When the Ostrogoths in Asia Minor under their leader Tribigild went into revolt because of some real or fancied slight by Eutropius, it was Gainas who was sent to deal with the disturbance. We have no evidence that Gainas and Tribigild had connived beforehand, but the two men soon realized that theirs was a rich opportunity. There was unrest all around the barbarian periphery of the empire, and it must have been common knowledge that Alaric was managing to use the great ministers who were trying to make him their tool. The Huns were in movement again, and the Persians were in a threatening posture. Gainas and Tribigild must have sensed that the time was ripe for sending out some kind of call. Slaves would certainly flock to them, and probably almost anybody with barbarian blood in his veins would feel a quiver of excitement. So, indeed, it turned out. In Asia Minor noble cities were plundered, and hapless citizens were slaughtered.

Ambassador Synesius, meanwhile, had been waiting to enter the royal presence to offer the gift of a golden crown from his fellow citizens and to deliver an oration that he had been polishing, perhaps in consultation with his friend the prefect Aurelian. At this point the summons came. Synesius's speech was not the flattering effusion that indolent Arcadius must have expected, if indeed he had given it any thought at all. He may have dozed through it, but the effect on the two groups of antagonists was electrifying. For the pro-Romans it was nothing short of a manifesto, and for Gainas and his supporters it was a declaration of war.[17] Synesius painted a stirring picture of what a real emperor ought to be. He thought much more highly of bald old Emperor Carus back in the third century, sitting on the ground in his bedraggled, sun-faded purple to share repulsive rations with his weary troops, than he did of a modern emperor who dressed like a peacock and left government to eunuchs and defense to untrustworthy Goths. Arcadius must rouse himself and put the barbarians to work in the fields or send them back across the Danube. He must make the army Roman once more.

Eutropius discovered that he had no defenders, only attackers in both parties. Possibly moved by Synesius's oratory, Empress Eudoxia, who owed her own lofty station to the hated lord chamberlain, appeared before her husband, demanding the dismissal of Eutropius. Eudoxia was half-barbarian herself, but let us not forget that her barbarian blood was that of her splendid father, Bauto the Frank. Gainas also called for the dismissal of Eutropius as the only way to pacify Tribigild, the offended Ostrogoth.

A melodramatic scene ensued. Eutropius cowered under an altar, while the patriarch of the city thundered a scathing sermon. The emperor's soldiers ignored the claim of sanctuary and dragged the miscreant away. Eutropius was deprived of all his possessions and banished.

Next came a struggle between Aurelian and his supposed brother "Typhos" for the office of praetorian prefect, which had fallen vacant in the general upset. To the elation of his party Aurelian was appointed, but that was not the end of the matter. Gainas and Tribigild became open allies and marched on Constantinople. Gainas was arrogant enough to demand that the emperor come out to meet him at Chalcedon; the emperor was weak enough to comply. There Gainas demanded and received the powerful office of master of soldiers and secured the prefect Aurelian and two other leaders of the antibarbarians, whom he retained as hostages. "Typhos" succeeded Aurelian. The patriarch John Chrysostom persuaded Gainas not to execute his hostages but to banish them instead.

Gainas triumphantly entered Constantinople to begin a period of fumbling domination. He had no objectives, no vision, no plan for handling the explosive situation. His only recorded move was a call for a church for Arian worship within the city walls, but here again the patriarch was persuasive and coaxed Gainas away from the idea.

Students of crowd psychology could hardly find a better example of what can happen when two population groups ignorant of each other's motives and harboring built-in prejudices are forced into close association (most of the following account of the expulsion of the Goths is based on Albert Güldenpenning's interpretation of Synesius's *Egyptian Tale*, which he considers historically trustworthy).[18] Gainas, vacillating by nature, grew increasingly anxious and irresolute to the point of becoming ill. We almost feel tempted to call his illness psychosomatic. His indecision communicated itself to his Goths, who began walking timorously in the streets of Constantinople, afraid to move about alone for fear of murderous attack. The people of the city also walked in dread, circulating rumors that Gainas was planning to take over the banks, set fire to the Great Palace, and so on. Panic spread without any basis; the appearance of a large comet was enough to banish reason.[19] Finally, using his ill health as an excuse, Gainas departed from the city to pray at the nearby shrine of John the Baptist. His men began drifting after him, taking along their families and wagons loaded with goods. Rumors flew even more thickly. The alarmed city population began senseless preparations for putting out fires, for flight by ship, even for suicide. It took only the yammering of an old beggar woman by the city gate to touch off a mighty brawl in the early dawn. Terrified barbarians and furious citizens soon were engaged in a melée that ended when a clamorous horde of Goths was hopelessly trapped in a church. The roof was fired and crashed down on the multitude within.

Gainas now fled in earnest, only to find his escape route blocked by Fravitta, the pro-Roman Goth. Moreover, the lands that Gainas thought of as his homeland had fallen to the Huns. The Hunnic leader Uldín attacked and dispatched Gainas's wretched head to Emperor Arcadius as a gift. He was rewarded with handsome presents and a treaty, while Fravitta was elevated to the rank of consul for the year 401 and allowed to celebrate a triumph.

Güldenpenning thinks that Gainas had the power to effect a total reversal in the state, to achieve at least a sort of independence similar to that of the Visigoths. His failure lay not only in his own wavering personality and the inequality and tribal differences among his followers but also in the passive resistance that the East was able to oppose to him, with its extended borders, difficult terrain, and many cities. In Güldenpenning's opinion this conflict, which was followed by a slow retrogression of the Germanic element, can be justly regarded as a turning point in the history of the Eastern empire. He observes that the relative ease with which the powerful adversary was brought down must have shocked Alaric and the other Goths into reluctance to proceed once more against the East. [20]

Alaric turned his face toward Italy.

ROME AND RAVENNA

A BOUT half way through the period of Stilicho's control in the West, the enthusiastic people of Rome rewarded him with a monument in the Forum, but when we examine what remains of that monument today, still standing in a position of conspicuous honor in front of the Curia, we see that his name and titles have been purposefully effaced, no doubt by the same once-grateful people. Stilicho was a traitor, they said. He brought in the barbarians. He was party to dishonorable alliances with Alaric. He wanted to make his own son Eucherius emperor. He was an enemy of Christianity. He burned the Sibylline Books. If all this is so, the end of Stilicho's story makes no sense. His loyal bodyguard would have fought for him to the death in Ravenna when his enemies, riding the crest of antibarbarian sentiment, managed to convince Emperor Honorius that his great minister was his most dangerous foe. Instead of allowing any action to be taken on his behalf, Stilicho stepped forward in stern obedience to the emperor's sentence and suffered himself to be decapitated. Did he value the empire more than his own life?

There are two ways of looking at almost everything that Stilicho did, depending upon the bias of the contemporary writer or our own intuitions. Many take sides with unscholarly passion. There is little doubt that Stilicho was ambitious and that he was hard enough not to blanch at the idea of murder, but whether or not self-advancement was the mainspring of his existence is another question.

He started off in a fortunate position, as a member of an elite corps known as *protectores*, a personal staff of the emperor, generally made up of young barbarian nobles and Romans of good family. His Vandal father had held fairly substantial rank in the auxiliaries of the Roman army under Emperor Valens. The *protectores* enjoyed the curious distinction of being among those who were allowed to "adore the purple." In other words, they were admitted to the very presence of the emperor (Theodosius, in Stilicho's youth), where they would touch and kiss his royal robe.[1] In spite of the obvious advantages of such a post, Stilicho did not begin his rise to power until he returned from a diplomatic mission of some sort and was noticed by Theodosius's favorite niece, his adopted daughter, Serena. The young lady was so struck by Stilicho's good looks and impressive height that she announced in no uncertain terms that she intended to marry him. Theodosius could deny Serena nothing: the wedding took place, probably in 384. After that Stilicho headed the imperial guard and then moved higher and higher in military rank, though the sequence and dates of his promotions are hard to follow.

By the time Theodosius decided to erect the huge Egyptian obelisk as an embellishment to the Hippodrome in Constantinople, Stilicho's position was such that it was natural to depict his little son Eucherius on the elaborately carved base that supports the great shaft, standing beside the emperor in the royal box along with young Honorius (see plate 39).[2] The panegyrist Claudian makes a point of referring to Eucherius as the emperor's grandson. Even at his tender age the youngster was engaged to Theodosius's daughter Galla Placidia, while Stilicho's little daughter Maria was to marry Honorius when she reached an appropriate age. It should not astonish us, therefore, that Theodosius on his deathbed entrusted Honorius's guardianship and regency to Stilicho, as the best-qualified member of the royal household.

It would be helpful to know more about Stilicho's wife, Serena. She was not in the least hesitant about using spies and embroiling herself in public business. It is possible that some of the actions that brought down so much wrath on Stilicho may have been inspired by his impetuous wife. The fleeting glimpses that we have of her are so suggestive that it is tempting to fit the pieces together arbitrarily. Just how much did Serena have to do with the destruction of the Sibylline Books, for instance? This alleged crime of Stilicho's ranked in its enormity with Nero's matricide, in inflamed pagan minds.

Pagan or Christian, no one scoffed at the Sibylline Books. They were of such hoary antiquity and their commands had been obeyed to the letter for so many centuries that they could not be lightly dismissed even in a Christian empire. Physically they were flimsy enough, their mysterious verses palely written on palm leaves or linen, so faded that special priestly custodians were obliged to copy and recopy them as the centuries passed. Emotionally and spiritually, however, they were practically indestructible. They had been reverently consulted in time of plague, famine, and crisis almost from ages past man's imagining, and through them religious bonds had been established that welded together distant parts of the empire. The point to be considered here is that in the days of Hannibal the message derived from the oracular verses had been that the Great Mother goddess should be brought to Rome from Asia Minor to expel the invader.[3] If we skip from 205 B.C., when that took place, to the time of Serena, we find that she audaciously entered the temple of the

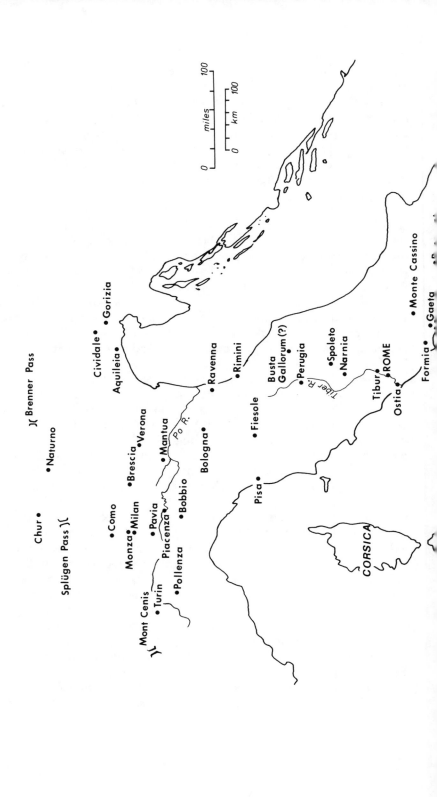

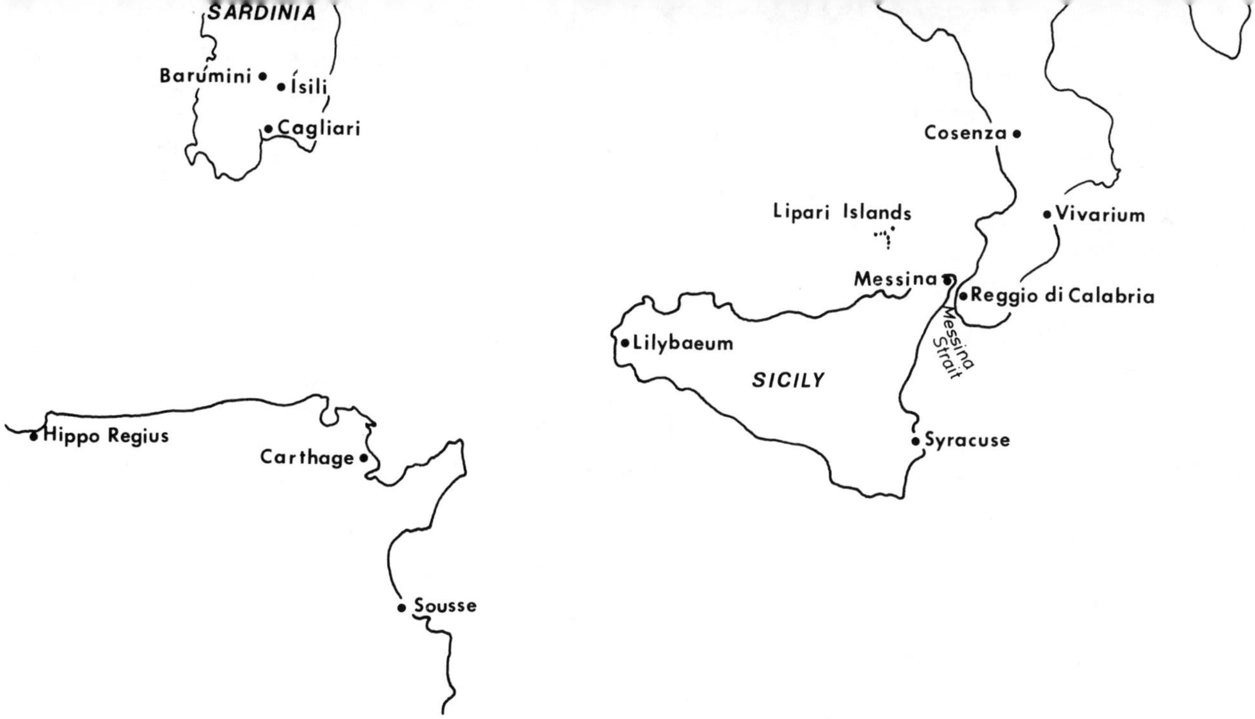

SARDINIA

Barúmini • • Ísili
        •Cagliari

Cosenza •

Lipari Islands

Messina
Messina
Strait

•Vivarium

•Reggio di Calabria

Syracuse

SICILY

•Lilybaeum

Hippo Regius

Carthage
•

Sousse

Italy

Plate 39. Eucherius, son of Stilicho, with Theodosius I and young Honorius, panel at the base of the Egyptian obelisk in the Hippodrome, Istanbul.

Great Mother when she accompanied Emperor Theodosius to Rome, stripped the cult statue of its necklace, and emerged wearing the glittering ornament while a vestal fulminated.[4] Is it too audacious at this distance to entertain the notion that it may have been Serena, not Stilicho, who wanted the Sibylline Books burned?

Admittedly, Stilicho had his own ample reasons for such destruction. The Sibylline Books had become instruments of antibarbarian propaganda,[5] and Stilicho was already under oblique attack from pagans and Christians alike because of his ambiguous relationships with Goths, Huns, and Alans. Nor did people forget that Stilicho himself was half Vandal. Barbed comments were coming from all directions. About a year before Stilicho's downfall an angry Jerome took up his pen and wrote a piece of exegesis on the Book of Daniel in which he managed to epitomize what people were coming to feel about barbarians. The feet and toes of the statue in Nebuchadnezzar's dream were part iron, part clay, "which clearly refers to our time. Verily, just as at the beginning nothing was stronger or harder than the Roman Empire, toward the end nothing is weaker, since in civil war as in war against various nations we need the help of the barbarians." Jerome's monastic establishment in Bethlehem was anything but a retreat from the world.[6] The scholar was at the heart of a vast communications network, in contact with some of the most powerful families in Rome. What Jerome wrote swiftly became common knowledge to the senators. Shortly before Stilicho's fall Jerome seems to have written a faint-hearted retraction, which he mentions in a subsequent work, *In Isaiam*. In that paper he asks his friend Pammachius to intervene with the emperor on his behalf. Someone in Stilicho's still-powerful entourage must have expressed displeasure.[7]

Like Stilicho, Alaric the Visigoth inspires reluctant, somewhat tentative admiration. His motives are obscure to us, but we reflect that we hear about him only from his enemies. Both men seem to have had a wider vision than that of most of their contemporaries. They had something more than their own private gain in mind. Both seem to have been struggling toward an impossible, dimly understood goal of mutual accommodation. Stilicho never cut down Alaric, and Alaric in turn seems never to have so much as dreamed of trying to destroy the empire. His approach was negotiation first, for the sake of a home for his people. Among his own Visigoths, Alaric was no dictator. In accordance with tribal custom he consulted with his council of "optimates" (to use E. A. Thompson's term for tribal elites) and was accompanied by them at parleys. He did have one characteristic that alarmingly suggests the dictator: he sometimes heard a mysterious Voice.

How different the course of history might have been if Stilicho and Alaric had occupied the stage alone. Such an idea is pure nonsense, unfortunately. There were the two emperors. There were the jealous ministers in the East, an increasingly hostile Senate in the West, growing antibarbarian sentiment at Honorius's court, fierce anger among some of the soldiery, Alans and Huns and Ostrogoths and Vandals stamping around in Gaul, an upstart emperor there, a rebel in Africa, and churchmen busily spinning webs of intrigue.

Alaric appeared in Italy for the first time in the year 400, leading a huge wagon train.[8] The news that he had set foot on Italian soil and massed his people near Aquileia, at the head of the Adriatic, was enough to generate panic. Honorius and his courtiers babbled about fleeing from Milan to Gaul to save their skins, while in the Eternal City there was feverish activity, with special attention to the crumbled encircling walls.

Stilicho was able to stop the stampede away from Milan. He himself hurried off for reinforcements. His army must have been woefully inadequate, because it took him the better part of a year to collect a sufficient force, stripping the Rhine frontier and even calling in troops from as far away as Britain.

Such as they are, the records of the time are hopelessly muddled. There can hardly be said to be a consensus even today concerning the course of events or what lay back of them. Historians are perplexed. Why did Alaric linger as long as he did in Venetia? He could not have moved rapidly, hampered as he was by old people, women, children, and all their impedimenta. This was a migration, not an invasion. Stilicho seems to have been able to relieve Milan, but why, we wonder, was the major engagement with Alaric at Pollentia (modern Pollenza)? It is almost due south of Turin and is an extremely odd place to be if you have passed through Aquileia and are heading for Rome. The location suggests that Alaric may have been trying to beat his way to Gaul, though it seems to be fairly well established that there was no talk of Gaul as a place for Visigothic colonizing until much later.[9]

After the bitter, possibly drawn battle at Pollentia, at Easter, 402, Stilicho appears to have ordered Alaric to quit Italy, but there was another battle at Verona in which Alaric fared much worse than he had at Pollentia. He was in personal danger; his horde was demoralized. He turned back whence he came and apparently spent several years in Epirus in Stilicho's pay.

Stilicho, meanwhile, had to drive off much fiercer onslaughts by much more ferocious barbarians (mostly Ostrogoths) under the leadership of one Radagaisus. These Goths also moved with long, lumbering wagon trains, which made military maneuvers extremely difficult.[10] Armed outriders could reconnoiter, but the body of invaders could not move effectively against an organized army. This time Stilicho showed no compunction in destroying fellow barbarians, despite what his enemies charged with respect to his gingerly handling of Alaric. Using a force of Huns, Alans, and Goths under Alaric's sworn enemy the violent Sarus, Stilicho penned Radagaisus near Fiesole and starved him into submission by the simple expedient of blocking the narrow defiles from the valley pockets in which he was trapped. Some of Radagaisus's followers escaped, but it was essentially an operation of destruction. A few remnants of the host were sold into slavery.

What would one do with a slave in a world gone awry? For one thing, an alarming amount of abandoned land was standing idle for want of people to cultivate it. The population of the empire had been steadily diminishing for generations. There had never been a proper recovery from the plague outbreaks, the famines, and the general disorders of the latter part of the third century.[11] Emperor Theodosius had been so concerned that he had offered to give full title to anyone who would farm abandoned land for two consecutive years. Who would be able to buy slaves in such a situation? Only those who already had tremendous holdings and did not need to engage in intensive cultivation of the land. Wealth among the landholding senators could still be staggering. In a contemporary satire one of the characters remarks, "What I'd like to do now is add Sicily to my little bits of land, so that when I go to Africa I could sail there without leaving my own property."[12]

There would have been a place for those stubborn Ostrogoths who so uncooperatively allowed Stilicho to starve them to death. It would have been helpful if they had surrendered while they were still in reasonably good condition, because slaves did not breed well in captivity, and the wealthy needed them. An aristocrat was supposed to move about like an oriental potentate with a retinue of bodyguards, in a train swelling his progress as he passed through the city, "tearing up the pavement," as Ammianus said, in a lofty silver coach. Statistics are undependable at best, but sobering evidence exists that there was at least one slave, if not two, for every free male in the city of Rome.[13]

As we are learning day by day, a large city is vulnerable in many ways. This was true of Rome, where the splendor and daring of public structures was in stark contrast to the living quarters of ordinary folk in the walled metropolis. The wealthy had their palaces and gardens, but most of the others—except the slaves, who lived in cellars beneath the municipal buildings or slept under the stairs in their masters' houses—were crammed into multistoried apartment houses, firetraps of the worst sort.[14] There were not only the fire hazard and the danger of building collapse but also the dismal fact that no one above the ground floor had access to water other than public supplies in the street. The squalor and din of the tiny apartments were bound to produce a restive, surly population, the kind that is always on the verge of an outbreak. It is not difficult to imagine the mood of a man who has been tramping the city all day as an itinerant barber, ready to set up his chair and shave a customer on a street corner, or of an exhausted load carrier coming home to such a place for the night.

Christian piety was becoming a disruptive force, indirectly setting at odds the laboring freemen, the slaves, and the poor who depended on a dole. It also generated anger and trepidation among the aristocrats. This disquiet stemmed from the enthusiasm of a clique of blueblood ladies whose love of the Lord, coupled perhaps with boredom and a vague gallows sense of impending doom, led them to rejection of accepted property values. Urged on by the foremost ascetics of the day (Paulinus of Nola, Rufinus of Aquileia, and his enemy Jerome), the ringleaders among the headstrong Roman ladies, who were related by the complex ties of senatorial intermarriages, quickly became dissatisfied with mere retirement from what has been aptly called a "competitive salon culture."[15] Giving away one's silks and jewels and wearing a hair shirt under a simple gown was no longer enough.[16] They shattered the accepted social pattern in a way that can only be described as fanatic. As early as 385 the lady Paula took her daughter on pilgrimage. They went first to Palestine, where Paula indulged in unseemly transports at the sight of holy relics, and then moved on to visit the holy men of the Egyptian desert before returning to the Mount of Olives, where Paula established her convent. Melania the Elder, the most famous of these early ascetics and the most determined maker of pros-

Plate 40. The Clivus Scauri, Rome, second–third centuries. Aside from the monu-
mental ruins in the Forum, which afford no impression of everyday life in the city,
little remains from our period in modern Rome, but the Clivus Scauri has survived. This thoroughfare leads to the aristocratic quarter where such luminaries as
the Anicii and the Symmachi had their palaces. The Clivus Scauri was part of the
property of Gregory the Great. He converted his estate into a monastery called
Saint Andrew the Apostle. Here we see the façades of multiple dwellings; apartments occupied the upper floors, while shops with their back rooms were on the
ground floor.

elytes, likewise traveled the pilgrim route to the desert before betaking herself to the Holy Land. In later years, when she learned that her namesake granddaughter wanted to adopt the ascetic way, she hurried back to Rome to encourage her. It was the resolution of Melania the Younger that had the strongest repercussions in Roman society, at a time when Rome could least withstand any additional strains and tremors in her foundations.

As Roman fortunes went, Melania's was not excessive. Her home was on the Mons Caelius, in the most exclusive residential quarter of the city, where the Anicii and the Symmachi and Laterani had their palaces. She had estates in Campania and Apulia and in Spain, Gaul, and Britain, as well as in Sicily, Africa, Mauretania, and Numidia. Her biographer, who knew her well, stated that she had 24,000 slaves, 8,000 of whom she freed. No modern historian appears to be inclined to challenge these figures. There have been many futile attempts to arrive at a modern monetary equivalent of Melania's annual income, which was said to amount to 120,000 solidi (the solidus was a gold coin). If she were to unload all that at once, the market would be seriously shaken.

Melania was barely twenty years old, and her aristocratic husband, Pinianus, was just twenty-four. Their two children had died in infancy. Since it was their intention to live henceforth as celibates, the presumed heir to their holdings was Pinianus's brother Valerius Severus. His move to block the young couple showed comprehension of the forces at work in Rome. Shrewdly he incited Melania's slaves to revolt in protest against their impending sale to strangers. Melania's own understanding of the situation was somewhat blurred. She proposed to sell her slaves apparently to have more money to give to the poor. That, by the way, was not a unique example of confrontations in which slaves sided with the aristocrats and freedmen sided with the church.[17] Melania, foreseeing other uprisings among the slaves in farflung provinces, sought some legal means to solve her problem. In Roman law full financial competence was not attained until one's twenty-fifth year, and the only legal way to circumvent the law was by means of a venia aetatis, obtained through the prefect of the city in his capacity as presiding officer of the Senate. Melania and Pinianus must have realized that Valerius Severus was not alone in his opinions and that there was little likelihood that the Senate would assist them, concerned as its members always were about any possible threat to the price structure. They found another way, though in the end it probably had a lot to do with the dreadful death of Stilicho's wife, Serena.

In the summer of 404, soon after Melania's father, Publicola, died, leaving a still greater fortune in her hands, Melania applied for an audience with Serena. The story of this interview is given at length in the biography of Melania. The narrator says that he heard it many times from Melania's own lips, and indeed it is not unlikely that he himself was actually present. Serena

Plate 41. The Aurelian Walls of Rome, near the Porta Ardeatina. The Aurelian Walls were begun in 271 and completed about ten years later. The circuit is eighteen kilometers. In the portion shown here, the walls are about four meters thick and twenty meters high. Originally there were 381 towers at thirty-meter intervals. In 403, Stilicho directed extensive restoration of the walls to preserve the city against the Gothic threat. Belisarius undertook still further refurbishing (Giuseppina Sommella Bede, ed., *Le mura di Aureliano a Roma: esposizione documentaria organizzata dal Centro internazionale per lo studio della cerchia urbane*).

was overwhelmed by the piety of Melania, who appeared before her garbed in black, with her head covered. Melania had found precisely the advocate she needed. Serena, whom the biographer naïvely calls "the empress," promised to go at once to Emperor Honorius to obtain a directive whereby the intricate process of liquidating Melania's vast holdings could begin. Responsibility would be delegated to the various competent provincial magistrates. The Senate does not appear to have been consulted, even in a courteously vacuous, pro forma way.

No one, not even Serena, had the money to buy Melania's palace, but it was stripped bare of its costly marbles, some of which were given to Serena in gratitude for her assistance. It is interesting to see that the great lady accepted the marbles only after she had virtuously refused some precious necklaces, with the comment that, since all these things were consecrated to God, it would be "sacrilege" to take them. Presumably Serena remembered that her daring action in taking the Great Mother's necklace had infuriated the pagans. It would not be wise to inflame the Christians as well. Melania's palace was never sold, but fell in ruins at the time of Alaric's sack of the city. She went first to Sicily, thence to Africa, where she owned an estate at Tagaste (Augustine's birthplace). In 417 she moved on to the Holy Land and established a monastery there. She died in 439.

Rome's time had not quite yet come, but Stilicho was living in a nightmare. Alaric had met failure in his two ventures into Italy, but he had caused extremely severe dislocations. Stilicho had had to respond to his incursions by stripping the Rhine garrisons. There was no longer any protection to speak of against all those hordes jostling in the north.

The Alans, migrating north from Pannonia along with the two branches of the Vandals (the Asdings and the Silings), were first to reach the Rhine, under the leadership of their two kings, Goar and Respendial. Here we find Goar offering his services to Rome. The Asding Vandals, advancing in the wake of the Alans, were cut off by Franks who were still defending the Rhine in their role as Roman federates, whereupon the Alans under Respendial joined in the battle and saved the Vandals from destruction. The combined horde of Alans and Vandals fell on Trier, sacking it before moving on to Reims, Amiens, and Arras. The Burgundians meanwhile were swept along by the general turmoil and settled temporarily on the left bank of the Rhine.

When we read contemporary accounts, we are led to think that all the unfortunate cities in the path of the Alans and Vandals were utterly demolished (this is the picture that Salvian presented). If, on the other hand, we follow along with historical reconstructions based on archaeological evidence and documents, we are inclined to believe that the cities survived fairly well.[18] Whether or not the physical destruction was drastic, we can be sure that there was much human misery (see plate 42).

There was no earthly chance that the East would respond to a call for help. Empress Eudoxia had unwittingly seen to that before she died by entering into a dispute with John Chrysostom, the patriarch of Constantinople. This quarrel, like many other quarrels in which churchmen were concerned, ultimately involved not only the empress and the patriarch but also the archbishop of Alexandria, Coptic monks from the Nitrian desert, the bishop of Cyprus, and ultimately the pope and the emperor of the West, to say nothing of rioting mobs on the streets of Constantinople who threw Egyptian sailors into the

Plate 42. The top of the amphitheater at Arles. When we contemplate such massive construction, we can only wonder at the popular notion that the barbarians had the means to destroy the great cities of Gaul.

harbor. The story is long, complex, and fascinating in an involuted Byzantine way, but what we need to extract from it is the knowledge that in the end John Chrysostom was banished. From his exile he called on Pope Innocent I to act on his behalf. Innocent's envoys were treated with inexcusable violence, and Emperor Honorius was moved to address at least three letters of protest to his imperial brother. Emperor Arcadius did not deign to respond. Stilicho saw in all this a perfect justification for closing the ports of Italy to ships from the East. In modern terms the two halves of the empire were in a period of cold war.

Possibly this hardened situation had something to do with Alaric's next move. The East showed signs of strengthening its position in Illyricum; he may have thought that he was in danger of being trapped in Epirus. In 407 he took his forces north again, presumably in the expectation that Stilicho would cross over and join him in open war against the East. At this point Stilicho received an erroneous report that Alaric had died and a true report that the usurper Constantine had arrived in Gaul from Britain. Stilicho had to revise whatever plans he may have had about Illyricum and Alaric in order to dispose of the usurper immediately. He dispatched fierce Sarus the Goth and a force of barbarians, but they were unable to accomplish their mission and returned to Italy, harassed all the way through the Alps by brigands (Bacaudae) who lurked in the mountain passes.

Almost simultaneously with Sarus's defeat Alaric appeared on the very frontier of Italy, demanding recompense for all his efforts. His emissaries pointed to the long, difficult trek to Epirus, the fruitless and rather dangerous wait there, and now the return trip. In response Stilicho hurried to Rome, where he made a most extraordinary revelation to the assembled Senate. He produced a letter from Emperor Honorius to prove that Alaric had indeed been in the service of the West and went on to say that Honorius had abandoned the Illyricum project because his own wife, Serena, had urged the emperor to do nothing that would further jeopardize any prospects of peace between him and his brother Arcadius.[19] The Senate granted Alaric the 4,000 pounds of gold that he demanded but did so with bitterness. Stilicho was no longer a hero and defender; he had become a hated master.

Just as in Constantinople at the time of Gainas there was now at the court of Honorius an antibarbarian party. Its leader, Olympius, was very close to the emperor. He was both underhanded and pious; we can see that Stilicho had become wary of him. To counter one of Olympius's few well-founded charges, namely, that Stilicho was tolerant in religious matters, Stilicho suddenly revived laws that had been on the books for a long time but had fallen into abeyance and issued new decrees against heretics. The latter were addressed especially to Africa, where Donatists and orthodox Catholics were always at each other's throats. Why bother with Africa, so far away? We are forgetting the close mesh of communications that existed among the churchmen. These actions of Stilicho's did not help him much, and he did not even receive credit among the Catholics for his sudden zeal. Augustine, writing to Olympius after Stilicho's fall, expressed the hope that the laws that had come into force in Stilicho's time might continue, adding politely that he assumed these laws to have been the work of "our most godly and faithful emperor." It may be worth noting that Augustine was engaged in correspondence with Olympius even before Stilicho fell.[20] In another effort to hold things together under his feet, Stilicho appointed the pagan aristocrat Nicomachus Flavianus as prefect of the city. Both maneuvers must have been highly encouraging to Stilicho's enemies. Their quarry was beginning to show signs of desperation.

It was not only at the court and in the church that Stilicho was running into trouble. There was a Roman core in his army, comprising mostly Italians who had been recruited at the time of Radagaisus. They were hostile, feeling that Stilicho passed over them time and again to promote barbarians. They were underpaid, or not even paid at all, and the fact that the treasury was drained to give Alaric his gold had not brightened their prospects. It was not helpful that the Ravenna garrison was under the command of Sarus, Alaric's enemy. How must Sarus have felt when he saw Alaric triumphantly departing with 4,000 pounds of gold?

Emperor Honorius, meanwhile, suddenly grew stubborn, as if he had acquired a mind of his own. He had drifted into the orbit of the anti-Stilichonians and also, oddly enough, had come under the influence of his foster-mother, Serena, whom he disliked. Serena seems to have been loyal to Stilicho; however, she was frantic in her conviction that the fate of her husband and herself hung on the life and well-being of the emperor. Honorius was saying that he wanted to leave Rome, where he had resided since his triumph following the defeat of Radagaisus. He was not at all sure that the peace with Alaric would hold, and he thought that he would feel safer in fortified Ravenna. Stilicho was convinced that he would be more secure where he was. Honorius started off defiantly for Ravenna, asserting that Serena thought he was right to do so.

Before the emperor could reach Ravenna, Sarus and his barbarians mutinied. According to the historian Zosimus, Stilicho instigated the uprising to frighten Honorius and show him that the army was not his to command, but the modern consensus seems to be that Sarus erupted spontaneously in anger at the thought that Alaric's star was rising. Stilicho was able to control the situation, and Honorius continued on his way, but while he was still on the road, another complication developed.

In May, 408, Emperor Arcadius died, at the age of thirty-one. Here is one aspect of the times that is difficult for us to assimilate. Men died early and suddenly in those days, often in what looks like mid-career.[21] It is pointless to talk about anything as purposeful as a career in the instance of Emperor Arcadius, but the problem remains. We unfairly call the late Roman Empire stale, worn-out, and unimaginative, not pausing to think how hard it must have been for such youthful people to do anything other than follow traditional ways. It takes time to work out a new theory of government. Perhaps it was no accident that the Roman emperors who did make determined efforts to change existing patterns were those who had lived at least into middle age, Diocletian, for instance, or Constantine the Great or, later, Constantius III.

To their chagrin, Stilicho's enemies imagined him taking over the reins in the East, where the new emperor was a small boy. Would Stilicho, who just days before had seemed to be tottering, suddenly begin uniting the two empires under his sole control, as he claimed Theodosius the Great had directed thirteen years before?

The new question concerning the movements of Emperor Honorius now became, Should he or should he not go to Constantinople to assume the guardianship of little Theodosius II? The antibarbarians did everything they could think of to bolster the emperor's courage. They may even have been the ones who urged him to go to Pavia, to show himself to his "Roman" army. Honorius indeed started off with that intention, but once more the barbarian soldiers mutinied, this time at Bologna, where he had halted temporarily. That was clear evidence of the raging mood of the troops on whom Stilicho had to rely; the mere sight of the turmoil was overwhelming for Honorius, who scurried back to the counsels of Stilicho.

Under extremely stressful conditions Stilicho hammered out a coherent plan, but it would work only if many ordinarily unreliable people proved dependable after all. Alaric, for example, was to be named master of soldiers and directed to head an expedition into Gaul. His mission there was twofold: destruction of the usurper Constantine and the expulsion of the Vandals and the Alans. He would be backed up by new, strengthened military bases to be set up at Mainz and Strasbourg, which had not been hit as hard as Trier. Stilicho himself would go to Constantinople to tender the kindly ministrations of a kinsman to the bereaved little eastern emperor.

Honorius, meanwhile, would be the mainstay, bulwark, and embodiment of empire. He would proceed to Pavia to instill enthusiasm and gladness into the hearts of the restive Roman troops, telling them that now they would have the good fortune to march out shoulder to shoulder with the barbarians, as brothers under Alaric. This was quite an assignment, but Honorius was unimaginative enough to believe that he could handle it. We may assume that Stilicho had his private thoughts. In August, 408, he sent the emperor off, accompanied by his own best, most-trusted officers. That was some protection for Stilicho, but in the final analysis everything would depend on Honorius, who swayed with every wind that blew.

All the ugly charges that could possibly be aimed at Stilicho were now on the lips of his enemies. He was obviously planning the takeover of the East, the downfall of Honorius, the destruction of the church, and the enthronement of his own son Eucherius (who, by the way, had never held any but minor posts). The Christians were more violent in their attacks than the pagans were.[22] As Honorius moved toward Pavia, Olympius the courtier managed to divulge all sorts of "facts" that gained the emperor's avid attention.

To his consternation Stilicho next learned that there had been a massive uprising at Pavia. His best commanders and all those who were close to him had been murdered before the eyes of Honorius. Stilicho believed at first that the emperor too had been assassinated. His reaction was to consider taking his barbarians to Pavia to exterminate the criminals, but then he learned that Honorius was alive and safe. He himself was far from safe. He hesitated. Leading barbarians against a force largely made up of Romans, in the presence of the emperor, would be tantamount to treason.

Stilicho turned back to Ravenna, only to learn that the commander there had orders from the emperor to arrest him. Loyal men helped Stilicho flee to a church for sanctuary.

The story of Stilicho's final hours has been twisted this way and that. It is a fact that Honorius sent two orders, the first stating that Stilicho was merely to be taken into custody. It is a fact that when Stilicho honored this order a second message was instantly produced commanding his execution. It is a fact that Stilicho offered no resistance and that he was ignominiously beheaded then and there (in Ravenna on August 22, 408). Whether Stilicho had become suicidal or felt bound by some unknown oath to Theodosius I or was the victim of his own warped view of the world or was any of the other things that have been said speculatively about him,[23] we can at least agree that he had been placed in one of the truly impossible situations contrived in the course of human events.

The immediate aftermath of Stilicho's death was a horrible wave of anti-barbarian violence, mostly directed at the families of the Goths stationed in northern Italy. As many as 30,000 enraged barbarian warriors straightway stormed off to join Alaric, calling for vengeance. Only Alaric's enemy Sarus stayed behind, with his own men. Alaric showed admirable restraint. He sent a proposal to Honorius and his new minister, the triumphant Olympius. He stated that he was willing to withdraw to Pannonia if a certain sum of money was given to him and hostages were exchanged. The reaction to this suggestion was negative. Alaric did not waste much time. In contrast to his earlier incursions, when the Visigoths traveled with all their gear like people on a trek to new territory, he seems to have brought along only his warriors and their necessary equipment. Early in the fall of 408, just weeks after Stilicho's death, he advanced rapidly down the Flaminian Way, heading for Rome, with panic surging ahead of him like the waters of a flash flood. The citizens of Narnia, at which the road passed over a gigantic bridge, were frightened enough in their extremity to offer sacrifices to the old gods in the Etruscan manner. This act was rewarded by a splendid thunderstorm that deflected the enemy host (see plate 43).[24]

Terror was rampant in Rome. The Senate under its pagan prefect of the city, Pompeianus, reacted with vindictive irrationality, ordering that Serena be strangled. The historian Zosimus expressed satisfaction about the appropriateness of the manner of her death. He observed that the noose was applied to "that very neck around which she had hung the Goddess's ornament."[25] A public appeal was made to Pope Innocent I: Might Rome emulate the example of Narnia and offer pagan sacrifices? Innocent is said to have consented on condition that they be made in secret, but since only a public rite could be expected to bring results, the idea was abandoned. This anecdote may be a pagan fabrication. Innocent appears to have been in Ravenna at the time. It was at about this stage that the Senate initiated a process for expropriating Melania's remaining property (Melania had fled to an estate in Campania).

Plate 43. Ponte d'Agosto, Narni, Umbria, Italy. "Narnia is only 350 stades distant (about 90 kilometers) from Rome. . . . The road to the west . . . spans the river and provides a passage over it at that point. This bridge was built by Caesar Augustus in early times and it is a very noteworthy sight: for its arches are the highest of any known to us" (Procopius of Caesarea *History of the Wars* 5.17.8–11). At Narnia (modern Narni), Etruscan rites were performed to ward off Alaric and his invading host. An effective thunderstorm resulted. Pagans in Rome were eager to defend the Eternal City by performance of similar rites.

This followed closely on the heels of Emperor Honorius's decree that commanded confiscation of the property of Stilicho's adherents, but Melania must have been something of a traitor in her own right, in the eyes of the senatorial class. It is hard to imagine just what use could be made of jewels and palaces in those desperate days. During Alaric's siege bread rations were reduced to nothing. There is said to have been cannibalism in the city at the time when Pompeianus was killed by a starving mob.

In shame the Senate had to bow to Alaric's demands. He would accept as ransom for the besieged city no less than 5,000 pounds of gold, 3,000 pounds of silver, 4,000 silk tunics, 3,000 scarlet-dyed skins, and 3,000 pounds of pepper.[26] The Senate also undertook to urge Emperor Honorius to consider an alliance with Alaric and to furnish noble hostages. We can imagine the Visigoths hastening away in December toward Etruria, gloating over their good fortune, their ranks swollen by the thousands of escaped slaves who straggled joyfully after.

Alaric waited in southern Etruria, and precisely nothing happened. In great anxiety Rome sent a delegation to Ravenna to prod Honorius. Among the envoys was Priscus Attalus, a friend of Symmachus and like him a pagan in the old aristocratic style. Probably the Senate included him because he was an admired orator; the emperor was deaf to oratory. Even to Honorius and Olympius it was clear that Rome needed defenders. A force was accordingly transferred from Dalmatia, but Alaric intercepted it and killed most of the soldiers.

Reinforcements also came to Alaric from across the Adriatic. They were led by his kinsman Athaulf, whose troops included Huns and an elite band that had once been part of Radagaisus's horde.[27] They had to fight a pitched battle with Honorius's Hunnic mercenaries near Pisa, but they managed to cut their way through.

Olympius fled to Dalmatia. He was replaced by his opponent Jovius, who had once been loyal to Stilicho—if "loyal" can be correctly applied to a man who changed sides so often. Early in the spring of 409 he was Honorius's praetorian prefect. He was something of a friend of Alaric's too, and for a while he urged on the emperor a policy of peace. He even went so far as to arrange a meeting at Rimini.

This time Alaric said that he wanted the status of federates for his people and practically all the territory on the far side of the Adriatic. He wanted money and annual grain supplies. Jovius suggested to the emperor that these demands might be subject to negotiation. If Alaric were given an honorary title, he might soften somewhat. Honorius was a proud Roman at heart; he said no. The refusal insulted Alaric, who again marched off toward Rome.

Once more a mission was sent to Ravenna, and once again Alaric made a proposal. He would accept the province of Noricum alone, not a particularly

Plate 44. Storage jars (*dolii*) in a garden at Ostia, Italy. The *dolii* were used for bulk storage of grain or oil shipped in from provinces overseas to supply Rome. This garden is at the bottom of a court enclosed by an apartment house. The windows overlooking the garden recall Augustine's moving account of the last night of his mother's life. They were resting at Ostia in preparation for a trip to Africa (Augustine *Confessions* 9.10.23).

good source of tax revenue for the emperor.[28] Unfortunately, Honorius had reprimanded Jovius for probarbarian leanings, and in his zeal to prove his loyalty, Jovius had sworn the mightiest oath he could imagine—on the emperor's head—that there would be nothing but battle to the death between him and Alaric.

Off marched Alaric again, at the close of 409, this time to call on the citizens of Rome to rally to him. The citizens jeered. He then blockaded Portus, on the Tiber, threatening the city with starvation. Portus was the place where African grain was unloaded.

The senators had second thoughts. They cunningly agreed to a plan whereby they would proclaim an emperor, one of their own, who would be more amenable to Alaric. The choice fell on Priscus Attalus, the orator who had represented Rome in a delegation to Ravenna not long before. He accepted Arian baptism and received the purple from the Senate. Attalus took his new responsibilities seriously. The citizens of Rome were "in good spirits," according to the historian Olympiodorus, because he appointed good administrators. Only the rich Anicii were apprehensive, uneasy about the possibility of a restoration of paganism. [29] As a matter of fact, Attalus did reopen the temples and gave churches to the Arians. Ancient Rome might rise again. The pagans must have welcomed the silver medallions struck by Attalus: they portrayed Victoria romana on her globe. The new praetorian prefect, Lampadius, and the new prefect of the city, Marcian, were members of Symmachus's coterie, like the new emperor himself.

There remained the nagging problem of the grain supply. Africa was under the control of one of Honorius's men, Heraclian, who had been rewarded with a high position in return for the death blow that he had dealt to Stilicho with his own hand. Alaric wanted to send Goths across to Africa to attack Heraclian, but Attalus refused to make such a move. He explained to superstitious Alaric that the auspices were against it, but his own thinking may have been a bit more subtle. Gothic control of Africa might spell doom for the empire. If a Roman force was in control, it would still be the beneficent empire that graciously fed the lowly barbarians. Attalus persuaded Alaric that the best course would be to send a Roman contingent to Africa while he and Alaric together went to Ravenna.

Panic set in at Ravenna, but reinforcements miraculously came from the East, sent by Anthemius, the praetorian prefect for Theodosius II. News then arrived that the African expedition had failed. Alaric again talked of sending Goths, but Attalus and the Senate, just as stubbornly Roman-minded as Emperor Honorius, would have none of it. It would be indecent to send barbarians against a Roman province. Irked by the insulting behavior of both emperors, Alaric deposed the one he had in hand. In the summer of 410 he ostentatiously stripped Attalus of the purple and again tried to reach some sort of settlement with Honorius.

For once it seemed that reasonableness might prevail. A conference was arranged at Ravenna in July, 410, to be attended by both Honorius and Alaric. But, as we observed in the case of Constantinople, the barbarians did not present a united front. Alaric's enemy Sarus was inflamed by the idea of Alaric sitting down with the emperor. He dashed in and broke the truce, attacking Alaric's camp. Alaric stormed off toward Rome in a rage, thinking that Honorius must have known about Sarus's plan beforehand. The time had arrived for him to obey his insistent inner Voice: "Thou shalt penetrate into the City. Delay not, Alaric." Somehow the Salarian Gate was opened—perhaps by barbarian slaves inside—and the unthinkable event occurred.

The shock generated by the sack of Rome is almost impossible to match in all subsequent history. In our own time, as country after country went down before Hitler, we might have been almost as numbed if London had fallen. Rome was a majestic goddess to many people and to ever-growing multitudes she was the holy city of Saint Peter. The trampling of this place beneath the feet of marauders was the monstrous end of the world. Pagans and Christians alike sought some meaning behind it all and blamed each other for the outrage.[30]

The sack of Rome lasted less than a week, perhaps no more than three days. In spite of the remarkable respect that the Goths showed for consecrated altar vessels, and despite the limited destruction of buildings,[31] there was violence of the ugliest kind, much of it inflicted by slaves who joined in, and many victims lay dead in the streets or were carried off into slavery. Wealthy refugees contrived spectacular escapes; soon they were relating their lurid adventures in Carthage and Jerusalem.[32] Laden with booty, the Visigoths moved south along the peninsula. Plunder was fine, but the main difficulty remained. Alaric's people were hungry. Plans were drawn to cross by way of Sicily to Africa, the province running over with oil and grain, but the horde was not to reach the promised land. Their boats foundered in the Strait of Messina, and shortly thereafter, before the end of 410, Alaric unexpectedly died.

Death has a way of arousing atavistic impulses. The wailing Goths put aside Christianity and mourned Alaric much as their pagan ancestors would have celebrated a fallen hero. Slaves labored to deflect the Busento River from its bed, and there Alaric was buried with a wealth of captured treasure. The river was allowed to course back over him, and the slaves were killed, partly in tribute to the dead, partly to make sure that no one would ever disturb great Alaric or take away his golden hoard.

NARBONNE, BARCELONA, AND ARLES

W E are about to meet two men who were far ahead of their times: a new-style barbarian and a new-style Roman. Both died before the first quarter of the fifth century had passed, before their ideas had come to fruition, yet it is intriguing to see what breed of men the times could produce.

The first was Alaric's handsome successor, his kinsman Athaulf the Visigoth. The second was Athaulf's opponent, the unprepossessing but vital Roman general Constantius. The former made Emperor Theodosius's daughter Galla Placidia his captive and then his queen. The latter rescued her, made her his wife, and through her became an emperor of the West.

It is a pleasant change of pace to read a love story. Athaulf was enchanted by his fair young prisoner, and the royal lady returned his love, disdaining ugly General Constantius, who was also bewitched by her. Such was Athaulf's courtliness that he refused to make Placidia his bride without the consent of her half brother Emperor Honorius. For this reason the couple yearned for each other for almost four years in the style of true romance. This is delightful, but the truth is that Galla Placidia was a valuable piece in a complex chess game, and Athaulf was well aware of it.

Just what Athaulf did during the first fourteen months after Alaric's death is not known. Some people imagine that Rome was sacked again, though the general weight of evidence suggests that the Visigoths may have lingered for a while in southern Italy and then straggled toward Gaul, which they had reached at last by the year 412. Athaulf took along two potentially useful people, Galla Placidia and Attalus, Alaric's deposed emperor.

A horde of Visigoths headed by a warrior king could not have anticipated a warm welcome from the other bands of newly arrived barbarians. In 411, Gaul was harboring a usurper from Britain, Constantine III, whom Honorius felt constrained to recognize; a Caesar at Arles, Constantine's son Constans; a puppet at Tarragona, Maximus, who owed his office to Constantine; and that puppet's independent general, Gerontius. Although the usurper Constantine III was disposed of in 411 in the purposeful campaign of General Constantius, Gaul could not be described as tranquil, because the downfall of Constantine had been followed almost immediately by the acclamation of a new usurper, a man of high-born Gallo-Roman stock. This individual, Jovinus, owed his elevation to the Burgundians and the Alans, but he had strong support from the Gallo-Roman aristocrats, especially those of Auvergne.[1] Because of a fresh emergency in Africa, General Constantius had to abandon Arles, which he had so recently snatched from Honorius's enemy, leaving it open to Jovinus and his swarm of Alans, Burgundians, Alamanni, and Franks (all of Gaul and even Britain fell to him).

The timing of Athaulf's arrival is interesting, suggesting that he may have had a plan of some sort that involved Jovinus. He may even have come to Gaul on Jovinus's invitation. Former Emperor Attalus is thought also to have had a hand in the affair, possibly in hopes that by good management he might himself at least become a Caesar in Gaul, after having lost out in Italy when Alaric stripped him of the purple.[2] He is supposed to have encouraged Athaulf to offer his services to Jovinus.

Whenever the situation in the story of the Visigoths becomes tense, we can depend on it: Sarus will appear. While Athaulf and Attalus were negotiating with Jovinus, Sarus arrived with about twenty warriors to offer his own support to Jovinus. Since Honorius had slighted him in some way, he had become the enemy of the legitimate emperor.

Athaulf overreacted—or rather he reacted in the way that was customary in a blood feud. He sallied forth at the head of an enormous force to cut down Sarus and his pitiful little band. Sarus was snared in a net (a Hunnic stratagem), after which he fought furiously until he died.[3]

Parleys between Athaulf and Jovinus made no progress and broke off when Jovinus made his own brother Sebastian his colleague. In disgust Athaulf immediately dispatched emissaries to Honorius's representatives. If he was given territory in southern Gaul and grain, he said, he would undertake to send the heads of Jovinus and Sebastian to the emperor, and he would also restore Galla Placidia to Ravenna.

Honorius assented. Any prospect of a respite in Gaul would be welcome in Ravenna. Heraclian, the count of Africa, who was supposed to be deeply loyal to Honorius, had suddenly revolted. Maybe he had had dishonorable intentions all along. More pressing for him must have been the circumstance that the star of the Illyrian general Constantius was rising. This would cause him serious alarm, for Constantius was known to be bent on the extinction of Stilicho's enemies.[4] Heraclian stood high on that list; it was his hand that had delivered the death blow to Stilicho. Constantius had already eliminated the wily courtier Olympius, having his men hack off the miscreant's ears before clubbing him to death (some of Stilicho's officers had been treated in precisely that way by Olympius). Perhaps with this unpleasant episode in mind Heraclian stopped the grain supply and sailed across the Mediterranean at the head of a fleet said to be so enormous that we cannot be expected to believe the figure. According to Orosius he had 3,700 ships.

Heraclian was roundly defeated in a battle on the road leading to Ravenna. He fled back to Carthage and was killed there. His name was expunged from official records, and his fortune was turned over to Constantius, who used it to celebrate his accession to the rank of consul (the hero was made consul three times—an extraordinary honor—and then became the emperor's patrician). It must have been a time of fierce exultation for that resolute, remorseless man.

Of necessity the grain shipments had been disrupted. The supplies that Honorius had promised to send to Athaulf were not forthcoming, even though Athaulf had kept his part of the bargain by destroying Jovinus and Sebastian. Very well, then, Athaulf would not surrender Galla Placidia.

By this time Constantius had begun nurturing ambitions, as heroes often are inclined to do. He was a true Roman, and he loved Galla Placidia; he ought to have her hand. Was there not a sentiment abroad that Constantius was meant for the purple?

Athaulf made a quick first move in the fall of 413. He occupied Narbonne, and there, early the following year, he married Galla Placidia without waiting any longer for Emperor Honorius's consent. As a ceremony intended to symbolize the fusion of two peoples, the wedding was adroitly handled.[5] Handsome Athaulf arrived in the scarlet cloak of a Roman general. Following him were fifty silk-clad pages, gifts to the bride, at whose royal feet they heaped a glittering treasure of captured Roman gems and gold fit for the most barbaric of queens.

Athaulf had a more sophisticated view of his situation than Alaric had had. He is reported to have said to a friend that he had come to realize that his barbarians were incapable of obeying laws and that they needed the restraint of the Roman system. Whereas he had originally planned the utter destruction of Rome, he now wanted to restore and strengthen the empire. This little fragment of a conversation in Narbonne does more than cast a revealing light on the mental processes of a barbarian king. Even the way that we learn about it is illuminating. According to the Spanish historian Orosius, Athaulf's interlocutor was "a wise and religious person" from Narbonne. Orosius met this individual in Bethlehem, where he heard him relay Athaulf's remarks to Jerome. Athaulf and his Visigoths were Arians. It is unlikely that Jerome would ever have received an Arian or that a man like Orosius would have described an Arian as wise and religious. It is reasonable to conjecture that Athaulf's friend was an orthodox Catholic. The conciliatory message must have been deliber-

Plate 45. Mosaic in Corporations Square, Ostia, where offices of seventy shippers' representatives were marked by distinctive designs in the pavement. The office of the Narbonne shippers shows cargo being loaded from a dock at the home port. The harbor of Narbonne silted up long ago.

ately planted for transmission over the efficient, widespread communications network of the church.[6]

Just as Athaulf was more sophisticated than his predecessor Alaric, so his Roman adversary, the military man Constantius, was infinitely more sophisticated than his own admired former commander Stilicho. When we look at the work of Constantius, we are struck by its coherence; there was no more piecemeal handling of the problems of the empire. It was management in the modern sense. Whether Constantius's perceptions were accurate enough to warrant use of the term "insights" is beside the point, nor is it important that his decisions were not uniformly wise. The ability to see things whole and develop an overall plan was not characteristic of his day.

It is odd that a man of so much forcefulness who dominated the history of his own epoch should flicker through histories of the period so elusively, sometimes without so much as one entry in a comprehensive modern index. This elusiveness can be explained in part by the circumstance that most of his actions were veiled, taking the form of edicts and decrees issued over the signature of vague, indifferent Honorius.

Not unexpectedly, Constantius's first action was purely military. He attacked Athaulf in the spring of 414. Athaulf had arranged his affairs so that it almost looked as though Constantius were trying to unseat a legitimate regime. Attalus had been made emperor again and installed in a court at Bordeaux, with an impressive array of officials under him. The Visigoth understood that at all costs he had to support Narbonne, his crucial port of entry, but the Roman general made effective use of a blockading fleet and outmaneuvered him. In the course of a retreat to Bordeaux an attempt to assault the town of Bazas had the effect of splitting off Athaulf's contingent of Alans, which was coaxed into defecting. This was a military loss to Athaulf, but it was much more troublesome that the scales were tipped against him among his own followers, because the Alans had been the strongest pro-Roman faction.[7] Now hotheads were in a position to overthrow the man who would not have been reluctant to bring them under the sway of Rome.

Athaulf led his people in retreat down into Spain, where he occupied Barcelona, but even there bad fortune stalked him. Food was in dangerously short supply. Hope gleamed for one brief moment. A son was born to Placidia and Athaulf. They named him Theodosius, to signify the blood tie that they wanted to strengthen, but within days the sorrowing parents had to follow a tiny casket to its burial place.[8]

In that same year, 415, Galla Placidia had more trials to bear as the plots against her husband came to a head. His archenemy Sarus was dead, but the knife that was plunged into Athaulf's body was driven home by one of Sarus's men. He could not have been acting alone in this gesture of revenge, because the next king of the Visigoths was Sarus's violently anti-Roman brother, rather than Athaulf's own brother. The new king was not much more than a ruffian. He lasted only a week, but in that time he forced Galla Placidia to stumble along in the dust beside his horse as his captive.

A duly elected king succeeded this lout. King Wallia, like Alaric before him, tried to take the Visigoths across to Africa, but, being no seamen, they foundered in the Strait of Gibraltar, just as they had foundered several years before when they tried to go to Sicily. Wallia had to sue for peace.

By the agreement that was worked out, poor Galla Placidia, still a pawn, was prosaically ransomed for 600,000 measures of grain. Since that would be an annual allowance for 15,000 men, we have a gauge of the size of the force that Wallia was to lead forth to subdue the Vandals, the Alans, and the Suevi, who had migrated to Gaul with the Vandals and the Alans.[9]

Galla Placidia's story was far from over. She was escorted back to Honorius, and on the first day of the year 417 the emperor placed her unwilling hand in that of Patrician Constantius. As brother-in-law of the emperor, Constantius now had an even firmer grasp on the reins of power than before, though his authority had been unchallenged since the downfall of Stilicho's scheming enemy Olympius seven years earlier.

Constantius had recovered Gaul from the swarm of would-be emperors, expelled the Visigoths to Spain and put them to work for the empire, and secured Africa. Rome had regained a large measure of her glory with astonishing speed after Alaric's departure. Gaul, however, had been badly mauled, and the northern parts were lost, while ties with Britain had been practically severed. An enormous task of reconstruction lay ahead.

Constantius does not seem to have been as wrapped up in the problem of barbarians as we might expect him to have been. He was aware that the empire would have to depend militarily on barbarian federates more than ever, because the actual forces that Romans could muster had been depleted to an appalling extent. Contemporary military lists in the *Notitia dignitatum* show that new units had to be raised, including about a dozen barbarian regiments. Possibly to cover up this dependence a bit, Constantius engineered a directive whereby nobody was to appear on the streets of the Eternal City with long hair or fur garments characteristic of the barbarians.[10]

In the main, Constantius's piercing gaze seems to have been fixed on the flaws in Roman society rather than on the rude peoples who had broken in. If indeed all sorts of alarm bells were clanging in his mind, it might be worth our while to try to understand how the world must have looked to him.

Our first bewildered impression is that he must have been an ardently religious man because his major undertakings frequently involved ecclesiastical matters, but if we think about the close interlocking of church and state in those days, we see that religion in itself was not necessarily Constantius's chief concern. When we first hear of his involvement in church affairs, the downfall of Rome at the hands of Alaric and his Goths was impending. Constantius wrote to Carthaginian authorities, in the name of Emperor Honorius, with instructions aimed at eradication of the schismatic Donatists, whom he chose threateningly to call heretics. Heresy or schism was not the problem: the urgent need was for peaceful conditions and a loyal citizenry who would ensure a steady flow of grain from Africa to Rome.

Donatism had long been a thorn in the flesh of the African church and had become a rallying point for social misfits and rebellious reformers. Even today reputable historians argue that the Donatists and their terrorist fringe, the Circumcellions, were protonationalists who wanted to break away from the empire. Constantius must have seen them in this light, though the concept of nationalism is far too modern and would not have occurred to him. His emissary Marcellinus, who was dispatched to Carthage to supervise a conference between Catholics and Donatists, carried crisp, no-nonsense instructions that earlier decrees in favor of Catholic law were to be enforced, upon removal of all "seditious superstition." [11] Little is heard of the Donatists after that momentous meeting.

The church in Gaul was in need of a strong hand if it was to function as a mainstay of imperial order. Ever since the brutal execution of the Spanish pietist Priscillian by order of the secular authority at Trier when Maximus the usurper was emperor (385), there had been two parties in the church in Gaul. Martin of Tours, we remember, had been involved on the Priscillianist side and had narrowly escaped becoming ensnared himself on that account. There were those who looked askance at the saintly bishop. They disliked his unkempt appearance and his ascetic ways and wondered whether he was a Manichee or engaged in the practice of magic. [12] Even Brice, a member of Martin's own monastic community, who was destined to succeed him as bishop of Tours, railed at times that Martin was a madman. Martin obviously enjoyed enthusiastic support from the common people. A contemporary of his named Postumianus told Sulpicius Severus:

> Our fellow men who have had in their midst such a marvelous saint have not been worthy of him. But I am in no wise accusing the laity. Only the clergy, only the bishops, ignored Martin. And these envious and jealous men ignored him intentionally, for they well knew that if they praised his virtues they would be forced to know and abhor their own vices. [13]

From Martin's time on, two factions refused to share the sacraments. The Priscillianists, as Martin's followers were called, were puritans and pietists. They imposed harsh rules on themselves and demanded equally rigid self-denial from others. Given to fasting, continence, and incessant prayer, they were beginning to draw the attention of more worldly individuals, who questioned their own materialism after the sack of Rome and the incursions of the hordes into Gaul. Possibly because they were antiestablishment people, the

Priscillianists supported the usurper Constantine III when he came over from Britain and set himself up at Arles, whence he was ultimately dislodged by General Constantius. The bishop of Arles at the time of Constantius's siege was Héros, a friend and disciple of Martin's. In a spirit of charity, Héros gave the defeated usurper asylum and attempted to shield him by ordaining him into the priesthood. Constantius captured Constantine nevertheless and roughly deposed Héros, putting his dependable friend Patroclus in his place. Patroclus's reputation was not particularly savory, but in view of the custom of using bishops as a kind of secret police, installation of such a man on an episcopal throne was not novel.[14]

At first glance, we might suspect that personal animosity of the conquering general toward the protector of his adversary was at work here, but Constantius appears to have made suppression of the Priscillianists a studied matter of policy. For instance, another of Martin's disciples also fared badly and was deposed, presumably by the spontaneous action of his congregation. This was Lazarus of Aix, who had brought charges against Martin's conservative successor, Brice, in a move intended to drive him into exile. Brice was returned to his see in 417 by Pope Zosimus, who had been installed under the aegis of Constantius in that year.[15]

The two deposed bishops, Héros and Lazarus, journeyed together to Palestine, but the metropolitan bishops of Marseilles, Vienne, and Narbonne, all members of the Priscillianist faction, remained. There was so much antagonism between Priscillianists and the majority conservative party that accusations and counteraccusations were flying, with scandal piled on scandal.[16]

Bishop Patroclus of Arles (Constantius's protégé) presented himself in Rome early in 417, the year of the marriage of Constantius and Galla Placidia. The bishop was a man of inordinate ambition. Whether or not he had received a signal of some sort, he must have been aware that the current pope would not last long. Innocent I had been in office for about sixteen years. There was no harm at all in being on the spot, on the chance of a papal election. Innocent died, and Patroclus was able to ingratiate himself with the most likely candidate, Zosimus, who was Constantius's man.[17] Zosimus and Patroclus fitted together in a highly congenial manner. Zosimus wanted the churches everywhere to acknowledge the supremacy of the Roman see, and Patroclus wanted to have all the churches of Gaul under his domination. Zosimus seems to have listened approvingly to Patroclus's argument that Arles should have the primacy in Gaul because it had been the seat of Trophimus, the reputed "apostle" of Gaul. That was the kind of argument that Zosimus could utilize in asserting his own position as the successor of Saint Peter.

Just three days after his consecration on March 18, 417, Zosimus issued an astounding decree in favor of Patroclus that ran counter to all tradition and could not be justified in the light of any powers accorded to the See of Rome by imperial authority, since the days of Valentinian I. By the terms of Zosimus's order, the Priscillianist bishops of Marseilles, Vienne, and Narbonne were deprived of their metropolitan status, and Patroclus was free to rule with a heavy hand. He alone would have the authority to consecrate bishops in the provinces of Viennensis, Narbonensis Prima, and Narbonensis Secunda. We can imagine that Constantius felt confident that his man would quiet the situation in the Gallic church. Parenthetically, we note that this order was tacitly withdrawn by a successor in 422, the year after the death of Constantius.

Zosimus likewise ordered that any member of the clergy who wished to travel outside Gaul would have to furnish a passport for that purpose, duly signed by the bishop of Arles. These *litterae formatae* were elaborately coded as a means of detecting forgeries.[18] Constantius and his appointee wanted order and quiet, but why was it necessary to seal off the Priscillianists? For one thing, it might be unwise to allow free intercourse between Gaul and Britain.

There is a statement by the Greek historian Zosimus which has been interpreted to mean that the British established an independent government shortly before the fall of Rome.[19] Under the stress of Alaric's presence in Italy, Emperor Honorius had sent a letter to the British *civitates*, telling them that they would have to look after themselves. That was in 410, possibly before mid-August, when Constantius came into a position of power. It is impossible now to determine what the British reaction was, but fragments of contemporary writings allow us to guess that there was a fierce upheaval, involving rival factions that tried to fill the vacuum produced by this abrupt cessation of civil administration. Most of the soldiery had left for the continent earlier, either recalled by Stilicho or taken along in the forces of the usurper Constantine III. A bloody account, incongruously entitled *De vita christiana* (ca. 411) seems to allude to lynch-mob activity, as one power group assailed another.[20] Popular unrest was almost endemic in the West. There had been peasant uprisings in Gaul off and on for many generations. In the early years of the fifth century the rebels and runaways became more assertive than ever before. Their ferocious insurrection in 407 spelled disaster for the western part of Gaul. They were actually separatists, the Bacaudae, with their own outlaw style of justice and their own defiant self-government. In his first year of power as a member of the emperor's household, Constantius saw to it that the Bacaudae of Armorica (roughly modern Brittany and the territory around the Loire) were severely suppressed by military action. Constantius must have suspected that there were some connections between the independent people of Britain and the Bacaudae. In such a situation the nonconformist Priscillianist clergy might function as go-betweens. Martin's own Tours was in Bacaudic territory, and the church had managed to maintain a frail existence in Britain; it was known to be in touch with the Gallic clergy.[21]

The reform movement was strong in both Britain and Armorica, fueled by the preachings of a British monk, Pelagius, who had crossed over to the mainland long before to raise his voice in Rome, where he gained a following among influential people. Ideas attributed to him were shockingly subversive, clashing not only with those of Augustine but also with Jerome's. The implications must have been deeply disturbing to Constantius.[22] The man in the street could not be expected to understand the subtleties of the arguments, but he would surely hear talk that sounded like an attack on the validity of baptism and an assault on the idea of original sin. He might even think that when Pelagius spoke of *gratia* he was referring to corruption and favoritism in high places (the word could mean that). Suppose people were suddenly to believe in their own worth and refuse to accept their lot fatalistically. In the long run the Pelagians might undermine accepted social arrangements. One man, a firebrand known later as "the Sicilian Briton," was turning out letters that were decidedly inflammatory. "Abolish the rich and you will have no more poor," he wrote wrathfully, pressing Christianity back to its primitive socialistic simplicity.[23] The empire could not afford to be *that* Christian. "Abolish the rich!" What a slogan, to catch hold in a populace already made desperate by the burden of taxes, already looking at the Bacaudae with envy and even a certain amount of sympathy.

The Bacaudae had been suppressed in Armorica, to be sure, but suppression would not end the matter if British Pelagians were to find a way to spread their dangerous ideas in Gaul.[24] There was already too good a climate for rebellion there, a point illustrated by a strange story in Sulpicius Severus's biography of Martin. Among the venerated shrines in the Loire Valley, Sulpicius relates, there had been one in honor of a "martyr" whose anonymity made the holy Martin suspicious. As an experienced necromancer Martin was able to summon the shade of this unknown individual and demand information concerning name and credentials. The ghost confessed that, alas, to his shame he was no martyr; rather, he was a brigand who had been executed for his misdeeds. Through the veil of hagiography we see the Celtic hero cult at work, with elevation of a Bacaudic leader to the ranks of the blessed.[25]

Pelagius had passed through Carthage after the sack of Rome and moved on to the East without having caused any disturbance in Augustine's territory. Augustine seemed to think well of him, but then unsettling word traveled back from the exiled bishops Héros and Lazarus that Pelagius was a heretic. The case was referred to Pope Zosimus, who was gratified by such deference. To the confusion of modern historians, he sent word to the agitated African clergy that, so far as he understood the matter, Pelagius and his colleague Caelestius were orthodox in their beliefs.

Zosimus had made a dismal error: his royal patron would not automatically side with the enemies of Héros and Lazarus. He had a larger view of the

Pelagians, since he regarded them as disturbers of the peace. On April 30, 418, an imperial rescript went out, banishing Pelagius and Caelestius. The bishop of Rome executed a rapid about-face. Constantius's ire had been kindled partly by riots that had occurred in Rome itself, but he made no bones of the fact that he had no use for intellectual subversives under any circumstances. "They consider it is a sure sign of being lowborn and commonplace to think the same as everybody else, and a token of exceptional expertise to undermine what is unanimously agreed." [26] Considerable damage had already been done to the unity and discipline of the church. Eighteen bishops in the heart of Italy had become defiant and were sent into exile. The turmoil continued, and another severe rescript had to be issued in January 421, in the wake of more civil disorders in Rome.

Constantius had found a reliable man at Arles who could be depended upon to maintain ecclesiastical order in Gaul at least. He had another stalwart at the upper end of the Rhone Valley axis,[27] in the person of Bishop Germanus of Auxerre, who, unlike Patroclus of Arles, was an entirely upright and conscientious public servant.

There is much confusion about the actual functions that Germanus may have performed before 418, when he was suddenly elected bishop of Auxerre by popular acclaim, to succeed Bishop Amator, but there is enough in the shadowy near-contemporary biography that has come down to us to suggest some fascinating possibilities. At the very least, it may be apposite to note that the late Bishop Amator had been another of Martin's friends and that the unexpected election of an unwavering supporter of the establishment like Germanus as his successor seems to follow a familiar pattern. Germanus came from a background that precluded any ties with nonconformists. He is thought to have been a lawyer, native to Gaul (probably of Celtic stock) but trained in Rome. He may have been a military governor in Bacaudic Armorica, though scholarly disputation on this point has been hot and indecisive. If he actually had once been the dux tractus Armoricani et Nervicani, as some scholars believe,[28] details of the varied and busy life of this extraordinary saint would be explained. His two missions to Britain, which ostensibly were against the Pelagians, had curious military overtones. On the first mission he organized local citizens in an Easter battle against invading Picts (the famous "Hallelujah Victory"), and on the second he had contact with a man named Elafius, who may have been a latter-day Belgic dux commanding what was left of some of the forts of the Saxon Shore, possibly near the Isle of Wight or Winchester. The miraculous foreknowledge of Germanus's approach, ascribed to demons, could then be explained. Such forts customarily communicated by semaphore signals. As a commander in Armorica, Germanus would once have had the matching Saxon Shore forts of Gaul under his authority.[29] There was certainly something military in his encounter with a troop of Alans in Armorica, some years after Constantius's death. As federates the Alans had set off on a punitive expedition against the Bacaudae. Germanus personally forced their leader, King Goar, to halt and subscribe to an agreement whereby he would desist from further action until new orders arrived. The determined old bishop then traveled to Ravenna, intending to enlist the attention of Emperor Valentinian III, but the strenuous trip was too much for him, and he died. Constantius's widow, the Augusta Galla Placidia, herself prepared Germanus's body for its journey back to Auxerre, treating his worn garments with reverence. One of the garments was an old military cloak.

The interesting thing about the role of Germanus in what must have been Constantius's grand design for unification is not only his activity in Britain but also the connection with Bishop Hilary of Arles that developed in the years following Constantius's death. Hilary was struggling with excessive zeal to sustain the kind of authority for himself and his see that had been arranged for Patroclus. Germanus seems to have been in full accord with him.[30]

Mention has been made of some hazy evidence of involvement in military affairs when Germanus went to Britain. It was generally accepted at one time that Britain was abandoned absolutely by the Romans in 410, but that is not necessarily true. Entries in the *Notitia dignitatum* relate to military organization in Britain that must have been either in place or at least contemplated later than 410. Also at the Saxon Shore fort Richborough there are impressively large stores of coins from the time of Honorius. Taken together, the *Notitia dignitatum* and the coins indicate that Constantius may have initiated a military reorganization aimed at the recovery of Britain[31] and at control of a Bacaudic movement there. It is tempting to speculate that Germanus might have been a key figure in all this, as a former commander of forces in Armorica.

What other pieces of Constantius's overall plan for the West can be found? What about his recall of the Visigoths from Spain in 418? This move cannot be shown to have been a response to anything initiated by the Visigoths. It must have been a matter of Roman policy, pure and simple.

Wallia and his Visigoths had been successful and were in the midst of a mopping-up operation in Spain. Had they become powerful enough to be viewed as a threat? Perhaps they were brought back into the heart of Gaul so that some constraints could be put on them. Or were they being rewarded for work well done? The work was not yet completed. If indeed they had to be controlled or rewarded, it is strange that they were moved into "the very marrow of the Gallic provinces," as Salvian called it.[32] What kinds of arguments could have been offered to the proud landowners of Aquitania in their fine villas to induce them to relinquish their lovely, fertile holdings? We reflect that the traditional terms of *hospitalitas* for quartering troops were drastically revised when the Visigoths returned to Gaul. Instead of the customary one-third of the produce from the land, they received two-thirds of the land itself,

Plate 46. Amphitheater of the Three Gauls, Lyons, France. A precedent existed for the provincial assembly constituted by Honorius and Constantius in 318. Three centuries earlier the amphitheater shown here had been built at Lyons as a meeting place for representatives of sixty Gallic nations. The structure was repeatedly remodeled and enlarged. It was the scene of gladiatorial spectacles, and it is popularly believed that Christians were martyred there in 177.

leaving the dispossessed Gallo-Romans with a scant third of their original spacious properties. It is difficult to imagine quiet acquiescence, unless the alternative was drastic indeed. Is it possible that the manpower shortage had become so acute that there could be no other solution, or are we once more confronting the Bacaudae? Cogent arguments have been presented by E. A. Thompson to show that the latter was indeed the case.[33] Forces planted in Aquitania could not have been expected to fend off Franks and Alamanni, who were far away in the north or beyond the Rhine, says Thompson. If the Visigoths were supposed to be acting as defense against the Vandals, would it not have been more appropriate to leave them where they were, or at the very most to place them as a buffer in the northern part of Spain? To move them north of the Garonne was a curious piece of strategy. According to Thompson's theory, Saxon sea raids must also be ruled out, on the ground that they were a rarity in the period in question. The remaining threat would come from the recently subdued Bacaudae in the Loire region. These people had staged their most impressive insurrection at the time of the major barbarian breakthrough. They could be suspected of a propensity for cooperation with the barbarians.

The Visigoths were deliberately put on prime agricultural land. As Thompson points out, from that day on the Visigoths could not defend their own interests without at the same time defending those of their Gallo-Roman hosts. The Bacaudae would not see any reason to join forces with the Visigoths because of the obvious split into opposing groups, have-nots and haves. There was another implicit advantage. Gradually the more powerful Visigoths would lose their sense of tribe and become class-conscious, looking down on their own, lowlier people as mere tenants and peasants. Thompson calls Constantius's solution "brilliant." The belligerent Visigoths were tamed and converted into fairly stable agriculturists, as well as effective military forces.

Constantius must have been aware that, in spite of all the potential advantages, the Gallo-Romans crowded off their lands would not be delighted by the new arrangement. Once again we see that his fertile brain thought of everything. He had a plan that might go far to allay the pain of the aristocrats. Specifically, he undertook to give the Gallo-Romans a feeling that their concerns were important to the imperial court. He had taken a few steps in this direction as early as 414, when his military efforts against the various usurpers and barbarians were beginning to show results. The poet Rutilius Namatianus, a Gallo-Roman of distinguished family, was appointed prefect of Rome in that year.[34] Constantius's most important measure, meant to bring the members of the senatorial class back into a loyal, comfortable relationship with Rome after the upheavals in which the usurpers, especially Jovinus, had received support from that quarter, was the revival of the Council of the Seven Provinces of the Diocese of Viennensis. The new council included Aquitania, where the Visigoths were established. Emperor Honorius's *Constitutio* restoring the council, dated April 17, 418, is a famous one. It refers glowingly to Arles, where Constantius, *parens patriciusque noster*, was in residence, calling the city a metropolis. It was here that an annual month-long assembly of officials and landowners was to be convened. The document was "conceived in a liberal spirit" and may have resulted in the elimination of abuses.[35]

Constantius became an Augustus in 421. By that time, he and Galla Placidia were the parents of two small children. Since Honorius was childless, "noble boy" Valentinian would be emperor someday, even though the court of Constantinople refused to acknowledge the elevation of Constantius and Galla Placidia. That must have been a frustrating, rather humiliating time for Constantius, who disliked the formality of the court and the stiff, uncomfortable clothes he had to wear. He and his empress did not get along well, and people commented that the Augustus was stingy and disagreeable. He died in the fall of 421—of boredom, suggested Thomas Hodgkin. Another scholar, Felix

Burckhardt, expressed the opinion that the death of Constantius was perhaps the greatest misfortune that struck the West in the fifth century, up to its final collapse.[36]

All the hard work was rapidly undone. Almost immediately the Visigoths assaulted previously accepted boundaries, and there were new troubles with the Bacaudae. Before long it was all too patent that the empire had become both decentralized and barbarized.

By 423 peculiar things had happened at Ravenna. Once, it has been said, almost incestuously fond of each other, Galla Placidia and Honorius had quarreled, and she had fled with Valentinian and her daughter Honoria to Constantinople. The quarrel may have had a personal basis, but there may also have been a split at Ravenna into a barbarian party and a Roman party, the barbarians rallying around the Augusta who had once been their queen. She still had her own little army that had followed her from Spain, plus *bucellarii* (a private army) inherited from Constantius. These people brawled in the streets with the Roman faction. The final split may have involved two rival candidates for Constantius's now vacant office of military commander-in-chief. Honorius backed an officer named Castinus, who seems to have detested Galla Placidia, while the Augusta favored her friend Boniface, a general who had performed with great éclat in Gaul. These two men are known to have had a furious falling-out just before an expedition was to set off against the Vandals in Spain. Castinus received the command. Boniface abruptly departed for Africa, where he seems to have established himself as an independent governor. He had been serving in Africa for some time and had ties there to draw on. Augustine, for example, was one of his friends.

It was after this altercation that Placidia and her children left for Constantinople. Emperor Honorius died in 423. In spite of all the upheavals in his long reign, he died a natural death. Gibbon reported it prematurely in his narrative, with the wry comment that the man was so boring that his demise might be overlooked in the proper chronological place. Four-year-old Valentinian was supposedly heir to the throne unless Theodosius II claimed it for the reunification of East and West. Theodosius was intelligent but rather languid and not likely to exert himself.

Once again a usurper appeared. Like Eugenius back in the days of Theodosius I, John was a notary. Not much is known about him, but it is suggestive that an antibarbarian party should support a candidate with the qualifications of a literary background and some ability in marshaling Latin words, just as in the case of Eugenius.[37]

General Castinus, who sided with the upstart, sent most of his available troops to Africa to immobilize Boniface there, and John's constable, the clever general Aëtius, was dispatched to Hunnic territory to round up a defensive army should Theodosius decide to attack.

The historian Procopius calls Boniface and Aëtius the last of the Romans. If this characterization is accurate, we must revise our thinking about "Romans" somewhat. Both Boniface and Aëtius were entangled with the barbarians, and as with Stilicho, motives are masked. We might make the general, qualified observation that Vandal Stilicho kept the Visigoths from gaining a permanent foothold on Italian soil during his lifetime whereas Roman Boniface must be held partly responsible for the loss of Africa to the Vandals, and Roman Aëtius must be remembered for bringing Huns into the very heart of the empire.

Aëtius, as we saw, had been sent to enlist the Huns on the side of the usurper John. He was a good man for the assignment because he had close ties with the Huns. The son of a prominent cavalry officer, Aëtius in his youth had been of sufficient value to be twice a hostage, first to Alaric the Visigoth and later to the Huns, among whom he stayed long enough to become familiar with their language, their military tactics, and their leaders.[38] All of this happened before the unification of the Huns under Attila.

Aëtius returned leading 60,000 Huns, three days too late. In his absence Theodosius had sent an army under the command of two capable Alan officers, the usurper John had been captured and executed at Aquileia on Galla Placidia's order, General Castinus had gone into exile, and little Valentinian III had had the diadem bound around his innocent brow. Acting as regent, Placidia now confirmed Boniface as governor of Africa, with the rank of *comes*.

With his formidable Hunnic mercenaries, Aëtius was strong enough to force peace with Placidia. His Huns were dismissed with a handsome donative from the Augusta, and Aëtius himself, promoted to the rank of *comes*, was sent to Gaul as military commander.

So far we have not paid much attention to Africa. We know that it was Rome's major granary. We have seen that Gildo's rebellion prompted Roman action in the time of Stilicho. We know that both Alaric and Wallia tried to lead the Visigoths there, as if to a promised land. We remember that Heraclian was tempted into using Africa as a platform for his own rebellion. Religious schism in Africa, we know, was taken seriously by Constantius. With Boniface there and the Vandals lined up on the Spanish shore, it is time to look at Africa more closely.

CARTHAGE AND THE
HIGH PLAINS OF AFRICA

O N the eighteenth day of May in the year 411, less than a year after Alaric plundered Rome, 565 African bishops convened in the city of Carthage under orders from Constantius to thrash out their antagonistic positions before an imperial commission. We see at once that this was a different continent and that the problems were not those of the Roman heartland, but we should remember that affairs in Africa were to affect the empire much more deeply than the sack of Rome ever did.

The African church was Western with a difference. One peculiarity was the extraordinary multiplicity of its bishops. How could one province produce or need 565 bishops? Surely that must be a gross misreading of some blurry palimpsest. No, the minutes of the conference of 411 exist, and there are names in the document to match that figure.[1]

The early history of the episcopate is hopelessly confusing, but it is known that, in Africa at least, it was considered absolutely necessary to have a bishop in every community.[2] In other parts of the empire the proliferation of sees had been more or less brought under control by the actions of various councils, but old ideas persisted in Africa. Besides, the bishops assembled at Carthage represented two factions, orthodox Catholics and schismatic Donatists. Especially in the backcountry of Numidia there was likely to be a "shadow" Catholic for every Donatist. Consequently, the number of attending bishops was almost double that of the communities they represented.

This confrontation had a special occidental flavor. It was not based on a clash over dogma of the kind that repeatedly rocked the Eastern churches as they fought out their christological positions. The Carthage meeting may have been called for political reasons, since a split in Africa could have serious repercussions in Rome.

It appears that the trouble between the Donatists and Catholics may have been a matter of temperament, as far as the Africans were concerned, but it also revolved around the hard question of how a universal state church ought to

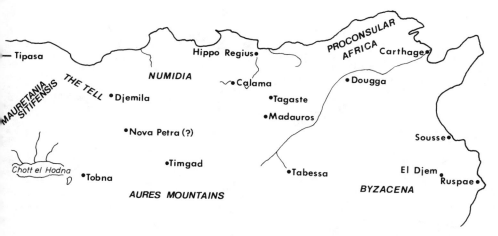

North Africa

operate. In a troubled age, that entailed a struggle toward some definition of Christian perfection.[3] On one side were the rigid Donatists, who believed that the church should demand—and have—priests who were willing to undergo torture or death for their faith. Many of the best intellects subscribed to this demanding code.[4] On the other side were the Catholics, who felt that a church that had become as wide as the civilized world would have to soften its holiness a little and accept the ministrations of people who had not always been able to measure up in time of persecution.

Africa had its peculiarities. It also had its glories, in a triad of giants, all illustrious fathers of the church. One of them, Augustine, was to play a major role in the conference at Carthage and would emerge from it in triumph. The other two, Tertullian and Cyprian, had lived and died before Christianity became a state religion. Even then the church had been enough of a force to elicit a reaction from the empire, and that reaction had taken the form of persecution. For better or worse, the response of Tertullian and Cyprian, against the background of African conditions, was much more than tragic heroism. Between them they laid the foundations of Catholicism as it was to be built in Europe in the Middle Ages.

The church was evolving even in Tertullian's time, though we could not expect that a man living in the early third century would have grasped a concept like that. Even if he had understood that institutions evolve like living organisms, Tertullian would have rejected the idea. Instinctively he was holding onto the past. "A prince among rigorists," he has been called.[5] We jeer at the puritanical ways of people like Tertullian, with their abhorrence of fri-

Plate 47. The ruins of Roman Cuicul, Djemila, Algeria. At the conference of Carthage in 411 the Catholic bishop from this city reported that a Donatist bishop had opposed him there but that he had just died. The city was comparatively prosperous in the fourth and fifth centuries. Many of the inhabitants were retired veterans. The domed structure is a Catholic baptistery.

volities such as the theater and the circus, but we forget what those institutions were at the time. Tertullian describes the circus in a way that unmistakably puts him among the spectators, "laughing" while a suffering wretch mockingly costumed like the god Attis was publicly castrated for the crowd's enjoyment. We have Augustine's story of his dear colleague Alypius, whose friends dragged him to a gladiatorial contest against his will, with the horrifying result that he was irresistibly transformed into a raging member of the mob. Small wonder that when persons of any sensitivity were confronted with the nature of their addiction to these disgusting events they felt such revulsion that only the cool, cleansing waters of baptism and close association with others who had withdrawn into a life of serenity and purity could restore them.

Tertullian became a Christian around the year 195. He embraced his new faith with a passion that contrasted oddly with the precision of his elegantly analytical mind. He equated Christian practice with the revelation of the

Gospel, convinced that there had been no accretions, no change, since the days when Jesus walked the earth. The teaching of the church in Africa, Tertullian felt, was precisely the teaching delivered to the apostles. It should be preserved at the cost of martyrdom if necessary. Tertullian established the essential rightness of tradition:[6] he championed the idea that there should be no concession to outside pressure. It remained for Cyprian of Carthage, like Tertullian a spokesman for a growing Latin faction not only in Africa but also in Rome, to put the control and government of the church into the hands of the bishops, by establishing the principle of apostolic succession.

Bishops were latecomers in the ecclesiastical scheme. In Africa even the distinction between clergy and laity came late and was still rather nebulous in Tertullian's day.

Cyprian's own election is interesting because it ran counter to the very rule that he himself laid down, namely, that bishops of neighboring sees should elect a new bishop and that this action should be ratified by the congregation.[7] In other words the shift to the principle whereby grace was dispensed from above occurred in Cyprian's own lifetime. We do not need to involve ourselves in the complexities of the argument; what concerns us is the practical application of it, whereby the authority of the bishops became paramount. Gibbon has many unkind things to say about Cyprian, but in fairness it does not seem that Gibbon ever tried to put himself into the bishop's shoes. He thinks that everything in Cyprian's career, including his martyrdom, indicated a ruthless drive for personal power.

If a visible church is to be sustained, it must be held together in the face of persecution. It must also remain steady in the swirling currents that persecution stirs up among the survivors. It was precisely the post-persecution problem that concerned Cyprian.

As persecutions go, the Decian episode 249–50 was well managed. Emperor Decius was an intelligent man who understood that apostates were much more valuable than martyrs. All a Christian had to do to reinstate himself was appear before the appointed commissioners,[8] who, after witnessing a token sacrifice, were prepared to issue *libelli*. These documents were certificates which stated that the petitioner in question had duly offered wine and incense. Drastic persuasion could be applied, but if people understood the emperor's wishes and were sufficiently alarmed, they would conform. The *libelli* of an extant collection are so nearly uniform in wording that they have the look of standard government forms. Those from villages in the Egyptian Faiyūm show how anxiously and submissively the little people presented themselves for certification. The situation must have been much the same at Carthage.

Cyprian's difficulty came from the "confessors" who had adamantly refused to bow to the emperor's will and had suffered valiantly under horrible maltreatment because of their heroic stubbornness. There had been confessors in the

African church all along; they constituted a kind of elite.[9] With the Decian persecution the number of confessors increased spectacularly, and lapsed members of the flock who wanted to return to the bosom of the church importuned these notably holy, distinguished people to intervene for them. Some of the confessors were humanly arrogant and irresponsible in their perfection, taking it on themselves to decide whose sins should be remitted. Cyprian believed that only a bishop should act on behalf of the Almighty, after long and prayerful consideration of individual cases. It was an exquisitely delicate business in the eyes of those who accepted Tertullian's stern teachings. Forgiveness could come only from God, who was not a particularly generous being. Were God and the confessors truly of one mind? How would it all turn out, on the Last Day?

The confessors wrote letters addressed to the bishops on behalf of the lapsed—for a friend, perhaps, or a family—but then for more and more individuals until one Lucian capped it all by sending a letter to Cyprian in the name of all the confessors: "We have given peace to all persons who shall bring you a satisfactory account of their doings since the offense."[10] Cyprian stood firm, but other bishops relented. In the end even Cyprian had to relent a little, proposing that time should be taken for everyone to calm down. Eventually he was able to conduct a meeting at Carthage, where the consensus was that only those who had actually sacrificed, not those engaged in some sort of subterfuge, should be required to wait until the hour of death for absolution. Meanwhile, those unfortunates were to live a hard, depressing life of penitence. At still another conference (May, 252), when new persecution loomed, there was a general amnesty for all who had been steadfast in penance, but that should not be construed as a weakening of Cyprian's position on episcopal authority. It was a victory, because the bishop himself, not the confessors, issued the pardon.

It is revealing that the imperial rescript against the Christians that burst on the church in the year 258 under Emperor Valerian was conspicuously directed against bishops. Theirs would be the death penalty. That was in startling contrast to the customary set of Roman law: severest bodily punishment was usually meted out to the lowly, whereas persons of high rank were likely to escape with confiscation of property. We must assume that Valerian had become aware of a challenging development of personal authority within the church, something that might be a threat to his own power.

Cyprian now laid down his life, no doubt aware in his last moments that sainthood was his. As he bent his head to receive the stroke, he was surrounded by the faithful, who held out bits of cloth that were to be tied to his body, to soak up his immediately hallowed and restorative blood.[11]

The trials of the African church were far from over, though the subsequent chapters had nothing to do with empire-wide persecution. The troubles came to a head after Christianity had become the recognized state religion. Events might have been quite different if the African congregations had not been so convinced that grace was to be dispensed only within the church and that the bishops themselves should be in a state of grace because they were the channels of divine will.

We have arrived at the age of the Donatists. The Donatist movement took its name from one of its leading spokesmen, Bishop Donatus the Great of Carthage, whose name is a latinized form of a Punic name signifying "Given of Baal." [12] He came from the southernmost edge of the Numidian High Plains. When he first appeared in Carthage (around the year 311), the faction that he was to head for more than forty years was already taking shape. At that stage the austere Numidian churches were banding with the fanatic street rabble of Carthage in a struggle that concerned the consecration of a new bishop, Caecilian, who once in the stress of persecution had allowed certain books belonging to his church to be confiscated by the emperor's deputies. The Numidians called him a *traditor* (one who has handed over something) and proclaimed that he was unfit for office (see plate 48). Having assembled in a synod, they elected a bishop of their own. Constantine the Great, who was emperor at the time and somewhat overconfident in his new role as head of a Christian state, tried to resolve the affair in a series of conferences—at Rome in 313, at Arles in 314, and at Milan in 316. Each time the *traditor's* election was upheld, and the Donatists seethed. The situation worried along until about 346, when Donatus felt strong enough to approach Emperor Constans with a request for recognition of himself as *the* bishop of Carthage, probably on the ground that by that time he was the senior bishop in the city. [13] The emperor responded by sending a commission to Carthage to study the situation. The two imperial notaries arrived in Africa in the following year and were conspicuously gracious to the Catholics, thereby setting off wild rumors. The scenes that ensued in Numidia when the envoys arrived were appalling. Troops had to be called out. There were riots and massacres, and the body of a bishop was flung down a well. It is hardly astonishing that Donatism was proscribed. The Donatists then sent delegates to protest, headed by one Bishop Marculus, who must have spoken his mind too freely. He and other delegates were bound to pillars and flogged. Riots broke out in Carthage, and it appears that regular troops were called in. That ostensibly ended the horror, because Donatus went into exile, but the flame was kept alive. Marculus, the bishop who had been flogged, became the hero of the Numidians. The vast basilica built at Nova Petra, the site of his suffering, soon became a place of ardent pilgrimage.

A lot of ink has flowed in development of the notion that people like the Donatists were protonationalists, using a movement within the church as an expression of separatist inclinations, but that sounds much too sophisticated for the times. Earnest churchmen were not even sure just how the church should be organized. The minds of simple herders and olive cultivators in the

Plate 48. *Traditio legis*, detail of a sarcophagus, fifth century, Abbey Church of Saint Victor, Marseilles, France. *Traditio* conveyed the idea of delivery of instruments or symbols into the keeping of worthy persons. It was against this background that the Donatists objected to weak bishops who handed over sacred writings to persecuting authorities, calling such bishops *traditores*. The motif of *Traditio legis* was adapted from imperial iconography. Jesus is depicted handing over a scroll to Peter, who receives it with "muffled hands," as a courtier would accept a gift from an Eastern emperor.

dry, remote steppe country of northern Africa may not even have grasped the notion of empire.

Characteristically, the physical attacks by the fanatic fringe group known as the Circumcellions were aimed primarily at the instruments of economic woe—creditors, extortionists, tax collectors, and slave owners.[14] The action was anti-Roman in the strict sense because the targets were mostly Romans, but the argument against the theory of deliberate separatism seems to lie in the circumstance that the leaders could barely communicate with the rank and file of the movement. The theoreticians may well have had a strong point, that the Roman brand of Christianity was a social betrayal of the ideas of the early church, but these intellectuals wrote and spoke Latin, the language of the oppressors, whereas the people of the High Plains spoke a Libyan dialect. Note, for example, Augustine's letter to Bishop Crispinus, who had forced eighty Christian slaves to be rebaptized as Donatists: "Let them hear us both, our statements then being written down and, after being attested by our signatures, translated into Punic for them."[15] "Deo laudes!" the blood-curdling cry of the Circumcellions, was probably all the Latin they knew.

As far as the idea of African separatism goes, when we look at the intellectuals in Carthage, we find that Manichaeism had considerable attraction for them. Although the church viewed the religion of Mani with hostility and alarm, many members of the orthodox community were in fact associated with it at one time or another. Adolf Harnack suggests that Manichaeism may have appealed to "cultured" individuals who wanted rational explanations. He observes that it may have been especially popular in Africa because of the Semitic (that is, Punic) element in the population.[16] Augustine himself, who was part Berber, was a Manichaean for nine years.[17]

There is another factor that deserves consideration. Manichaeism was viewed with deep suspicion not only by the church but also by the state. Subversive ideas were infiltrating those Christian communities that were in contact with Syria, where Manichaeism was strong. In his Christian apocalypse Lactantius wrote: "The name of Rome that now governs the world will disappear from the earth. The East will be master, and West the slave."[18] It would be too much to say that the Carthaginian Manichees desired the downfall of Rome, but they were perhaps not attuned to the concept of an eternal empire.

Population splits and alien undercurrents antedated the African Donatists and Manichaeans. Long before the Romans arrived, Punic settlements extended shallowly along the coast and penetrated inland through the valleys near and below Carthage. In this fertile region the seagoing Phoenicians found in themselves an unexpected talent for farm management and developed large country estates that were worked by slaves. Behind the forbidding coast lay the northern spur of the Atlas Mountains (the forested, rocky Tell). That region was also fertile, but on the south, curving around Carthaginian territory, came the semiarid High Plains, where the Berbers lived. By the time of the Roman conquest the Berbers had begun to abandon transhumance in favor of specialized cultivation of barley and olives, which could be grown successfully with careful water management, but such activity had little in common with the large-scale farming of the valleys. Even today there are two Berber terms for the olive tree, one of which is a true Berber word and refers to the wild olive, while the other derives from the Semitic and refers to the cultivated plant.[19]

What we call Algeria was never smoothly integrated with the rest of Roman Africa, or Romanized, or even de-Berberized. It has been said that the Berbers "saw all other races in and will see them out."[20] The timelessness of Berber civilization can be explained by geography: the valleys are high, narrow, and short. They are not routes for trade and the entrance of alien civilizations.[21]

Is there something in the High Plains that nurtured fanaticism, something there that made the population rigid and uncompromising? The same region at a later time was the source of strength for puritanical brands of Islam.[22] Except in African centers that were in direct communication with Rome (Leptis Magna, for example), the veneer of Roman civilization must have been thin. In pagan times most towns had temples to Saturn and Caelestis, but it would be an error to think of that as evidence that the easygoing Roman gods had been welcomed just as they were. Saturn was depicted in Africa as a sour old man who ruled fiercely as eternal and omnipotent. He was much closer to Baal, the deity brought in long before by the Phoenicians, or to the Tripolitanian deity called Gurzil, whose name was a war cry and whose idol was wet with the blood of sacrifice on the eve of battle. Originally, African Saturn had no actual temples that would have been the due of a proper Roman god. When temples were subsequently built for him, they had a somewhat Roman look on the exterior, though their internal structure was not Roman at all. These edifices were sited on heights outside the towns, as at Thugga (Dougga), where originally there had been a sacred enclosure dedicated to him.

Caelestis was not Roman, but she was not wholly Phoenician either. Her Punic counterpart was Tanit (see plate 49). Like Saturn, Caelestis was formidable. Worship of both deities required submission—in Punic times to the point of human sacrifice, as the tiny bones of infants in the sacred enclosures called the Sanctuary of Tanit ("tophets") attest all too clearly.

When the Berbers made an abrupt shift to Christianity late in the third century, the event was not so much a conversion as a transformation of the popular religion. The Berbers never shed their feeling that worship was ritual appeasement of divine wrath. There was nothing incongruous to them in the way they welded their Christian tradition and ritual onto what had previously been Saturn's. They whitened their altars and their martyrs' shrines, just as they had previously whitened cult objects in Saturn's sanctuaries.[23]

Bad management and greed must have thrown the roughly treated fanatical Donatists and the fatalist peasants into each other's arms. We see this particularly in the time of Valentinian I, when a notorious governor stirred the anger of the Donatists by his use of military force against them, simultaneously goading the plains people into open revolt by his rapaciousness. The story of the sufferings of the people around Leptis Magna as Ammianus tells it could probably stand for other regions also. Appeals for help became entangled in the machinations of the unscrupulous governor, and instead of an intelligent response from the emperor there were merely ineffectual inquiries and investigations. "Even Justice herself has wept," says Ammianus.[24]

Peasants and Donatists alike responded to the call of the Moorish rebel Firmus. When the formidable Count Theodosius (father of Theodosius the

Plate 49. The sign of Tanit, precinct of Tanit, Carthage, Tunisia. Tanit was a celestial goddess, the consort of Baal Hammon. Submission to her will entailed human sacrifice, evidence of which remains in her sacred enclosure. Although she was distinctively Western, she was the "descendant" of Phoenician Astarte. Tanit's symbol is enigmatic, comprising a triangle topped by a disk from which it is separated by a horizontal arm, and a crescent that points downward, or a crescent and disk on a ribboned staff.

Great) arrived to quell the uprising, he faced a complicated situation. It took him about three years of hard fighting to resolve it, even though he presumably had the loyal support of the Catholics and the wealthy landowners. He was able to control Catholic strongholds like Tipasa without much trouble, but he had difficulty with the Donatist centers. Firmus is said to have sent Donatist clergy as emissaries to parley with Theodosius on at least one occasion.[25]

Firmus the Moor called himself "rex" and rode "mounted on a tall horse, his purple cloak trailing out and spreading wide."[26] (According to Procopius, the Moors, who remained essentially tribal, had a certain awe of the empire as a mysterious embodiment of authority: "It was a law among the Moors that no one should be ruler over them, even if he was hostile to the Romans, until the emperor of the Romans should give him tokens of office." These gaudy symbols included a staff of silver covered with gold, and a silver cap "like a crown, held in place on all sides by bands of silver," as well as a white cloak, golden brooch, embroidered tunic, and gilded boots.)[27] Imposing and daring as he was, royal Firmus won over some of Theodosius's own troops and accepted a Roman officer's collar to wear as a diadem, as had Emperor Julian not long before. Firmus failed in the end, and like an antique Roman "he decided by a voluntary death to spurn with his foot his desire to live," and his body was brought to Theodosius on the back of a camel.[28]

The aftermath of all of this shows that the part that the Donatists had been playing was known. The new proconsul appointed for Africa in 376 was instructed to forbid the Donatists to assemble for worship. Their bishops again went into exile; however, the new *comes Africae*, victorious Theodosius, suddenly and inexplicably became an object of suspicion, and was beheaded at Carthage in the same year. The highest office in Africa was transferred to a confirmed Donatist, who simply ignored the emperor's further instructions in church matters. All of this is most strange. The question has been worked over elaborately, with blame assigned variously to the emperors Valens, Gratian, and Valentinian I; the Frankish general Merobaudes; and so on. We should not, however, overlook a hint from the contemporary historian Orosius, who seems to say that the Donatists had a hand in the death of Theodosius. There is no convincing proof. We can only contemplate the swift change of Donatist fortunes and wonder.[29]

By the year 393, Africa had a new *comes* in the person of Firmus's brother Gildo, who presumably won the honor as reward for loyal support during the late disturbance. Theodosius I was emperor, and, as we know, it was his way to trust barbarians. Gildo's use of power was without precedent in Africa. He understood the mechanics of delivering or withholding grain shipments and of playing East against West in the power struggle between Ravenna and Constantinople. He seems to have had other economics-oriented ideas. If grain was held in Africa, obviously the price of it would go down locally. Also enormous imperial estates could be confiscated, to be parceled out in what we might call a program of agrarian reform, for the benefit of the Circumcellions. Gildo had a colleague in this effort, the "mitered barbarian," fiery Bishop Optatus of Timgad. That powerful Donatist leader was a revolutionist. He dictated redistribution of lands and also welded the Circumcellions into a paramilitary force for use in repressing his rivals.[30]

Poor wretches: the Circumcellions are branded as crazed suicidal fanatics, bloody terrorists, the scum of a desperate peasantry. As the core of a supposed nationalist movement they have less credibility than their nearest counter-parts, the Bacaudae in Gaul. They were a curiously heterogeneous group, difficult to identify. For one thing, there is the problem of social stratification. Certain laws in the Theodosian Code seem to indicate that the Circumcellions were property owners, because they were made subject to heavy monetary fines. They could not, then, have been at the very bottom of the heap; in that case the imposition of fines would have been fruitless. They have even been called "the highest group of the rural population." Some scholars think that they may have been olive cultivators, more or less the backbone of the economy of the High Plains.[31] Many were wanderers like the Bacaudae, for the same reason—namely, because the hand of the tax collector lay heavily on them. Some are known to have been migrant agricultural workers, while others were escaped slaves. Some Circumcellions were even orthodox Catholics.

What we see across the centuries is likely to represent the extremes. Not all the Circumcellions were religious fanatics, but it was they whose performance was the most colorful and conspicuously horrifying. The fanatics renounced the world and all its works, living in poverty around the "cells" (churches and shrines), where, as archaeologists have been able to demonstrate, there were stores of food for their use, though not enough to support them continuously. The Circumcellions wore a vaguely monastic dress, indulged in ritual drunk-enness, and were capable of mass suicide. Murder and pillaging was a way of life for them. Even Augustine narrowly escaped being ambushed by them.

It is beyond question that the Donatists made tools of them. In the time of Gildo's uprising (when Stilicho was still in power), the Donatists and the African Catholics remained at an impasse.[32] By throwing in their lot with Gildo, the Donatists strengthened themselves so much that Augustine, the champion of orthodoxy, was unable to attack them.[33] In the end Stilicho tri-umphed over Gildo, who either was executed or committed suicide. The Do-natist firebrand Optatus was also killed. It was after this, in 401, that Stilicho's brother-in-law Bathanarius became *comes Africae.*

By 404 the situation was again out of hand. Donatists were using Circum-cellions to fight their battles, and Catholics were taking hostages. A delega-tion of Catholics went to Ravenna. Severe penalties against the Donatists were demanded, as well as military protection of Catholic property. Stilicho re-sponded by pronouncing Donatism a true heresy, in the name of Emperor Honorius. No death penalty, to be sure (the Catholics did not want any more martyrs)—mere flogging with lead-tipped whips ought to suffice.

With Stilicho's fall in 408 the resentful Donatists came out of hiding. Once more there were riots and murders, and a Donatist bishop came to Augustine's own town, Hippo, escorted by Circumcellions.

Augustine must have been aware of stirrings in the wind, because it is

Plate 50. Mosaic of an African basilica, date and place of origin unknown. The conference of 411 at Carthage took place in an edifice like this. The actual site of the conference, a vast, seven-aisled church, can be seen today only in barest outline. Paris, Musée du Louvre MA 3676. *Courtesy of Musée du Louvre, Paris.*

known that he was in urgent communication with Olympius, who masterminded Stilicho's overthrow. After the recall of Stilicho's brother-in-law the replacement as count of Africa was Heraclian, who was soon forced by the complexities of his own situation to set out against the empire with a fleet, in full rebellion.

Before that fatal move the curious drama of confrontation was played out in Carthage. Honorius's (that is, Constantius's) summons to this meeting just months after the sack of Rome, states coolly that "among the major concerns of our Empire, respect of Catholic law remains either the first, or our sole concern." [34] Perhaps there was not so much sangfroid as one might think: Catholic law at that stage must have been about the only tie holding the empire together.

The conference was presided over by Marcellinus, a friend of Augustine's. We recall that he had been instructed to bring an end once and for all to religious discord in Africa. That was no easy assignment. The Donatist bishop of Nova Petra had no intention of letting anyone forget what his people had

Plate 51. Basilica of Justinian, Sabratha, Libya. The basilica was built of masonry robbed from Severan structures that had been destroyed by desert marauders. The *ambo* (pulpit) was cut from a cornice of the Capitolium. Sabratha was the only one of the three great cities of Tripolitania to send a Catholic bishop to the conference of Carthage in 411.

suffered in the past at the hands of the emperor's deputies. In identifying himself, the bishop told Marcellinus that he had no Catholic rival in his see, "for Marculus is there, whose blood God will avenge at the Last Day."[35]

Politicians to a man, those prelates. Any modern practitioner of the strategic art of delay and obfuscation must admire the process of attrition that evolved around the mere seating of delegates. Perhaps "seating" is not the right word; the Donatists loftily refused to sit, stating that Jesus had stood at his trial. Marcellinus must have been a model of endurance and tact. How else could he have kept his equanimity in the face of the stupefying roll calls, the endless challenges of delegates, the convoluted arguments?

Archaeological evidence suggests that, although Augustine's eloquence won the day and judgment went against the Donatists, who were fairly quiet after the conference, they survived in Numidia. It may be significant that they fared there somewhat better than the Catholics did when the Vandals came in.

Marcellinus himself was summarily beheaded in 413 in a purge following the execution of the rebel Heraclian. He does not appear to have been involved with Heraclian at all. As in the execution of Count Theodosius, there is a lurking suspicion of a vindictive denunciation by Donatists, but no proof exists one way or the other.[36]

Four years later Augustine sent a letter to Galla Placidia's loyal friend Boniface indicating that the Donatists were reported to be sounding out Gothic mercenaries in Africa as potential allies. He thought he saw signs that they were looking for points that they might have in common with Arians, since both were branded as heretics.[37] Like his revered Ambrose of Milan some years before, Augustine understood secular power. He was extending the principle of ecclesiastical dominance in affairs concerning the state church to include the formidable application of military authority in the interests of orthodoxy. Augustine was an earnest pastor, but mixed into his concern for the welfare of his flock as individual souls—not least his friend Boniface, the frontier commander—was his confident belief that all possible forces should be mustered to protect and sustain the Catholic church. This idea, flowing out of Africa and stemming from the Donatist situation, was to have dire effects in Europe at a later day.

The first of Augustine's surviving letters to Boniface is addressed to him as a soldier of the Lord. Boniface had been disconcerted by his orders to suppress the Donatists, whose threat to the church he did not understand too well, and he had asked Augustine for enlightenment. Augustine's response used quotations from the Scriptures to justify military service against the barbarians (meaning the Moors), but on the whole he did not have much to say about the Donatists. Soon afterward he wrote again, setting out his whole case against the Donatists, describing them as a menace. This letter also conveyed the information that the Donatists were approaching the Arians to look into possibilities for an alliance of sorts. Presumably the Arians in question were Boniface's own Goths, who made up part of his command on the southern frontier of Numidia. Boniface may have absorbed Augustine's information with considerable attention, in a way that Augustine would not have foreseen or intended.

There is much disagreement about Boniface's title and status in his early years in Africa. He must have been either a *praepositus limitum* (commander of a sector of the frontier defense system called *limes*) or a *tribunus* (administrative

Plate 52. The chott (salt lake) of Sidi El Hani, east of Kairouan, Tunisia. It was in such a forbidding area that Boniface held his original African command.

officer).[38] Such an officer was subordinate to the *comes Africae* (Boniface's subsequent rank under Galla Placidia). He was stationed at Tobna, in the desolate region of the salt chotts, or lakes, commanding a band of local *limitanei* (see plate 52). These were landowners, obligated to the performance of military duty on the frontier. Their rights were not hereditary, but they enjoyed certain advantages such as tax exemption. They were not so much an army as a population under arms, ready to respond to enemy incursions. They were never much Romanized: there are fourth-century inscriptions that show only Moorish names.[39] Boniface also had Gothic federates under his command. These auxiliaries theoretically were part of the army of the empire, but they were fairly independent.

We have it on Augustine's authority that with these troops Boniface was successful against desert bands. He was popular with his men and approved of by the Catholic clergy. This obscure commander was not destined to live out a long career beside the salty, windblown chotts, however. His emotions, his religious beliefs, and his military and political obligations suddenly began to clash, partly because of events in his personal life, partly because of events in Ravenna. By the time all these matters had been ironed out, the Vandals were in possession of Africa. Even today Boniface is largely blamed.

Sometime before 422, Boniface lost his wife. In his gloom he toyed with the idea of becoming a monk. Much upset, Augustine and his friend Bishop Alypius set out on the difficult journey to Boniface's station at Tobna. Neither cleric was young, and Augustine was a notoriously poor traveler. The mere fact of the trip conveys a sense of urgency. They came to him to offer a counter-proposal. Live chastely like a monk but stay in the world, they said: serve as a defender of the church.

It was at about this point that affairs in Ravenna began to dominate the life of Boniface. He was summoned to the court and ordered to go to Spain in an expedition against the Vandals under the command of a rival officer, Castinus. The assignment was not at all to Boniface's liking, and an angry shouting match ended with Boniface's precipitate return to Africa. He looked like a fugitive or rebel, but in spite of his arrant insubordination he seems to have extracted the title *comes Africae* from Honorious. The affair came close on the heels of the death of Emperor Constantius. With the added complication of Galla Placidia's partisanship it may be that the emperor was unable to think of any other way to resolve the conflict.[40]

In the midst of all this commotion Boniface suddenly acquired a new wife. The bride's name was Pelagia, which tells us nothing. She was a barbarian—a Goth according to most scholars, a Vandal princess and a member of Gaiseric's own family according to some others, though the argument is not convincing. Boniface is said to have made a trip either to Italy or to Spain to marry her. She was an Arian, which deeply disconcerted Augustine. Although he comforted himself with the knowledge that she became a Catholic before the wedding, the daughter of Boniface and Pelagia was baptized Arian. Pelagia was rich; that much is clear. Perhaps the most important thing about her was that her dowry included a large military bodyguard, her *bucellarii*.

We have met *bucellarii* fleetingly before. Rufinus collected a bodyguard of Huns in Constantinople when he came into conflict with Stilicho. His is the first documented case of the assembling of such a private force. Stilicho later had his own loyal Hunnic guard, and Galla Placidia in Ravenna had *bucellarii* who may have been with her ever since her days as queen of the Visigoths. She also had a train of armed Goths who had been in the service of her late husband, Constantius.

When we think of bodyguards, we tend to imagine small groups, but that is misleading in regard to *bucellarii* (see plate 53). They could constitute a sizable cavalry troop, occasionally numbering in the thousands. There is no exact translation for *bucellarii*. The term vaguely indicates that these men consumed the same quality of fine bread that their leader ate. The term appears only in the fifth century, though such followers of military leaders had been known as far back as Tacitus, who described what may have been the Germanic predecessors of the *bucellarii*.[41] By the fifth century they were no longer elite young noblemen but had become mercenaries picked from any walk of life because of demonstrated ability. They were mounted units, closely associated with their chiefs, always near them in the field.[42] They looked utterly un-Roman: we can see them today on the base of the Egyptian obelisk in the Hippodrome of Istanbul, attending their emperor and gravely eyeing us, their long hair resting on their shoulders, and impressive bullae hanging about their necks as insignia. We see them again in glowing color in the mosaic at San Vitale, in Ravenna, where they press into the church in the train of General Belisarius and Emperor Justinian.[43]

Through his marriage to the rich Pelagia, Boniface had acquired *bucellarii* of his own in Africa. During the usurpation of John that followed the death of Honorius, Boniface held Africa for Galla Placidia and her son. The large military contingent that John was constrained to send to Africa must have helped weaken that usurper, thus assisting the army from the East. We would expect honors to be heaped on Boniface after Placidia had become the established, legitimate regent, and no doubt those were Boniface's expectations also, but confirmation of his post as *comes Africae* was the only acknowledgment of his loyalty.

The trouble was that the position of the Augusta was precarious. The West had reached a phase in which the most prized office was that of commander-in-chief with the concomitant rank of patrician. Stilicho and Emperor Constantius had set the pattern. Galla Placidia moved cautiously among the many traps that beset her path, trying to balance Boniface, ensconced in Africa with his control of the grain supply, and Aëtius with his Huns massed just across the border. To maintain some kind of uneasy equilibrium, Galla Placidia chose a nonmilitary man, the courtier Felix, to be her prime minister, a choice that by no means solved the problem, because Felix, although competent, was calculating and ambitious.

We sense that in the ensuing struggles no one had a clear view of what constituted the Roman Empire or what it might be, now that Constantius was dead. Take Placidia herself: she was a thoroughgoing conservative, concentrating all her force and effort on the problem of imperial prestige for her son. She was not inventive enough to do anything other than juggle one faction or individual against another. What about the great landowners, bloated as they still were with incredible wealth? Theirs was a monumentally self-serving greed. They understood tax shelters, if anyone ever has. Their concern was to shield their enormous fortunes from the grasp of the tottering empire, a con-

Plate 53. *Bucellarii* in attendance on Theodosius I, base of the Egyptian obelisk at the Hippodrome, Istanbul. The *bucellarius* is always to be recognized by his long hair and the bulla around his neck. He invariably stands close to his commander. See also plate 60.

cern to which Placidia had to bow because their power was equal to if not greater than hers. The church? We have seen Augustine corresponding with the powers in Ravenna and manipulating a military commander. The generals engaged in a naked power struggle. Although in the course of it Aëtius admittedly managed to hold Gaul, and Boniface kept the grain flowing to Italy in the time of Galla Placidia's need, there is nothing to show that either man had any aim beyond securing the prize that had become worth far more than a diadem. The hero of the late Roman Empire was the peasant, says Lynn White, but since most individuals did not enjoy the benefits of urban life, they would feel no stake in the city or loyalty to it.[44] We cannot look for understanding of problems of empire in that sector. That greatest of urban centers, the Eternal City, had been parasitic for generations: not much in the way of vision could be expected from the bureaucracy with its ties to the aristocrats. The soldiers of the rank and file probably had no notion at all of what was at stake. Their pay, their booty, their rations—that was about as far as their thoughts were likely to go.

Felix, as head of the government, applied his power for his own aggrandizement. This man was no Stilicho, no Constantius, though in fairness it must be admitted that he did bear in mind the interests of the empire well enough to see to it that the Huns were expelled from Pannonia. That may merely have been a move against Aëtius, however. He also set about the business of eliminating his rivals, beginning with the not particularly admirable Bishop Patroclus of Arles, the late Constantius's protégé to whom Placidia was loyal. This part of the story is hazy, but it seems that at the time of John's usurpation the Visigoths moved against Arles, possibly on the invitation of Bishop Patroclus. Just what motivated the Visigoths is hard to say; an attack on the ports would have been more profitable to them. Perhaps they were in league with their former queen, as some historians believe. In any case, Felix sent Aëtius to push the Visigoths back into their own territory, and Bishop Patroclus was bloodily murdered in 426.[45]

Next Boniface was summoned to Ravenna to render an account of his doings in Africa. The misdeeds are not specified, but a letter of Augustine's indicates that Boniface had become entirely preoccupied with his foederati and *bucellarii* and the fortification of towns near the coast. His Goths were unruly, terrorizing the local population. Besides, as Augustine wrote: "What shall I say of the devastation that is being wrought by the African barbarians? They meet no opposition as long as you are taken up with the difficulties of your own situation and take no measures to avert this calamity."[46] Moorish tribes are known to have crossed into Roman territory around 428. Boniface may have found it expedient to establish some Berber chieftain in control of the roads that extended from the Hodna region westward into the High Plains (there was a strong native kingdom there in Vandal times).[47]

Boniface had no inclination to honor Placidia's summons, which was doubtless instigated by Felix. There is no need to accept the wild yarn of Procopius to the effect that Aëtius treacherously poisoned the minds of Placidia and Boniface so that they were unable to trust each other.[48] The plot runs along well enough without an Iago.

Felix grasped the opportunity that the recalcitrance of Boniface presented. He dispatched a force to Africa to deal with the rebel, who was officially designated a public enemy. Boniface emerged victorious, able to supply himself with weapons captured from the defeated expeditionary force. In the following year a large army of Goths headed by a "comes Africae" named Sigisvult arrived. We contemplate the spectacle of a Roman civil war fought almost exclusively by Goths on African soil.

Placidia eventually decided to send out peace feelers to bring Boniface back into her orbit. Amicable relations were restored, and Boniface once again was the comes Africae in good standing.

The count of Africa was not a man to be envied in the year 429. In May of that year the Vandals, who had been contenting themselves with sporadic raids against the Balearic Islands or Mauretania, moved en masse from Spain to Africa. One story goes that Boniface, under attack before his return to Placidia's favor, had invited the Vandals to come to Africa. He was said to have dealt directly with the two Vandal kings who ruled the Vandals and the Alans in Spain. In another version of the story Felix's general Sigisvult likewise sent word to the Vandals that they would be welcomed if they were to come over to subdue Boniface. Still another version simply states that when Gaiseric became the sole king of the Vandals he saw that Africa was ripe for the picking. On the whole the last looks like the most reasonable interpretation of the events.[49]

In spite of their unappetizing reputation, the Vandals did not spend their entire lives ravaging the civilized world. The term "vandalism," which has become attached to acts of wanton destructiveness, has nothing to do with them. It was coined by Bishop Grégoire of Blois, who was talking about the French Revolution, not about the struggles of wandering folk in the time of the great migrations.[50]

Before landing in Africa, the Vandals had suffered many trials in Spain. Romanized provincials were there, ready prey for their raids, but the Suevi had come along too, and relationships with those people were not smooth.[51] At their backs the Vandals had their traditional enemies the Visigoths, then commissioned by Ravenna to control if not exterminate them. As targets of Constantius's intricate policies, the Vandals, the Alans, and the Suevi jostled about in their cul-de-sac, and conditions were difficult indeed. Immediately after Constantius's death General Castinus was sent to Spain, in command of a large force directed against them. Although the Vandals routed Castinus, they were still menaced by the Visigoths, and they knew that Ravenna could be expected to pounce again someday. The triumph over Castinus may have served as a signal to the Vandals that at that moment the empire was unusually weak.

They beat back the Suevi in a savage engagement and then turned their attention to the logistics of crossing water, all eighty thousand of them. Most figures indicating the numbers of barbarian hordes are unreliable, coming from the fevered minds of Romans who saw twenty barbarians where actually there was one, but this time the count must have been more trustworthy than usual. There had to be an accurate determination of the number of vessels needed for the crossing to Africa.

How would one go about transporting eighty thousand individuals with their horses, livestock, and household gear across a strait some fifteen centuries ago? Plenty of fanciful theories have been offered to account for this astounding performance. At one time it was common belief that Boniface had furnished a war fleet. At another time it was assumed that the Vandals had been able to commandeer an enormous flotilla of Spanish merchant ships. These ideas have since been demolished. Christian Courtois concluded that they must have taken the shortest possible route, near Gibraltar, shuttled across by small fishing craft. The operation rather recalls the rescue of the British army from Dunkirk in 1940. Two or three men handling a small boat could ferry four or five Vandals and their gear, negotiating a sixty-two-kilometer round trip in twenty-four hours. If there were five hundred fishing boats, which is not beyond possibility, the Vandals and Alans could have arrived in force on the beaches east of modern Tangiers by the end of thirty-two laborious days. [52]

Did "a huge host of savage enemies armed with every kind of weapon" actually swarm all over Mauretania and the African provinces, as Possidius reports in his biography of Saint Augustine? [53] That seems about as unlikely as the orderly sailing of a battle fleet. The Vandals trickled across in the general direction of Carthage. The progress was so slow that members of the clergy were able to escape, taking refuge in Gaul, where there was some worry that they might be Donatists. [54] On the whole the population—Donatist or otherwise—seems to have remained passive. No indication of resistance is known.

Traces of the Vandals are to be found at various points along the way. It took them a full three months to travel seven hundred kilometers. Women and children and the aged could not move along at an efficient pace, and the host had to fan out into foraging parties to sustain itself. Seven months were required to negotiate the next twelve hundred kilometers. Gaiseric and his people arrived before Hippo in May or June, 430, just months before the death of Augustine. However slow and lumbering the advance of the invaders may have been, their slowness cannot be attributed to any blocking action by the Berbers. When we consider the general desperation of the Circumcellions, we reflect that in some ways the Vandals must have looked like liberators.

At Hippo, Boniface was unable to mount a defense. It almost seems that the only combat force at his command comprised his Goths and *bucellarii*. At most he had about twenty thousand mercenaries.[55] They could not all have been concentrated at Hippo, since he was responsible for the general safety of the frontiers against the Moors. For fourteen months the Vandals laid siege to Hippo, where Boniface was trapped. Possibly he had come there at Augustine's request, to protect the episcopal see.[56] Augustine's ideas on tactics tended to be tinged by his concern for the orthodox establishment.

Help was eventually sent out from Constantinople under the command of Aspar, the general who had disposed of the usurper John at Aquileia. Whether Aspar and Boniface ever actually engaged Gaiseric in combat is a matter of scholarly dispute. If they did, in anything other than minor skirmishes, it appears that Gaiseric must have been victorious, but the victory did not help him much because his followers were beginning to suffer from disease. It was a familiar situation for which modern epidemiology has a perfectly lucid explanation. There is no need to mention miracles to account for the melting away of a besieging army. A stable community of a given size develops its own natural immunity to infections that may be lethal to outsiders who come into contact with a virus that is new to them. The very fact of communal existence offered about as much protection as a turreted wall. In the end the siege of Hippo was lifted, and the Roman forces were able to extricate themselves from their humiliating position with a semblance of dignity. Aspar appears to have withdrawn to Carthage, where he remained for the next few years. He was an Alan, and Gaiseric was "King of the Vandals and Alans": the two leaders are known to have exchanged gifts, and nothing in accounts of their subsequent relationships suggests much hostility.

Boniface, meanwhile, departed for Italy with his *bucellarii*, summoned once more by Galla Placidia, who needed him badly. The Augusta was losing the desperate contest with her alarming general Aëtius. By this time he had so much obvious power that barbarian embassies were going directly to him, not to Galla Placidia. Felix had been murdered on the steps of a church in Ravenna, presumably at the hands of Aëtius's henchmen.[57] Shortly afterward Aëtius had renewed his earlier ties with the Huns, restoring territory to them that Felix had been able to wrest away only a few years before. Placidia angrily tried to dismiss Aëtius, but his military exploits against barbarians both in Gaul and along the Danube were so spectacular that she had to reward him with the consulship. While Aëtius was away campaigning once again, Placidia thought that she saw her chance. She hurriedly recalled Boniface from Africa and invested him with Aëtius's offices.

Aëtius raced back to Italy to prevent Boniface from reaching Ravenna. The clash, which occurred at the fifth milestone beyond Rimini, made it clear to everyone that Placidia was far from master of her situation. The engagement has been described in such a way that we think of hand-to-hand single combat in the medieval style, but in all likelihood it was in fact a miniature war fought by *bucellarii*.

Boniface was mortally wounded, even though he was the victor. Aëtius, who retired to the security of one of his fortified country estates, is said to have emerged after the death of his rival cynically to marry the widowed Pelagia, thereby co-opting Boniface's *bucellarii*.[58] Only murder, it appeared, could dispose of Aëtius, but that was not to occur for some years. Meanwhile, the Vandals consolidated their position. Aëtius never showed any inclination to attack them. As before, his preoccupation was with Gaul, his true power base. It is not astonishing therefore, to find a treaty being arranged at Hippo in the year 435.[59]

Gaiseric had an acute sense of timing. His shift from Spain to Africa followed the defeat of Castinus, and his next major move was triggered apparently by a Roman defeat at Toulouse. He immediately broke his treaty and moved on to Carthage, which he was able to enter without striking a blow on October 19, 439. The sense of timing was still there sixteen years later, when the Vandal sack of Rome followed directly upon the murder of Emperor Valentinian III.

The regnal years of the Vandal kings date from the capitulation of Carthage.[60] Gaiseric was much more kingly there than he had been as chieftain of a wandering host. Double kingship had been characteristic of the Vandals in Europe, but Gaiseric ruled alone. Ancient traditions were discarded: gone was the tribal council. This is our first chance to see what happens when a barbarian kingdom becomes established on Roman soil. In the initial stages we know that there will be violence, unrest, cruelty, and sorrow, but we anticipate something exciting to result from the novel arrangement.

There could be no abrupt change, obviously. When we think of the great landed proprietors, the Donatists and the Catholics, the Manichaean intellectuals, the simple Berbers of the High Plains, the fierce Circumcellions, the "barbarian" Moors, the tradespeople from the East, and now the blond Vandals, accustomed for a generation to a life of rapine and struggle, to say nothing of their comrades the Alans, those dramatically displaced nomads of the steppe, all wandering through the streets of Carthage, we can well imagine that almost everyone must have been in an acute state of cultural shock.

VANDAL AFRICA

T HE Vandals ruled Africa for a century. Even by the time of the dispersal there had been astonishingly few changes. The period of Vandal domination was not dull and flat, but it might have had a more vivid tone.

Gaiseric was the dominant figure. This man had a fearsomely cunning intelligence, with an uncanny comprehension of emerging political forces. Procopius refers to him as the cleverest of all men.[1] According to Jordanes, "He was a man of deep thought and few words, holding luxury in disdain, furious in his anger, shrewd in winning over the barbarians and skilled in sowing the seeds of dissension."[2] It is odd that in popular estimation he has been so overshadowed by his Hunnic contemporary Attila, because he was infinitely more adroit. Moreover, the aftereffects of his manipulation of the strands that were supposed to bind the empire together were much more enduring than those of Attila in his brief appearance on the European stage.

Unfortunately, Gaiseric had no more comprehension of what a new world order might be than did any of his adversaries overseas. His thought was so concentrated on the narrow problem of security for his people and the filling of their hungry mouths that not once did he look about him to assess the potentialities of the complex administrative tools that he had seized from Rome. The apparatus offered no challenge to his mind. His duty was exclusively that of the tribal chieftain, centered on the distribution of booty that included whole fertile farms and estates, not just the usual captured flocks and occasional troves of coin and tableware.

Gaiseric's land distribution caused much heartache among former owners because they were simply ordered to clear out, but from the conqueror's viewpoint it was rigidly in line with custom. In the immediate vicinity of Carthage farmlands were doled out among Gaiseric's people in equal or equivalent shares, and farther away in the more inaccessible regions Gaiseric took over huge estates as his own rightful domain. In this way his Vandals were not too scattered, and the warriors could make a quick response in an emergency. Compared with the total population, they were few. Once these matters had been attended to, Gaiseric was free to direct his energies to random plundering expeditions, though he was a sea hawk now, with the Carthaginian fleet and shipyards at his command. How the inhabitants of the cities and towns and countryside were to hobble along was no concern of his.

On the African side, after the initial shock of being conquered and dispossessed, the people seem to have been sufficiently resilient and self-reliant—or passive—to get along by improvising. If there were no longer the usual local administrators, someone stepped in and filled the breach—a local churchman, perhaps. Farming and marketing seem to have gone on as before, though it is not clear what medium of exchange prevailed. There were still merchants from the East in Carthage. The postal service appears to have continued its operations. Inevitably someone collected taxes. On balance one has the impression that life may have been a shade less trying for the poor than it had been before the arrival of the Vandals. Nothing more is known of Circumcellion activity, for example. The Donatists and the Catholics presumably closed ranks because now they had a common enemy in the Arians.

The Vandals were not deliberately destructive. They left Augustine's library at Hippo untouched, and the dilapidated appearance of the towns in later times cannot be laid at their door. It was the Moors, those ultimate barbarians, who were responsible for most of the damage, helped along by the Byzantines, who grabbed any available dressed stone for their fortifications. The Vandals moved into the cool, handsome country villas; enjoyed the fruit trees and the leafy parks; and rode happily to the hunt on their *tamga*-branded horses (see plate 54).

How did the villagers fare? It will be worth our while to look for a few minutes at the "Albertini tablets," records of small transactions between insignificant, vaguely Romanized folk with strange African names like Gibalus and Fotta, in an unidentified community somewhere south of Tebessa. We should look at the tablets if for no other reason than to admire the scholarship that has been applied to them. A whole fifth-century microcosm has been constructed from this difficult material.[3]

All dealings in the obscure little community were carried out with some degree of formality. Purchasers and sellers had access to scribes and witnesses, and everything was set down in rather tortured Latin. Apparently a kind of "social reconquest" was under way about fifty years after the original Vandal takeover. The Albertini records may refer to transactions that occurred under Gaiseric's more tolerant successor, King Gunthamund. One family seems to have been in the process of buying back original properties from which its members had been expelled in Gaiseric's day. Returning now with cash in hand, the family was acquiring the old homestead bit by bit—here an oil

Plate 54. Mosaic showing a barbarian, probably of the Alans, mounted on a *tamga*-branded horse, fifth century, from the foot of the Bordj-Djedid hill at Carthage. The use of the *tamga* was carried from the Asiatic steppe to Africa. The rider has used a cross *fourchée* as a brand. See also plate 25. *Courtesy of British Museum, London.*

press, there a tiny scrap of land with no more than a tree or two (fig, almond, olive, or oak) on it. Identifying notations, "by the irrigation ditch," "along the conduit," "at the well," indicate that in earlier times the then-prosperous owners had managed the estate carefully. Presumably they hoped to do so again. We are left with the uncomfortable feeling that the little people, squatters perhaps, would lose their grip and lapse into their pre-Vandal condition, the state that bred the Circumcellion bands. What then would become of a bride named Geminia Lamarilla, whose dowry of veils, bracelets, and earrings is mentioned in the Albertini tablets?

As we look at this retrograde, or at least stagnant, situation, the question arises, Why was this encounter of two cultures so barren? The trouble must have been that there was only a glancing encounter, not a fusion or interaction. There was nothing to bridge the void that divided them. Why not the church? We think of Ambrose of Milan, of whom the barbarian Arbogast could say with conviction "He loves me."[4] The nature of the African church was uncompromising. There is also the discouraging fact that the one Roman notion that the Vandals heartily endorsed was that of a state church—an Arian one. In the early days of Gaiseric's reign Catholics and Donatists alike underwent humiliation and torture for the sake of their golden treasures, and many churches were confiscated. That was war, but when the Vandals settled into their new life, they were avid to protect themselves from Catholic contamination. Under Gaiseric's son Huneric, it is said, special police stood outside Catholic churches, armed with grappling hooks to tear off the scalps of any Vandals or persons in Vandal clothing who ventured into the forbidden building (the Vandal kings affected gorgeous Eastern silks, but their retainers were required to wear barbarian dress, even though they might be African).[5]

We turn now to the life of Saint Fulgentius for a disconcerting view of Africa under the Vandals.[6] He represents the wealthy aristocracy, as opposed to the obscure farmers of the Albertini tablets. Fulgentius's grandparents fled to Italy at the time of the Vandal conquest, and their extensive holdings were confiscated. Part of their property was turned over to an Arian church, while the rest presumably went to Gaiseric himself. So far that is what could have been anticipated, but for unknown reasons the part that had been in Gaiseric's possession was restored to Fulgentius's parents. After the death of his father Fulgentius managed what was still a prosperous estate with its complement of slaves. Born about 462, he was not quite out of his teens. His education was that of a wealthy member of the senatorial class, with grounding in both Greek and Latin literature. Incongruous though it may sound, the youth was able to lead a carefree life of festive banquets, theater parties, and hunts with other rich young blades, some of whom were Vandals. Still further to confuse the picture, Fulgentius was an official tax collector with a staff to assist him.

The writings of John Cassian somehow came into Fulgentius's hands; acquaintance with the sober thought of the desert monk fired him with the desire to enter monastic life. To be a Catholic monk was not a safe career even under the more easygoing Vandal kings. As monk and later as abbot Fulgentius was associated with a succession of small, sternly ascetic establishments that were either broken up on order of the Vandals or destroyed by mountain tribesmen. Twice he was banished to Sardinia. Between times Fulgentius managed to pay a visit to a holy hermit on a tiny island off Sicily and go on pilgrimage to the tombs of the apostles in Rome. While exiled in Sardinia, he busied himself with correspondence and tract writing, serving as secretary to the colony of banished churchmen there. Spurred on by a letter to these clerics from the famous Scythian monks who were deeply immersed in religious controversies at Constantinople and in Theodoric's court at Ravenna, Fulgentius penned no fewer than seven books against Faustus of Riez, the most celebrated of Gaul's "semi-Pelagians" from the monastery at Lérins.[7]

To cap it all, Fulgentius was summoned to Carthage by King Trasamund, who fancied himself a theologian and chose to indulge his curiosity about Catholicism by conversing with the bishop. During his two years in Carthage, although he was constantly under surveillance, Fulgentius was able to supply morale-giving comfort to the African Catholics. Eventually he was released from his Sardinian exile and managed to die peacefully at last in his own see in the year 527, having lived sixty-five extraordinarily varied years.

The most interesting aspect of Vandal rule, especially under Gaiseric, was the entrance of this new, untried kingdom into the complex world of diplomacy. The first venture was an obvious one. Gaiseric engineered a lasting agreement of some kind with the powerful general Aspar, who, in all his years as the dominant figure at the court of Constantinople, had never made so much as a gesture against the Vandals. As we observed before, Aspar was an Alan, and Gaiseric had assumed the title *rex Alanorum*. There were, however, other moves on the diplomatic front that were more subtle and showed some grasp of the principle of the balance of powers. Gaiseric's problem lay in the circumstance that he had two enemies across the sea, namely the Romans and the Visigoths. His first move was to accept the daughter of the king of the Visigoths as a wife for his son Huneric, thus establishing a somewhat wavering alliance between the two previously hostile nations.

So far we are on relatively firm ground, but when we try to penetrate further, we are thrown into an exasperating morass. The only clues are embedded in some of the most soggy writing ever turned out by a court poet. Panegyrics are almost never great art, but the products that rolled from the pen of General Flavius Merobaudes are unusually depressing. Quite unintentionally, however, Merobaudes does show us what Valentinian's court at Ravenna was like, and a very unflattering picture it is. Let us leave the intricacies of linguists' arguments in competent hands and take it more or less on faith that we have arrived at the year 446, looking in on what must have been an extremely awkward gathering. In a gorgeous mosaic-ceilinged room, arrayed in stiff, awe-inspiring clothing, the emperor and his courtiers brace themselves against the torrent of fulsome praise pouring from Merobaudes' lips, all in honor of his patron Aëtius (whom Emperor Valentinian will murder one day). The court has been listening politely for some time to the orator's stately descriptions of Aëtius's triumphs over the Bacaudae in Gaul, his heroic successes in the north, his pacification of the Visigoths, the relief of Narbonne, and so on and so on and so on. Now comes this:

> The occupier of Libya had dared to tear down by exceedingly fated arms the seat of Dido's kingdom. . . . he has taken off the garb of an enemy and has desired ardently to bind fast the Roman faith by more personal agreements to count the Romans as relatives for himself, and to join his and their offspring in matrimonial alliance.[8]

Merobaudes' listeners must have been biting their lips, hardly knowing where to look.

The precise timing is not at all proved in the welter of interpretations of Merobaudes' effusions. In the year 442 a pact had been drawn up acknowledging Gaiseric's legal claim to Carthage. Romans and Vandals became allies. The West recovered the more barren and remote parts of Africa in return for this recognition. It must have been in the year of the pact or shortly thereafter that Emperor Valentinian III formally betrothed his daughter Eudocia, who was about five years old, to Gaiseric's son Huneric, who was already married to a Visigoth princess. It was this tidy arrangement that Merobaudes celebrated so glowingly.

Who could have proposed it, and why? It could be argued that Aëtius saw that the best policy for keeping Gaiseric in check would be to cultivate good relations with him. That would remove any pretext for attack on Sardinia or Sicily or even on Italy itself. Aëtius would want to keep Vandal-Visigoth enmity alive.[9] On the other hand, it is not even certain that Aëtius had much to do with the treaty of 442, let alone with Eudocia's engagement to Huneric.[10] Such a marriage might be a personal threat to Aëtius, in view of his own ambitions (he demanded that Valentinian's younger daughter Placidia be given to his son Gaudentius). Possibly the emperor would have found the marital alliance with the house of Gaiseric to his own liking, as a means for counterbalancing the influence of Aëtius. Let him call in his Huns: he, Valentinian, could then summon Vandals. Either way Gaiseric would gain. He could be reasonably sure that no serious effort would be made to dislodge him from Africa.

By the terms of this arrangement a Catholic and an Arian were to be married. The deeply pious Galla Placidia was still alive, and there is little reason to think that her son would have been less devout than she.[11] For reasons best known to themselves, Valentinian III and Gaiseric must have seen fit to overlook this aspect of the situation. Another matter bothered Gaiseric. Huneric would have to be freed from his marriage to the Visigoth princess. Gaiseric quickly made the useful discovery that his hapless daughter-in-law was trying to poison him. He hustled her off to her father in Toulouse with her ears cropped and her nose horribly mutilated. The Visigoths at once became embittered because of this disgusting treatment of their royal lady.

Rome had by no means acquired a loyal friend. Gaiseric had sacrificed his tentative alignment with the Visigoths, but there were other barbarians with whom he might connive. What about a Vandal-Hun axis, for example?

Attila had his own brand of diplomacy, if we are willing to honor it by that name. It consisted almost exclusively of extortion. The first embassy from the West that approached him somewhere near the Save River about 434 had found him sharing kingship with his older brother Bleda. The two kings conducted the whole interview on horseback. They demanded tribute and extradition of subjects who had fled to Roman territory so that they might punish (that is, crucify) them.

Attila murdered his brother shortly thereafter (probably in 445) and then became sole ruler of a congeries of tribes. He settled down to the agreeable business of extracting gold from the treasury of the weak eastern emperor Theodosius II. Staggering quantities of gold came to him from the coffers of the East. He received embassies at a permanent court, housed in elaborately carpentered buildings (probably the work of Goths). Choral processions of young girls honored him with song, ceremonial banquets were held, bards celebrated his valorous deeds, and clowns performed for the amusement of the guests. The strictest protocol was observed under the unsmiling eyes of a ruler whose plain dress and wooden table service emphasized the gulf between him and his courtiers in all their frivolous glitter. Attila's demands continued monotonously to be for more and more gold and for return of those under his rule who had run away to seek shelter in the empire.

Gaiseric is said to have suggested craftily to Attila that the Visigoths in Spain were his rightful subjects and that as escapees they ought to be chastized. The news that these fugitives from his supposed wrath could no longer count on assistance from the Vandals would have caught Attila's interest.[12] Attila had other grounds for attacking Gaul and Spain, but this looks like a barbarian's reason, in harmony with his constant call for the return of fugitives.

One of Attila's immediate excuses for moving into Gaul was his concern in the contested succession to the leadership of the Ripuarian Franks, who were just beginning to coalesce. There is no certainty who the late king may have been, or even who his two rival sons were, for that matter. The historian Priscus met the younger one in Rome, and described him as a downy-cheeked lad with luxuriant blond hair tumbling over his shoulders.[13] For once Aëtius and his emperor saw eye to eye, jointly supporting the cause of this youth. It was he who became the Frankish leader, though the older brother had put his case before Attila, who had received him favorably.

Attila's final reason for open hostility was about as bizarre as anything else in that extraordinary epoch. Perhaps the news of the impending marriage of Valentinian's daughter to Gaiseric's son had reached him. He was inspired to press the ridiculous claim that Valentinian's flighty sister Honoria had actually proposed to him. He had her ring, he said, and he rather thought that Gaul would be an appropriate dowry. It is impossible to know what may have been in Honoria's mind. Offhand, J. Otto Maenchen-Helfen's impatient rejection of the story as "Byzantine court gossip" seems acceptable.[14] J. B. Bury, on the other hand, thought that Honoria's aim was purely political, that she wanted to be a queen in Gaul. He suggested that Honoria was not a pretext but rather the key to Attila's policy.[15] Honoria's own mother, Galla Placidia, had been a

Visigoth queen in her day, and Honoria's niece would some day sit on the Vandal throne. Honoria's chance of becoming a Hunnic queen was not necessarily great. Attila's principal wife, Kreka, was secure in her position, and it would not be easy to displace such a lady, but, cloistered as she was with her wearisome nunnish aunts, Honoria may have found even the notion of being a concubine in a royal harem attractively exotic and adventurous. [16]

The Eastern emperor Theodosius II, who was accustomed to complying with Attila's incessant demands, wrote to Valentinian that he ought to hand over Honoria forthwith. This proposition infuriated the Western emperor, who seldom had an opportunity to be master in his own house. Honoria was rapidly married off to a safely inoffensive nobleman, and that is the last we hear of her.

The upshot of all this was that Attila did indeed ride down into Gaul, causing much havoc, though the importance of the expedition has been overblown by the attention devoted to the picturesque leader by Corneille, Raphael, and Verdi. The advance of the Huns was bloody. Metz was savagely treated, and so was Reims. Paris was spared, it was said, by the efficacy of Saint Geneviève's prayers. The target was Visigoth territory, and therefore the host swept on.

After some hesitation the Visigoths were convinced that they were indeed under attack, whereupon they joined Aëtius's scanty forces from Italy. The hastily assembled army that confronted Attila included Burgundians and Franks, as well as Bacaudae and those Alans who had broken off from the barbarian invaders long ago to settle in Gaul. It was enough of a force to cause Attila to have second thoughts: he drew back to Troyes.

It is reported that on the eve of the conflict (in June, 451) Attila had his shaman examine shoulder blades of sheep. The cracks in the magic bones yielded the ambiguous information that the Huns would lose the battle but an enemy leader would fall. This account, taken from Priscus, is surely genuine. [17] It reflects practices that had come down to Attila from ancient days when his ancestors ranged the Chinese borderlands.

The battle was a horrendous one, with the loss of thousands of lives. At the end Theodoric, the brave king of the Visigoths, lay dead under a heap of his slaughtered warriors. He was mourned by wailing, dirge-chanting barbarians before their new king, Thorismund, led them back to Toulouse, on the advice of Aëtius.

Attila had been prepared to do away with himself on a fiery pyre made of stacked wooden saddles rather than fall into the hands of his foes, but Aëtius followed Stilicho's tradition of keeping potential allies alive, and Attila was allowed to escape. Huns had been useful before and might well be so again. "The Goths through fear put their hope in God, and we through presumption put ours in the Huns," commented Salvian bitterly. [18] In an odd way Attila himself put some faith in the Christian deity. As he retreated, he is supposed to have taken saintly Bishop Lupus of Troyes along as far as the Rhine, "for his own safety and the well-being of the army." Lupus was released when they reached the river, but not before Attila's interpreter informed him that Attila wanted to be remembered in the bishop's prayers. This story appears in a latter-day life of Lupus, but there is a tinge of truth in it. There the interpreter is called Hunigasio; according to the entirely reliable historian Priscus, who visited Attila's court, the interpreter's name was Onegesius. That comes remarkably close. [19]

The Huns had been seriously weakened. It is a puzzle, therefore, that Attila led them into northern Italy the following year. [20] This time a violent epidemic was his undoing. He turned back, but fearful destruction had been wrought at Aquileia, following a three-month siege. Milan was also occupied and so thoroughly stripped that the Hunnic wagon trains could barely groan along under the weight of the booty.

The church extracted glory from the Hunnic retreat. Pope Leo the Great, accosting Attila somewhere near Mantua, reportedly impressed the Hun so deeply with his majestic, holy bearing that the invader immediately dropped his plan to pillage the Eternal City. Thomas Hodgkin accepted the story. [21] He attributed a sort of "magnanimity" to Attila that allowed him to be satisfied by the bare fact of an enemy's acknowledgment of his own greatness. In the words of Jordanes, "Beneath his great ferocity, he was a subtle man." [22] Maenchen-Helfen, on the other hand, documents his own theory that the pope's errand had to do with ransoming prisoners taken at Aquileia. [23] If so, this was actually a time of humiliation.

The Hunnic peril ended with disconcerting abruptness in 453, when Attila died ignominiously of a nosebleed in excessive celebration of his wedding to a new bride. The description of his spectacular funeral has survived. The chieftain's body lay in a tent of Chinese silk, while riders circled it, and a dirge was chanted. Men gashed their faces and tore their hair. A wild revel, a *strava*, followed. Then the body was placed in three nested coffins, bound with gold, silver, and iron (such coffins were also used by the Hsiung-Nu, a Chinese people possibly related to the Huns), [24] and gemmed weapons were massed on them. At the end the slaves who prepared the tomb were killed, just as Alaric's had been destroyed at the Busento.

Emperor Valentinian must have begun to look speculatively upon his hated patrician Aëtius at this point. Would the Huns be too engrossed in their own power struggles to care about the fortunes of a Roman general? Valentinian gave himself a moment of freedom by murdering Aëtius, fatally forgetting that Aëtius had faithful *bucellarii*. He recklessly took these men into his own service. In March, 455, before many months had passed, two of them attacked and killed him.

Through all this the Vandal king had been biding his time. Whether or not Gaiseric's activities had actually set in motion the train of dramatic events, the outcome was in his favor. In Gaul the Visigoths were in some disorder. So were the Huns, and so was the Western empire. Theodoric the Visigoth was dead. Attila was dead. Aëtius was dead. Valentinian III, the last of the Theodosian dynasty, was dead. The new emperor, Petronius Maximus, had been implicated in the murder of Valentinian. To secure his shaky hold on his new office, he forced himself as husband on Valentinian's widow, Eudoxia, and also speedily arranged another highly injudicious marriage, that of his son to Valentinian's daughter Eudocia, the girl who had been engaged for so long to Gaiseric's son Huneric. This was a gratuitous insult to the Vandal king. We hardly need trouble ourselves about the veracity of the story that Empress Eudoxia had sent for him. The situation was a barbarian's dream come true.

When Emperor Maximus learned that Gaiseric's fleet was heading across the sea, he tried to make his escape, but a raging mob cut him down. Gaiseric and his Vandals along with Moorish troops appeared at the gates of Rome in May, 455. Once again majestic Pope Leo valiantly confronted a barbarian invader, but this one was not to be deflected. Gaiseric agreed not to put the noble city to the torch and not to permit a general massacre, but that was the sum of his concessions. Prisoners were taken by the thousands, including many young persons and artisans, especially those skilled in making weapons. Important political prisoners were also taken, among them Aëtius's son Gaudentius, the empress, and her two daughters. Eudocia at last became Huneric's wife.

The inventory of lost treasures is deplorable. Mere gloating possession may have been an end in itself—as indeed it may have been for the original, aristocratic owners. It is apparent, however, that the idea of a hoard imbued the barbarian psyche (think of the *Volsunga Saga* or even the later *Nibelungenlied*). As far back as Herodotus we find the statement that the ancient Scythians not only guarded their sacred gold but "yearly offered great sacrifices to its honor."[25] In an almost mystic way possession of a treasure was equated with the energy of the tribe. This fixation must have been part of the Hunnic mentality. The Vandals, far from their tribal home and remote in time from tribal tradition, appear to have sustained a similar atavistic drive, even in distant Africa.

For two weeks the Vandals methodically sought out and stowed onto their ships everything portable and precious still to be found in public and private Rome—everything from jewels to gilded roofing materials. After this it would not be possible to speak of the city's metallic luster that Prudentius and Claudian praised. Today there must still be a sprawl of statues, cargo that sank on the way to Carthage,[26] lying on the floor of the Mediterranean.

A few things here and there escaped. Pope Leo is said to have been required to surrender gleaming golden altar vessels with his own hands, but he managed to salvage some gigantic silver urns that had been gifts of Constantine the Great. At a later time he had them melted down to furnish the bare altars of robbed Roman churches with simpler vessels.[27]

For the third time tremulous Rome lay helpless before a barbarian. Like Alaric and Attila before him, Gaiseric seems to have had no thought of establishing himself there as a permanent ruler, though in the year 455 he was certainly the most powerful man in the Western world. Alaric was driven on in search of food for his hungry host, while Attila was turned back by an epidemic and possibly also by superstitious fear of Rome the Eternal. What about Gaiseric? He knew that no barbarian should ever wear the imperial purple, but he was not a man to be swayed by custom. Perhaps even Gaiseric felt awe before timeless Rome. He withdrew to Carthage, content to carry on as before with his booty and his power to threaten anyone whose land edged the Mediterranean, including the Adriatic.

One of his ventures after Rome was a novelty, or in any case an imitation of the ways of emperors. He took possession of Sardinia, which lay between him and his most powerful rivals, the Visigoths, and established a defensive colony there, using Moors just as in the old days the Romans had defended their northern frontiers with Goths. On the whole the policy served its purpose fairly well. Sardinia was an unmanageable place at best. A wild country, peppered even today with stone huts and mysterious fortifications, it had been used by the Romans as a place of exile for recalcitrant or disgraced citizens. The native population was divided into two factions that were in continuous conflict—sedentary farmers on the plains versus nomadic herders in the mountains. This condition still existed in the time of Pope Gregory the Great, who referred to the mountain people as *barbaricini*.[28] Compounding the problems of this rough situation, Gaiseric introduced his Moorish colonists along with their families. Procopius thought that they were rebels deported from Africa as punishment, but the present consensus is that it was a true colonizing effort. Under Gaiseric's heavy-handed Arian successors, Sardinia again became a place of exile, but the banished Catholic clergy do not seem to have fared too badly there. They had their churches, their library, their small monastic communities, even their councils.

The end of the Vandal story in Sardinia is an ironic reenactment in miniature of the troubles that the empire had with Africa in the days of Gildo and Boniface. In 533 the governor, Godas, revolted. This rebel, a former slave in whom Gelimer, the last of the Vandal kings, had placed too much trust, suddenly declared himself an independent ruler and sent a request to Constantinople for support. When he heard of this, King Gelimer's reaction was prompt but ill-advised, since the forces of the Eastern emperor, Justinian, were already gathering for the expedition to help Godas. Gelimer dispatched his brother Tzazon to Sardinia at the head of what apparently was the entire

Vandal force. Tzazon came ashore at Cagliari and executed Godas.[29] Unfortunately for the Vandal cause, Tzazon's letter reporting this action fell into the hands of Emperor Justinian's general Belisarius, and the fleet that had been intended for support of Godas's insurrection was quickly rerouted to Carthage.

Almost a century had passed since the arrival of the Vandals on African shores. Gaiseric had parried the first efforts by the empire to launch an effective attack, and after his death there had been something of a standstill.

Immediately before Gelimer there had been two Vandal kings, first Trasamund (496–523) and then Hilderic (deposed in 530), whose reigns had been characterized by the alarming circumstance that on the fringes of Vandal territory the Moors were going from strength to strength. Their inroads were becoming increasingly destructive, and it is their "vandalism" that is popularly laid at the door of the Vandals who were its victims.

King Trasamund was an indolent man, fond of poetry and the good life. Flattering courtiers made a kind of *roi soleil* of him, but in truth he was not particularly inspiring. His wife, Amalafrida, was a force, however. She was a sister of powerful Theodoric the Ostrogoth, who was busy in Ravenna winding a wonderful skein of marital alliances. He sent Amalafrida to her new home accompanied by a royal retinue. Her *bucellarii* numbered "a thousand of the notable Goths as bodyguards," who were "followed by a host of attendants amounting to about five thousand fighting men."[30] Her dowry included Lilybaeum (Marsala) and the territory surrounding it, in Sicily.

When Trasamund died, a flaw in the Vandal system became painfully obvious. This was "tanistry," their principle of royal succession laid down by Gaiseric on his deathbed. The throne went to the oldest male in the royal family, not necessarily a descendant of the deceased monarch.[31] The advantage lay in the avoidance of accession of infant rulers, but that was offset by the advanced age of the new king, Hilderic, the rather faded son of Huneric and Eudocia.

Perhaps in wistful memory of his unhappy mother, who had ended by fleeing to Jerusalem, half-Roman Hilderic was vaguely pro-Catholic and anti-Goth. He abandoned the alliance with Theodoric that had been cemented by the marriage of Trasamund and Amalafrida and began instead to make overtures to Emperor Justinian in Constantinople.

There was outrage among the Goths. Widowed Amalafrida was accused of fomenting trouble; although she escaped to the Moors, her death followed so swiftly that there is little doubt that she was murdered. All her retainers were killed. Vengeance from Ravenna might have been formidable, but Theodoric died, leaving a little boy with a regent, Theodoric's fine daughter Amalasuntha, who could do no more than write a strongly-worded letter of protest.

King Hilderic did not last long: there was a military coup in Africa (even the Vandals tired of him), and he was flung in prison. The throne went to his cousin Gelimer, who, as we know, experienced difficulties with a rebellious governor in Sardinia.

Emperor Justinian was indignant. Hilderic was his friend. His preparations for a holy war for the recovery of Africa received a handsome if unexpected lift in the news that Gelimer's forces had been dispatched to Sardinia to deal with the rebel governor. Popular enthusiasm was given a boost by the announcement that this was to be a war to the death between Catholics and Arians.

We have an entertaining little sidelight here on the ways of propaganda. According to Procopius, a bishop reported having had a dream in which God instructed him to rebuke Emperor Justinian for not protecting the Libyan Christians. For African consumption, on the other hand, the story had local color: it was one of their own martyrs, Bishop Laetus, who appeared directly to the emperor himself in a dream.[32]

Those who watched the departure of Belisarius and his expeditionary force from Constantinople did so with prayerful misgiving, as well they might. Belisarius still stands high in the ranks of the great military men of history, but he was to have a complex problem disciplining and controlling a motley collection of warriors as they entered a land so full of crosscurrents that even liberators might be unwelcome. He could count on his own fourteen hundred or more *bucellarii*, but the federates and their argumentative commanders were bound to be unruly, impulsive, and even cowardly. The sailors too had their own decided notions about winds and landing places, while the troops en route to Africa showed their apprehension in the face of the invincible Vandals by declaring that they were afraid of the sea and "would turn to flight if a hostile ship should attack them."[33] Then the Hunnic archers—six hundred of them, all tremendous fighters—felt that they had been tricked into coming. They feared that the ultimately victorious Romans would use them as an army of occupation and that they might be "compelled to grow old and die right there in Libya."[34] The federates and the Huns were much interested in booty. Belisarius had to remind them repeatedly that they were on a rescue mission and were not under any circumstances to attack the Libyans who were Romans and allies.

As we read Procopius's eyewitness account of the events following the African landing, we share his amazement at the general ineptitude on both sides. By all the laws of logic Gelimer and the Vandals should have won. The Romans were split up, confused, out of contact with each other and their ships. They were even routed in one engagement. That in spite of all of this they managed to beat their way north from their landing place and march triumphantly into Carthage can hardly be attributed to their brilliance. One contingent, which had driven off some surprised Vandals, killing Gelimer's impetuous brother Ammatas, who had not kept to his timetable, rushed headlong toward Carthage and thus separated itself from the body of Belisarius's army. The Huns had an unexpected encounter with another troop, commanded by Gelimer's nephew Gibamund. They exterminated those Vandals with gusto. This action demolished an excellent attacking movement that Gelimer had devised, but since the success was not reported to Belisarius, the latter could not profit from it. The forces were traveling on more or less parallel routes, concealed by intervening hills. All the skirmishes were necessarily impromptu. Gelimer's own large force clashed with federates who were in the van of Belisarius's main army; these federates fled back to Belisarius in panic, sweeping along the *bucellarii* in their pell-mell retreat. At that point, as Procopius says, Gelimer had victory in his hands. He could have broken Belisarius or pressed on to Carthage to capture the separated contingent there. What he actually did was halt in his tracks over the dead body of his brother Ammatas to lament and wail and then to supervise a fitting burial for the hero. He was burying his potential victory also.

The people of Carthage were not quite as jubilant as an army of liberation might have wanted them to be. As Belisarius strode into the palace and seated himself on the Vandal throne, he found that the first citizens clamoring to see him comprised a shouting, infuriated mob who "made the charge that there had been a robbery of their property on the proceding night by the sailors."[35]

Gelimer and his remaining men fled to Numidia, where they waited for the return of Gelimer's brother Tzazon, who had been urgently recalled from Sardinia.

Historians seem to be united in their disdain for Gelimer. The man was neurotic, they say, rather in the style of Richard II as Shakespeare portrays him. There seems to be more behind Gelimer's behavior than neurosis, but if *he* was neurotic, we must go on to say that so were all the Vandals, to judge by the evidence of Procopius's narrative. For a century the Vandals had been a minority group in an alien culture; a situation like that can generate mass neurosis.[36] Consider Gelimer's letter to Tzazon that recalled him to Africa: "It was not, I venture to think, Godas who caused the island to revolt from us, but some curse of madness sent from Heaven which fell upon the Vandals. . . . Valor straightway departed and fled from the Vandals, taking good fortune with her."[37] Consider also the woeful meeting of Tzazon and Gelimer. It was not just the king who was distraught. It was the whole Vandal army, reverting to the primitive feelings of a lost, abandoned people:

> For Gelimer and Tzazon threw their arms about each other's necks, and could not let go, but they spoke not a word to each other, but kept wringing their hands and weeping, and each one of the Vandals with Gelimer embraced one of those who had come from Sardinia, and did the same thing. And they stood for a long time as if grown together. . . . nor could those who came from Sardinia bring themselves to ask about what had happened in Libya.[38]

A second engagement was fought between the Romans and the Vandals at Tricamaron. It was much like the first, characterized by general confusion, incipient revolt, disorder among the Romans, and a lost chance for Gelimer, who suddenly bolted with a few followers for the cold, distant mountains. Belisarius's men were drunk with victory, captured treasure, and "extremely comely" young women. The spectacle of noble Belisarius "desperately appealing to the discipline that no longer existed"[39] is far from elevating.

Of the Vandals only Gelimer held out. A trusted Roman officer, Pharas, was assigned the arduous task of capturing him, but Gelimer was practically inaccessible in his Moorish mountain fastness. There was a curious exchange of friendly letters. Pharas indicated that Gelimer would be treated kindly by Emperor Justinian. He wondered whether the royal Vandal fugitive might not have lost his good judgment, "steeped as you are in misfortune." Gelimer baffled Pharas by his response: he asked for a loaf of bread, a sponge, and a lyre. The bearer of the letter explained that the king had tasted no baked bread since his flight to the Moors, that his eye was infected and he needed a swab, and that he had written an ode on his tragic fate and wanted to accompany himself while he chanted it. "A brittle glory shineth in this face: as brittle as the glory is the face"—yes, we must admit that there was a touch of Richard II in this man.

Gelimer surrendered at last, laughing uncontrollably, overcome by the irony of his situation.

Africa was a bitter place from start to finish. Only two references to laughter have appeared in this whole chronicle: first, the derisive laughter of a Roman circus crowd enjoying the spectacle of human misery and now the harsh self-mockery of a defeated Vandal king.

After having been paraded in his purple through the streets of Constantinople, Gelimer was graciously given an estate in Galatia, where he lived out his days. Let us hope that he found a lyre.

The Vandals had never been numerous at any time, yet it is strange to realize that they disappeared. Their extraordinary career ended in deportation. Some were incorporated into the army of the East, as a cavalry unit called "Justinian's Vandals," for campaigns against the Persians. Four hundred of them made a dramatic escape during their transfer to Syria by forcing the ships' crews to take them from Lesbos back to Africa.[40] They arrived to find a mutiny spreading among the unruly army of occupation. There were about a thousand Arians in the Roman army, Procopius says, whom Vandal priests had worked into a state of insurrection.[41] After this uprising was controlled, the remaining Vandals were deported, and the Vandal women who had married Roman soldiers were dispersed into slavery. A few Vandals followed the leader of the revolt to join the Moors. There are blond Berbers in North Africa today who are descendants of the Vandals, according to some writers, but that is

Plate 55. Byzantine church, sixth century, Leptis Magna, Libya. After the recovery of Africa by Belisarius, the cities once again became magnificent. At Leptis a basilica built in the period of Septimius Severus was remodeled. An altar was placed in the southeast apse and closed off by a chancel rail made of pilasters from a Severan arch.

unlikely. There were blond Berbers in Africa before the coming of the northern barbarians.[42]

In the final analysis it was the Moors who were the intractable barbarians confronting the empire in Africa. This was no new situation, and although through the centuries the most elaborate schemes to exclude or contain them were developed, it was one barbarian problem that the Romans never resolved. We might ponder this, wondering how much weight it may have had in the final loss of Africa to Islam.

Aerial photography shows how extensive the defense system was, dating back at least to the time of Emperor Hadrian. There was a great interlocking apparatus consisting of the actual *limites* (border fortifications and outposts) and the *fossata* (ditches and walls). These frontier defenses were held by local populations under arms in Boniface's day. The Vandals destroyed town walls as a matter of policy, but the menace from the desert marauders became so great that some towns defended themselves by building their houses tight together like a wall, with a locked entrance (Procopius describes such a town, below

Sousse). With the Vandals gone and control of Africa in the East, the frontier system was strengthened and elaborated as chains of forts were joined to fortified towns, with larger towns behind them as backups.[43]

All the blandishments of diplomacy and lavish gifts plus earnest exhortations of the clergy were used to supplement the military effort. Solemn tribal oaths of allegiance to the emperor carried little weight.

There were intervals of peace under the occasional competent Roman governor, but the empire bled itself white in an interminable guerrilla war, marching its heavily armored men in unsufferable heat against lightly armed desert cavalry that could swirl away in the dust. The enemy might be penned up in a walled town, but then he simply slipped out through a rear gate. Confrontations could be picturesque—Roman horses rearing and whinnying in terror at the odor of crouching camels ranged in a ring to protect the Moors. It was a situation for which there was no acceptable solution.

In the very year in which he put down the mutiny of the army at Carthage and deported the last of the Vandals, Belisarius was already heavily involved in Italy, where the affairs of the Ostrogoth rulers had become so badly snarled that Emperor Justinian felt that his opportunity for recovery of the West had come.

We return now to the continent of Europe, to see what happened in Italy after the sack of Rome. The transformation during the relatively brief Vandal era is startling. A threshold had been crossed, and the world of antiquity was left behind forever.

Color plate 1. *Diatreta* (reticulated) glass beaker, third–fourth century, from Braunsfeld, a suburb of Cologne, West Germany. Most known specimens of this glass are from the Rhineland or are assumed to have been carried to distant parts of the empire by high-ranking officers. It is conjectured that such glass was produced in only one atelier. The technique is a matter of argument. Either several layers of different-colored glass were cut through to make the outer network and the lettering on the lip, or the layers were made separately and joined to the body of the vessel with small welded posts. The lettering here reads, "Drink so that you will live well." See also plate 13. Cologne, Römisch-Germanisches Museum 60.1. *Courtesy of Römisch-Germanisches Museum, Cologne.*

Color plate 2. Funerary column at Igel, near Trier, West Germany, ca. 250. Detail showing baled textiles lashed on a wagon.

Color plate 3. A Gallo-Roman country house. Wall painting from a living room in a palace in Trier, fourth century. The wings of the building are connected by a colonnaded "breezeway." The master of the house, who wears the hooded cloak of the Treveri and carries the characteristic stave, is greeted by his servants. Trier, Rheinisches Landesmuseum 43.5. *Courtesy of Rheinisches Landesmuseum, Trier.*

Color plate 4. The Pamirs, near Pendjekent, Tadzhik Soviet Socialist Republic. The name originally meant something like "long valleys" and did not refer to the mountains. The Pamirs provided throughways for all manner of folk, including the Huns. Evidence of this remains today in the colorful ethnic mixture to be seen in the region.

Color plate 5. Inhabited scroll (a vine scroll curving around figures of animals, *putti*, and so on), detail of a mosaic from the Great Palace of Constantinople. The human head emerging from the foliage is so realistic that it "has the appearance of being done from life," according to David Talbot Rice, who suggests that the subject may have been a Goth (Rice, *A Concise History of Painting from Prehistory to the Thirteenth Century*, p. 67). Istanbul, Mozaik Müzeleri.

Color plate 6. The Forum, Aquileia, Italy. Strategically positioned at the head of the Adriatic, Aquileia was "the second Rome," an imperial residence from the time of Augustus to that of Theodosius, with all the magnificence that such status entailed. It was here that the usurper John was captured and executed on Galla Placidia's command. The city suffered destruction at the time of Attila's incursion into Italy, but it was restored by the Ostrogoths. Ultimately it declined in favor of Venice.

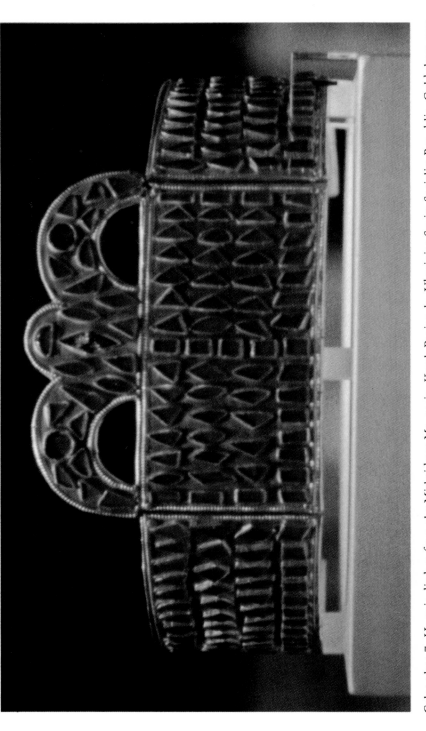

Color plate 7. Hunnic diadem from the Mithridates Mountain, Kerch Peninsula, Ukrainian Soviet Socialist Republic. Gold sheet over bronze is decorated with flat almandines in 257 cloisons and green glass pieces in two round cells and a lozenge on the top ornament. It is said to have been found in a grave next to the skeleton of a man with an artificially deformed skull (Maenchen-Helfen, *The World of the Huns*, pp. 300–301). Cologne, Römisch-Germanisches Museum D374a. *Courtesy of Römisch-Germanisches Museum, Cologne.*

Color plate 8. Temple of Saturn, Dougga, Tunisia. The temple was erected in A.D. 195 on the site of a Punic temple consecrated to Baal.

Color plate 9. Demarcation between desert and fertile valley at Deir el-Bahri, Egypt. This startling contrast is seen all along the Valley of the Nile.

Color plate 10. Cattle, detail of a wall painting, Church of Saint Proculus, Naturno, Italy, 770–830. The cattle, led by herders (not shown) are presumably to be placed under the protection of Saint Proculus. The paintings at Naturno are the oldest found thus far on Germanic soil. The artwork in this tiny church shows a combination of conflicting influences, including Celtic-style ribbon interlace and figure treatment that suggests some contact with classic art. The artist probably came from a location north and west of Naturno (Theil, *St. Prokulus bei Naturns*).

Color plate 11. Wall painting in the tomb of the nobleman Userhat, Thebes, Egypt, showing a Christian cross added above the head of jackal-headed Anubis. Monks and hermits made use of abandoned tombs and temples. They were careful to hallow them by painting or inscribing crosses on walls and roofs and defacing images of the ancient gods. We find evidence of similar practices in lands where the influence of Egyptian monasticism penetrated. See, for example, plate 73.

Color plate 12. The nuraghe of Ísili, Sardinia. Remains of thousands of these prehistoric stone towers can be found in Sardinia, some of them (for example, those at Barúmini and Sant' Antine) of powerful, cyclopean construction. It is thought that the nuraghe of Barúmini could shelter two hundred individuals. Like the brochs of Scotland, they are hollow, with staircases in the walls. See also plate 79.

Color plate 13. "Beehive" monastic huts on Skellig Michael, off the southwest coast of Ireland in the Atlantic, ca. fifth century. The huts were constructed without use of mortar, with evenly corbeled roofs, and they are still solid today. Little remains to show what the housekeeping arrangements may have been, except for stone pegs that extend from the inner walls, on which the monks hung the book satchels that they customarily carried. Each hut housed two or three monks. Small Skellig, a gannet sanctuary, lies in the middle distance.

Color plate 14. Mediobogdum, Roman fort, Hardknott, Cumberland, England. The fort was an outlier of the northern defense system, commanding the Esk Valley. It was built during Hadrian's reign (A.D. 117–38) and was manned by the fourth cohort of Dalmatians (Charlesworth, *Hardknott Roman Fort*).

Color plate 15. Gilt-bronze Visigothic fibula (clasp), one of a pair, from Tierra de Barres, Spain, ca. 550. The bronze is overlaid with gold sheet, and blue and green stones and garnets are set in cloisons. The boss in the center is a crystal cabochon, and the bird's eye is amethyst. Baltimore, Walters Gallery of Art 54.422. *Courtesy of Walters Gallery of Art, Baltimore, Maryland.*

Color plate 16. Throne of Pope Gregory I (590–604), Gregory the Great, in the Church of San Gregorio Magno, Rome.

Color plate 17. A Frankish helmet, called a *Spangenhelm*, from a nobleman's grave at Planig, near Kreuznach, Rhineland, West Germany, early sixth century. The conical helmet is built up from leaf-shaped segments attached to an iron frame. It originally had cheekpieces and a nose guard. Such helmets are thought to have been imported from northern Italy, deriving originally from Iranian prototypes. As the cross unmistakably shows, the owner of this helmet was a Christian. *Courtesy of Mittelrheinisches Landesmuseum, Mainz, West Germany.*

OSTROGOTHIC ITALY

RIGHT up to the moment when Emperor Valentinian III plunged a blade into him, Aëtius remained formidable, wealthy, and unscathed while the empire shattered around him. Unlike his hardworking predecessor Constantius, he was never a mender. The best that can be said of him is that he was true to his class and that the fortunes of Gaul were his primary concern. Throughout his long career Aëtius supported the interests of those who could not have been expected to make sacrifices for eternal Rome or the house of Theodosius, though they glorified in their own somewhat effete *romanitas*.

Aëtius had his original power base in the Hunnic kingdom in the time of Rua, from whom the sovereignty passed to Attila and his older brother Bleda. It was to Rua that Aëtius fled in 432, after the debacle that ended in the execution of the usurper John and the victory of Galla Placidia and her son Valentinian. The sixty thousand Huns recruited by Aëtius on behalf of John were enough of a threat to cause Galla Placidia reluctantly to accept Aëtius as her *comes* for Gaul, though obviously she was wary of him.[1] From that time on, Gaul appears to have been Aëtius's power base. He rapidly became the hero of the landowning senatorial class there, who recognized him as one of their own.

Attila was supposed to have been a friend of Aëtius in the beginning, a friendship difficult to credit, even though negotiations and gifts are mentioned. One of Attila's gifts to Aëtius was a Moorish dwarf who had originally belonged to Bleda, whom Attila had murdered. Attila detested the very sight of the dwarf. We might ask skeptically whether Attila was not making a somewhat backhanded gesture in parting with him.

It is true that in 437 Hunnic mercenaries were supplied to hunt down Bacaudae in Armorica under Aëtius's officer Litorius and to slaughter most of the Burgundians in that same year, but the supposed friendship between Attila and Aëtius must have suffered a severe jolt two years later, when Litorius's bad judgment led to the annihilation of his whole Hunnic contingent in a

189

bloody engagement with the Visigoths before Toulouse. Aëtius found himself compelled then to renew Constantius's treaty with the Visigoths, who were never friends of the Huns. After that he had to look around for other sources of barbarian military strength.

Aëtius needed a buffer against the increasingly hostile Visigoths, and likewise against the Bacaudae. He chose Alans for this mission, planting one group under their leader Sambida around Valence along the Rhone in 440 and another, under Goar, in the Orléans region, an arrangement that cut Armorica in two. This strategy may have been cunning, as far as control of the Bacaudae was concerned, but the local proprietors refused to divide their estates with the Alans and had to be forcibly ejected.[2]

The next settlement of barbarians worked more smoothly. In 443, Aëtius called in the remnants of the Burgundians who had survived the vicious Hunnic attack of 437, moving them down from the Rhine into Sapaudia (Savoy) so that they might act as a shield against local brigands and also as protectors of the Alpine passes to Italy, in the event of belligerent action by the Visigoths. The landowners found the Burgundians more acceptable. The Alans were primitive steppe people, the only non-Teutonic tribe ever to settle permanently in Gaul. Perhaps the Burgundians seemed less alarming, in spite of their unsettling practice of skull deformation in imitation of the Huns, whose subjects they may have been at one time.[3] The origin of the Burgundians is uncertain, though it is agreed that they were not steppe people. They drifted down from the general area of Denmark, and spent some time in Thuringia.

The landowners may have regarded the Burgundians as a ready reservoir of soldiers to replace the vanished class that had been soaked up by its system of large estates with tenants. It even appears that ultimately they came to appreciate the advantage of extending the Burgundians' holdings into the Lyons region to avoid otherwise heavy burdens of self-defense.[4]

At first glance it might seem that Aëtius was indeed in difficult straits if he needed to quarter foreigners among the self-consciously Romanized Gallo-Romans. But the Gallo-Romans were also self-conscious Gauls. Just one short generation before, many of them had rallied around Jovinus, a Gallic usurper who very nearly gained control of the West.[5] He was a member of a prominent Gallo-Roman family, but he had been elevated to the purple by none other than the Alans and the Burgundians.[6] There must have been Gallic aristocrats in Aëtius's day who could think of Burgundians as old comrades-in-arms. The bitterness of the defeat of Jovinus lingered in the generation after Aëtius. In a letter to a friend Sidonius refers to the time of their grandfathers, when Dardanus, who had engineered the break between Jovinus and Athaulf, was praetorian prefect of Gaul. Sidonius calls Dardanus a man abhorred for fickleness, pliability, and faithlessness—"all the vices together."[7] The dreadful fault appears to have been loyalty to Emperor Honorius.

Plate 56. Burgundian "Daniel buckle" from Verges, near Chalon-sur-Saône, France. According to the story of Daniel's second ordeal among the lions, as related in the apocryphal *Bel and the Dragon* 4.22–41, an angel snatches up the prophet Habakkuk, who has just baked bread for his farmhands, and carries him by the hair of his head from Judea to Babylon, where he is able to feed the starving Daniel. The two characters are clearly labeled on the buckle: "Danfe Profeta" and "Abbacv Profeta." Daniel prays while two lions lick his feet. Habakkuk holds the bread. *Courtesy of Musée national des antiquités, Saint-Germain-en-Laye, France.*

It would be excessive to say that Aëtius deliberately fostered Gallic separatism, but he certainly did nothing to discourage the aristocrats' tendency toward independence. Emperor Valentinian III issued decrees aimed at equitable distribution of financial burdens, placing more of the load on the shoulders of the senatorial class. There is no evidence that these decrees were enforced. The Gallic aristocrats probably were receiving signals from Aëtius that it would be a matter of indifference to him if they were to shrug off responsibility and ignore the emperor.

It would be interesting to know what the Burgundians thought of this. They saw themselves as loyal federates as far back as 413, if not earlier. It is true that they had followed Jovinus down into Gaul, but with his defeat they had returned to the north to accept lands on the Rhine assigned to them by Constantius.[8] Some scholars appear to believe that the unsophisticated, untutored Burgundians thought that they were being loyal to Rome all the time, since they did not comprehend the implications and complexities of usurpation. In any case, Aëtius made an extremely clever move, putting loyal if naïve barbarians in place and at the same time cushioning the aristocrats with the feeling that their uncouth guests might see eye to eye with them concerning the place of Gaul in the overall scheme of things. When Attila led his Huns toward Orléans, it was helpful to have federates on hand who knew from personal experience what the Huns were like.

In spite of his conviction that it was his destiny to rule the world, Attila arrived in Gaul to find that Aëtius had been able to patch together a tough makeshift army. Gaul stood, and Attila withdrew. After that the scene shifted briefly to Italy, where the Huns made another incursion that was quickly followed by the death of Attila, the murder of Aëtius, and the retaliatory murder of Valentinian III.

Among the Romans, Aëtius had a would-be rival. Petronius Maximus had reaped many an honor in his day—twice consul, twice praetorian prefect of Italy—and it therefore was not unreasonable to have the diadem swiftly conveyed to him on the death of Valentinian. There was salacious gossip involving his wife and the emperor, but it is safe to surmise that, although he was not out to avenge the desecration of his connubial bed, Maximus may yet have had something to do with Valentinian's murder, because his was a vaulting ambition.[9]

One of Petronius Maximus's major weaknesses was the Roman army's lack of confidence in him. Since he had no large body of barbarians supporting him, his rapid downfall could have been predicted even without the arrival of the Vandals. Shortly before the Vandal attack he had dispatched an ambassador to the court of the Visigoths, seeking assistance from that quarter. The man he selected to represent him was the right one, Flavius Eparchius Avitus, who had ties of friendship with the king of the Visigoths and who was also formidable in his own right. He had a long and honorable record of military service under both Constantius and Aëtius, and he was highly respected.

When Avitus arrived at Toulouse to cement relations with the powerful barbarians on behalf of his new emperor, he learned to his consternation, and possibly also with a certain expectant inner glow, that Emperor Petronius Maximus had been cut down by a Roman mob and that Rome was in no condition to furnish a successor.

It comes as something of a shock to realize that remote Toulouse might have become the new hub of the West. Here we are in the unprepossessing court of Theodoric, the Visigothic chieftain, among the elders assembled at dawn for their customary daily meeting. "Their dress is unkempt. Tarnished and greasy are the linen garments on their lean backs," as fastidious Sidonius puts it.[10] The scruffy group did in fact have the power to designate a new emperor. The Visigoths offered the purple to Avitus as an ally, not as a puppet. He was in a stronger position than Jovinus had been. Jovinus, we recall, had to rely on the politically untried Burgundians and Alans. This time the Gallic aristocrats closed ranks wholeheartedly since there was no longer any imperial apparatus in Rome.

Avitus responded with an admirable combination of alacrity and circumspection, ready to assume the reins and not restrict himself to the government of Gaul, a task that would have been easier. He met with a hastily assembled band of senators whose spokesman addressed him urgently, recalling with no little asperity that they had "deemed it a hallowed duty to cling to that shadow of Empire."[11] In July, 455, Avitus became emperor by acclamation and soon afterward appeared "sorrowing" before the troops to accept a military collar and other tokens of his new dignity.

We owe this information to Avitus's enthusiastic young son-in-law Sidonius, who accompanied the new emperor to Rome and delivered an unrealistically optimistic panegyric on the occasion of Avitus's entry into the office of consul for the year 456. Avitus was a stranger in Rome; high-ranking provincials sometimes lived out their entire lives without ever setting eyes on the great city.[12] Sidonius's panegyric was intended, therefore, to present Avitus to his new public, rather in the way that a modern keynote speaker might display an unknown candidate and his platform at a political convention. Sidonius drew hearty rounds of applause and was rewarded by the signal honor of the erection of a bronze statue of himself in the "poets' corner" of Trajan's Forum. In his old age Sidonius treasured the memory of this recognition.[13]

As a stranger and beginner Avitus stumbled and made serious errors that quickly alienated the Romans. He gave positions of trust to old friends. The two new patricians whom he created were both Gallo-Romans. He surrounded himself with a bodyguard of Visigoths. When he went back to Gaul for some obscure reason, he left an excellent opening for his rivals, restive senators, and a hungry populace. The people complained that there was not enough food to go around and demanded the expulsion of Avitus's train of Visigoths. The Visigoths themselves were not too helpful to Avitus's cause. They demanded their pay before they left. Avitus is said to have caused the remaining bronze statues in the city to be melted down and the metal sold to meet this claim. Irony of ironies: what became of Sidonius's statue? The senators professed to be outraged by the destruction of the remaining shreds of Roman glory, but there was much more below the surface. As in Constantinople in Gainas's day and again in Italy under Stilicho, there was a strong current of antibarbarian feeling, aimed this time at Avitus's Visigoths, but the reaction was also against Avitus himself as a Gallo-Roman. We see this in the attack on one of Avitus's patricians, who was murdered at Ravenna. In cold fact the Senate was unwilling to accept any other than a *Roman* emperor.

They were not averse to all barbarians. They held Ricimer, the grandson of a Visigothic king, in high regard. He was something of a public hero because of his glorious exploits against the Vandals off Sicily and Corsica. As a barbarian he was not eligible for imperial office, but he was willing to support his colleague Majorian, an Illyrian officer with whom he had served under Aëtius, in the unseating of Emperor Avitus.

Avitus made a plucky effort to defend himself, but the force that he led was miserable. His appeals to the Visigoths were without effect: they had lost interest in him and had gone off campaigning in Spain instead. After his defeat Avitus was allowed to become a bishop; learning of the ugly attack on his patrician at Ravenna, he took it as a warning and fled back toward his homeland. His death en route to Gaul was probably not a natural one.

Majorian might have been a strong constructive ruler, like other Illyrians before him. He was aware of the seriousness of the problem of Gaul and the menace of the Visigoths and the Vandals. He introduced some imaginative reforms and handled the Gallic situation with considerable tact. During the interregnum following the overthrow of Avitus, the Gallo-Romans, bitter over his fate, rallied in Auvergne, but to their dismay their next candidate stepped aside in favor of Majorian. After a showdown at Lyons, Majorian emerged in control. He was magnanimous and conciliatory. Sidonius, who had joined the insurgents, was able to choke down his disappointment and pronounce another panegyric. He even dined at Emperor Majorian's table, flourishing his poetic talents and what he regarded as his wit.

There appears to have been a kind of economic revival in southern Gaul at this point. André Loyen, who calls Majorian "a noble figure," attributes this recovery to the emperor's vigorous efforts.[14]

Unfortunately, it had been Ricimer's intention to rule through a puppet: he soon found Majorian unacceptable. When Majorian made his way back to Italy, he recklessly left his barbarian auxiliaries behind, a move that was his undoing. Ricimer attacked, captured the emperor, and finally, in August, 461, decapitated him. Bishop Ennodius, contemplating the modest stone that marked Majorian's grave, commented ruefully that bad emperors were the ones for whom pyramids and mausoleums were built.

Next came a series of nonentities who wore the purple only at Ricimer's pleasure and died in various uncomfortable ways after brief terms of office. The few men who might have been strong enough to oppose him were hampered by the threatening posture of the Visigoths. The Vandals too had to be reckoned with: Gaiseric had his own candidate for the throne in the person of Olybrius, the husband of Valentinian's daughter Placidia (Gaiseric's captive). We have little sense that the Romans had much to say in directing the course of events.

In 467 a new emperor arrived in Italy, sponsored by the Augustus of the East. Emperor Anthemius was a Greek, not too attractive to the Romans for that reason, but his chances of survival seemed brighter than most because Ricimer married his daughter. By 472, however, the situation had deteriorated to such an extent that there were virtually two rulers in Italy, Emperor Anthemius in Rome and Ricimer in Milan. In the end, in a complex series of maneuvers, Anthemius was deposed, and Gaiseric's candidate, Olybrius became Ricimer's new puppet (Olybrius died two months thereafter). Ricimer then laid siege to Rome for five months, and Anthemius was captured and beheaded.

This nightmarish period ended abruptly when Ricimer died a few weeks later—oddly enough, a natural death. Confusion now became general. Ricimer's Burgundian nephew Gundobad succeeded him as military commander and in 473 set up a puppet emperor, Glycerius, in the approved style. The East withheld recognition, and a more appropriate Augustus was sent out from Constantinople, Julius Nepos, who was proclaimed emperor in Rome in 474. Emperor Glycerius hurriedly became a bishop.

In a roundabout way we come once more to the Huns. Attila's court in its heyday had been a magnet for adventurers and soldiers of fortune. Attila had made good use of the more energetic and sophisticated people who offered him allegiance, no doubt convinced that they were better equipped to cope with the complexities of imperial courts than his tribesmen would be. He had two secretaries or ambassadors, Edecon and Orestes, who figure prominently in Priscus's narrative of negotiations with Attila. Edecon was a Hunnic-speaking leader of the Scirians, a Baltic or Sarmatian folk who regularly fought on the side of the Huns. Orestes, although a Hunnic subject, was Roman. These two participated in the mission to Constantinople, where the emperor's chief eunuch tried to arrange for the assassination of Attila by bribing Edecon. Edecon accepted the money, turned it over to Attila, and was sent back to the eunuch bearing the incriminating bag that had held the gold. He confronted the eunuch in the presence of the agitated emperor, who was forced to listen to a searing message from Attila.

When the Hunnic kingdom broke up after Attila's death, the soldiers of fortune moved on. Edecon's son Odovacar lingered in Gaul after the Battle of the Catalaunian Fields and then turned to Italy when he found himself squeezed out by Visigoths and Franks. He took part in the siege of Rome under Ricimer, in which Orestes also participated.

Orestes advanced to the rank of commander-in-chief, replacing Gundobad, who shifted his own base of operations to Gaul to become king of the Burgundians. Orestes proceeded to drive out the weak Emperor Julius Nepos, who fled before him to Dalmatia in 475. In October of that year Orestes solemnly invested his young son Romulus Augustulus with all the glorious trappings of imperial power and for one year held control as regent for the boy. Romulus Augustulus was not a legitimate emperor by any stretch of the imagination, in spite of his ancient Roman names. In the view of the Eastern Augustus, Nepos was still the Western Augustus, even though he was cowering in Dalmatia.

Orestes had not taken over Italy singlehandedly. The military force that he commanded largely comprised a heterogeneous assemblage of barbarians from Hunnic territory, Heruls and Scirians, among whom was the officer Odovacar, the son of his old friend and companion in adventure Edecon. Odovacar became a central figure when the troops confronted Orestes with a promise he had made to settle them in Italy. Orestes brushed them aside, and mutiny was the response. The soldiers chose Odovacar as their king. That in itself was an anomaly because they were no unitary tribe, only a mixture of mercenaries. Odovacar's title, rex Herulorum, had little or nothing to do with his own origins. [15]

Odovacar did not hesitate to attack Orestes, who was overcome and killed in 476. The victor then pushed on to Ravenna, where he kindly but firmly deposed the boy emperor, sending him on his way to the comfort of a fine villa in the south.

This sequence of events—the mutiny, the murder of Orestes, the deposition of Romulus Augustulus—has popularly been considered to embody the actual fall of the Roman Empire. The idea does not make much sense. The East was still very much a going concern, and the West had been a shambles ever since the entrance of the Vandals into Africa. The year 476 indeed marked a turning point, but it might be more accurate to observe that it marked the definitive break between East and West. From 476 on, the ranks of Roman aristocrats were roughly split into two groups. One hoped to gain independence for the West with the help of allies in Constantinople. The other relied on the barbarians. The East pursued a policy aimed at domination of the West, while the barbarians wanted at least the recognition of the East, if not their independence from it.

The illiterate, fur-clad rex Herulorum devised an interesting solution to his problem. Odovacar had to manage the affairs of his barbarians, placate the Romans, fend off the Vandals, and if possible introduce some kind of stability. Even the most astute and practiced of politicians would have found it quite an assignment. Was it really necessary to work through a puppet emperor? Odovacar thought not. His first move was to persuade the Roman Senate to send two leaders to Constantinople with the imperial insignia, which they were to present to Emperor Zeno on behalf of Romulus Augustulus with the statement that the lad had abdicated voluntarily and that it was the sense of the Senate that there was no longer any need for a separate Augustus in the West. Zeno should henceforth be emperor of the united lands. Odovacar himself could be given the authority of viceroy and the title of patrician.

Emperor Zeno responded by reminding Odovacar of the existence of Julius Nepos. He had words of praise for Odovacar, however, for his submissive act in sending the diadem to Constantinople. He declared that if the emperor of the West had not already granted the rank of patrician he himself was prepared to do so. Odovacar was still marked a barbarian: he never received permission to don Roman dress.

Ostensibly, Odovacar's pragmatic solution was satisfactory to all concerned. The barbarians received land and their elected king was de facto ruler of Italy. The senators erected a façade of acceptance of the situation; some of them may have found consolation in Odovacar's consistent selection of Roman aristocrats for high civil office (see plate 59).[16]

A settlement of sorts was effected with the Vandals, who relinquished Sicily in return for an annual tribute. Odovacar's general policy revolved around a system of treaties with all barbarian rulers, in Europe as well as Africa. It is a pity that no details of his rule are known.

Judgments on Odovacar vary. German scholars of the last century claimed him as one of their own, calling him a pioneer and trailbreaker, the outstanding phenomenon of the migration period. J. M. Wallace-Hadrill, writing in the present century, discounts Odovacar's successes, saying that most Romans loathed him because "he belonged to the terrible people."[17] It must be recognized, however, that after thirteen years of Odovacar's domination there were still prominent Romans (for example, Pierius, the *comes domesticorum* who stood by him at the disastrous Battle of the Adda) who were willing to give their lives in his cause. Whatever Odovacar's talents or shortcomings may have been, he was the first barbarian ruler who seriously attempted to administer, not just plunder, Roman territory. He was a trailbreaker in this much at least, that the Eastern empire received an impetus from him, perceiving his rule to be a model that might be turned to account in handling the dreadful problem of the Ostrogoths.

Once more the East stood in danger of being trampled, and once again, like the Visigoths and the Huns, the troublemakers were shunted westward.

The problem presented by Theodoric the Amal and the Ostrogoths had been compounded by a rival Ostrogothic leader, Theodoric Strabo ("the squinter"). Emperor Zeno had tried every scheme he could devise, adopting Theodoric the Amal as a son, making war alternatingly on the two Theodorics, alternately making one or the other an ally, but all to no avail. Sometimes one Theodoric or the other was against him; sometimes they even joined forces. For a while it appeared that Theodoric Strabo would emerge victorious in the strife between the two Ostrogothic factions. Emperor Zeno thought he saw how the tide was running and put Strabo in command of the army, deposing the infuriated Theodoric the Amal. This situation ended suddenly in 481 with Strabo's death when his horse threw him. The remaining Theodoric, no longer held in check by Strabo or anyone else, laid waste to Macedonia and Thessaly. At that point, in 488, Zeno was inspired. If Theodoric would undertake to dispose of Odovacar, he could take Odovacar's place as viceroy of Italy.

Odovacar was not a man to go down supinely. It required three years of hot campaigning to defeat him, and even then Theodoric could bring about his opponent's death only by a ruse. The two men had negotiated an unrealistic agreement that they would rule jointly. Theodoric was admitted to Ravenna on those terms. Still a true barbarian, in spite of a period in his youth when he had lived as a hostage in the sophisticated Byzantine court,[18] he nursed an obsession to avenge the death of some of his elite followers who had been lured into Odovacar's net. Theodoric invited Odovacar to dinner and sprang on his guest in bloody satisfaction, destroying him with one violent slash of his sword.

Hardly an auspicious beginning; yet there is much to suggest that as the years went by, Theodoric mellowed so much that the noble Bishop Ennodius was moved to extol the virtues of this prince and even to find the required justification for the murder of Odovacar and his followers. In a panegyric delivered in Theodoric's presence, Ennodius said that "the counsel you took secretly was already approved by all the people. The order for the greatly desired massacre was sent to the most distant provinces." Such a stark pronouncement could have been based on only an appreciation of Theodoric's difficult problem. Time and again before he entered Italy, the Ostrogothic chieftain had seen how easily imperial diplomacy could fluctuate, and for the sake of stability he had to wipe out all possible contenders surviving from Odovacar's line or among his followers. This was a Christian century, but there was general recognition of the grim fact that morality is a peacetime luxury.[19]

The people of Italy were better off under Theodoric than they had been for centuries.[20] Looking back to Theodoric's time as a golden age of peace and plenty, recalling how free they had been from Vandal attack and how he had built up a chain of alliances for the good of Italy, men of later generations proudly remembered his restoration of aqueducts and public works, his interest in beautifying their cities. There is a record of Theodoric's unbarbaric indignation over the theft of a statue at Como: "It is vexatious that while we are laboring to increase the ornaments of our cities, those which Antiquity has bequeathed us should be diminished by such deeds as this."[21] There was praise too for his evenhandedness in dealing with barbarians and Romans. It would be too much to say that he tried to merge the two peoples; he understood their deep-seated antagonism. He reserved military careers and defense matters to the barbarians and tried to sustain their war-mindedness by forbidding them to send their children to school. As Procopius explained it, "If the fear of the strap once came over them, they would never have the resolution to despise sword or spear."[22]

Civil posts went to the Romans. Like Odovacar before him, Theodoric was able to lure competent aristocrats to his court. Most of them must have been members of an anti-Byzantine coterie in the Senate.[23] For many years Theodoric's Romans served him faithfully.

Toward the end of his life events that had their roots in the remote past came to plague the old monarch, who responded in a way that has given historians reason to judge him a merciless murderer who reverted to type. Was the philosopher Boethius a saintly martyr, the victim of an aging Arian ruler's paranoia? Not much more than a century separated the execution of Stilicho the Vandal at the command of the Roman emperor Honorius and the execution of Boethius the Roman for treachery to a barbarian king. That short, stormy period had witnessed a series of staggering events: Alaric's sack of Rome; the loss of Africa to the Vandals; the partition of Gaul among Visigoths, Burgundians, and Franks; the tyranny of Ricimer; the takeover of Italy by Odovacar; and the officially sanctioned implantation in Italy of the Ostrogoths under Theodoric. It is bewildering to realize that there had been time enough and energy enough for churchly brawling.

The scope of this book precludes consideration in detail of all the currents of religious contention that swirled throughout the whole period of the later empire, but we could not honestly feel that we knew what the age was like if we were arbitrarily to ignore those commotions, which in a way were the very stuff of life. We have an especially instructive example here in a vastly complicated case that involved the fiery convictions of Eastern prelates and bitter rivalry between the sees of Constantinople and Alexandria, all laced with political infighting by Roman senators and an Eastern emperor's wily calculations. The empire could not tolerate such strains, yet there was no avoiding them, given the temper of the various protagonists. The strands of this contention tightened into a knot in Theodoric's time. One spectacular result was the action of that firm, hitherto just ruler, who pounced on two of the most honored and trusted Romans at his court and peremptorily ordered their brutal execution.

Let us consider the religious picture, the better to understand the tragedy of Boethius and his father-in-law, Aurelius Memmius Symmachus. It seems preposterous that grown men could become so furiously embroiled in esoteric argument. Few people were capable of the cool aloofness of Procopius, who wrote, "I consider it a sort of insane folly to investigate the nature of God." [24] Especially in the East, sharp, subtle minds were unable to resist the fascinations of christological argument. Like a nest of puzzle boxes, each problem opened to disclose another. The theory of the interrelationships of the divine and human natures of Christ could be teased out into a near infinity of contradictions: Logos and flesh—perfect man and suffering deity—one will or two—indwelling Logos or eternal Logos incongruously swaddled as an infant—Mary with God in her womb—human, resurrected redeemer. These ideas were relentlessly spun to the most impossible lengths: Jesus himself might have been interested to learn that whereas he spat as a man his spittle was divine. Christology had become "an armory of poisoned weapons" [25] not only for a few elite theologians but also for worldly individuals who exploited the controversy in pursuit of complex ends that had little or nothing to do with salvation or morality or faith.

The most ruthless of the power seekers before Theodoric's time was Dioscorus, the patriarch of Alexandria and virtual ruler of Egypt. Dioscorus should have been able to rely on the general support of the papal see, but he overreached himself. As a matter of policy Rome usually sided with Alexandria against the parvenu See of Constantinople to maintain a balance of power. That the bishop of Rome held the true primacy had been fairly well settled, largely by the masterly legalisms of Pope Leo I. [26]

Dioscorus's predecessor Cyril had won a resounding victory over Constantinople in a prior trial of strength. The formidable Nestorius, bishop of Constantinople, lost because Rome injected herself on the side of Alexandria. The emperor had tried to intervene at the Council of Ephesus, in 431, but that body was scandalously divided into two rival camps over which he had no control. Nestorius was deposed and Cyril hailed as "the new Paul." A council called by the emperor retaliated by deposing Cyril.

Nestorius had earned the deep enmity of a large non-Hellenized population in the East with a vivid background of a cult of a Great Mother. He was reviled because of his objection to the use of the epithet Theotokos (God-Bearer) for the Virgin Mary because it appeared to reduce that holiest of women to the status of a mere vehicle. He thought that the epithet Christotokos would be preferable. Perhaps it is unreasonable to wonder why Nestorius could not get a fair hearing at Ephesus. Of all places Ephesus was Mary's city. She was queen there, the veritable successor to all the great female deities, including Artemis.

Cyril managed to ride out the threat of deposition and came at last to be

Plate 57. Coptic Annunciation, wood, Egypt, fifth–sixth century. Mary
was an object of devotion in Coptic Egypt. This touching fragment of a
decorative panel shows her turning away from her spinning with startled
eyes, incredulous and bewildered. The pose is Egyptian: Mary stands in
Byzantine representations of this subject (*L'art copte, Petit Palais Paris 17 juin
15 septembre 1964* [catalog], p. 111). Musée du Louvre E 145. *Courtesy of Musée
du Louvre, Paris.*

venerated as a saint, whereas Nestorius was murdered, after much hardship and abuse in a desert exile. Centuries later it was still a common belief among resentful Egyptians that no rain ever fell on Nestorius's grave because of heavenly wrath.[27] His sin was not heresy but rather the generating of quarrels that led to the Council of Chalcedon.

There was another council before Chalcedon—the Robber Synod of Ephesus in 449, where Dioscorus scored a triumph that bore the seeds of the ultimate downfall of the patriarchate of Alexandria because it led the bishop of Rome to take a fresh look at the balance of power. The reasons behind the calling of this meeting are obscure. Although an elderly archimandrite named Eutyches seemed to be Dioscorus's target, it was probable that Dioscorus was after bigger game, the patriarch of Constantinople.

In alarm Pope Leo charted a new course. He supplied a volume of dogma, couched in terms that left no doubt concerning the identity of the true head of the church. His *Tome* broke no new ground, but implicit in it was the old idea of two natures of Christ in one person. To quote Adolf Harnack, "The unity is neither made intelligible by Leo, nor did he consider what was the supreme concern of pious Greeks in this matter, namely to see in the humanity of Christ the real deification of human nature generally."[28] Dioscorus presided at the emperor's command and took advantage of his position to brush Leo's *Tome* aside.

The patriarch of Alexandria had with him a band of trusted terrorists. Just how violent these fanatic Egyptian and Syrian monks actually were is hard to judge. The patriarch of Constantinople, who died soon afterward, was said to have been trampled. A Roman deacon ventured a protest at one point and had to flee for his life. The mere presence of ruffians had a sobering effect on the delegates, who deposed the patriarch of Constantinople with meek unanimity and accepted Dioscorus's nominee as a substitute. Such then was the Robber Synod. Harnack says that a body that *more than any other* gave expression to the underlying feelings of the Eastern church should not be branded as a robber synod, in spite of its brutality.[29]

Emperor Theodosius II died not long after, in July, 450. He was succeeded by his devout and headstrong sister Pulcheria, who chose Marcian to be her consort. The new reigning couple had no appetite for domination by the See of Alexandria, but they had to rely on outsiders because the settlement engineered by Dioscorus had quieted the East considerably. In Alexandria, Dioscorus knew how the winds would blow and did his best to prevent recognition of Emperor Marcian in Egypt. Marcian responded by addressing Pope Leo, formally transferring the primacy of the Eastern church from Alexandria to Rome and stating that he was prepared to summon a new council to undo the work of Ephesus. Pope Leo preferred to let his *Tome* do its work: the Robber Synod would be defused if Dioscorus's name were expunged from church records. This suggestion did not appeal to Marcian, who badly needed to show his authority as emperor and assert some independence of Rome. A council was called for 451.

This was the Council of Chalcedon, for which latter-day Egyptians blamed Nestorius in his grave. The problem with the council was that the dispirited bishops were now required to show solidarity with the emperor and negate the tenets of Cyril and Dioscorus, which more or less embodied their true feelings. Under severe pressure from the emperor these unhappy souls adopted the formula "Alike in his divinity and perfect in his humanity, alike truly God and truly man . . . two natures unconfusedly, unchangeably, indivisibly, inseparably. The property of each of the two natures is preserved." All over the East devout persons felt that the Blessed Virgin had been affronted. In their eyes she was holy. To say that she was merely a vehicle for an indwelling savior was to deprive her of her holiness and likewise deprive her devotees of the object of their adoration. The church of the East had been deprived of its faith, Harnack comments gloomily.[30]

The Egyptians in attendance at Chalcedon were terrified. We cannot go home, they said. We shall be killed if we subscribe to this. The record of succeeding decades provides woeful evidence of the accuracy of the prediction. Not only Egypt but Syria also reacted with revolt and violence. The fumbling efforts of later emperors to find ways of healing and uniting the Eastern church merely created a schism between East and West. The schism lasted from 484 to 519 and was at the root of Theodoric's trouble with Boethius.

A well-meaning emperor could cause havoc. Emperor Zeno, who had invited Theodoric to unseat Odovacar, thought it in his power to quell the dissent that followed suppression of the dogma laid down by Dioscorus. His *Henotikon* (482) appears to have been the handiwork of two conniving patriarchs, Acacius in Constantinople and Peter Mongus, who had been hand in glove with Dioscorus's unsavory successor, Timothy the Cat, but the emperor must bear the blame for it. The *Henotikon* was underhanded: it was ostensibly addressed to the Egyptians, urging a return to the fold, but it implied that Chalcedon might have been an error. That was an open door for repudiation of Leo's *Tome*, should anyone want to look at it in that light. Leo's successor, Pope Simplicius, indignantly understood the *Henotikon* that way. Acacius and Peter Mongus were going too far, acting as though they possessed the authority that belonged to him alone as head of the papal see. He excommunicated the two and thereby precipitated open schism.

From the time of Simplicius's successor, Felix III, Roman senators were journeying to Constantinople to make contact with the colony of pro-Roman exiles from Ravenna.[31] They wanted to encourage malcontents in Constantinople to join hands with them, with the ultimate goal of fusing the churches of Rome and Constantinople, to the detriment of Theodoric's position as ruler

Plate 58. Coptic stela from Idfu, Egypt, fifth–seventh century. The introductory "Sole is God" was a Monophysite formula. The imperial eagle has acquired a cross in place of the conventional olive branch, and around its neck the Coptic carver has supplied a bulla closely resembling the magic clasp that the ancient Egyptian gods held out to the dead pharaoh (Gayet, *L'art copte*, pp. 99–101). British Museum, Department of Egyptian and Assyrian Antiquities no. 1790. *Courtesy of British Museum, London.*

of Italy. One reason for the strength of Rome at the time, as in the days of Odovacar, was the absence of a true focal point of imperial authority.

Emperor Zeno died in 491. The day after his death he was replaced by Anastasias, appointed by the widowed Augusta Ariadne, who married him within a month. The choice was popular at first, but before long Anastasias's ecclesiastical policies stirred up the wrath of the pro-Chalcedon population of Constantinople. Some vociferous monks (called "the Sleepless" because of their perpetual chanting) were fanatic on the subject. The new emperor was inclined toward opinions that were popular in Alexandria and Syria, but at least initially he considered it his duty to support the *Henotikon*.

These were lively times in Constantinople. The city of Alexandria has the reputation of having had the most volatile and vicious crowds in all of history, but Constantinople could be a violent place too. A Monophysite monk, Severus of Pisidia, had come to town with a band of followers. He and his men became bolder and bolder and began injecting their own version of the Trisagion ("Holy, holy, holy, Lord God of Hosts") into the chanting in the church. The orthodox were outraged; in November, 512, there was an unseemly shouting match ending in a riot in which, inevitably, people were killed by the emperor's troops. Next the populace proclaimed a new emperor.

Anastasias boldly presented himself before the howling mob at the Hippodrome. At the end of a wild scene the fickle crowd implored him to put on his crown again. Brave as he was, Anastasias was getting along in years and perhaps not as subtle in judgment as he should have been. He deposed the moderate patriarch of Antioch in favor of the Monophysite Severus, who gave every indication of being in a mood to persecute the adherents of Chalcedon. The situation touched off a serious armed revolt in Thrace, where the supporters of Chalcedon were in the majority.

The Thracian rebels had a strong leader, a Scythian general named Vitalian. There is some question about Vitalian's motives, but it must be agreed that he appears to have kept his eyes firmly on dogma and not to have used his position to advance himself. His situation changed abruptly with the sudden death of Emperor Anastasias in July, 518. The new Augustus, Justin I, was not astute enough to hold power in his own hands. Before long the rule was divided between Justinian, Justin's clever young nephew, and Vitalian. These two were the chief proponents of union with the church of Rome. Papal delegates arriving in Constantinople recognized Vitalian as first among the faithful.

We now meet a relative of Vitalian's, the Scythian monk Leontius.[32] Vitalian is described as the "protector" of Leontius and his fellow Scythians, who came to Constantinople early in 519 to lodge a complaint against certain bishops in their province. The Scythian monks were known for a formula of their own devising, "Unus ex trinitate passus carne" ("One of the Trinity suffered in the flesh"), which seemed to offer a bridge for reconciliation between Chalcedonians and the recalcitrant Monophysites. Justinian was a man of long vision. He developed a grand design for the recovery of all the territories lost to the barbarians. Part of this scheme apparently included reunion of the churches of East and West, under the control of the emperor at Constantinople. He took a keen interest in the "Scythian formula" for this reason.

This long narrative seems to have little to do with Theodoric and his honored former consul Boethius (see plate 59) and Boethius's father-in-law, Symmachus. There is indeed a connection, however. William Bark sets out the evidence, showing that theological treatises tentatively attributed to Boethius are genuine and that Boethius supported the position of the Scythian monks.[33] Theodoric must have been entirely unsuspecting, loading honors on Boethius and his family until incriminating letters came to his hand that revealed that "Boethius was in close contact with those who strove for an ecclesiastical harmony which they hoped would be followed by political unification based on the destruction of Theodoric's power."[34] Bark paints a picture of a Roman aristocrat who would experience no mental conflict in accepting the highest honors at the hands of a barbarian whom he wished to destroy. The combination of theological and political activity brought Boethius to a grisly death and the reputation of saintliness.

Theodoric himself, if we follow Procopius, met a bizarre end, triggered by remorse. A balefully staring cooked fish presented on a platter looked to him so much like Boethius's murdered father-in-law that Theodoric rose from the table in horror, staggered off to bed, and died.[35] His kingdom and his people could ill afford to lose him. Justinian managed to have his way at a terrible cost for the Italians whom Theodoric had ruled carefully and well for more than thirty years.

The next ruler of the Ostrogoths, Theodoric's intelligent daughter Amalasuntha, might have been equally competent, but circumstances were against her from the very start. Her status as regent for her young son Athalaric was dangerous for her, with Goths at the court snapping at her heels. She tried to have him taught along lines similar to those of her own "liberal-arts" education, but the courtiers thought that the arts of war were of primary importance and took Athalaric away from her. Before long he was hopelessly debauched, diseased, and unfit for any kind of reasonable life. To add to Amalasuntha's troubles, the system of barbarian alliances based on a network of royal marriages that her father had worked out so carefully was breaking down, mostly because of the rapacity of the Franks. Right at home was her own scheming cousin Theodehad, who had become a major landowner in Tuscany and was in communication with Justinian, now emperor, offering to turn over his holdings in exchange for gold and high rank at Justinian's court. That prospect of a life of ease was demolished when Amalasuntha forced him to restore his lands

Plate 59. Flavius Manlius Boethius. Leaf of a consular diptych. Boethius, consul in 487 under Odovacar, was the father of Anicius Boethius, who was executed for suspected treason by command of Theodoric. Absence of an imperial bust from the scepter may indicate that this consulship was not recognized by the Eastern emperor (Delbrueck, *Die Consulardiptychen und verwandte Denkmäler*, 2:62). *Courtesy of Museo del età cristiana, Brescia, Italy.*

to their rightful owners. She earned his undying animosity by this move and solidified Gothic support behind him.

Amalasuntha enjoyed power. She was capable of unscrupulous action herself, as she demonstrated when she commissioned a triple murder to dispose of troublesome courtiers who were trying to pull her down.

When her worthless son Athalaric died, Amalasuntha made a grievous mistake: she offered the title of king to her cousin Theodehad on condition that the actual power remain in her own hands. Theodehad appeared to consent, but Amalasuntha's days were numbered. It is generally thought that Theodehad and Empress Theodora, Justinian's scheming wife, were of one mind on the imprisonment and death of Amalasuntha. Soon after she was incarcerated, the royal lady was strangled by henchmen of the three leaders whose murder she had instigated.

In this bare outline Amalasuntha does not seem especially worthy or admirable, but if we read her letter to Justinian on the question of Sicily, so direct and handsome in its composition that it reminds us of scholarly Elizabeth I of England, or if we read Procopius's estimate of her, we halfway condone the murders that she judged to be necessary. Procopius had this to say: "Amalasuntha administered the government and proved to be endowed with wisdom and regard for justice in the highest degree." Her murder, he says, was "an act which grieved exceedingly all the Italians and the Goths as well. For the woman had the strictest regard for every kind of virtue." [36] We contemplate her mild round face and deplore the violent death she died.

Justinian grasped at the death of Amalasuntha as a valid excuse for war against Theodehad and in 535 gave appropriate instructions to General Belisarius. The Goths were much more difficult to conquer than the African Vandals had been, and the protracted struggle visited calamity after calamity on the cities and countryside. Indeed, this was the nadir of the fortunes of Italy, which had prospered under the Ostrogoths.

Before we close this complicated chapter, we must pay our respects to one of the great men of the era, Cassiodorus Senator. He was a Roman aristocrat who revered the ancient heritage. The old gentleman was following in the footsteps of his forebears. His grandfather was a *notarius* and tribune under Valentinian III and took part in an embassy to Attila, in the company of Aëtius's son Carpilio. His father was a financial officer for Odovacar, as well as governor of Sicily and praetorian prefect under Theodoric. As Hodgkin put it, Cassiodorus himself "sat at the cradle of the Ostrogothic monarchy and mourned over its grave." He was successively *quaestor*, *consul ordinarius*, and *magister officiorum* under Theodoric and praetorian prefect under Amalasuntha.

It is Cassiodorus's misfortune that he is chiefly remembered for the mass of incredibly stuffy documents that he rolled out for the signature of King Theodoric. As we look at them, we do indeed wonder what the barbarian ruler may have thought of the stupefying array of metaphors that Cassiodorus habitually marshaled as a frame for such minor matters as instructions to a slow-moving official to hurry up with a grain shipment. [37] It must have given Theodoric a dizzying feeling that he was master of a wondrously erudite folk. His Roman subjects, on the other hand, were presumably equally dazzled by the evidence that their barbarian monarch had such a complex mind. It is easy enough to laugh at all this, but the motive should be respected. If something of the old learning could have been infused into the thought of the newcomers, Cassiodorus would have done well.

There seem to be traces of his work everywhere. How much inspiration did Theodoric take from Cassiodorus in the restoration of ancient buildings and public works? Again, who initiated the early revision of Roman law? Theodoric's *Edictum*, issued about 500, was intended "for the common benefit of all, whether barbarians or Romans." The document constitutes a primitive effort to wrestle with problems inherent in a society in which two cultures must mingle. It is a pity that Cassiodorus's Gothic history is lost. From what survives in Jordanes's *Getica*, we gather that the intention had been to foster mutual respect between Romans and barbarians.

Cassiodorus was a friend of the philosopher Boethius. Both men had a serious reverence for classic Greek and Roman thought, believing that it should be preserved in the Christian era. We are all much in debt to Cassiodorus for the work of his advanced old age after he retired to a monastery, when he might have considered himself entitled to well-earned rest. He had returned to his birthplace, a remote and lovely estate at the bottom of the boot of Italy, on the Gulf of Squillace. There he established two monasteries, one for ascetic retirement and a better-known one for a more active life of service. The latter is conventionally referred to as Vivarium because of its fishponds, in which live fish were impounded in seawater for the use of the monastery. It was a peaceful spot, "hanging like a cluster of grapes" on the mountain slope. There was a small, rippling stream, and there were orchards and well-tended flower and vegetable gardens, dovecotes, and beehives. There were accommodations for weary travelers and poor people in need of shelter, and a pair of churches built in the Eastern style. This establishment is charmingly pictured in miniatures that accompany early editions of Cassiodorus's *Institutiones*. [38]

Cassiodorus wrote his *Institutiones* as an introduction to a course of liberal arts for his monks at Vivarium. He wanted them to know secular Greek and Latin literature as a background for the study of the Scriptures. He also wanted them to be familiar with the various sciences. Cassiodorus has been described as "the first man in Italy to recognize the possibilities of the convent as a school of liberal culture." [39] He thought of his monastery as an asylum for the humanities in a violent and threatened world. He proceeded laboriously to assemble a library to give his copyists the best available material. Manuscripts were purchased from such distant places as North Africa, or borrowed from scholarly friends.[40] As a guide for transcription Cassiodorus—well into his ninth decade—set down exact rules for the treatment of corrupt texts. He did not object to neat correction of letters that had obviously been miscopied, but he believed that any tinkering with the Scriptures to put the divine message into smoother idioms should be avoided at all cost. Cassiodorus was an orthodox enough Christian to act as censor with respect to heretical writings. A supposedly anonymous commentary on thirteen letters of the apostle Paul looked suspiciously Pelagian to him. He carefully expurgated offending passages to salvage an otherwise useful piece.[41]

His library was ultimately dispersed, but important items were destined to survive in the distant northern parts of the monastic world, where they would be reverently handled and preserved. The Venerable Bede even used a Bible that once belonged to Cassiodorus (the famous *Codex grandior*), as well as a version of a manuscript that may have come to Cassiodorus in a roundabout way from the pen of Saint Jerome himself.[42] Bede had a familiarity with classic literature that suggests the effect of the labors of Cassiodorus. When we come to a discussion of events in the British Isles, we shall find that the connecting link was the Northumbrian abbot Benedict Biscop, who traveled widely and with great determination through the hazardous terrains of eighth-century Gaul and Italy, gathering treasures for the monasteries of Wearmouth and Jarrow.

Cassiodorus then, in spite of his amusing, pompous language, was a man of a dawning age. The rule of his monastic house was based on the stern old ascetic principles laid down by John Cassian, who derived his own ideas from those of the holy Desert Fathers whom he had known. Cassiodorus was so old that in his youth he must have talked with people who had seen Attila the Hun with their own eyes. He had witnessed the destruction of Rome, yet he had done his level best to support the potentially disruptive Ostrogoths. He lived in an era when classical literature, though it had its champions, was viewed suspiciously in many quarters and unknown in others. He was a contemporary of Saint Benedict of Nursia, and he must have been aware of the growing might of the monastic movement that would bear Benedict's name. Through all of this, in a period of fear, change, and uncertainty, Cassiodorus never lost his nerve. He never lost sight of the essentials. He stands for the best in an age that was at once terrible and full of portent.

LOMBARD ITALY

A CHILD born in the year of Amalasuntha's murder (535) grew to adulthood accustomed to terror, hunger, and the sight of death. If he had the misfortune to be an urban child, his chances of growing up at all were fairly slim, because the cities of Italy underwent famine, plague, assault, and massacre in that period as warring armies tramped back and forth along the great highways. Rome was captured five times, suffered devastating sieges, saw her walls partly demolished, was reduced at one time to a population of about five hundred, and indeed lay deserted for forty days. Milan, in 539, lay helpless before vindictive Goths who wiped out the male population and consigned the women to slavery under their Burgundian allies. "In the long series of deliberate inhumanities recorded in the annals of mankind, the colossal massacre of Milan is one of the most flagrant," writes J. B. Bury.[1] In Naples the starving people were mere wraiths whom a conquering Goth had to protect from their own dangerous voracity by devising a rationing system. At Pavia invading Franks slaughtered women and cast their bodies into the river—as human sacrifice, Procopius thought. Even small communities had their fill of siege horror.

Country life was no better. People began wandering wretchedly from one part of Italy to another in search of food. In Tuscany they subsisted on acorn bread. Procopius said that fifty thousand died of starvation around Pavia. His stark account of what he saw there matches anything we have read in our own day from Bangladesh or the Sahel: skin clinging to the bone, blackened ghosts, looking like burned-out torches, insane stares. Weak wanderers grasping at tufts of grass, too feeble even to pull up that miserable substitute for nourishment, "they would fall upon the grass and their outstretched hand and die." The bodies were not laid in earth, but carrion birds left them untouched since there was not a shred of flesh on them worth scavenging.[2]

The actors in this painful drama were Belisarius and Narses on the Byzantine side, with Emperor Justinian and the Augusta Theodora offstage (see plate 60). On the side of the Ostrogoths was Totila, their king. Belisarius entered the scene fresh from his conquest of the Vandals, which was topped off by his triumph in Constantinople, where he displayed his captive, King Gelimer. Even today military experts speak respectfully of the Byzantine general, whom they rank among the greatest of all time. The judgment might be questioned, because Belisarius had a consistent history of difficulty with insubordinate troops and commanders. We saw evidence of this in the Vandal campaign, and indeed it was already an old story. When Belisarius first assumed command of an army, in Persia in 530, his Hunnic commanders Sunicas and Simmas with their six hundred horsemen impetuously forced him against his better judgment into what proved to be a losing battle, at Callinicum. It is true that during his two Italian campaigns Belisarius was given niggardly support from Constantinople in supplies, soldiers, and money, but even so the feature that stands out is the quarrelsomeness of his officers.

Belisarius was a valiant man in the field, and his loyalty to the emperor was unswerving. It is regrettable that Justinian was too jealous to be able to return that loyalty, because he owed his very throne to Belisarius and his *bucellarii*. When Justinian's rule was seriously threatened by the Nika revolt in Constantinople, which grew out of an uproar between the two factions of the city's racing fans, the emperor, who was "a man of bold vision but apparently limited physical courage,"[3] could not rely on his own standing army. It was Belisarius and the men attached to him who worked their way through smoldering ruins to attack the mob in the Hippodrome. By that time, in 532, Belisarius had amassed a fortune large enough to sustain what amounted to a private army. In later years, Procopius tells us, he surpassed the generals of all time, equipping seven thousand of his own elite retainers, each of whom "could claim to challenge the best of the enemy."[4]

Belisarius could be imperious. Although he had only about five thousand armed men with him in besieged Rome in 537–38, he did not hesitate to send a message to the Ostrogoth king Witigis, encamped beyond the walls with an overwhelming army of mailed warriors, that "Rome belongs to us of old. You have no right to it." During that same stressful period, while he was supervising the repair and reinforcement of the city walls and the placing of a floating mill system for grain, Belisarius brusquely deposed the pope. In fairness it should be explained that this peremptory behavior may have been dictated by his thoroughly corrupt wife, Antonina, whose blindly infatuated tool Belisarius was. Antonina was a friend of the equally corrupt Empress Theodora, who was intent on undoing the work of unification that occupied so much of her husband's thought and attention (she was a Monophysite). To be fair to Antonina in her turn, it must be granted that she could be efficient and helpful. When Belisarius entrusted administration of the commissary to her, she performed well.

Plate 60. Belisarius in the train of Emperor Justinian. Mosaic in the Church of San Vitale, Ravenna. The emperor enters the church with General Belisarius on his right and Bishop Maximianus on his left. *Bucellarii* are in close attendance at the left.

Belisarius could be a hero in the Homeric style. Before the gates of Rome, driven from his command post in the general turmoil, "the whole decision of the war rested with him," because the Goths had spotted his big gray horse with its white blaze and shouted to each other to kill the man on the *balan* (their word for such a horse). The beleaguered general fought back furiously in "a display of valor such, I imagine, as has never been shown by any man in the world to this day."[5] When he and his men finally extricated themselves and rushed to the Salarian Gate, calling on those inside to open up, the tower guards saw only a bloody, dust-caked man, whom they failed to recognize. Crushed against the locked gate by the oncoming Goths, Belisarius bellowed to his exhausted followers that they must charge. This they did with such vigor that the confused Goths believed that they were being assailed by a fresh new army bursting from the city. They fled in panic. This battle, Procopius tells us, had begun early in the morning and continued at that desperate pace until dark.

Belisarius was constantly hampered by the insubordination of his commanders, but he himself disregarded the intentions of his emperor, with devastating results. By 540 the war against the Ostrogoths had reached a strange stage: the Goths were losing, yet their situation was far from hopeless because of the fluid state of affairs outside Italy. Almost simultaneously the Franks and the Byzantines approached King Witigis with alluring proposals. The greedy Franks sent envoys offering military assistance, with the suggestion that the two barbarian kingdoms divide Italy among themselves. The emissaries from Constantinople offered to let Witigis keep all of Italy north of the Po River. On the face of it the latter proposal seems most peculiar, but there was the circumstance that Justinian had to contend with his dangerous Persian foe and probably wanted to withdraw Belisarius for combat in the East.

The Goths accepted Justinian's bid, but Belisarius refused to sign the treaty, though his officers urged him to do so. The Goths responded with an unexpected move of their own. Witigis would abdicate, they said, and Belisarius himself could become king of the Ostrogoths. Belisarius now proceeded to demonstrate his loyalty to the emperor in his own way. He allowed the Ostrogoths to believe that he would accept their astounding offer, but when he entered Ravenna in May, 540, he rejected the whole scheme. He was not in any way a political animal, and it has been observed that outside his own military métier he would have felt uncomfortable in a position of supreme power.[6] He departed for Constantinople, taking along King Witigis and the royal treasure of the Ostrogoths. If he anticipated a reenactment of the triumph that marked his return from Africa with the Vandal king as his prize, he was disappointed. The emperor received him coldly. It is possible that Justinian saw just how much damage had been done by this flagrant disregard of diplomatic initiatives. The Ostrogoths had not surrendered; they would surely elect a new king and carry on somehow. It took another twelve ghastly years to eradicate them.

The second leading figure whom we should know is Totila, elected king of the Ostrogoths in 541, following two others who had not been conspicuously successful. Like Belisarius, Totila generally receives high marks from the historians, who praise the sweep of his tactical moves, his generosity, and his humane treatment of conquered Romans. Thomas Hodgkin calls him "the noblest flower that blossomed upon the Ostrogothic stem."[7] Bury counters by noting that a man who revives a seemingly lost cause and abruptly fails at the end of a long series of successes is bound to appeal to popular imagination but that we should not overlook the atrocities committed by Totila, such as the wanton mutilation of Demetrius, governor of Naples. Bury goes on to intimate that Totila was just one more perfidious barbarian.[8]

In the long run Totila shows up well, considering the times (Procopius apparently saw it as nothing extraordinary that Belisarius punished some

Huns in his African army by impaling them).[9] To counterbalance the disgusting episode of Demetrius, is the incident concerning Boethius's widow, Rusticana, who wandered forlornly from door to door as a beggar, like many other members of the senatorial class in Rome. Totila's Goths wanted to kill her because, they said, she had been instrumental in the destruction of statues of their revered Theodoric, as vengeance on the man who had brought death and disgrace to her husband and her father, Aurelius Memmius Symmachus. "Totila would not permit her to suffer any harm, but he guarded her safe from insult." [10]

There is a consensus that all barbarians stood in almost reverential awe of Rome. Totila's attitude toward the immortal city was therefore anomalous. When he entered Rome late in 546, he ordered the demolition of the noble city walls, possibly in imitation of Gaiseric's tactics in Africa.[11] He further expressed his intention to make a sheep pasture of the place. The ancient structures would be burned and leveled. A letter from Belisarius gave him pause. This communication has a distinctly modern ring. How many times, in the halls of the United Nations Building, have not similar ideas been voiced? "Insult to these monuments would properly be considered a great crime against the men of all time. . . . A reputation that corresponds with your conduct will be your portion among all men." [12] Totila read the letter over and over and was finally convinced. Even so, the Ostrogoth had no comprehension then of the strong propaganda value of possession of the city and marched his army off to other fields, leaving the mournful, deserted streets to echo to the cadence of the tramping feet of Belisarius's entering troops. When Totila came again to Rome in 549, he had arrived at a clearer understanding. He had received another letter, this one from a Frankish king curtly rejecting Totila's suit for his daughter's hand. The Frank informed Totila that the Ostrogothic leader "never was nor ever would be king of Italy" since he had let Rome fall to the enemy after having captured it.[13] This time Totila hurriedly set to work on reconstruction, summoned the Senate, and even symbolically presided at a horse race, indicating in this way that life would once more pulsate in the metropolis.

Totila met his match in the person of a new commander-in-chief, the chamberlain Narses, who replaced Belisarius after his second recall. We see Totila for the last time in 552, on the eve of the fatal battle of Busta Gallorum, when he was using every device he could imagine, stalling for time while he awaited expected reinforcements. It is not often that we have the opportunity to see a genuinely happy barbarian. There stood the two armies in battle array, confronted, waiting. Out between them galloped King Totila, magnificent in glittering mail, mounted on a splendid charger, to perform "the dance under arms," [14] making of strategic necessity an occasion to display himself in all his glory. His horse cantered in wide circles, first left and then right, while the gorgeous rider shot his javelin so high that it hung quivering in the air before it dropped back into his hand. Totila tumbled about on the horse's back, while the armies stared. When we remember how much brutal violence accompanied a concerted attack on generals in the field, we see that there must have been a rigid code governing these things. Nobody so much as drew a bow to shoot Totila down. But he died in battle that very day. His jeweled cap and drenched bloody garments were dispatched to Constantinople, there to be placed at the emperor's feet.

Totila had a brave successor, Teias, the last king of the Ostrogoths, who fought a tremendous fight at the foot of Vesuvius in 552. Narses had him cornered, and the well-equipped Byzantine forces had blockaded him so effectively that the Goths were without access to water. Tame surrender was not for Teias: he and his men issued from their retreat, attacking. As the leader Teias personally sustained the onslaught of enemy spears. Shield after shield bristled with them, and he had to hand them over for replacement. Possibly his arm tired at last. In any case he was slow in accepting a fresh shield and fell mortally wounded. Although his severed head was immediately displayed to the Goths, these hardy ones fought on into the following day before acknowledging their powerlessness. Even then their emissaries told Narses that they would not submit. They wanted to go peacefully beyond the boundaries of the empire. Narses agreed and permitted the warriors to take along the money and gear that belonged to them.

Narses is our third dominant figure. Historians tend to refer to him as "the Eunuch," as though castration were the most important fact about this complicated, intelligent man. It indicates something of his probable lowly origin and lets us know that he must have had the kind of excessive drive that sends people up the social scale, but it traditionally implies the sly meanness that characterized so many officials of the Byzantine court. That is unfair. Narses, though money-loving, seems to have been uncommonly moderate and honest. It would be more to the point to refer to him by his titles, grand chamberlain and patrician.

Narses was already getting on in years when Justinian first dispatched him, as grand chamberlain, to Italy at the time when Belisarius was supposedly in command. Belisarius had great difficulty in adjusting to the presence on the battlefield of one of the highest civil officers of the empire. He had trouble enough with insubordinate commanders at all times, and Narses was not in the habit of accepting commands. Their efforts in Italy tended to cancel out each other. In a shuffle arranged by Justinian, Belisarius was recalled, and Narses became supreme commander. He had better equipment, more money, and greater authority than Belisarius ever had. He made efficient use of his resources, pressing through to victory over the Ostrogoths in short order.

Although not a military man Narses was imaginative in battle, as well he had to be because in addition to the Ostrogoths he confronted the Franks who streamed across Italy in search of booty. The Franks used horrible weapons for close combat: not only their distinctive throwing ax but also the *ango*, a spear with curved barbs. The *ango* could be hurled or jammed into an opponent's shield and used as a handle to pull the shield away, exposing the victim to a blow of the ax. At Rimini, when Narses found that much damage was being done to his cavalry in this way, he averted disaster by taking a leaf from the Alans. He abruptly ordered a feigned retreat and then regrouped his forces and attacked. A contemporary historian commented uneasily that this was hardly worthy of a general of the empire. It was more appropriate to a Hunnic chieftain, he thought.[15]

Narses understood the value of old-fashioned Roman discipline and drill. During interludes between hostilities he saw to it that his men underwent systematic practice in horsemanship and infantry maneuvers, even in shouting the war cry. Imposing Roman discipline was something of a feat in itself. Narses had to harangue Heruls, Huns, and Isaurians, the backbone of his army, telling them that he, their Armenian general, expected every man to be worthy of his Roman ancestors. The positive response of the troops is one more testimony to the enduring power of the name of Rome.

Narses had the ungrateful task of administering reconstruction of the ravaged country. For twelve years he wrestled with problems inherent in decayed cities, desolate farmlands, and an exhausted population. No one would have been capable of responding with gratitude or appreciation. Inevitably a delegation went to Constantinople to tell the emperor that "where Narses the Eunuch rules, he makes us subject to slavery." They would prefer to be servants of the barbarians, they said bitterly. Rumor has it that Narses responded to this attack by inviting the Lombards to occupy Italy, though there is little to substantiate the charge. People need scapegoats. Stilicho was blamed for incursions by Goths and Huns, and Boniface was accused of luring the Vandals to Africa. If we look ahead we find the Venerable Bede having similar things to say about Vortigern, on whose shoulders he lays the blame for the Saxon invasion of Britain.

The charge against Narses sounds silly. He was recalled by the busybody Empress Sophia in 567 (her husband, Justin II, was a cipher). It was only logical for the Lombards to take advantage of the general unrest. Those who said that Narses enticed the Lombards with a description of the wonderful fertility of Italy overlooked the fact that the Lombards had been able to see it for themselves, when they came there in strength to fight under Narses in 552. They had been sent home after the victory over the Ostrogoths, but it is entirely likely that Lombards had been talking about Italy and keeping a watchful eye on it since that time.

The Lombards poured into northern Italy in 568, just a brief sixteen years

Plate 61. Ivory throne of Bishop Maximianus, Ravenna, Italy, detail. The throne was almost certainly a gift of Emperor Justinian, to mark the reestablishment of Byzantine power in Ravenna and to designate the bishop as the emperor's representative. It was probably sent to Ravenna in 547 (Beckwith, *Coptic Sculpture, 300–1300*, p. 48). The carvings were executed in either Alexandria or Constantinople. The peacock was a symbol of immortality. For an entertaining account of Augustine's experiment to determine whether the flesh of the peacock is actually incorruptible, see his *City of God* 21.4. *Courtesy of Museo arcivescovile, Ravenna, Italy.*

after Narses's reconquest of the peninsula in the emperor's name. There were not many Lombards, even though they called themselves an army; however, their presence put forces into play that far exceeded their own disruptive power.[16] They came in as conquerors, meeting little opposition. The very idea of accommodating themselves to existing institutions or incorporating themselves into the structure of the empire did not occur to them.[17] Their set of mind was wholly barbaric. Pillage was one of the chief delights of their warfare. The most valued treasure that their king possessed was a drinking vessel made from the skull of a detested enemy. The Lombard historian Paul the Deacon saw it a century later, when it was still a royal treasure: "I speak the truth in Christ. I saw King Ratchis holding this cup in his hand on a certain festal day, to show it to his friends." This looks like an odd throwback to the ancient Scythians, whose similar behavior was described by Herodotus.

The invaders never managed to conquer all of Italy. They scooped out territory for themselves in the north and along the backbone of the peninsula but were unable to drive Byzantine forces from the Adriatic strongholds. They never permanently cut the corridor between Ravenna and Rome. Lombard territory was divided into "dukedoms," some of which subsequently became so strong that they were virtually independent, notably Friuli, Benevento and Spoleto.

Tribal defenders, along with their families, were stationed at points where they could keep a lookout for possible attackers. There are still traces of these arrangements. The name of the pre-Italian Lombard unit, *fara* (a group of families on a war footing for raiding purposes) persists in such modern place-names as Fara d'Adda and Farra d'Alpago. The many churches dedicated to Saint Michael—274 of them—are Lombard. These Arian establishments usually were on heights, dominating the churches in the lowlands dedicated to Saint Martin by Catholics.[18]

A formal land settlement inevitably had to follow the first ugly months, but the Romans could not expect anything like the arrangement with the Ostrogoths, the former "guests" who had preempted one-third of the land and left the rest in Roman hands. The Lombards had an entirely different concept of the relationship between man and the soil. This was the idea of the *gewere*, which entailed a multiplicity of uses and aspects for the same area. Thus it was possible for one individual to have a *gewere* for the actual piece of land, another for the trees growing on it, and still another for its springs and wells. All of this must have spelled utter confusion to the Roman mind, because in Roman law *dominium* was indivisible.[19] Scholars have never agreed on the interpretation of the few sparse lines in the sources that supposedly tell what happened. The present consensus appears to be that the Lombards demanded and received one-third of the products of the soil and may not necessarily have lived on the land themselves. The unfortunates who had to deliver the products of their labor were not much better than serfs, but at least the peasants were not reduced to slavery in the Roman meaning of the word. A slave in Lombard tradition was a person, not a chattel. References in later Lombard law codes may concern the Romans, though they are never specifically mentioned by name. The *aldii* (probably the Romans) were half free.[20]

The dukedoms must have had a promising look of anarchy to bureaucratic minds in Constantinople, though the system was presumably nothing new to the Lombards. Before they entered Italy, they divided their territories into cantons. The patrician Longinus at Ravenna, possibly hoping that everything relating to the Lombards would come crashing down, appears to have entered into some dubious dealings at the Lombard court in the early days of the

Plate 62. A Lombardic Virgin Mary, eighth century, the Duomo, Cividale del Friuli, Italy. Detail of a Visitation scene on the so-called Altar of Ratchis. The Virgin has a cross on her brow to indicate her sanctity. *Courtesy of Museo archeologico nationale, Cividale del Friuli, Italy.*

occupation. When King Alboin's queen, Rosamond, brought about the murder of her lord for the colorful reason that he had forced her to drink a toast from his famous cup, which was made from the skull of her royal father, she and her accomplices fled at once to Ravenna. Conveyances seem to have been provided to speed them on their way, and when they arrived in Ravenna, Longinus received the queen cordially.

Constantinople launched various other attacks in an effort to recover Italy. Emperor Tiberius sent an expeditionary force in 575, perhaps believing that the Lombards had been fatally weakened by lack of central authority. Their second king, Cleph, had been murdered the year before, and administration had gone to the hands of thirty-five dukes, most of whom were deeply distrustful of each other. The Lombards proceeded to chop Tiberius's army to bits and kill the commanding officer. Next the emperor encouraged envoys from Rome to try their hands at bribing some of the more powerful dukes or, failing that, hiring Frankish mercenaries. Tiberius could not do much more: he had his hands full defending the East.

Tiberius's successor put pressure on the Franks and Burgundians, to no avail. In 584, Childebert of the Frankish kingdom of Austrasia accepted a handsome sum from Emperor Maurice and marched against the Lombards. This endeavor turned out to be a fiasco when the Lombards refused battle, and the potential enemies made peace instead. By that time the Lombards again had a king, Authari, who significantly gave himself the Roman military name Flavius, presumably to indicate that there was going to be stability on Italian soil. It remained for the Holy See, a century and a half later, effectively to stir up another Frankish dynasty for the sake of managing "the unspeakable Lombards."

In 586 a new office was created, that of exarch, at Ravenna. The exarch was to be commander-in-chief of the Byzantine Empire in the West. He had about the same kind of authority that Theodoric the Ostrogoth had possessed, except that an exarch could be recalled at the emperor's pleasure, whereas Theodoric, the king of his people, could not be easily dislodged. The exarch Smaragdus managed to work out an agreement for a cessation of hostilities, but war broke out again when a new Lombard king was chosen. He was King Agilulf, the former duke of Turin, the second husband of Authari's widow, the pious Theudelinda. After Agilulf's accession little is heard of any positive action from Constantinople. The effect was to turn the remnants of Byzantine Italy into a frontier. The traditional field army tended to merge with locally recruited garrison troops, because no more forces were forthcoming from the East. In this new arrangement the locals inevitably came under the jurisdiction of the eastern military commanders, since they were now part of the Byzantine defense establishment. We might almost think of protofeudalism.[21]

Edward Gibbon contemptuously dismissed the Italians as "pusillanimous" in the face of the Lombards, not considering how drained everybody must have been feeling. Even staunch Pope Gregory, whom we still rightly call "the Great," wavered when he looked over the walls of Rome to see people with halters around their necks being dragged off to slavery. He moaned, "My soul is weary of my life. . . . My soul melteth away for very heaviness."

The long struggle to recover Italy had given the lower classes time and reason to nurture anti-Greek sentiments. Resentment had grown during the short reconstruction period, directed against the tax collectors, those living symbols of an emperor's cynical concern for the well-being of his distant subjects. Why not submit to new masters? Could they be any worse?

The upper classes may have nourished an unreasoning hope that the crude, shaggy people would somehow vanish into thin air. Alaric and his Visigoths had failed in Italy, and so had Attila and his Huns. Even valiant Teias's shields could not prevent the Ostrogoths from coming to grief. Wary Romans buried their treasure and scurried off to Constantinople in the belief that some fine day they might return in peace. Their property, alas, has been recovered by archaeologists' spades.

As opposed to unreasoning hope for worldly serenity, there was also a kind of gallows mentality abroad. Overwhelmed by endless waves of woe, many accepted the doomsayers as the true prophets. The best course would be to hand over one's land and riches to the church, an act signifying submission to the divine will.

Whatever the thought processes may have been, the result was the same. While the peasant remained immobilized and braced himself for the worst, the townsman was pressed into military service under a Byzantine commander, and the aristocrat who might have spearheaded a defense effort disappeared. More specifically, the Roman Senate disappeared, its long history that reached so far back into antiquity simply trailing off into nothing. The Senate was still a functioning body in 579, when a delegation was sent to Constantinople to call urgently for help. In 593 the pope stood alone, lamenting, "Ubi enim senatus?" "Where is the Senate?" The Senate is gone.[22] Undoubtedly many senators and members of their class were felled in the course of the first Lombard incursion. Some survivors lingered on in Italy, having no civil responsibility but solacing themselves with empty titles that could still be purchased at the Eastern court. Many exiled themselves. For all intents and purposes the Senate and the aristocrats had departed. Moreover, the Senate could not easily be renewed. Emperor Justinian's Pragmatic Sanction of 554 left only four offices in the West that carried membership in the Senate—that is, the Senate at Constantinople.[23] Inevitably, with the stalemate between the exarch and the Lombards, and in the absence of any civil authority in Rome, it devolved upon the church, with valiant Gregory at its head, to fill the breach.

What resources precisely did the church have, in this desperate time?

Once there had been huge patrimonies, stretching almost as far as the remotest reaches of the empire. On the soil of Italy those church lands in territories dominated by the Lombards were as good as lost, at least for the time being. The Arian conquerors had no interest in the preservation of Catholic properties. In territory under Byzantine control the situation was not much better, because military officials were unscrupulous enough to exploit their position. They did not hesitate to force churches to lease their lands for a token payment, after which the payment was conveniently forgotten.[24]

Church lands in Gaul were generally administered from Arles, a system which presented difficulties because of the location, and those in Africa, Sardinia, and Corsica were not particularly productive. Sicily, therefore, was the chief source of revenue and grain. Pope Gregory's own family holdings were there; he had turned them over to the church when he abandoned public life, as he thought, to become a monk. It may have been his familiarity with these family holdings that allowed him to manage the Sicilian lands so well for the benefit of the Roman people.

In the final analysis the greatest resource of the church and the forsaken population of Rome was "God's consul," frail, determined Gregory, who, though he might moan, groan, and weep, never knew how to give up. No one ever ascended to the papal throne in times more dire. Gregory's predecessor had died in a plague, which was the aftermath of a terrible flood that had caused the Tiber to overflow, wrecked the granaries, and even released a swarm of serpents that hurried down to Ostia in the wake of a large dragon, if Gregory of Tours is to be taken at his word. The plague continued to ravage the city. Eighty victims dropped dead right in the church, during a penitential that the new pope was conducting. Duke Ariulf of Spoleto was moving inexorably against Rome, and the city was jammed with frightened, hungry refugees.

The embattled Gregory handled this crisis firmly, prayerfully and boldly going far beyond his competence as head of the church. Political instincts were alive in this former prefect of the city, a monk who had been unwillingly drafted for his high office. We find him addressing a letter to General Velox, telling him that, whereas he had been prepared to send the general soldiers required for frontier service, he had held them in Rome for defense of the city. He was ready to relinquish them, he wrote, but Velox would do well to confer with the other generals in the field, with a view to possible joint action. Specifically, the pope wanted the Byzantine forces to attack the Spoleto region to turn back Ariulf.

Gregory ventured further into military affairs by personally appointing a military governor for the threatened town Nepi. The peremptory letter that he sent to the people of Nepi left little doubt that Rome had a commander: "Whosoever resists his lawful commands will be deemed a rebel against us."[25]

In the following year, 592, Gregory again gave tactical instructions to the generals, but before there could have been any response to his letter, Duke Ariulf himself appeared on the scene. Both Rome and Naples were menaced because the duke of Benevento was cooperating with Ariulf. Gregory's reaction was to appoint a tribune for Naples, with orders that the city garrison obey this man's commands. Since there still was no action from either Ravenna or Constantinople, Gregory took the inevitable step and personally entered into peace negotiations with Duke Ariulf. He appears to have bought him off with five hundred pounds of gold from the church treasury. Rome was saved from the shoddy fate of becoming the property of a bloodthirsty Lombard duke, but both Ravenna and Constantinople were deeply angered. Peace between Spoleto and Rome was anything but desirable in their view.[26] The exarch deliberately broke Gregory's truce and marched into Lombard territory to take the key city, Perugia.

A year later, 593, the new Lombard king, Agilulf, had consolidated his power sufficiently to turn his attention to Rome, which still loomed as the greatest though most fateful of all prizes. Rome lay under siege once more, but not for long, for Agilulf had to keep a watchful eye on his northern lands. He had already proved his point by recapturing everything that the exarch had taken the previous year, including Perugia. Agilulf and Gregory probably never met on the steps of Saint Peter's, as legend would have it, but it is interesting to learn that Gregory sometimes referred to himself as "the Lombards' paymaster."

By 595, Gregory had given up hope that Ravenna would ever abandon its obstructionist tactics. He arrived at the point of threatening to negotiate directly and on his own with the Lombard king. The reaction in Constantinople was explosive. There was a furious exchange of letters. Gregory could lose his temper at times, and he lost it now:

> If I had been aught but a fool, I should never have endured what I do endure for this place amid the swords of the Lombards. As to my report concerning Ariulf, that he was ready with all his heart to come over to the Republic, I am accused of being a liar. I was robbed of the peace which, without any expense to the State I made with the Lombards. . . . There was a worse affliction when Agilulf came. . . . an excuse is sought for blaming us because forsooth the supply of corn was deficient.[27]

There was quiet on both sides after this outburst, but Gregory continued to boil whenever he thought of the exarch. He wrote to one of his bishops that "his malice is worse than the swords of the Lombards."

Pope Gregory was not young, and his health was always precarious, for he suffered from intermittent fever and dysentery. Sometimes the mere thought of all of his burdens brought him close to the breaking point. This found expression in exasperation over small matters. He wrote to his steward: "Thou hast sent me one sorry nag. . . . That nag I cannot ride, he is such a sorry one."[28] Yet this was the man who found the strength to administer not only the church but also the distant Sicilian estates and to manage the poor relief, the distribution of the dole, the housing of refugees, the restoration of aqueducts, the repair of city walls, the ransom of captives, and the dispatch of a mission to far-off England—yes, even the composition of a torrent of homilies and pastoral letters. His Sicilian stewards had to be on their toes. They received detailed instructions about the disposition of barren cows and the care of indigents in their neighborhoods. Above all, they were admonished to do justice to the peasants.

Gregory died in the hope that a better day might be dawning. There had been one more violent clash when a new exarch attacked the Lombards and carried off King Agilulf's own daughter. The infuriated ruler made an alliance with those threatening enemies of the East the Avars and laid about him angrily to capture and reduce Padua, Mantua, and Milan and to close in on Ravenna. A new exarch—Smaragdus again—was sent out, and he, assessing the situation realistically, concluded a truce that was supposed to last for three years. It was in this period that the exhausted Pope Gregory died, rousing himself for one final feeble effort, to send a loving letter to King Agilulf's queen, Theudelinda, whose son had been baptized in the Catholic faith.

This prince of the church was a personage to be reckoned with not only in the City of God. Gregory often signed himself "The servant of the servants of God." Gibbon says uncharitably that "his devotion, and it might be sincere, pursued the path that would have been chosen by a crafty and ambitious statesman." Gregory's weak body housed much more than the soul of a crafty statesman. There were two indomitable spirits in him, that of an antique patriot and that of an emotional, God-fearing monk endowed with an almost modern social conscience. It may be no accident that Gregory's stately throne with its carved motifs from a distant classic past stands today in a tiny chapel opposite a bleak little stone cell that is said to have been his own. Those stern senators whom Livy described would have understood Gregory and would never have questioned his motives. Seated all day long like statues in the doorways of their homes, almost eight hundred years before Gregory's time, holding their wands of office, they did not so much as glance at the rough, pillaging Gauls who roamed the forsaken streets. Rome must not be surrendered ever.

King Agilulf survived Gregory until 615. From that time, in spite of the wistful hopes of the exiles and their families, the Lombards were to be in control of central Italy for more than a century and a half. We do not need to follow every step of the way because the pattern was more or less set. It is worth our while, however, to look at the traces of the gradual Romanizing of the Lombards.

A succession of Lombard kings viewed themselves as lawgivers. Rothari was the first of these (his *Edict* was published in 643). Next came Grimwald, in 688, and then Liutprand, who added more than 150 titles to the Lombard legal code between 713 and 735. The last contributions were by Ratchis in 745 and 746 and Aistulf in 750 and 755. The society reflected by Rothari's laws was still deep in barbarism, but some of the legislation, no doubt set down for practical purposes, was an entering wedge for more civilized ideas. The problem was that Lombard society was small; it would not do, walled around as the Lombards were by alien forces, to continue indulging in their traditional suicidal practice of the vendetta. Honor is honor, but now it was to be satisfied by monetary compensation, not by blood feuds. The laws offer us vivid glimpses of the Lombards going about the solemn business of administering the new justice:

> Blows on the head, breaking bones (per bone) 12 *solidi*. No count to be taken above 36 *solidi*: and the broken bones are to be counted on this principle, that one bone shall be large enough to make an audible sound when thrown against a shield at twelve feet distance on the road.[29]

By the time of King Liutprand the legislation was framed in such a way that it becomes evident that there was doubt about the validity of proof of guilt by torture. At least there was provision for some kind of restitution of payments, should it turn out that an innocent person had been punished.[30]

It remained for the church to introduce the idea that there was a third party in all disputes. No matter how the contenders might settle their differences, God must have satisfaction. There had to be penance—fixed tariffs here also, corresponding to the magnitude of the offense against the deity. Once the Lombards accepted this inherently ethical approach, they were on their way out of barbarism.

Rather unexpectedly the Lombards became great protectors of the church. The first to receive land and protection from the Lombards were outsiders in a way, rather like their sponsor, the Catholic schismatic Queen Theudelinda. These people were the Irish *peregrini*, led by that formidable saint Columban, whose checkered career had taken from his homeland across Gaul to Luxeuil and from there, banished by the Burgundians, to Italy. Theudelinda and Agilulf received him kindly at Pavia and allowed him to establish a monastery at Bobbio, in the hills not far from Piacenza. Columban was always one to speak his mind. He had refused to bend to orthodox bishops in Gaul, he had infuriated a Burgundian queen by telling her that her illegitimate grandsons were the offspring of a harlot, and he had sent a rather impertinent letter to the pope on the question of the date for the celebration of Easter. Once settled in Lombard territory, Columban informed Pope Boniface IV that the schism among the Catholics over the Three Chapters controversy was a matter of concern to Agilulf and Theudelinda. This schism revolved around the efforts of Emperor Justinian to find a solution to the problems caused by the Council of Chalcedon. Columban thought that Boniface was wrong to follow the policies of his predecessor, since "perchance the Watchman [a pun on the name of Pope Vigilius] did not watch well."[31]

Columban's ideas on penance were appallingly harsh, but that did not deter people from flocking to him. Individuals who thought that retribution could be computed by the thud of a bone against a shield may not have found Columban's punishments as dire as they seem to us. It was Columban's Bobbio mission that insinuated into the Lombard consciousness the notion that there had to be an accounting with God. They were still barbarians, but the minds of the Lombards were no longer in the German forests.

In the end the Lombards went down before the Franks, who were called in by the pope in desperation. King Aistulf was defeated by Pippin the Short. Then came Charlemagne, and the last Lombard king, Desiderius, was taken captive at Pavia in 774.

When the Lombards fell, one man who had flourished in the general excitement and hurly-burly of a royal court fled to Monte Cassino to become a monk. Paul the Deacon, as we know him, emerged less than ten years later to put the case of a dispossessed brother of his before the Frankish king. About three years later, his mission accomplished, Paul returned to Monte Cassino, where he settled down after all the glories of life at Charlemagne's distinguished court to write his history of the Lombards. Paul celebrated the national traditions of his people and their cultural union, as he saw it, with the world of orthodox Christianity. With profound sincerity though not too much accuracy, he revealed to his readers how fortunate the Lombards were to have come into the orbit of true Christians. The theme was embroidered to show the underlying spiritual meaning of old tribal legends and mold them into a form in which Byzantine, Roman, and Carolingian ideas intermingled. In other words, Paul the Deacon was a forward-looking man. This Lombard monk was one of the first Europeans.

Monasticism had taken firm hold in Europe by Paul the Deacon's day. Let us now consider that great movement, from its beginnings in the Egyptian desert.

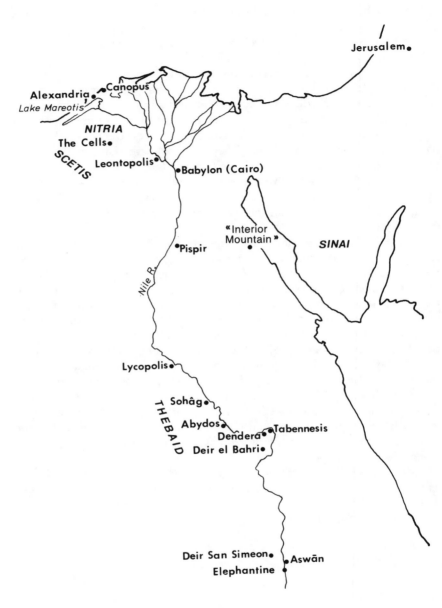

Egypt

DESERTS
AND HOLY ISLANDS

IN Athanasius's time, Alexandria was a teeming cosmopolitan center with a
mercurial street population. Riots and violent clashes were endemic, yet
through the jostling mobs there strode people of vast calm and erudition who
had been drawn to the city by the famed schools and libraries. Alexandria was
elitist, a forcing ground where acute minds could test and examine ideas from
all over the world. Hellenistic philosophy was strongly represented, as were
the Eastern mystery religions and Judaism. Christianity itself "grew wild," [1]
burgeoning there in myriad forms. Even remote India contributed in a tenuous way to the rich intellectual mixture.

Of all the lands that encircle the Mediterranean, Egypt was the ideal place
for nurturing the seed of monasticism. The tendency to the contemplative life
was there long before the Christian Era. As far back as the twelfth century B.C.
we find this writing: "Thou sweet Well for him that thirsted in the desert: it is
closed to him who speaketh, but it is open to him who is silent." [2] Chaeremon,
in the first century of the Christian era, wrote of those who

> chose sanctuaries as the place in which to study philosophy, since to dwell with the
> statues of the gods was in harmony with their utter longing for vision. . . . They
> gave up their existence to contemplation, and trained themselves to endure hun-
> ger and thirst and scanty food for all their life. [3]

Although abstinence from animal food became generally associated with
asceticism, it was peculiarly Egyptian and was not foreign to the population as
a whole. The reason for it may lie in the ancient joining of the various *nomes*
(districts) by a process of political fusion. Each *nome* had its own animal totem;
with unification all animals may have come to be respected. This might account for a popular taboo, but perhaps the explanation of the ascetics' self-
denial is more complicated. They may have had some acquaintance with the
vegetarian practices of the Buddhists. Trade relationships were established
with India very early, and merchants coming up the Red Sea and overland to
Alexandria might have brought such ideas along. [4]

Plate 63. Clay lamp showing Alexandria harbor, second century. British Museum BM 527 (Townley Collection). *Courtesy of British Museum, London.*

In Judaic tradition the idea of purification and withdrawal for the sake of revelation was as old as Moses' ascent of Sinai. We need only remind ourselves of Jehovah's specific demands when the people of Israel had been assembled at the foot of the mountain.[5] Philo of Alexandria, who combined the blood of Greeks and Hebrews in his veins, offered a new twist. He went beyond Greek intellectualism, adding the Jewish notion of revelation and mystery: "The injunction to free oneself from sense and strive upward by means of knowledge remained, but . . . only ecstasy produced by God himself was able to lead to the reality above reason."[6] It is not astonishing to find that the more intense seekers after truth who were familiar with Philo's teachings should adopt asceticism as the way to higher wisdom.

As we move into Christian times, we find a group of Jewish ascetics (the Therapeutae) living a communal life on a hill near Lake Mareotis, not far from Alexandria. Philo's *De vita contemplativa* is our only source of information about them. Philo himself must have spent some time among the Therapeutae,[7] though the course of his life was to take him into the swirl of public affairs both in Alexandria and abroad. Perhaps he found that he did not have a true vocation for such a demanding existence. He says that, although he often went into the wilderness to concentrate on some subject, he "derived no advantage from doing so." His mind persisted in straying, "scattered or bitten by passion."[8] The Therapeutae were deadly serious in their pursuit of mystic truth. They had disposed of their possessions and lived in a simple, severe community, following a rigid ritual that included song and sacred dance. They consumed ceremonial meals together that consisted solely of leavened bread, hyssop, salt, and clear water. This life comprised their whole duty as "servants of God" (the name Therapeutae has the double meaning "healers" and "servants"; according to Hans-Gottfried Schönfeld, the name was probably made up by outsiders, not members of the sect, and meant "servants of God"). It seems unlikely that there was ever any contact to speak of between the Therapeutae and the Christians, though some historians once followed Eusebius in his judgment that they were the precursors of the Christian monks. In any case, this example of asceticism, which seems to have persisted in organized form for a long period, could not have failed to contribute to the general trend.[9] The link in the chain is provided by Origen of Alexandria. His rigorous self-denial must have been widely publicized because he was a prominent man. Certainly it was to have its counterparts in the desert, though Origen himself was a city dweller and in fact spent about half his active life in Caesarea, not in Egypt. He took Jesus' words with the sober conviction that the master meant precisely what he said, as reported in the Gospel according to Matthew.[10] In line with this belief Origen castrated himself, never owned more than one garment, went barefoot, and slept on the hard floor. His days were devoted to the labor of teaching and writing, his nights to the study of the Scriptures. Unlike many Egyptian monks, Origen did not let his austerity become an end in itself. He remained a prodigious scholar right into his old age, when persecution killed him.

Perhaps Origen would not have been troubled much by the friction that arose in later times among the desert monks, evidenced by an undercurrent of resentment against scholarly Greek speakers displayed by Copts recruited from the ranks of the lowly townspeople and the fellahin. Origen thought that Christianity offered a twofold way, one for simple sinners, who required healing and redemption, and another for the pure in soul and body, who sought the unveiling of the mystery implicit in the life of Jesus.[11]

If Origen supplied a link to monastic asceticism in general, the link to anchoritic practice was provided by Hierax of Leontopolis. The lifetimes of Origen and Hierax overlap somewhat, but Origen left Egypt in the year 232, and the date of Hierax's birth is 245 at the very earliest.[12] Therefore, there was no possibility of any interaction between them.

Hierax was a canny old hermit who lived in a cell not far from the first milestone beyond his native city in the Nile Delta. He had far-ranging knowledge, including Greek science, astronomy and the healing arts, and possibly magic as well. He supported himself as a calligrapher; he was able to exercise his skill well up into his ninth decade because his eyesight never failed him, and his hands remained steady.

Hierax knew the Bible by heart. He decided that the only truly innovative feature to be found in the New Testament was a change in the status of marriage. Those who married could not expect to enter the kingdom of heaven. This stern preachment attracted a following.

Sources concerning the Hierachites are dim and difficult. They must have been just one of many small Christian sects in Egypt. They were bound to die out, because they did not permit anybody to worship with them who had not wholly accepted their way. It would be false to think of them as schismatics or heretics because there was hardly any established dogma as yet. There were few people in Egypt with authority to enforce "right thinking." It is important to be aware of Hierax because he foreshadows things to come. Like Antony and the cenobitic abbots, Hierax was a Copt, in whom the ethnic character of the Egyptians was unmistakable. Again like Antony, Hierax had a following, which is an indication that the notion of an anchoritic life had already become seductive and that a strong personality could sway many persons. It almost seems appropriate to speak of the beginnings of a movement.

Hierax was a solitary. His life exceeded the bounds of early Christian practice, in which at that time self-denial and marriage had been able to coexist. If his idea should catch hold, it was radical enough to present a problem to the church. Monasticism was bound to teeter on the brink of the unacceptable as the church became embroiled in secular affairs. It is not difficult to see that someday the conflict between prelates and independent monks might become critical.[13]

Meanwhile, the stage was set for a strange drama in the desert. No matter how hard they tried, the monks could not escape the world, and in turn the world could not escape them. Their kindness, their gentleness, their zeal, and their fanaticism all had an effect on the outsiders who importunately broke in on them. For better or worse no man could escape into silence.

Monasticism was shaped as much by the physical geography of Egypt and the course of political events as by the extraordinary personality of Antony and the great cenobitic leaders. Egypt is a slender stalk of a country, bearing the flaring flower of the Nile Delta at its northern end. If flight became necessary for any reason—whether philosophical or political—there lay the desert, just inches away, ready to engulf the fugitive for indefinite periods in its tremendous silence. Again, because of the geography of the Nile Valley, even those who fled were still accessible to anyone persistent enough to follow (see color plate 9). A hermit like Antony would have to solve the problem posed by swarms of eager disciples.

The Egyptian desert has little in common with the glowing desert of the American Southwest, with its reds and golds, its dusty green of sagebrush and juniper, and the hypnotic rolling motion of the tumbleweed. In Egypt the desolate pale expanse of shale, sand, and flint that flanks the lush ribbon of vegetation along the riverbanks is appalling in the stark threat of its motionlessness.[14] In such a surrealist landscape Antony met a centaur, and many of his fellow "athletes of God" who built their little domed cells in the wasteland were familiar with the sight of demons.

Why would anyone deliberately set himself down in such a place for a lifetime of exile? Behind this terrible effort by simple, unlettered folk was the atavistic pull of magic.[15] In spite of the despair and loneliness, and in spite of the boredom that weighed down like a stone, a desert recluse's life was one of hope because he was substituting the formidable magic of his own personal holiness for the sterility of ritual purity. By ceaseless fasting and sexual abstinence he proposed to tear a heavenly crown of martyrdom through the iron gates of life, and by mystic ecstasy he might even have a foretaste of the bliss that would be his reward. Although the monk would have been first to deny it with tears and protestations, he had high hope of personal salvation.[16] There were valid practical reasons, too, for making an escape to the desert in the fourth century. Sometimes it was not the soul but the body that required saving. The last official persecution ended in 312, but the tax burden was so intolerable that whole communities are known to have taken cover either in the desert or in the Nile Delta swamps, rather as the Bacaudae in Gaul fled in response to similar pressures. The fugitives may have drifted into monastic communities for the sake of anonymity and protection, not necessarily out of spiritual longing.

The Peace of the Church unexpectedly gave an impetus to the monastic movement. With the picture of the sufferings of martyrs and confessors bright in their memories, and with the conviction that those fortunate few would surely pass through the heavenly gates, people sought martyrdom for themselves. What better way than to withdraw to the desert and challenge the horrible demons lurking there?

Saint Antony was a trailbreaker. He was born around 251, while Decius was emperor. In his boyhood he may have heard first-hand stories of what the last great persecution had been like. No doubt he was an impressionable youngster. Otherwise, why at age twenty did he feel so strongly that the words of the Gospel read in church were specifically intended for him? "If thou wilt be perfect, go and sell all that thou hast . . . and follow me." He gave away his worldly goods and lived a sober life in his own village, sheltering himself in a shed at the bottom of his garden, earnestly visiting the hermits living on the outskirts of the village to learn from them. His private temptations were gradually overcome in this way. He then moved up onto the next rung of the difficult ladder to purity. He had to brave the demons who, driven from his mind, now lay in wait for him outside. He went forth to meet them, just as Jesus had gone out to confront Satan in the wilderness at a similar stage of his own training. Antony moved from his little garden shed to a tomb outside the village.[17] The demons were real to Antony; we may as well accept them. Like Antony, the demons were a product of Egypt. They had none of the threatening grandeur of fallen angels, as did those of Syria. Their malevolence was expressed in earthy, primitive kinds of mischief-making. Their favorite prank in attacking the unwary was to assume a disguise. They could appear as beautiful women or giants or almost any other kind of individual. They sang, hissed, jibbered, snarled, and even chanted psalms. They might appeal piteously for help, as the "boy" who said that he was pursued by hyenas; that particular demon, unable to overcome the resolution of his would-be victim, lost his temper and went off in a huff, dissolving himself into "wild asses galloping off and kicking up stones."[18] Another demon managed to hide inside a bandaged mummy, to tease a saintly man who had bedded down for the night in a cave and was using the mummy for a pillow. That demon failed too because the intrepid monk thumped the mummy and ordered him to shut up.[19] Antony's demons beat him into insensibility. His friends thought that he had died and took his limp body to the church for funeral rites, but he revived and feebly insisted on being taken back to the scene of his ordeal. He won his victory at last, only to move on to a still more difficult challenge. This time he moved out onto the desert. An abandoned fort was his abode for the next twenty fearsome years. When his friends ultimately broke down the entrance of his solitary habitation, Antony emerged with a firm step, composed in mind and body. As Athanasius expressed it in his famous biography, Antony was "all balanced."[20]

Antony had become that most wonderful of beings, a free man, free as Adam before the Fall. His face shone, but not with the frightening luminosity that made it necessary for Moses to veil himself after his encounters with the Almighty. Antony's cheerful countenance was that of a man who could say with disarming simplicity, "I no longer fear God: I love him."[21] Old Antony himself was lovable. He performed miracles of exorcism and healing, and he was immensely wise, but it was his human kindliness that made people eager to be near him and live like him. Under his touch the desert indeed became a city, peopled by those who flocked to his side.

He was soon surrounded, there at Pispir on the Nile. It was no life for an anchorite. Antony left the "Outer Mountain" colony that had coalesced around his cell. On impulse he traveled eastward with a caravan, halting at his "Interior Mountain," a small oasis not far from the Red Sea. It was a quiet solitude, in which Antony lived for the next forty-three years, tending his tiny garden plot, weaving palm-leaf mats, loving the place and communing with his God. People tried to follow him even to the Interior Mountain, but the journey was a hazardous one. The old saint preferred to take the risk himself. He walked to the Outer Mountain at irregular intervals of days or weeks to offer consolation and advice to the monks living there and to the visitors who patiently awaited his coming.

This concern for others was typical of Antony, who never managed to become wrapped up in his own soul. Whereas some of his imitators spent a lifetime gazing into eternity, Antony was able to shift his attention to the world and the demands that it continued to make of him. He always stood up for his principles. When there was a new flurry of persecution, he deliberately went down to Alexandria to comfort and encourage the confessors in their stress, willing to share their martyrdom for a good cause. He was aware also of the problems that his friend Athanasius confronted in the Arian controversy. Antony was supposedly illiterate, but he had scribes handy: he sent a letter to the emperor on Athanasius's behalf when the prelate was exiled for the first time. The letter did not help much, but the emperor did at least respond courteously. When Athanasius was finally allowed to return, Antony made a point of going to Alexandria to show solidarity with his friend.

Antony was intensely interested in developments in monastic life. Although the ways of the great cenobitic founders Amoun and Pachomius were not his way, he approved and expressed encouragement. In the year 338, when he went to Alexandria, Antony probably also visited the growing monastic community at Nitria, to find out how things were going there. Nitria, more or less a gateway to the desert for one who was outbound from Alexandria, was undergoing a population explosion. Abbot Amoun was worried about providing quiet and solitude for those of his community who wanted it in a setting not unlike that of modern urban sprawl. Within a few decades thousands of monks would be living in Nitria. Amoun and Antony talked about the matter, and one afternoon they set out together to walk away from the settlement, onto the true desert. They plodded for twelve miles under the blazing African sun (Antony was eighty-seven years old) and planted a cross in the wilderness, marking a place where monks could be alone and yet have some tenuous contact with their fellows at Nitria. That was the beginning of the Cells, which were to become world famous.[22] Yet even at the Cells there would be no escape.

With such a multitude the solitary life that Antony led and that many of his admirers craved for themselves was a practical impossibility. They found a compromise in the broad arrangements of the Nitrian community. Those living at Nitria were organized loosely in "stations," where as many as 250 monks might live apart or in pairs, meeting once a week for worship and a shared meal. They had a communal bakery and agents who took the products of their labor (ropes, mats, and linen) into Alexandria to sell in exchange for supplies. There appears to have been a priest at Nitria from an early date. The monks had a rough system of discipline, evidenced by whips that hung from palm trees at the meeting place. They had a guesthouse in which visitors could stay—sometimes for periods that stretched into years. Nitria offered a testing place where those who dreamed of a harder ascetic life at the Cells could go into training and toughen themselves.

At the Cells the forms of asceticism could be bleak. There were terrible excesses, especially in the early days. One man punished himself for having killed a mosquito by banishing himself to a marsh, where he lived naked among stinging insects for half a year, to return at last almost unrecognizable in his disfigurement.[23]

About forty miles beyond the Cells lay Scetis, the ultimate place of voluntary banishment.[24] Originally one lone hermit lived there, but he was followed even to that desolate hell of blinding heat: Chaeremon lived in a cave at Scetis, twelve miles from the nearest water. It seems unthinkable, yet it is a matter of record that by the time fashionable tourists began seeking out the holy recluses four communities had been established at Scetis.

Antony kept an attentive eye, though from a distance, on still another development: the surge in the monastic population hard by the Nile in the Thebaid.[25] The enormous settlement around Tabennesis (near modern Dendera) was the creation of the Coptic convert Pachomius, of whom Antony remarked that "he goes the way of the Apostles." Tabennesis was not intended to be a training ground like Nitria. The commitment there was to a lifetime of work and contemplation in a cenobitic setting. Of necessity a fairly formal character gradually evolved, and the community acquired its own written "rule." Parenthetically it should be noted that, although these monasteries had a rule, there was never a monastic order like that of the Benedictines either in Egypt or in those countries that were to take their inspiration from Egypt. At Tabennesis there were set hours for assembly and prayer, set kinds of instruction (all members of the community were required to learn to read), and set work routines, because in such a motley gathering there were many who were incapable of directing themselves. Tabennesis, with its complex of barracks and service buildings had something of the air of the headquarters of a modern thriving agribusiness. Swineherds, camel drivers, grain harvesters, reed gatherers—each had a place. Within the community were those with special skills who served their fellows—carpenters, metalworkers, shoemakers, tailors, and so on. Boats came and went, transporting the linen produced in the mills for sale in Alexandria.[26] All the linen woven by the monks, all the tanned hides, all the baskets and rope and other products that they offered for sale on a competitive market must have had a serious effect on regular industry in Egypt.[27]

Women lived in convents separate from the men's communities. The life of the recluse seems to have been hard on the women: they quarreled a lot and were shrill with each other at times. At least two are known to have committed suicide.

The Thebaid was Athanasius's hiding place on two occasions. His enthusiasm for the monks therefore lay not only in his personal friendship with Antony but also in grateful memory of his protectors. He appears to have written his biography of Antony while he was in hiding there for the second time.[28]

When Athanasius went to Rome in 340 to plead his case, he took along two monks, Ammonius Parotes and Isidore. Ammonius was one of Nitria's famous four "Tall Brothers." Ironically, this man dreamed the impossible dream of complete withdrawal from the world, yet he went obediently to the Eternal City. He it was who starved himself for salvation's sake; cut off his ear, thereby making himself ineligible for episcopal office;[29] and applied red-hot irons to his flesh to subdue desire. During his stay in Rome he stubbornly refused to visit the holy places except the tombs of the apostles, and persisted in his silent contemplation. Not so the second monk in Athanasius's party. Isidore became acquainted with "the entire Roman Senate and all the wives of the great men," including the lady Marcella.[30]

The names Antony, Pachomius, and Amoun were soon on the lips of many in the Eternal City. Roman names became familiar to the monks in their desert retreats, for converts like Paula and the lady Melania sought them out. Several grand personages, after tracking the great ones to their cells and insisting on conversing with them and showering them with gold, moved up to Palestine, there to settle around the holy places in monastic colonies fit to receive visiting bishops and royalty.

Acquaintance with Isidore and the enthusiasm generated by the story of Antony brought on a fever of emulation that raged among the self-consciously elite Romans of the senatorial class, especially the aristocratic ladies of untold wealth and piety like those who were to be so receptive to Saint Jerome and

Pelagius. Rome was fertile ground for the ascetic movement, but whereas in Egypt the population was temperamentally ready for what might almost be called a mass migration, a special group in Rome was the mainstay of monasticism. These individuals were undergoing their own crises in a changing world. In a word the great pagan families were in the throes of becoming Christianized. In the time that followed Symmachus's struggle to save the Altar of Victory and Emperor Theodosius's defeat of the usurper Eugenius, there were still many unhealed wounds, but the pagan aristocracy was as impressively viable as ever. This class looked back with proud nostalgia to the old Roman past when blue blood and stern *gravitas* were one. It placed great store on iron discipline.[31] The long-term solution was the slow conversion to sober Christianity, but meanwhile family life showed the strain. Many of the aristocrats had Christian wives who indulged their piety in a kind of reverse conspicuous consumption, giving lavishly to the poor, endowing churches, and so forth. The husbands looked on with some indulgence, evidently thinking that pagan tradition could be entrusted to their sons. The women, on the other hand, were dissatisfied and bored and sought some distinctive pattern of behavior that would set them apart. They responded to the example of the Egyptians by giving away their jewels, gold, and silk and retiring into the privacy of their elegant homes for prayer and edifying conversation. The lady Marcella was one of the first: she made her beautiful palace on the Aventine into a retreat. Soon headstrong ladies were giving away large estates that they controlled, much to the consternation of the pagan members of their families (we remember the story of Melania the Younger and the reaction of her family and the Senate).

The movement disturbingly assumed the character of a fad, and a loud public outcry occurred at the funeral of young Blaesilla, a daughter of Paula the Elder, whom Marcella had converted (that is, conversion to asceticism, not a turn from paganism to Christianity). Blaesilla undertook such rigors in her fasting that she died from a disease that must have been akin to anorexia nervosa.

There was something a little contrived about the monasteries of Jerusalem and Bethlehem.[32] Take the establishment of Melania the Younger, for example. She lived there in impressive abnegation, never bathing, humbly washing the feet of visitors, spending her nights in the study of elevating texts, yet, according to Palladius, she was wealthy: "She sold off everything she had, . . . keeping only her holdings in Sicily, Campania, and Africa." It is interesting to read that she arranged at her monastery "to do herself some of the daily work of her slave women, whom she made her associates in her ascetic practices." Paula the Elder made a practical division of the members of her establishments according to class: highborn, middle-class, and lower-class women lived, worked, and had their meals separately. A lady of noble birth

DESERTS AND HOLY ISLANDS

was required to have as her attendant someone who had never been part of her earlier household, lest familiar conversation between maid and lady about former grandeur and comforts prove to be a temptation to the delicate aristocrat. Presumably the maid would not be as sorely tried by remembrance of things past.

The Visigoths' invasion of Italy precipitated an outflow of wealthy refugees, but even earlier the desert monks had felt the repercussions of theological quarrels in the empire. After the death of Athanasius in 373, Emperor Valens, an Arian, appointed an Arian patriarch for Alexandria. Egyptian bishops were sent into exile, and for some obscure reason Nitria was attacked by soldiers on government order, and monks were beaten to death. The Theodosian Code for the year of Athanasius's death states that those who tried to escape public duty by joining the monks in the desert were to be dragged out. Possibly that is the explanation for the attack on Nitria.[33]

There was also the troubling fact that heresy or the suspicion of it lay heavy on the solitudes. Origen's elaborate teachings had traditionally been accepted without much question by the desert monks. Evagrius of Pontus, the leading Origenist of his day, lived and wrote in the Cells for almost fourteen years without being challenged. The simple Copts were a little suspicious of Evagrius and his great erudition, and he was never quite one of them, but it was not until a year or so after his death that the real trouble began. By then Origenism had come under attack overseas, led by Bishop Epiphanius of Cyprus. Suspicion seeped back into Egypt, where Evagrius's Origenist companions, the "Tall Brothers," still lived. The Coptic monks were not clear in their minds just what the problem was with Origen's doctrines, but that was uncomfortably revealed to them in a pastoral letter from Theophilus, the patriarch of Alexandria, sharply condemning anthropomorphism. In shock the Copts asked bitterly how they could pray if they were forbidden to think of God in human terms. Was *that* what Evagrius and Origen meant? Only one group at Scetis accepted the offensive letter or even allowed it to be read to the congregation. Others stormed to Alexandria to demand a retraction, setting off riots in that excitable city. Theophilus timidly reversed himself, ordering expulsion of the Origenists. His convictions were never strong. Besides, he had come into personal conflict with the Tall Brothers and may have welcomed the opportunity to drive them out.

What happened next is anyone's guess. Theophilus claimed that the Origenists had armed slaves and seized and fortified the assembly places. The monks retorted that drunken soldiers had broken in, causing general havoc. In 401 the Tall Brothers departed at the head of a band of about three hundred monks. They went first to Palestine and thence with a smaller group to Constantinople, where they laid their case before John Chrysostom, the fiery patriarch who was in conflict with his empress. Once more the Tall Brother

Ammonius, that paragon of anchorites, was forced out into the world, as he had been more than sixty years before, when Athanasius took him to Rome. Ammonius died overseas.

Chrysostom's welcome of the Tall Brothers served only to speed his downfall. In his own way Chrysostom undermined much that Nitria stood for. At his hands holy men who traditionally fled from even the simple priesthood were consecrated bishops. That happened to Palladius, the indefatigable eager pilgrim whose *Lausiac History* tells us much about the old heroes of the wasteland. Chrysostom made one of Evagrius's disciples bishop of Ephesus. John Cassian, a Scythian monk who had spent many years at Scetis, was made a deacon; his feet were thereby set on the path that he was to travel in Gaul.

Around 407 desert tribes burst into the Nitria Valley, massacring most of the monks. Several years later the ascetic Arsenius, who was among the few who had escaped, commented mournfully that "the world has lost Rome, and the monks Scetis." Survivors straggled off to Palestine. A tiny handful of them may have reached Ireland. There seems to be no difficulty inherent in the notion that they went so far afield, since Egyptian monks could travel from Alexandria to African ports and thence to Spain. In the reign of Huneric, Catholics from Tipasa made their way to Spain, taking along the body of Saint Salsa. In the sixth century, when the plains of Africa were prey to Moorish brigands, African churchmen were to be found in the Spanish backcountry. Contact between Spain and Ireland must have been close; we find proof of this in the similarity of Irish monastic practices and those in the Celtic region of Spain known as Galicia. All this might account for the lines in a twelfth-century Irish litany, the Litany of Oengus the Culdee, invoking the "seven Egyptians who lie in Disert Uilaig."[34] The disaster at Nitria was more than a physical loss: it was a deeply wounding psychological blow, like the fall of Rome.

The monks who remained in Egypt seem to have been unable to recapture the quality of detachment and generosity that had been characteristic of many of the original desert fathers. Latent fanaticism must have been promoted by the events that had forced them into contact with the outside world. When they saw themselves mirrored in the admiring eyes of the fashionable Roman visitors, their thought must have been at least tinged with some hint of their own excellence.[35] Schism within the community and the departure of the Origenists must have tended to confirm in them a sense of moral superiority. Then came the attack by desert marauders, to supply the feeling that they were persecuted. Altogether it would not take much to make zealots of them, and indeed they became so. Within a decade or two some of the Nitrians were known henchmen of the bigoted patriarch Cyril of Alexandria, abetting him in his personal warfare against heretics, Jews, and pagans. Responsibility cannot with certainty be laid on Cyril for the sordid murder of Hypatia, the noble

Plate 64. Turreted wall, Monastery of San Simeon, near Aswân, Egypt.

pagan philosopher-mathematician, but we know that Nitrian monks participated in that vicious act in 415. Hypatia's death outraged the civilized world, even in times when most people had been battered into a state of indifference to horror stories by the repeated traumas of the day.

Monasticism continued in Egypt, especially in the Thebaid, but the early bloom of enthusiasm had long since faded. The spectacularly self-denying John of Lycopolis had his moment in the sun as adviser to Emperor Theodosius, but on the whole asceticism had become a stale formality. John's holiness was exceptional. There was a problem of homosexuality in the Thebaid, where monks had to be locked into their cells at night.

The menace of desert tribes was so continuous that the monasteries took on the aspect of fortresses. As it stands today, San Simeon, near Aswān, is enclosed in forbidding turreted walls (see plate 64). Once stones were piled right inside the gate for hurling at attackers. The gate itself was barred with enormous millstones propped against it, as Alfred J. Butler saw them in the late nineteenth century, when he visited the monastic strongholds at Nitria that had replaced the early, more primitive settlement.[36] Within the compounds were a few bored uninspired monks and, to keep the world at bay, heaps of ugly missiles. Everywhere else in the Roman world there was a struggle toward some kind of accommodation to inevitable change. Stern absolute resistance could be found only in the monasteries of Egypt and the East. Ironically, the monks and hermits remained outwardly unchanged but lost their splendid fervor when they were forced into contact with the ongoing human race.

What languished in Egypt blossomed freshly in another clime—in Gaul, where John Cassian, the monk from Scetis, ended his flight from the uproars of Constantinople and the Visigoth assault on Rome. Western monasticism had its roots in the East, but the monks of southern Gaul were men of the world, though some of them emulated the recluses of the desert by retiring to lonely caves. In contrast to the Copts, the men who gathered about Abbot Honoratus on the tiny islands of Lérins, offshore from modern Cannes, were aristocrats who had never planned to leave their homes or relinquish their power. No enthusiasm, not even Vandals and Alans, had driven them out of Trier and Cologne, where their senatorial dignity and vast wealth had given them the authority that accompanies inherited status. The later Frankish incursion into former Roman lands seems to have furnished the impetus. Here they were, voluntarily living as paupers in tiny huts, praying in humble little oratories, pinning their hope on God's mercy in the hereafter. Rejection of the world and all the ills that flesh is heir to is understandable, but it is also understandable that men of this imperious stamp might at least unconsciously be responsive to the possibility of recovering their secular power.

In Egypt an emotion-laden line was drawn between the educated, Greek-speaking monks and the peasantlike Copts. The demarcation in Gaul between sophisticated members of Honoratus's foundation at Lérins and the monks of Martin's monasteries along the Loire was a matter of class distinction, though admittedly among Martin's followers were also a few highborn individuals. It is odd to leaf through Sulpicius Severus's biography of Martin in vain search for a word about the men of Lérins. Conversely, in all the voluminous writings that flowed from Lérins, there is nothing that might suggest the existence of multitudes of monks centered around Tours. Yet, indeed, multitudes there were: more than two thousand persons marched in Martin's funeral cortege. There were blind spots on both sides.[37]

The situation in the Gallic church in the early fifth century was more fluid than we might imagine. Conversion to Christianity had occurred less than a century before. At the end of the fourth century only half the cities of Gaul had their own bishops. Consequently, the church presented a more or less open field to anyone interested in carving out a power base for himself. It was surely no accident that as the episcopal sees became established their territories closely matched those of former civil administrative units and were manned by the senatorial class. Emperor Constantius III had appreciated the value of such persons and had been firm in his policy of removing bishops who leaned toward the erratic, controversial Martin, replacing them with individuals whom he considered to be steady and reliable. His deputy Patroclus, metropolitan bishop of Arles, was on good terms with Abbot Honoratus of Lérins, whom he presumably recognized as a fellow aristocrat.[38]

Although Honoratus humbly practiced stern asceticism and had in fact chosen that life before the appearance of the barbarians in his homeland, there was always an aura of patrician grace about him. He could not be confused with Martin's frowsy followers, who were known to seat themselves self-righteously on episcopal thrones, clad in malodorous garments made of camel's hair.[39] This difference held true of the men who responded to Honoratus's call after the barbarian breakthrough. Upper crust they had been; upper crust they remained. The very fact that they assembled as a group seems to be indicative of a determination to survive collectively in a world torn asunder.

The date of the founding of Lérins is not known, but it was no earlier than the year 400, no later than 410 (see plate 65). In the period up to 435, Provence was immune to the barbarian incursions that were a threat or a reality everywhere else in Gaul. There was time to strike a few roots. By 434 at least four men had gone out from the little islands to become bishops. Honoratus, the founder, was the first. He was elected by popular acclaim in the prestigious city of Arles in 426. Arles had replaced Trier as the Gallic capital, and its bishop therefore was a metropolitan with far-ranging authority. On the death of Honoratus in 429 the See of Arles again went to a man from Lérins, Honoratus's strong-minded young kinsman Hilary. In the very year that Honoratus became bishop of Arles, Hilary's brother-in-law Lupus, who had come to Lérins just the year before, became bishop of Troyes, a see to which he brought great honor in his long career as a wise leader and an active political force. Even Attila admired him warily. In 434, Eucherius of Lérins was consecrated bishop of Lyons, a see equal to Arles in importance. It is difficult to believe that all this was fortuitous. The Gallo-Roman aristocracy was extraordinarily tight-knit. Bonds of common interest and experience were reinforced strongly by a complicated network of intermarriages. We have already noted the relationships among Honoratus, Hilary, and Lupus. Bishop Eucherius was related to the prefect Priscus Valerianus and through him to Emperor Avitus, the father-in-law of Gaul's famous poet-bishop Sidonius Apollinaris. In succeeding decades certain "mitered families" came to occupy most of the important sees. As the last of the Romans they dealt with barbarian kings and courageously defended their flocks.

The displaced northerners who fled to Lérins were among the first to find this route to authority in troubled times. We do them an injustice if we label them self-serving. They were earnest, brave, and strong at the very time when Gaul was in desperate need of just such stalwarts. Their drastically changed lives made them tap inner resources they could hardly have been aware of before. Studied rhetoric became impassioned utterance. Precious verse was

Plate 65. Above: Church of Saint Féréol, Îles de Lérins (Saint-Honorat), fifth century. The little church has a triple apse in the Eastern style and a primitive cupola, probably one of the first in the West. Below: Church of Saint Sauveur, Îles de Lérins (Saint-Honorat), fifth century.

discarded for hard argument, hammered out on the anvil of conviction. Fastidiousness of person was transformed into iron physical discipline. The Spenglerian notion of dying empires and depleted civilizations is contradicted by the lives of the magnificently resilient Gallo-Romans of Lérins, who had what David Riesman calls "the nerve of failure"—the courage to accept the possibility of defeat without being morally crushed by the prospect.[40] These heroic monk-bishops were sober about their new calling: they truly believed that God was punishing Gaul and that serious amends were due. Therefore, they fasted and prayed with fervor.

Being the men they were, they believed that their communities had to be orderly. They were soon casting about for some rules to follow, as they established monasteries in conjunction with their network of bishoprics that gradually spread up the Rhone Valley. Disapproving of the random ways of Martin's monks, they found guidance in the work of John Cassian, who set down for them all he could remember of the practices and sayings of the Desert Fathers. He also wrote a description of cenobitic monasticism that adapted ideas from the Nile Valley and Palestine to the different conditions in Gaul. Cassian's book was not so much a rule as a guideline. In this same spirit Saint Benedict of Nursia later incorporated much of it in his own "rule for beginners," which was destined to sweep over the monasteries of Europe and Britain.

Cassian was well acquainted with the existing forms of monasticism. As a young man he had left his home in Scythia Minor (known today as Dobruja, a region in Rumania and Bulgaria between the Danube and the Black Sea) to enter a monastery in Bethlehem. The lure of legendary Nitria was strong: he sought and received permission to visit the holy men there. The years in Bethlehem marked Cassian's only personal experience as a member of a true cenobitic community: Once in Egypt he moved out to Scetis, there to sit at the feet of the anchorites. The life of the anchorite was Cassian's ideal, but he was forced out of it, presumably by the Origenist troubles. After his departure from Egypt there was no turning back. John Chrysostom made him a deacon, and when he journeyed on from Constantinople to Marseilles, the bishop there made him a presbyter. Almost immediately thereafter, Cassian set about establishing a monastery close to the Church of Saint Victor. He appears, however, always to have felt more intimately attached to Lérins than to his own foundation. The request that he write a rule was addressed to him by Bishop Castor of Apt, who wanted to found a monastery. The introductory sections of Cassian's *De institutis coenobiorum* are dedicated to Castor, while the concluding ones are dedicated to Honoratus and Eucherius, whom Cassian calls his "brothers."[41]

The circumstances of Cassian's life do not preclude his awareness of Basil's cenobitic communities in Cappadocia (see plate 66). That founder had produced a written rule. He was convinced that cenobitic life was ideal in itself, not a stepping-stone to the perfect life of the anchorite. Basil's teachings were

Plate 66. Rock-cut chapel, Cappadocia, Turkey. Monks by the hundreds hollowed out cells for themselves in the volcanic cones that characterize the region.

sympathetically received in Italy, carried thence to Gaul by Martin of Tours and his mentor Bishop Hilary of Poitiers, whose exorcist Martin was before he absented himself to Ligugé to become a hermit. Basil had visited the Egyptian desert in his time but had never responded to its awful mystery as Cassian had.

Cassian made an effort to temper the severity of Egyptian practice, but the regime that he offered was still stiffly demanding. A monk was supposed to get along with about four hours' sleep and to sustain himself on the simplest fare. Cassian warned that fasting should not be undertaken merely to attract attention and admiration. The monk was to participate in a succession of long offices at which Psalms were chanted and lessons read, with intervals for silent contemplation. Nocturns—dawn office—morning office—terce—sext—none—vespers: "Seven times a day have I praised Thee" (Psalm 119). Without going into the intricacies of scholarly reasoning, we accept the statement that this order of offices combined practices then current in Palestine and Egypt.[42] Cassian indicated variations throughout these services, in both the number of chanters and the postures to be assumed by the worshipers, in view of the constant danger of drifting off to sleep.

The battle against sleep was but one of the monk's ceaseless struggles. Cassian enumerated in order the temptations to be overcome, each more difficult than the one before. His deadly sins were eight: gluttony, fornication, covetousness, anger, melancholy, *accidie* (boredom), vanity, and pride (Pope Gregory the Great reduced the number of deadly sins to seven and revised the order somewhat). Even after that the demons remained. Cassian's demons were the hosts of hell, the fallen angels, not those outrageous imps of the Egyptian desert. There was something human about them, in the intimate way in which they could insinuate themselves into a man's life.

In his book the *Collationes patrum*, an account of a series of conferences with the Desert Fathers, Cassian wrote movingly of mystic contemplation. The mind should strip itself down to one single thought: "O God make speed to save me. O Lord make haste to help me."[43] Continuous prayer, with exclusion of every thought except of the glorified Christ: a good Egyptian, Cassian believed that the soul could truly behold God.

Most of the sayings of the Desert Fathers are reported in the *Collationes* ring true. Cassian said that the memory of his days at Scetis was beginning to fade somewhat, but the words that he puts into the mouths of the wise hermits have a convincingly primitive quality. One section of the book, the thirteenth conference, is an anachronistic creation, dealing with a controversy that did not develop until long after Cassian's departure from Egypt. The topic is grace and free will; it reflects the disturbed frame of mind of people familiar with Pelagius's arguments against the severe Augustinian doctrine of predestination. Some of Cassian's friends at Lérins, especially Vincent, expressed their objections with considerable bitterness, in deep dislike of Augustine's frightening innovation. Cassian's own reaction was moderate. Quoting Genesis, he pointed out reasonably that, after the Fall, Adam knew *both* good and evil. He had acquired a knowledge of evil but had not lost his knowledge of good. His will might be sick, but even a sick, weakened will could perform healthy, healing acts.

These sane remarks were enough to put Cassian's name among those of the "semi-Pelagians," who were looked on with suspicion for centuries, but at the same time he remained in high favor in Rome, where Pope Leo I assigned him to the task of championing the cause of the orthodox faith against Nestorianism (we recall the trouble caused by Nestorius's complaint that people called the Virgin Mary Theotokos). Pope Leo held his friend Cassian in high regard, but the same cannot be said of his feelings about that hothead, Bishop Hilary of Arles.

Of all the men of Lérins, Hilary was the most complex. He had not even wanted to go to Lérins in the first place. He must have been quite a playboy, because the news that he was "turning out badly" traveled down from the north, alarming his older kinsman Honoratus so greatly that he made the hazardous trip to Trier to fetch him. Hilary rejected Honoratus's pleas, but at a somewhat later time he presented himself at Lérins. He reacted to the place by falling passionately in love with it.

Even today the objective modern visitor can understand the sudden over-whelming emotion. It is still a paradise on earth, just as Hilary said. He intended never to be expelled like Adam from this perfect garden. Bells chime thinly in the soft air at Lérins. The sea glitters, perhaps silhouetting a dark, long-legged bird perched on a rock beneath the fragrant pines near the shore. In the distance white-hooded figures move about deliberately with breviaries in hand or bend among the rows of cultivated lavender. Still "green with herbs, radiant with flowers," Lérins is a lovely spot, timeless and dreamy.

When Honoratus moved on to Arles to become archbishop there, he took Hilary with him, but the impulsive young man escaped his watchful eye and hurried back to Lérins. When Honoratus lay dying, Hilary went loyally to his side, but he turned and fled when it dawned on him that Honoratus's pointing finger meant that he was to be the next bishop of Arles. Reluctantly accepting the charge at last, Hilary threw himself into his work. The well-being and prestige of his diocese soon became his passion, though he still withdrew to the solitudes whenever he could, even when it entailed a thirty-mile walk barefoot through the dark night to return to his heavy episcopal duties at the required time. He drove himself unmercifully, fasting and keeping hands and mind busy. He read at mealtimes, knitted while he dictated, toiled in the saltworks of his monastery, and preached and exhorted his flock with all the ferocity and eloquence at his command as long as four hours at a stretch. Sooner or later a man of such extremes was fated to step beyond the bounds of reason. Hilary allowed himself to acquire an overblown conception of his power as metro-politan bishop. Arles still ranked high, even though the authority granted to Bishop Patroclus in the time of Emperor Constantius III had been pared down.

In all fairness it must be acknowledged that Hilary's actions were no doubt based on a conviction that the church needed rigorously ascetic leaders in a time of general disarray. That he had aligned himself with the "semi-Pelagians" also tended to make him distrustful of people in the more conserva-tive pro-Augustine camp. A mild excuse may be offered for Hilary's bold practice of calling synods as though he were the primate of all Gaul, in the sense that elsewhere in Gaul there were impotent laments that this essential apparatus was breaking down, but no one was doing anything about the prob-lem. In those uncertain times it took an extraordinary person with a capacity for quick, undoubting decision to accomplish anything at all.[44]

Hilary's high-handed way of selecting and consecrating bishops cannot be overlooked as trivial or justified by the times. A protest was presented to Pope Leo I in the case of the bishop of Besançon, whom Hilary had deposed, excom-municated, and replaced. In response to the news of this protest Hilary set out for Rome. He disdained any grand official conveyance that might have been due him by virtue of office: he walked in the dead of winter through the chill Alpine passes, spurning even a cloak, if his biographer is to be believed. His charisma failed him in Rome. Pope Leo subsequently wrote, in his detailed account of the affair for the benefit of Gallic churchmen, that Hilary had vociferously expressed his opinions before the Roman synod "in words that no layman should use, and no priest can listen to." Leo went on to note that Hilary reportedly had a habit of darting around in Gaul, bursting into churches where he had no authority, surrounded by a band of armed men. Trevor Jalland charitably suggested that travel in Gaul was more dangerous at that time than Leo may have realized.[45] We might inquire whether bishops of the conservative school may not also have been so escorted, in the style of Gallo-Roman aristocrats, who were accustomed to the service of armed retainers.

The Roman synod dismissed the charges against the bishop of Besançon that had been at the base of Hilary's action. Leo ordered that Hilary should lose his status as metropolitan; he could remain a bishop, but he was stripped of all competence for ordination. Leo reinforced the order by procuring an extraordi-nary imperial rescript directed to Aëtius, the military commander in Gaul, in the name of Theodosius II and Valentinian III. It seems likely that Leo's deci-sion had not met with universal approval in Gaul. The wording of the em-perors' document, dated July 8, 445, was strong and unmistakable in its intent:

> Since the authoritative decision of the sacred synod itself has confirmed the pri-macy of the Apostolic see as appropriate to Saint Peter, who is the chief of the

episcopal order and the glory of the Roman city, let no one presume to undertake any illicit act contrary to the authority of that see.

Hilary retreated, but he sent a number of emissaries back to Rome. One of his highly placed friends, Auxiliaris, wrote him a piece of worldly-wise, candid advice: "People do not take it patiently if we speak just as we think. The ears of the Romans are humored by a little civility." Bishop Hilary became quiet, punishing himself with terrible austerities. He died a few years later, a burned-out man.

Faustus, abbot of Lérins, was an entirely different kind of person. Lérins produced an extraordinary variety of gifted men, and the amiable Faustus was not the least of them. Not only his contemporaries but also Latinists today admire the lucid, expressive style of this British-born member of the community, who clearly had enjoyed the advantage of superb education in his native land. Faustus became bishop of Riez (Reqium) about ten years after Hilary's death. The time in which southern Gaul would remain a haven untouched by the barbarians was running short. Indeed, Faustus himself was exiled for ten years or more when King Euric the Visigoth came into control of Riez.

The interest of Faustus's career lies in the part he played in the "semi-Pelagian" affair and the reactions that his writings provoked in faraway places. He was much more outspoken than Cassian had been on the subject of divine grace and free human will, so much so that he was called a heretic and denounced by the "Scythian monks" who were involved in controversy at Constantinople and Rome in Boethius's day. In remote exile in Sardinia the Catholic clergy were stirred by letters from the Scythians into agreement with African Bishop Fulgentius that Faustus's ideas were "inventions, contrary to the truth, entirely hostile to the Catholic faith."

Faustus was banished from Riez because his diocese in southern Gaul came under the domination of an Arian king. Let us turn now to Gaul as a whole, to examine shifts in the balance of power as the barbarian kingdoms took shape.

SUB-ROMAN AND
MEROVINGIAN GAUL

SIDONIUS APOLLINARIS was optimistic when he pronounced his glowing panegyric honoring his father-in-law, Emperor Avitus, and received the warm plaudits of the admiring Roman senators. He was only about twenty-five years old. He must have had the heady feeling that, in spite of the turbulence of a world dominated by Vandals and threatened by Burgundians, Alamanni, Visigoths, Franks, and Saxons, his own future would be bright either in Rome or, better still, in his beloved native Gaul. Sidonius lived for about another quarter of a century (we lose track of him around the year 479), but in that period he had to become adept at political tightrope walking just to survive. We learn from his poems and letters that his fellow Gallo-Roman aristocrats shared his problem and solved it in various conflicting ways.

He was in trouble immediately after the death of Avitus, in his own city of Lyons. The citizens had entered into some kind of "conspiracy," as Sidonius later called it. There were two generals, both of whom were competent and powerful enough to command followings. The first, Marcellinus, seems to have been offered the diadem at Lyons, where the Burgundians actively supported his cause. The second general was Majorian, who enjoyed the favor of Ricimer the patrician, at whose nod emperors rose or fell. Marcellinus apparently stood aside because Majorian was his friend and colleague, but the people of Lyons were stubborn in their reluctant acceptance of Majorian. Therefore, they faced the prospect of a severe punitive tax.

As a member of the conspiratorial party Sidonius poured out a torrent of anxious welcome when triumphant Majorian arrived. The conquest was "for my benefit," proclaimed Sidonius. "I am fain to leap for joy."[1] The lengthy panegyric betrays inner anguish: Emperor Avitus, whose downfall had made way for Majorian, is not mentioned. Whether or not the desperate poetics moved him, Emperor Majorian was inclined to be lenient and lift the tax burden. Sidonius advanced in favor. He was back in Rome again in 460, in a

251

government post of some sort, but then, alas, Ricimer engineered the fall of Majorian, who was replaced by a puppet Libius Severus. Once more without a royal patron, Sidonius retreated to Lyons.

Defiance flamed again—double defiance this time. General Marcellinus refused to recognize Ricimer's contemptible tool and withdrew to Dalmatia, where he was a serious threat to the Ravenna government. He was practically independent yet had the protection of the Eastern emperor. In Gaul, Majorian's commander, Aegidius, offered stern resistance and threatened Ravenna from the west. Ricimer, himself a general of no mean ability, was on the defensive. Like his early predecessor Stilicho, Ricimer believed that Italy had to be held at all cost. The cost was higher this time because Italy was ringed around, with the powerful Vandals in control of Africa.

On the face of it we might expect to see Aegidius enjoying tremendous advantages in Gaul, in spite of the strength of the Visigoths and Burgundians. He was certainly the kind of man around whom patriotic Gallo-Romans could rally—he was one of their own. Aegidius's family, the wealthy Syagrii, had extensive land-holdings and were firmly meshed in the web of friendships and intermarriages that made the Gallic aristocracy a kind of fraternal network. Aegidius's grandfather was none other than Consul Afranius Syagrius, whose descendants at the time of Aegidius's rebellion included a kinsman and friend of Sidonius, the revered former praetorian prefect Tonantius Ferreolus. With such a background we wonder why Aegidius had so little local support to draw on. We comb Sidonius's letters in vain; Aegidius and his activities are nowhere mentioned. That is odd, because Aegidius had his share of fame not only in his own lifetime but even posthumously. In his own day he must have been known in Britain. It is generally agreed that the Venerable Bede erred when he wrote that the "groans of the Britons," the famous appeal for help against the Saxons, was addressed to Aëtius. The earliest known manuscript says that the appeal was sent to Aegidius.[2] He lingers on in hagiography also, as an antihero in the siege of Chinon in 463.[3]

Sidonius was about thirty years old when Aegidius began his rebellion. In other words, he was in what should have been his most productive and vigorous period in the service of his country. Yet if we judge by his writings, he frittered away the next six years as though what happened to Gaul were of no interest to him. We must judge cautiously, however, because Sidonius edited his correspondence for publication, and who knows what incriminating material he may have removed?

The whole picture is curious. Those Gallo-Romans who had been so churned up in the past in support of Jovinus or Constantine III or Avitus or Marcellinus or Majorian appear to have elected to abstain from any involvement in Aegidius's struggle. Instead, they engaged in a steady round of empty social activities and went about the countryside visiting each other, living a life that could be compared with the Roman idea of *otium* (gentlemanly retirement for quiet contemplation), meanwhile inditing the most insipid complimentary poems to each other.

Once in a while something slips through to make us suspect that the couriers who bore those elaborate greetings and erudite invitations may have been caused to memorize something of more pith and moment that could not safely be set down in writing. Possibly during those ostensibly carefree afternoons in agreeable shady porticos there was much worried argument and consultation. In response to a request from his friend the senator Catullinus, Sidonius offered an elegantly turned verse to the effect that this was not the time for a song dedicated to Venus, because he was surrounded by long-haired hordes with rancid butter in their hair who reeked of garlic and invaded his kitchen before dawn. Presumably these ill-smelling intruders had been quartered on him.

A year after he penned that poem, Sidonius visited his dear friend Pontius Leontius of Bordeaux. This gentleman lived in imposing state in a castle known as Burgus. Perched on the site of a Celtic fortified town, the castle was also elaborately fortified with walls and towers that could resist battering rams, catapults, mantlets, or other siege engines. His fortified estate was not unique: Sidonius's friend Aper likewise had such a fortress, and there also remained the older stronghold of the magnate Dardanus near Sisteron.[4]

Sidonius whiled away considerable time in the half-ruined city of Narbonne. The damage to the city that he describes probably occurred in earlier attacks, rather than during the most recent fray. At the latter time the populace remained relatively passive, and a Gallo-Roman count handed over the city to the Visigoths in return for assistance in quelling Aegidius.

While he was in Narbonne, Sidonius had access to King Theodoric II and became well acquainted with him. It is amusing to learn that the Visigoth, who was essentially a sober-minded fellow, could become so absorbed in a board game that his joy over a winning play could put him in a mood to dispose quickly of annoying transactions. As Sidonius explained it to his brother-in-law Agricola, in such a situation he might successfully ask for a favor that otherwise might not have been granted. We are not told what such favors were.[5]

It is possible that there was no longer any unanimity among the Gallic magnates. The fall of Avitus must have been a clear signal to them that a Gallo-Roman emperor would never be acceptable to Rome. Besides, there was the disheartening thought that it had not even been Gallo-Romans but Visigoths who first proffered the diadem to Avitus. Uneasy minds might focus on the disquieting role that the barbarians played in that one moment of Gallic good fortune and conclude that Visigoths or even Burgundians might incongruously be the hope of the world.

Plate 67. Visigothic sarcophagus, ca. 550, Narbonne. A characteristic of Visigothic work is the flattening of the acanthus. This appears to be the first example of interlace work known in France. Neither Visigoths nor Ostrogoths are known to have used it in Italy (Perkins, "The Sculpture of Visigothic France," pp. 103, 118; Puig i Cadafalch, *L'art wisigothique et ses survivances*, p. 70).

King Theodoric II was an admirable man. Sidonius was witness to that. He called the king "pillar and savior of the Roman race."[6] There was much latent power in Gaul. We think of Sidonius's letter to his friend Eutropius: "You are well furnished with horses, armor, raiment, money and servants."[7] If men with such resources at their command—and there were many of them—were to take the field for Aegidius, Gaul might rise again, but people wanted to wait and see. Aegidius has been called "a glorious exception" in a period when self-interest was the order of the day and virtue on the throne could not be tolerated.[8] He saw himself as the protector of Gaul, the avenger of Emperor Majorian. We remember that Majorian had not been the first choice of the Gallic aristocrats. Does this explain their indifference to Aegidius?

Ricimer, who was a master of the techniques of propaganda, managed to portray Aegidius as a mere upstart who should be destroyed. He also marshaled the barbarians shrewdly, planting the Burgundians at Lyons, where they were in a good strategic position to block any possible invasion of Italy. He dismissed Aegidius from his military command and put Burgundian King Gunderic in his place. He allowed the Visigoths, who were federates still, to understand that Aegidius was in insurrection against the rightful emperor.[9] The Visigoths moved willingly and forced Aegidius to engage his military contingents in Gaul, without any possibility of crossing the Alps.

Hemmed in as he was, Aegidius was pressed north into the Paris basin above the Loire, where of necessity he came into closer contact with the Franks. There he relied on a conglomeration of Alans, Sarmatians, and Armoricans and made good use of the three weapons factories near Soissons, which became his headquarters. The troops at his disposal were remnants of the heterogeneous force scraped together by Aëtius at the time of Attila's incursion. The arms factories had been established earlier, part of a series at Mâcon, Autun, Trier, Reims, and Amiens.[10] Soissons had escaped intact from the barbarian surge of 406–407. It had a mint, and it was an important administrative center.

In the last year of his life, 463, Aegidius made overtures to Gaiseric, proposing a Gallo-Vandal alliance against the hated Ricimer. It is possible that some of the proempire magnates of Gaul heard about this, distrusted Aegidius, and duped themselves into thinking that the destruction of this heroic man would be all to the good.

Aegidius fought hard and scored a fine victory at Angers over Odovacar's attacking Saxons, who apparently had been incited by Ricimer. At Orléans he was also victorious over the Visigoths under King Theodoric's brother. In that battle Aegidius had federates of his own: Franks from Tournai, under the early Merovingian chieftain Childeric. Reliance on Childeric was to have far-reaching consequences. Under Childeric's successor, Clovis, the Franks were able to take Soissons and its rich resources from Aegidius's son Syagrius, with sobering results for the Visigoths and Burgundians.

The story of Aegidius ends abruptly with his death by poisoning in 464, the year after Orléans. He remains a remote and shadowy figure, but we should consider that if it had not been for Aegidius the story of Europe might have been very different. Ricimer had reacted to his threat by expanding the territories of both Burgundians and Visigoths, and Aegidius had responded to that move by shifting his base close to the Franks. Caught between the Visigoths and the Burgundians, the Gallo-Romans came to appreciate the advantage of courting and encouraging a new force (pagan but not Arian), with the final result that Gaul became France, not Gothia.

In the face of impossible odds Aegidius managed to establish a Roman enclave in the midst of the barbarians. This island of *romanitas* survived precariously after him for nearly a generation, first under a mysterious Count Paulus (perhaps a commander of the Saxon Shore like Saint Germanus) and then under Aegidius's son Syagrius, whose strange story shows how barbarized

Gaul had become by the end of the fifth century. We shall return to Syagrius, but first we must follow the erratic fortunes of Sidonius Apollinaris.

If Sidonius ever entertained the notion that he might someday hitch his political wagon to the Visigothic star by promoting warm friendship with Theodoric II over their backgammon board, the idea was cruelly dashed in the year 466, when Theodoric was murdered by his brother Euric. The new ruler was an ardent Arian as well as an aggressively ambitious man who clearly intended to rule Gaul. Without repeating the complicated story of Ricimer's puppets, we can pick up the narrative with the appointment of Anthemius as emperor of the West. By a tremendous stretch of wistful imagination, his subjects could regard him as a rightful successor of the Theodosian line. Loyal Gallo-Romans chose to see him in that light and promptly, in 467, dispatched Sidonius to Rome at the head of a delegation to present the Gallic case to the court.

Sidonius wrote a long, highly entertaining account of his journey. Because of his prestige and his official mission, he traveled grandly by the *cursus publicus*, a system of official transportation that somehow had survived through all vicissitudes (Bishop Ambrose used it, we remember). Delays, Sidonius reported happily, were "not due to scarcity of post-horses but to multiplicity of friends." Over the Alps he went, on "a pathway cut through the snow" and along rivers where bridges were still in good repair.[11] At Pavia he transferred to a special boat that served the *cursus publicus*: there were relays of oarsmen on the route to Ravenna. Sidonius did not like Ravenna much. It was a noisome city because the seawater did not clear the sludge from the inland channels. It had no water fit to drink. The ancient Via Flaminia appears to have been in good order still, though by the time Sidonius reached it he was suffering from the fifth-century precursor of the *turista*, and his consciousness was so taken up by the extreme discomfort that his travel report degenerated into a list of cities between Ravenna and Rome. Perhaps that would have been the sequence of Sidonius's movements in any case, but in this situation he went directly to Saint Peter's Basilica to implore divine aid: "Straightway I felt that all sickness had been driven from my enfeebled limbs." He went at once into the city, arriving at the festive moment of Ricimer's marriage to Emperor Anthemius's daughter Alypia. The shout of "Thalassio!" (good wishes to a bride and groom) echoed everywhere, in theaters, markets, law courts, churches, camps, and playgrounds.

Once again Sidonius was able to bask in the bright light of public recognition. His newest panegyric, in honor of Anthemius, was rewarded by a glittering appointment: Sidonius became prefect of the city of Rome in 468. It was a formal bow by the new emperor to his Gallic dominions, but it was no empty honor. Sidonius soon advanced to the rank of patrician. He must have felt that at last he was fulfilling his moral obligation to his illustrious ancestors.

"There is nothing nobler than for a man unremittingly to combine mind, body, and estate in an effort to surpass his forefathers," he once wrote. [12]

Anthemius was bestirring himself to send armed forces against Visigoth King Euric. Who could tell what glories might lie ahead for the beloved homeland and for the family of Sidonius the prefect? Alas, not all Gallo-Romans were willing to put their faith in the new emperor. Before his term of office was out, Sidonius became painfully aware of it. His friend Arvandus, praetorian prefect of Gaul, was brought to Rome by an official delegation made up of other friends of Sidonius, who accused Arvandus of having made treasonous overtures to King Euric. The charge held, and Arvandus was condemned to death by the Roman Senate. It was a dreadful time for Sidonius, who was loyal in his friendships and made a serious effort to avert a tragedy. Arvandus was unaccountably insolent and arrogant, right up to the very moment of sentencing; his behavior has led some historians to conclude that he must have had Ricimer's secret approval. In the event Arvandus was not executed, but before this denouement Sidonius had completed his year in office. In 469 he slipped gratefully back to Gaul.

Conditions at home were grim. Sidonius wrote despairingly to his brother-in-law Ecdicius that one Seronatus (possibly the vicar of the seven provinces) was in league with King Euric, encouraging Visigoths to enter Roman territory. "He brags to the Goths and insults the Romans." The closing sentence of this sad little letter suggests that, since the emperor lacked the will and resources demanded by the times, the nobility might soon resolve to give up its country or take holy orders. [13] Indeed, in that very year, 469, the unhappy patriot and erstwhile man of letters became bishop of Clermont-Ferrand, where the local church had just received handsome donations of land from Sidonius's kinsman Avitus (not the late emperor).

By an ironic twist it was only after Sidonius ostensibly abandoned public life that he had the opportunity to show what a true patriot he was. These were dark days in Auvergne, which held out vigorously against Euric. The city of Clermont was besieged and in such desperate straits that the famished people plucked weeds from the city walls for nourishment.

There were two leaders in the four-year struggle for Auvergne: Sidonius and his brother-in-law Ecdicius, whose first exploit had all the bravura of folk heroism. With only eighteen armed men he burst out of the surrounded city of Clermont, startling the Goths into pell-mell flight. The jubilant townspeople nearly overwhelmed Ecdicius when he galloped safely back with all his troops, covered with the gore of slaughtered Goths. Shortly thereafter he collected and armed what Sidonius described as "a sort of private army" at his own expense, with only a little help from "great men" on the outside. [14] With this band Ecdicius was able to halt the previously unchecked pillaging forays of the Goths and annihilate "phalanxes of cavalry." The letter in which Sidonius recorded all this ends with a prescient plea. Ecdicius had been singled out by Anthemius, whose commitment was honored in 474, by his successor, Emperor Julius Nepos, to make the hero of Auvergne *magister militum* and patrician. At an earlier time Sidonius would have been single-heartedly exultant over this honor to a member of the family, but now he wrote, "Be quick to withdraw your duteous attendance from the dangerous intimacy of princes" (Burgundian princes in this instance, apparently).[15] With the very next spin of fortune's wheel Emperor Nepos had second thoughts and recalled Ecdicius. The post was handed over to Orestes, the adventurer who had once been secretary to Attila and was the father of Romulus Augustulus, the last Roman emperor.

Nepos had entered into complicated negotiations with King Euric that ended with the surrender of Sidonius's beloved Auvergne to the Visigoths. This was bitter for the staunch defenders of Clermont. Sidonius was plunged into the depths of woe, looking at "our hideously charred walls, our palisades of rotting stakes"[16] and recalling the efforts of people like the frail old priest Constantius who had painfully traveled from Lyons in the dead of winter to "return people their harmony" in the harassed city (had some citizens wanted to surrender?) and to bring spiritual consolation. Sidonius knew that it was the valor of his "luckless Arvernians" that had held back the Visigoths for so long. He wrote in sorrow to Bishop Graecus of Marseilles, who had had a hand in the negotiations with Euric, that the plight of Auvergne was "less miserable in war than it is now in peace. Our freedom has been bartered for the security of others. . . . Is this our due reward for enduring want and fire and sword and pestilence?"[17]

King Euric was a confirmed Arian. He soon hurried Bishop Sidonius off to prison in a fortress not far from Carcassonne. The imprisonment lasted about a year. Possibly through the good offices of his friend Leo of Narbonne, who was at Euric's court, Sidonius was released on parole about 476, though he was still banished from his see. Soon afterward he went to Bordeaux, which may have been Euric's capital.

Almost instinctively we brace ourselves for another panegyric. Not quite, though Sidonius did pen a monstrously long poem, which he enclosed in a letter to his friend Lampridius, who, like Leo, was faring well at court. If we are to take this poem literally, the Gothic capital had become the lodestone of the world, crammed with emissaries from places as remote as Persia, all suing for favor. The streets of Bordeaux were colorful, as people from all nations in their distinctive garb trudged up and down. King Euric graciously allowed Sidonius to go home to resume his duties as bishop of Clermont.

Leafing through the last of Sidonius's collected letters, especially those addressed to fellow bishops, we might believe that he had no appreciation of the responsibilities and potentialities of episcopal office. There are the same empty compliments that were characteristic of the "underground period," when Sidonius and his colleagues were waiting out Aegidius's time, only now the letters are carried to men who have become saints on earth, who are "gifted with a sweet and holy style . . . distinguished by the varied elegance of its vocabulary." As before, it appears to be logical to surmise that the carriers of these effusions had something to *say*. Sidonius indicates as much, referring to the insecurity of the roads because of the "commotions of peoples" and commenting that a courier is subject to sharp scrutiny and search.

A strain of despair runs through most of the later letters, but Sidonius was fully aware that the church offered the only route still open to a proud, public-spirited man. It was for this reason that he was so alarmed by the effect of King Euric's policies. The Arian ruler was methodically stamping out Catholicism in his domains by allowing the office of the bishop to lie vacant whenever an incumbent died. That had happened in Bordeaux, Périgueux, Rodez, Limoges, Javols, Eauze, Bazas, Saint-Bertrand, and Auch, Sidonius reported in consternation to the bishop of Aix.[18] He went on to describe crumbling church roofs and cattle chewing the cud in church vestibules and even cropping at grass growing up around the altars. Episcopal ordination must be allowed in Euric's territories, he insisted.

At one time Sidonius was asked by the people of Bourges to name a candidate for the office of bishop of that city. Sidonius made it clear in his nominating speech what kind of colleague he wanted in these difficult times. Not an ascetic monk, he said: such a man would be better qualified to intercede before the heavenly throne for the souls of men than to plead for bodies before earthly judges. Not a cleric, he continued. The picture that Sidonius drew suggests a languid seniority system in which long years of service rather than usefulness would warrant elevation to the episcopal throne. He selected Simplicius, the descendant of bishops and prefects, whose wife came from the illustrious family of the Palladii, "who have held professional chairs and episcopal thrones." Simplicius had demonstrated his worth as spokesman for Bourges before "skin-clad monarchs or purple-clad princes" and had once been cast into a Gothic dungeon. Not only this, but he had built a church for the city of Bourges. Such then was the metropolitan of Aquitania Prima whom Sidonius chose.

Sidonius used his own power with discretion, to resolve personal disputes or to help members of his flock caught in the press of circumstance. Otherwise, his efforts were probably confined to the business of keeping channels of communication open, with the hope that such channels would be useful at some future date.

One of the Sidonius's correspondents could recall a time when a bishop's power had been formidable. This was the venerable Lupus of Troyes, who traveled to Britain with Germanus of Auxerre on a mission of considerable import and who had negotiated with Attila for the protection of his city. Another recipient of letters from Sidonius, a younger man, was to wield tremendous influence in another twenty years or so. This was Remigius (Saint Remi), bishop of Reims, scion of a powerful northern family, who was to officiate at the baptism of Clovis, the brilliantly successful warrior son of Childeric the Frank.

In Sidonius's day the future of the Franks was still veiled. They had fought for Aegidius under Childeric at Orléans in 463, but what happened to them in the years before 486, when Clovis led them against the very Roman forces for whom their fathers had fought is a puzzle. Some of Childeric's following appears to have remained at Soissons under the command of Aegidius, but most went back to the Frankish base at Tournai. Perhaps Aegidius had enough authority simply to dismiss his federates when he no longer had need of them. There is an odd story that tells about an eight-year period during Aegidius's time in which Childeric was an exile somewhere across the Rhine. Two matched halves of a broken gold coin are romantically mentioned: delivery of the half that matched his own was supposed to be a signal to Childeric that the time for safe return to power had arrived. A mysterious friend, a Hun named Wiomad, is supposed to have acted as emissary, engineering the restoration of Childeric by way of the improbable route of Constantinople. It may be that Childeric actually had some tenuous relationship with the Eastern court, where Aegidius was clearly regarded with suspicion and antipathy.[19]

A Byzantine connection might account for some of the marvelous grave goods in Childeric's tomb. Most of those pieces are lost forever, but it is known that what now remains to dazzle us is only part of the great Tournai treasure. Glittering garnets and almandines from Pontic workshops adorned the warrior's sword and buckles, and there was a purse that contained more than a hundred gold coins, along with a collection of two hundred silver coins, a signet ring with a Latin inscription, and a cloak ornamented in Sarmatian style with a swarm of golden cicadas (the ancestors of Napoleon's bees).[20] Nothing in the tomb could be said specifically to symbolize kingship. There may have been some undefinable sacral character vested in Frankish kings, indicated perhaps by their long, flowing hair and the magical necklaces that they wore.

Succession to leadership of the Franks was hereditary. There was a smooth transition on Childeric's death to his fifteen-year-old son Chlodovech, whom we know better as Clovis. His Franks followed him willingly. Upon the demise of the formidable Visigothic ruler Euric in 486, Clovis found that the time was ripe to challenge Aegidius's son Syagrius.

Syagrius, king of the Romans—rex Romanorum. Gregory of Tours describes him so, and it seems safe to assume that Syagrius's contemporaries called him king. Romans traditionally spurned the title rex, having acquired a profound distaste for it in the time of the Tarquins. They used it condescendingly for barbarian chieftains, those useful, supposedly subservient federates of the empire. They also applied a diminutive form that we might translate as "kinglet" (*regalis*, *regulus*) to barbarian military leaders.[21] Syagrius had no office or standing within the imperial system; he was completely cut off from the court in Constantinople. He had no standing in the West either. Who, in an Italy ruled by Odovacar, the rex Herulorum, would have bothered to confer a title or an office on Syagrius? It must have been the barbarians in Gaul who dubbed him rex Romanorum, seeing him as one of themselves, the chief of a strong war band.[22] There were plenty of Frankish *reguli* in the north, not just Clovis.

Gregory of Tours thought that Syagrius had a hereditary kingdom at Soissons, no doubt because he was accustomed to the idea of hereditary kingship among the Franks and Burgundians. The territories that Syagrius held have never been well defined, but they must certainly have included the remnants of the imperial fisc. Such extensive lands would be very tempting to a man like Clovis, who could distribute them among his followers as rewards for service. Situated in the heart of prosperous farmlands and heavily wooded areas, Soissons was still a prime location. Its mint continued to strike coins; its arms factories were still productive. The truth of the matter appears to be that Syagrius was more a soldier of fortune than anything else. His responses to his adversaries were not those of a Roman military man; the important battle that cost him his "kingdom" was fought on strictly barbarian terms. When Clovis challenged him, Syagrius took the action that would be expected of the leader of a German war band. He exercised his right to select the battleground.[23] In sum, two chieftains on an equal footing were disputing territory, winner take all.

We may surmise that Syagrius was not sufficiently versed in the Roman art of strategy. Otherwise he might have made better use of his opportunity to choose the battlefield. The conflict ended in disaster for Syagrius, who fled for his life to take refuge under the uncertain protection of Alaric II, the new king of the Visigoths. Nothing can be found in the narrative to suggest that Syagrius could have hoped to inspire support anywhere among the Gallo-Romans. Clovis threatened timid Alaric, who shipped Syagrius back from Toulouse in chains, whereupon the unfortunate rex Romanorum was summarily executed in 486.

The Frankish band that Clovis inherited from his father probably was not much bigger than a force of five hundred warriors. The victory over Syagrius therefore marked a major turning point for him. About five years later Clovis was able to command not only Roman units but also military colonists who had settled in the region. These colonists were mostly Sarmatians and Alamanni,[24] which makes it something of an anomaly to speak of Clovis as a leader of the Franks. He had attracted more true Franks, to be sure, notably the

Ripuarians (Clovis himself was a Salian Frank). He had also acquired Syagrius's bureaucratic apparatus. Tournai was abandoned, and Clovis's new capital was at Soissons, where the old praetorium of the walled city became a palace, in which presumably scribes continued to grind out documents as before.

Here at last was the day that Sidonius and his friends had dreamed of for so long. By concerted action they might escape the Arian yoke, and, more important, Roman Gaul might rise to glory. There was a chink in the Arians' armor—their disunity. The churchmen of Gaul must have been acutely aware of it. Unconsciously the Arians tended to act like members of "national" churches, with little or no communication between like-minded clergy in other barbarian kingdoms. Although their adherents had control of most of Gaul—and of Italy, too, for that matter—they made no use of the potentials of church organization for purposes of intercourse or propaganda. [25] The Catholics would have been doomed by the power of their barbarian overlords if the Arians had joined forces against them. As it was, there was more than one instance of Catholics who were in trouble in one Arian kingdom yet were able to slip unscathed to another. A characteristic example is that of Bishop Aprunculus of Langres, whose preference for the Franks was so obvious that he aroused the suspicions of his Burgundian ruler, King Gundobad. Aprunculus was banished from his see but made way to Visigothic Auvergne, where he was kindly received and in due time became bishop of Clermont-Ferrand. [26] One of Aprunculus's own successors, Quintianus of Rodez, had a similar history. Quintianus was driven from his see by angry Goths but was subsequently rewarded for his faithfulness to the Franks by being made bishop of Clermont. [27]

The Catholics, meanwhile, maintained their network of communications, their "underground." During Syagrius's reign Sidonius wrote some of his fatuous letters to the bishop of Soissons. [28] No reference is to be found there either to Syagrius or to the Franks, but contact was being made with a key northern city in critical times. Who is to know what the messenger may have said when he delivered the letters in Soissons?

The bishop of Soissons was a member of one of Gaul's prominent "mitered families," a kinsman of powerful Bishop Remigius of Reims, who also took pen in hand. Remigius sent kindly, somewhat threatening words to Soissons, saluting the youthful new king of the Franks on the occasion of his accession. In a fatherly, rather patronizing way that is reminiscent of the letters of Bishop Ambrose to young Valentinian II, Remigius suggested that Clovis ought to defer to the bishops. A prosperous reign could be promoted in this way: the bishops, after all, came from families accustomed to running the affairs of northern Gaul, and it would be well to gain their favor. [29]

Clovis was enough his own man to allow his pagan followers to plunder Catholic churches at will, but before long there were indications that he was in the mood to make a concession or two. He married a Catholic, for one thing—the romance may have been helped along by Bishop Remigius. Clothilde was an orphaned Burgundian princess. She and her sister were the only Catholics in the family of her uncle, King Gundobad. Clothilde was an ardent, insistent missionary. She managed to prevail upon Clovis to allow the baptism of their firstborn son, and even the second one, in spite of the ominous death of the first while he was still in his white baptismal garments. Clovis rejected the idea of his own conversion. He had his warriors to think of. Besides, there was the murky matter of his possibly divine ancestors. It was all right to honor the local territorial deity, but to abandon his Frankish gods would be a risky step.

There are three serious difficulties in unraveling the story of Clovis. The first is the chronology, which is wellnigh hopeless. Scholars have warred over it for years. What confidence can be placed in judgments that sometimes must be based on the tense of a verb in a manuscript corrupted by copyists whose knowledge of Latin was admittedly faulty? The second difficulty hangs upon the circumstance that most of our information comes from a biased source. Gregory of Tours was a honest man, but he was possessed with a burning desire to prove that Clovis, from a very early time in his extraordinary career, had been the champion of true Christianity. There seems to be a general agreement now that Gregory placed Clovis's conversion too early so that all his bloody campaigns could be presented as victories for the glory and unity of the church. The third difficulty stems from the popularity of a modern thesis that Clovis was a man of unusual drive and vision, a man of clear-eyed purpose, who *intended to found the French nation*, whereas in reality, if we read closely, he was a greedy opportunist who seized upon whatever chances arose in the flux of any given critical situation.

After the capture of Soissons and the defeat of Syagrius, Clovis was in a much stronger position than before, but he faced serious danger still. He must have known that his energies would have to be directed to the satisfaction of his warriors with gifts of land and booty and to the problem of various Frankish bands not yet subject to him, if he was ever to be free of the threat of the Alamanni, who had a well-founded reputation for ferocity. It was still vivid in popular memory that the Alamanni had joined Attila; their cruelty had made as deep an impression as that of the Huns. By 455 they had more or less consolidated, spreading to the left bank of the Rhine and subsequently occupying land in modern Switzerland, Alsace, and upper Burgundy. Their warriors were brave and disciplined. They were contained by Theodoric and his Ostrogoths on the east, and by their allies the Burgundians to the south, but the Franks at Soissons must have looked like tempting prey for booty raids.[30]

For safety's sake Clovis took cover in the loose Arian hegemony of Theodoric the Ostrogoth, who, by a policy of marital alliances, was trying to make himself independent of Constantinople. Theodoric married Clovis's sister Audofleda about 493, while Clovis took Burgundian Clothilde for his own bride. It may have occurred to Clovis that a way to preserve a little independence lay in marrying a Catholic Burgundian, to mollify the powerful bishops in Frankish territory and at the same time make the Arian Burgundians and Ostrogoths a little wary.

The quarrels of the Burgundian royal house tempted Clovis, who as a kinsman could make such quarrels his own if he saw any profit in intervention. He would not be restrained by his Christian queen, "whose sanctity did not consist in the forgiveness of injuries," as Edward Gibbon remarks. King Gundobad had murdered Clothilde's royal father. Clovis answered the call of King Godigisel, who ruled in Geneva, for help in attacking his brother King Gundobad. The Burgundian said that he would pay an annual tribute for Clovis's assistance, and also hand over part of Burgundy. It is thought that the Gallo-Roman magnates and churchmen may have supported Godigisel even though he was an Arian, because their goal was the surrender of Burgundy to the Franks.[31]

King Gundobad managed to escape the trap that Godigisel and Clovis laid for him at Dijon, and fled to Avignon with Clovis in hot pursuit. A long siege of the city ensued. Enter a Gallo-Roman from the entourage of Gundobad, pretending to be a defector. He insinuated himself into Clovis's confidence and persuaded him to withdraw in anticipation of an annual tribute.

Not much came of all these alarms and excursions, except the firmer entrenchment of Gundobad, who promised to pardon his brother but saw to it that he was killed at Vienne, along with an Arian bishop. He also effected the massacre of Godigisel's supporters. Gundobad allowed the tribute to lapse, but Clovis was in no position to express outrage. He continued in uncomfortable alliance with the Burgundian king because the Alamanni still loomed ominously on his horizon.

The Alamanni finally boiled over into Frankish territory, and there was a furious battle (probably in 506) at a fortified place called Tolbiac, not far from Cologne. By that time the various Frankish tribes had acknowledged Clovis, but even with this massive support he was in sore straits. According to Gregory of Tours, the tide turned abruptly when Clovis desperately called on Clothilde's God. The enemy was routed, pursued by Clovis. Those who escaped sought asylum under the protection of Theodoric the Ostrogoth. Theodoric was disconcerted by the turn of events. He wrote to Clovis, rejecting his demand for the return of the vanquished. "Those wars of mine have been profitable, the ending of which has been guided by moderation," he observed sagely. Up to the battle of Tolbiac, Theodoric's policy of alliances had allowed him to put some distance between him and the East, but a new field of forces had developed. From that time on, the Alamanni ceased to play a significant part. Their own political organization had been amorphous, no doubt. The-

Plate 68. Baptistery at Cimiez, near Nice. The design of baptisteries of Clovis's time indicates the awesomeness of the ceremony performed in them. The candidate was led in through one door, stripped of his clothing, and immersed in the font. After his baptism, clad in new white garments, he was led triumphantly out through another door into the body of the church. The See of Cimiez persisted at least until the Council of Arles (554), where it was represented by one Bishop Magnus.

odoric found that henceforth he would have to contend not only with the Eastern emperor but also with Clovis the Frank.[32] We shall see that Emperor Anastasius appreciated the advantages of the new situation and reacted favorably toward Clovis.

According to Gregory of Tours, when Clovis told his queen about the miraculous happening on the battlefield at Tolbiac, she quickly relayed the information to Bishop Remigius. The two of them fervently urged the victorious king to enter the baptismal font. He finally did so, with great ceremony, on Christmas Day, along with about half of his Franks. The rest departed under another leader, never to return. This was a tremendous step that Clovis had taken. There is a whisper of what it may have meant to him in the words of Remigius, who solemnly intoned, "Mitis depone colle, Sicamber," which Jean Hoyoux translated, "Be humble, barbarian, and doff your necklaces"—in other words, relinquish your sacral character and magic powers.[33] The passage in Gregory's history that reports the great event calls the king "another Constantine." The news traveled far and wide. Before long, Clovis received a warm letter of welcoming commendation from the highly gratified pope in Rome.

Ironically, at that moment in history Clovis was in truth the only king who adhered to the Nicene Creed. Emperor Anastasius entertained some fairly unorthodox Eutychian views; all the other rulers were Arians. This was brought home to Clovis in a long letter addressed to him by that clever diplomat Bishop Avitus of Vienne, who stood high in the esteem of the Burgundian court but had not managed, despite his best efforts, to persuade King Gundobad to abandon his Arianism.[34] Avitus's letter would have to pass through Gundobad's hands for approval; in a way it was addressed more to him than to Clovis.

Even the salutation of Avitus's letter was artful. Instead of the customary stuffy "Your Glory," he hit on a marvelous expression. Clovis, that brutal warrior who could bash in a skull with his throwing ax without a qualm, that candid murderer and plunderer, was called "Your Subtlety." That was courtly flattery at its best.

Avitus's point was that the perspicacious ruler, despite heresies that attracted other barbarian leaders, had had the astounding discernment to recognize the true religion. He had had the brave clear-sightedness to break with his ancestors. Any objection on grounds of tradition would not be valid after the miracle of Clovis's conversion (this argument was not lost on Gundobad, who had long wrestled earnestly with the problem and with his conscience). Avitus chose his words with care, to emphasize the point that Gundobad would do well to follow Clovis's example because of the general holiness and rightness of such a move, not because his clergy and Roman subjects might betray him to the Franks. The message was clear enough. Clovis was chosen by God, Avitus went on enthusiastically, and he was sure to win victories in the name of the true church: "Your victory is ours." The bishop suggested that Clovis ought to engage in missionary activity because it was he who had miraculously been perceptive enough to see the healing effect of the one true religion on a mixed people (whereas by implication poor Gundobad could not even put his own royal house in order—most were Arians, but some were Catholics). Clovis had been chosen by God to be the arbiter, Avitus concluded. Clovis the judge had made the choice that all should follow.

Clovis was stirred. Before long he announced that it grieved him to think that so much of Gaul lay under the heel of the Arian Visigoths. It became clear that he was about to embark on a holy war. There had always been an implacable hatred between the Franks and the Visigoths. How splendid to be able to go forth against ancient enemies under the shield of Saint Martin of Tours.

No matter how strenuous our effort, we cannot possibly know what it

Plate 69. Rock-crystal pendant from Alzey, Germany. Crystal had magic properties in the eyes of the Franks. A crystal globe was found in the grave of Clovis's
father, and Frankish ladies wore pendants like the one above suspended from their
belts. *Courtesy of Mittelrheinisches Landesmuseum, Mainz.*

was like to deal with Saint Martin. His presence was palpable, his power awesome. The priests who served at his sanctuary in Tours must not have been far removed in popular estimation from the sibyls and oracles of old. Clovis and his army had to cross the Touraine to reach Alaric and his defending Visigothic host. Neophyte that he was, Clovis moved with extreme circumspection. He issued a command that, out of respect for Martin, nothing should be taken by the marching warriors but water and grass for fodder. One of Clovis's followers made a legalistic decision: hay is grass, and therefore there is nothing wrong in taking hay: "The deed came to the king. And quicker than speech the offender was slain by the sword." Perhaps execution of the pillager had not been enough to propitiate the insulted saint. Deeply concerned, Clovis dispatched some of his men to Martin's church laden with gifts, praying for a sign. As Clovis's messengers were about to enter the church, they did indeed receive a sign. There was chanting within. The voices rang out clearly: "Thou hast girded me, O Lord, with strength unto the battle." [35]

The battle was joined at the tenth milestone beyond Poitiers, at Vouillé. Alaric died at the hand of Clovis, and the Visigothic army retreated in disarray, but Clovis himself had a close call. Even Gregory does not say that Martin saved his hero. Clovis had stout armor, he reports, and a fast horse.

Clovis split his forces after Vouillé. He advanced on Toulouse and then attacked Carcassonne, where the Visigothic treasure was (see plate 70). Holy war was fine, but booty was better. The second part of his army moved on under the command of Clovis's oldest son, Theuderic, who had been born illegitimately many years before the marriage to Clothilde. Theuderic made his plundering way across Aquitania, joined Gundobad and his Burgundians, and laid siege to Arles. The Franks, by the way, appear to have been the only barbarians who used Roman-style siege engines. Presumably they acquired them at the factory in Soissons and found Roman-trained soldiers who knew how to manage them.

The siege of Arles was unsuccessful. Strong countercurrents ran among these most Romanized of the Gallic people, and some of them were partisans of the Visigoths. It almost seems to be stretching things to say that anyone in Arles was strictly pro-Roman, because loyalty to the empire would mean loyalty either to remote Constantinople or to Theodoric the Ostrogoth in Ravenna.

Caesarius, the bishop of Arles, had to expend a good deal of energy extricating himself from the web of accusations woven about him by unruly factions. Caesarius was one of the great men of Lérins. Like the others, he was almost larger than life in his formidable asceticism, his charity, and his charismatic personality. Such people can have enemies as well as devoted followers. Even before the Franco-Burgundian attack Caesarius had been de-

Plate 70. Visigothic tower base, Carcassonne, France. Carcassonne was a Visigothic stronghold. The rough, rounded base is Visigothic work.

nounced to the Visigoths. As a Catholic he was suspect; it was stated in so many words that Caesarius wanted Arles to join the Burgundians. The accusation resulted in exile, but King Alaric II became convinced of the bishop's innocence and restored him to his flock. The flock was not exactly a united or loving one. In the excitement of the siege Caesarius was blamed because a kinsman of his, an overenthusiastic young priest, slipped over the city walls to join the Franks. An enraged mob hauled the bishop from his house, fuming that they were to be hacked up and carried off to slavery simply because those fancy church aristocrats wanted to go with the Franks. They threatened to toss him into the river or throw him in a dungeon. Caesarius was locked up, but then the fury of the mob was deflected by the discovery that a member of the city's large Jewish community had tossed a message over the wall, offering to let in the Franks. The Catholics utilized the general confusion to clamor for the release of their bishop and succeeded in saving him.

Theodoric the Ostrogoth resolved the problem of Arles by sending troops, who routed Theuderic and his Franks, hurling them back up the Rhone Valley. When the dust settled, Theodoric the Ostrogoth turned out to be the real gainer. Provence and the rich Mediterranean ports were under his control, and the land connection to Visigothic Spain was likewise secured. Clovis raised his siege of Carcassonne, recognizing the realities of the situation.

Clovis was by no means a loser. He was in fair control of most of Aquitania, and his hands were unmistakably free in the north. He took a barbarian's satisfaction in having trounced a Visigothic king. As a Catholic he had a clear claim to the tremendous prestige of being Saint Martin's man. He lost no time expressing his recognition of that by going to Tours to offer captured booty at the shrine.

The Catholics had won too, and they in turn put on a magnificent show for their champion. In the great basilica of Tours a representative of Emperor Anastasias was on hand to give Clovis a diploma and a high-sounding title. Wearing a purple cloak, with a diadem binding his flowing locks, Clovis rode forth to shower gold and silver coins upon the eager multitude. The ceremony may not have been correct in every detail if, as some scholars believe, Clovis was made a consul (a consul should have ridden in a chariot, it seems).[36] It must have been a moment of high satisfaction for all concerned, however. A Roman title never was entirely empty in the estimation of even the most powerful barbarians, and it had significance for the Gallo-Romans (see plate 71).

The church did not come off scot-free. There were generous donations of land, but Clovis was firm in the matter of his own right to designate bishops, even overriding the judgment of his mentor Remigius.

Plate 71. Consular diptych (righthand leaf) of Flavius Anastasius, consul in 517. If Emperor Anastasius did indeed earlier confer a consulship on Clovis, the document announcing the honor would have been delivered in the leaves of a folding ivory cover. Clovis in turn would have announced the appointment to friends, using ivory diptychs as envelopes. Many diptychs have survived because they were used in churches to hold lists of persons for whom prayers should be offered (Delbrueck, *Die Consulardiptychen und verwandte Denkmäler*, p. 125 and no. 20, Anastasius 0 517). *Courtesy of Victoria and Albert Museum, London.*

Clovis died in 511, a Christian monarch whose body appropriately belonged in a church, but also a Frankish chieftain whose old traditions still held. His kingdom was his private property; it was therefore sliced up in equal portions for his four surviving sons. He had made sure that there would be no awkward problem of rival claimants. Gregory of Tours, who says that Clovis had his power from God because he did "what was pleasing in his eyes," reported that Clovis once gathered all his people and spoke movingly to them of the blood relatives whom he had slaughtered: "Woe to me, who have remained as a stranger among foreigners and have none of my kinsmen to give me aid if adversity comes." That was not an expression of grief, Gregory explained. It was a ruse, "if perchance he should be able to find someone still to kill." [37]

It was possible for a barbarian to hack up a magnificent bejeweled Gospel cover and divide the pieces arbitrarily, but even Clovis's ruthless sons appear to have respected established political divisions when they portioned out their father's domains. The part that went to Childebert I is a case in point. It almost looks as though it represented a survival, through the commands of Aegidius, Paulus, and Syagrius, of the *Tractus Armoricanus* as reorganized for defense purposes by Constantius III and Aëtius.[38] The *Tractus* had had Frankish troops stationed at Rennes in those days. With his capital at Paris, Childebert received Amiens, Beauvais, Rouen, Le Mans, Rennes, and Armorica. Theuderic, the oldest, assumed control of the northernmost part of Clovis's realm (Trier, Mainz, Cologne, Reims, Châlons, and Basel) with his headquarters at Reims. Clodomer took Troyes, Orléans, Tours, Sens, Angers, and Nantes, seating himself at Orléans. The youngest member of the quartet, Clothar I, received Noyons, Soissons, and Laon. His capital was Soissons.

"Capital" is a misleading word, because we immediately think of power centers as we know them. The Frankish kings were constantly on the move, each taking his entourage along in his royal progress from one "palace" (it would be more accurate to say hunting lodge) to another. They were busy rulers, but there was still plenty of time and energy for happy vigorous brawling and the pursuit of game.

Gregory of Tours was born in 538, not long after the division of Clovis's kingdom among the four sons. As bishop of Tours he lived in the prestigious spiritual center of the superstitious world of Gaul, through which all the greats and near-greats passed. Gregory knew them all, entertaining royal guests at his table, giving them sanctuary if need be, fending for himself as best he could. He took an old Roman's pride in his descent from a long line of distinguished bishops, but even so he was barbarized. His language was strange, with Hunnic words in it, and his mind had absorbed a kind of crude superstition that we never find in Sidonius or the bishops from Lérins. Amulets had awful power; every event had its signs and portents. A physician could not cure him, but drinking water with a little dust from Martin's tomb did wonders. Once, when his tongue was sore, the illustrious bishop went down to Martin's shrine at night and licked it, with excellent results. It is with Gregory's uncritical eyes that we are privileged to look at the surrealist world of the Merovingians.

Of all the barbarians the Franks provide the most jarring contrast to the Romanized populations of the empire. Had those elegant Gallo-Romans known what they were about, when they courted their bloody, unpredictable neighbors? In comparison to courteous Theodoric the Ostrogoth or Sidonius's Visigothic friend Theodoric II or earnest King Gundobad the Burgundian who resisted all of Bishop Avitus's theological arguments, the new royalty makes us feel that Arian devils have been traded for appalling witches.

The difficulty lay in the abruptness of the transition. The Franks were not subdued or chastened by their new responsibilities because they were incapable of comprehending them. Their differences had always been settled by fratricide and feud. They knew no other way. As Christian rulers they continued to scuffle over territory without a thought of political unity, which was an unknown concept to them, let alone political accommodation, which was an equally foreign notion.

"I am weary of relating the details of the civil wars," says Gregory plaintively, in the beginning of the fifth book of his history. He had ample reason to be weary. His church at Tours was a place of refuge; to grant the privilege of sanctuary in those times was to invite the wrath of the fugitive's enemies. When Merovech asked for and received asylum, King Chilperic sent messengers to Gregory: "Cast that apostate out of the church. If you do not, I will burn that whole country with fire."

Gregory once had to swear on three successive altars that he had not betrayed his secular lord. His word was accepted, but the Frankish kings and their followers were fairly casual about their own oaths. Theuderic instructed his henchman: "Go and swear an oath to Munderic that he shall go forth safe. And when he has come forth, kill him, and blot out his memory from our kingdom." [39]

In spite of oath taking, private disputes could be bloody affairs. In Paris perjury charges flew when the injured husband of an unfaithful wife took his case to the tomb of Saint Denis: "They drew their swords and rushed on one another and killed one another before the very altar. The holy church was spattered with human blood, the doors were pierced with darts and swords, and godless missiles ranged as far as the tomb." [40]

Insults could be outrageous: "We bid you goodbye, O King. We know that the ax is still safe that was driven into your brothers' heads." The king, "inflamed," ordered his men to pelt the arrogant legates with rotted horse manure, cow chips, and stinking refuse. [41]

Even the clergy were sometimes infected with the Frankish virus. The bishop of Trois-Châteaux was attacked by armed ruffians in the hire of the bishops of Embrun and Gap. His robes were torn, his servants were wounded, and his dinner service was carried off. The complaint lodged against the offenders before a synod called by King Gunthram at Lyons was solemnly heard, and the bishops were driven out, but King Gunthram thought well of them and soon restored them to their sees, where they resumed their boisterous ways. They were banished again by the king in response to public outcry, but when his own son fell ill, Gunthram once more recalled the bishops because he wanted their prayers. They were soon carousing as before.

The scandalous affair of the monastery at Poitiers[42] is so grotesque that it cries for illustration by Brueghel the Younger. Armed ruffians hired by the rebellious nun Chrodield (King Charibert's daughter) attacked the prioress and dragged her about by the hair, carried off the abbess, and set fire to the monastery. Chrodield, armed with a cross, defied the force sent by the local count to restore order, and in the melée hands, noses, and ears were cut off. Gregory of Tours was appointed to the tribunal summoned to handle the case. He presented a full, careful report. The abbess received her monastery back with honor. Chrodield and her followers were excommunicated.

Whenever we see the "lesser people," as Gregory calls them, they are in a state of insurrection, burning tax books, shouting for the execution of a bishop, brawling in the church porches, and ecstatically following "holy men" whose miraculous relics are mouse bones, bear fat, and other such wonder-working materials, or they are being massacred. Once we see them as a joyful multitude greeting King Bertram at Orléans, and we hear the discordant shouts of Syrians and Jews in the crowd acclaiming the ruler. There is a ghastly monotony: the little people are always victims of the great. There is only one terrible unity: the great, the clergy, and the poor all die of plague.

One tragic figure emerged. She was Queen Brunhilda, the wife of Clothar's son Sigebert. She was a Visigothic princess, beautifully educated and of high intelligence. It was her fate to be regent three times, first for her five-year-old son Childebert II after Sigebert's assassination, then for her grandchildren, Childebert's two sons Theodobert and Theodoric, kings of Austrasia and Burgundy, and finally for a great-grandson, the sole ruler of Austrasia and Burgundy. In the early years Brunhilda had to put down the bitter courtiers who refused to bend to a woman, a foreigner at that. Gregory tells us that at one point she armed herself like a man and dashed between her loyal supporter, Lupus of Champagne, and men who were attacking him with the words, "Do not for one man engage in a battle which will destroy the welfare of the district."[43] Ultimately she destroyed the attackers, one of whom died in his flaming stronghold. The other was stoned to death.

In the name of unity and order Brunhilda allied herself with King Guntram of Burgundy, persuading him to adopt her son Childebert II as his heir.

At all times Brunhilda had to fend off the attacks of the vicious Queen Fredegund and her hired assassins. Fredegund, the wife of King Chilperic, had been instrumental in the death of Brunhilda's sister (Chilperic's queen), whom Chilperic strangled so that he might return to the arms of Fredegund, his paramour. At one stage all of Frankish Gaul was controlled by Brunhilda and Fredegund, because the latter was then also a widow and regent for a minor son.

Brunhilda was hated, feared, and maligned, even equated with Fredegund in wickedness, but many respected and honored her, though they probably had little comprehension of her principles. She was trying to do the impossible—govern in a time when society was not governable. Alone of the Merovingian rulers she had inherited something of Roman tradition. For that reason she had the daring to break with barbarian tradition in the name of unity, when she insisted that Austrasia and Burgundy should not be divided but that one of her great-grandchildren should rule over both.

She lost in the final clash with the magnates of Austrasia and Burgundy and died a hideous death, tied to the tail of a wild horse that had been whipped to a frenzy. Brunhilda was a murderess, a splendid woman, and a great statesman.[44] Her tragedy was that she lived in an age that could not accept her ideas, but some faint understanding of her goals must have filtered through. Otherwise it is difficult to see why ancient Roman roads in France came to be known as the Chausées de Brunehaut. People must have known that she had nothing to do with their construction, yet they grasped in some dim way that she had tried to bind the country together and keep it whole.

The kind of unity that Brunhilda sought eluded the Merovingians, but an important fusion occurred in their time. Without the barrier of religion Franks and Gallo-Romans intermarried and rapidly lost their identity. For the first time it was the Romans who assumed barbarian names. Not only that—they abandoned use of the surname as well as the cognomen (family nickname).[45] This runs counter to everything we think we know of Roman pride. Imagine Sidonius naming a son of his something like Bodegisel and abandoning the cognomen that denoted his illustrious ancestry.

If Gallo-Romans had entered the melting pot, there were still some elements in the population of Gaul that were not assimilated. These were the Irish monks, the *peregrini*. One of them, sturdy old Columban, had mightily offended Queen Brunhilda and had been driven out, but in the last analysis the victory was his. The *peregrini* were the most impressive of all invaders, and their history is as curious as anything that we have considered so far.

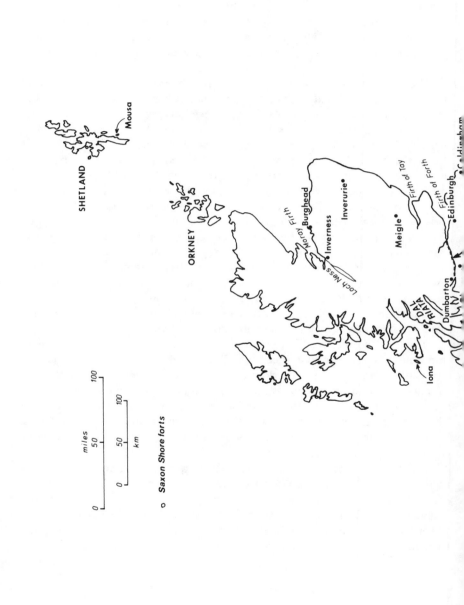

SHETLAND

Mousa

ORKNEY

Moray Firth

Burghead

Inverness

Loch Ness

Inverurie

Meigle

Firth of Tay

Firth of Forth

Edinburgh

Coldingham

DAL
RIATA

Dumbarton

Iona

miles

0   50   100

0   50   100

km

○   *Saxon Shore forts*

The British Isles

CELTIC OUTPOSTS
IN BRITAIN

DEMONS foretold the arrival of Saint Germanus when he crossed over to Britain on his second anti-Pelagian expedition (probably in 444). The prosaic explanation lies in the existence of a semaphore system on either side of the Channel, but we should be aware that fifth-century Britain is the territory of Merlin the Enchanter, a country where the true nature of persons and events can be hidden.

Not even the most learned specialist pretends that he has successfully ferreted out fact from the welter of scribal misinterpretations of bardic lore and errors or "improvements" in fragmentary chronicles and regnal lists that were handed down across the ages. The kind of orderly archival material that might have accumulated in Roman administrative offices vanished when the administrators were withdrawn, and all responsibility was left in the hands of inexperienced local people. Dates must be determined from much later "Easter tables," in which the correct posting of a movable holy feast was the major concern of the clerics who compiled them. A few marginal jottings here and there refer to a warrior king or a battle or a visitation of the plague, but there is no precision. At one stage the dates in the tables were based on the reigns of emperors. Later they were computed either on the assumed date of Jesus' incarnation or on that of his crucifixion: this in itself entails a shift that could swallow up a whole generation.[1] To make matters worse, even the events that the historian wants to pinpoint are vague and uncertain, possibly mythical. There are few inscriptions. Archaeological finds have not yielded much reliable information thus far. Documents emanating from the European continent offer little guidance.

Against a kaleidoscopic background of unlocatable battles, undatable invasions, and unrecognizable heroes with curious titles and dubious status, we might try another tack. Let us abandon the pursuit of accuracy and pick out patterns of action that denote response to problems known to have worried the

278

people of Britain in the fifth century, rather in the spirit of T. C. Lethbridge, who exclaims: "Let us not be so damnably cautious. . . . What does it matter if the dates are wrong and the names are all invented?" [2]

The times were critical. The usurper Maximus had removed large numbers of competent fighting men to Gaul in 383. Although there is shadowy evidence that he may have tried to leave Britain in a position of strength by placing control of whatever defensive forces remained there in the hands of local chieftains, the population was badly exposed to raids by Scotti from Ireland and Picts from the north. After 407, when the usurper Constantine III invaded Gaul from Britain, there was an even greater depletion of men under arms, and little or no help was to be had from the empire. The Saxon landings were soon to begin, first as a trickle and later as a flood. We remember that the people of Britain are said to have made some kind of attempt to set up an independent government in the first decade of the fifth century and that this effort was followed by a period of internecine violence. Popular unrest apparently took a form not unlike that of the egalitarian Bacaudic movement in Gaul. Although the church continued a frail existence, the issue of Pelagianism had split its thin ranks.

Raiders were surely more alarming than heretics. We may assume that the Irish Scotti occupied a larger place in the public mind than did the Pelagians, particularly if it is correct, as Charles Thomas asserts, that during the fifth and sixth centuries the number of Irish settlers in western Britain may have exceeded that of the Germanic settlers arriving in the east. [3]

The aggressions of the Scotti were formidable because they were slave raiders. Back in the days of the great Roman general Agricola, there might have been some chance of restraining them. Tacitus reported that his illustrious father-in-law was heard to comment on a number of occasions that Ireland could be "reduced and held by a single legion with a fair-sized force of auxiliaries." [4] It would be easier to hold Britain, he felt, if it were "completely surrounded by Roman armies." Agricola never took a legion across the sea to Ireland; three centuries after his day Britain was anything but secure, partly because of exposure to hit-and-run attack by the unsubdued people on the west.

Ireland remained barbarian, still in a undisturbed heroic age, with a tribal society that, though it was cut across by rival "kingdoms," had a certain unity owing to the peculiar geography of the island. It is rather like a shallow dish, rimmed around the shores. Inside the dish there is little to disrupt the continuity. Warring tribal factions under petty kings there might be, but the language, customs, and general societal fabric were one. It was the ultimate retreat of the Celts, a retreat to which pagan Rome, the Christians, and the Teutonic cultures that were sweeping across the European continent had had practically no access. Consequently, when Christianity arrived in Ireland, there was a fresh confrontation unlike anything that occurred on the Continent or on the British mainland.

There is an unsubstantiated hint that the Eóganacht dynasty that emerged at Cashel in the early fifth century may have been made up of former Irish colonists who were driven from North Wales at that time,[5] but this wispy thread is no indication of any strong contact with things Roman. At the most, expulsion of the colonists may show that there was some ripple effect from all the disturbances in Gaul and Britain.

Even in Ireland, change was in the wind. From the third century on, archaic tribal groups with primitive totemic names, translated as something like "bear people," "horse people," "boar people," and so on, were gradually pushed aside, subjugated or co-opted by more militant groups and alliances. The course of events is obscure, but the development that can be traced out was not as chaotic as it appears at first glance. In the shifting pattern "boar people" and "bear people" bound by allegiance to a dimly perceived deity were giving way to emergent entities whose bond was kinship and who defiantly called themselves by the names of doughty ancestors: the Connachta, descendants of Conn; the Eóganachta, descendants of Eógan; the Uí Néill, descendants of Niall Noígiallach, whom we call Niall of the Nine Hostages. A fairly rigid hierarchical system evolved, based on the tribal unit (*túath*) under a petty king (*rí*) who owed allegiance to an overking and so on up the line to a "high king" at Cashel, Tara, or Munster who embodied the whole in some ritualistic way, with close interlocking of the tribal units by specific duties and bonds encouraged by a complex system of fosterage. Life on the physical plane, however, was not much different at the dawn of the fifth century from that of centuries extending back into a dim Celtic dawn.

The Irish countryside today is pocked like a moonscape with the remains of thousands of tiny fortlets that were not much more than little earthwork circles. In their time these fortified structures were elaborate in varying degrees. A simple rampart topped by a timber palisade (*rath*) served to shelter a pastoral family against cattle raids. An artificial island (*crannog*) also was enclosed by a wooden palisade, here again functioning as a fortification of sorts. The larger strongholds (*cashels*) had stonework instead of timber and no doubt were more formidable to possible attackers. None of these fortifications had impressive dimensions. The largest, supposed to have been the seat of royalty, measured about two hundred feet across. Little has been found to indicate that the inhabitants were genuinely warlike people. Whatever warfare took place must have been sporadic and inconsequential cattle raids, despite the sagas that show how important acts of dauntless heroism in combat could be to the aristocrats. If the wars had posed a real threat to the life of the Irish populace, there would surely be something to show the existence of nucleated settlements for the sake of mutual protection, yet we know that when Patrick

Plate 72. The Chillingham herd of wild cattle, Alnwick, Northumberland, England. Records for this herd go back as far as the year 1200. The animals are entirely wild even today. Believed to be descendants of *Bos primigenius* (aurochs), they resemble the creatures herded in Ireland and Pictland in the days of Saint Patrick.

arrived on his missionary venture in the days of King Laogaire (or Lóegaire, a son of Niall of the Nine Hostages) there was nothing in all Ireland that even remotely resembled a town. Cities as we know them did not appear until the Viking era. It was the Nordic warriors who established the port of Dublin, for example.

Patrick had firsthand knowledge of Ireland when he embarked to spread the Gospel there, probably in 432, but that knowledge must have been limited, because a lowly swineherd would hardly have much opportunity to observe the workings of a complicated pyramidally organized society of kings and subkings, a great intellectual class of druids and historians and bards, and a wandering class of honored craftsmen. Patrick had been carried off to Ireland as a slave from what appears to have been a Romanized part of Britain somewhere in the north (it has been suggested that he may have been born at Bewcastle, on Hadrian's Wall), where his father held a position of trust in the civil service, and the whole family was Christian. After a dramatic escape the runaway somehow came into contact with the churchmen of Gaul. Some scholars believe that he sojourned at the island monastery of Lérins, while others make a fairly convincing case for Saint Germanus's monastic establishment at Auxerre. Patrick was inspired by a mysterious inner voice to return to the scene of his captivity with the message of truth. It is a pity that there is so little certainty about his mission. The timing of it and the possible identity of his sponsor are illustrative of the interlocking interests at work in Gaul, Rome, and Britain.[6]

We are within a year or so of Germanus's first visit to Britain (about 428), when the great bishop of Auxerre is supposed to have crossed the Channel to suppress Pelagianism. As we observed in another connection, there were strange happenings during Germanus's trips to Britain that seem to imply that his missions were at least partly military. He is thought to have been a dux in Gaul up to the year 418, when he was abruptly catapulted into the episcopate. The presumed former commander of the Saxon Shore system in Gaul, he appears to have sustained contact with the British Saxon Shore. His anti-Pelagian expeditions must have had a multiple purpose—the driving out of heretics and the quelling of popular unrest, and possibly also the strengthening of native resistance to invading Picts and Scotti.

A mysterious figure whose prime interest seems to have been the destruction of the Pelagian heresy has an undefined role in the stories of both Germanus and Patrick. This was the deacon Palladius. Because his office within the church was essentially administrative, Palladius had the attention of Pope Celestine in Rome. It is supposed to have been at Palladius's behest that Celestine designated Germanus of Auxerre to spearhead the anti-Pelagian effort in Britain. The intriguing aspect of this connection lies in the question of Palladius's identity. Was he, as Nora Chadwick suggests, the son of Saint Germanus's predecessor Exuperantius, the commander of the Gallic Saxon Shore? Chadwick, in an educated guess that she recognizes to be "fragile," admits that Palladius was a common name.[7]

For the sake of coherence let us accept her idea, agree that Palladius and Germanus may have had a community of interest deriving from Germanus's military command, and say that Germanus, the former military commander who was drafted to combat heresy, and Palladius, the antiheresy man whose father was a military commander, may have seen eye to eye on many issues.

No doubt it is merely a coincidence, but Patrick's forerunner in Ireland, known as the first bishop there, was named Palladius. He was consecrated the first bishop of Ireland by Pope Celestine, who, without military interests and presumably likewise without any thought of the potentials of a Christian mission as a means for quelling Irish raiders, would have been deeply concerned over the possibility that the sparse scattering of Christians in Ireland was going astray. Pelagians had been driven from the empire back in the days of Emperor Constantius III. It is not unlikely that some may have taken refuge in that place "where there is nobody beyond," as Patrick expressed it, a land that Rome had never touched militarily.[8]

Palladius went to Ireland in 431. Nothing more is known of him. We should remember that he went as a bishop to believing Christians, not as a missionary bent on making converts. Missionary enterprise was not characteristic of the church in those times. Palladius must have died within the year, and his unfinished work was taken up by Patrick, who had an entirely different idea of the task.

Patrick was not officially under the aegis of Rome. The historian Prosper, as a *notarius* to Pope Celestine, was well informed about the activities of the Holy See. He knew about Palladius but was silent about Patrick. Some scholars (notably Charles Thomas) believe that Patrick was sent out by the Church of Britain, while others believe that he was ordained a priest by Bishop Amator at Auxerre and consecrated a bishop by Germanus when it was learned that Palladius had died. Could it be that the devout but military-minded saint saw a strategic opportunity in enlisting the burning zeal of innocent Patrick? Did he think that a Christianized Ireland might be more readily dealt with, just as General Agricola long before had thought that a Roman-occupied Ireland might be more tractable?

Germanus's expeditions to Britain had not been crowned with success as far as putting down Pelagianism was concerned, the glowing account of his hagiographer notwithstanding. If he was indeed Patrick's sponsor, that might explain the coolness of British clerics toward the zealous missionary across the Irish Sea. Patrick seems to have felt throughout his career that his back was to the wall. He received no encouragement from the British church, where learned men scoffed at him for his rusticity and lack of scholarship. If we follow Bede's account in his *Ecclesiastical History* (1.17) of the meeting of Germanus and his adversaries in Britain, we see that these men were "conspicuous for riches, glittering in apparel." Such individuals would hardly feel that they had much in common with a former swineherd turned missionary.

There had been Christians in Ireland for a long time. Like Patrick they had been transported into slavery. According to Patrick himself, he was one of thousands. Christians there certainly were, but no church organization. There were loan words in Irish speech that had a Christian tone (*cáisc*, "Easter"; *caille*, "veil"; *vescor*, "vespers"; *sléchtad*, "prostration" or "genuflection"), but no word for "bishop."[9] Patrick had little to build on when he attempted to set up a diocesan system there.

A vivid ancient narrative describes an outraged king of Tara rushing out into the night in his chariot accompanied by his queen and his druid to confront Patrick, who had audaciously kindled an Easter fire on rising ground at Slane, not far from Tara.[10] Patrick met the challenge head on. He believed in the genuineness of druidical sorcery but knew that he was a greater thaumaturge because of divine power. He called down a fearsome darkness. The king's horses pounded away in panic, and the king was immediately converted to a wholesome belief in Christ. This wonderful story veils a less dramatic course of events. King Laogaire of Tara remained heathen to the day of his pagan burial (upright, in full battle gear), but he was a prudent person with a sense of the fitness of things. By ancient custom a king was responsible for a man without kinfolk, a "headless man" like Patrick, and Laogaire was aware that a place had to be found for such persons in the general order. Patrick and his followers were a new brand of druids perhaps. Bury suggests that toward the end of Laogaire's reign Patrick may have been invited peaceably to attend an assembly at Tara, where the problem could be thrashed out. In the end Patrick's growing communities were accorded the same kind of social footing as a *túath* ("family" or "tribe").[11] In this cautious way an opening was made for an interchange of ideas between the representatives of an archaic barbarian culture and the varied, elaborate civilization of Rome. Before long a process of mutual influence was under way. Ireland entered on the tremendous adventure of literacy (see plate 73), and the organized church was woven in a distinctive way into the very fabric of barbaric society, where there was a readiness for Christian dedication.

This is not to say that instant accommodation followed or that Ireland was Christianized overnight. Patrick was, however, able to move about in the north with the freedom customarily reserved to the privileged classes to establish his little "cities." Patrick's model was the traditional Roman one, wherein the center of a bishop's diocese was the city. In primitive Ireland, Patrick diligently consecrated bishops—350 of them—to preside over cities that might be nothing more than small enclosures with a hut or two for celibate priests, a little oratory, and perhaps a refectory.

In a way, by demanding celibacy of his priests, Patrick became the instrument for the introduction of monasticism among a dreamy, impulsive people who were to snatch at the novel, romantic notion of forsaking one's kindred for the love of God and the hope of salvation, though it is unlikely that he intended to do anything more than establish a firm core of committed workers who would go about the holy task of converting nonbelievers. How could he have foreseen that his converts would embrace the faith with such fiery enthusiasm that the face of all Ireland would be transformed, that ultimately this remote, illiterate people to whom he had been drawn so irresistibly would depart on an invasion of barbarized continental Europe, bearing not only the zeal of Christian teaching but also the culture of classic Rome that had come perilously close to extinction?

The readiness in Ireland lay deep in the traditions, even in the psyche of the people, but the traditions were such that Patrick's plan for a church based on the episcopate was destined for founder. Patrick's cities with their ruling bishops underwent an irrevocable change as time went by. They did not fit well into the Celtic tribal scheme, in which the nobles were the sole landowners and overlordship was hereditary within the *túath*. Aristocrats who generously set aside portions of their territories for the newcomers tended to regard the arrangement as an extension of control to a newly formed *túath*. The age-old

Plate 73. Stone abecedarium in the ruined church at Kilmalkedar, County Kerry, Eire. This alphabet is thought to have been carved for instruction of illiterate clerics. The letter *a* is broken off, but otherwise the alphabet is complete. It was customary for the first teachers of Christianity in Ireland to furnish their disciples with such alphabets. The letters *dni* signify *domini*. George Petrie thought that *domini* was added to consecrate a stone that had had some earlier pagan association (Petrie, *The Ecclesiastical Architecture of Ireland: The Round Towers*, pp. 134–35).

custom whereby any male in a given *túath*, within certain prescribed limits of kinship, was eligible to be king was gradually extended to encompass the office of abbot. Bishops remained independent in the performance of sacerdotal duties, more or less as tribal high priests, with an "honor price" (a sum to be paid by an assailant in the event of death of the victim) equivalent to that of the king, but abbots who administered the monastic communities were *coarbs* ("heirs") of the founder. In the Celtic tradition of tanistry [12] the abbot designated his own successor. In subsequent centuries we find long lines of abbots, all drawn from a single family (not infrequently a royal one). We also find it characteristic of the church in Ireland that by and large it was the abbots who held the power. We see this pattern with particular clarity when we come to the great abbot Columba (Colum or Columcille) of Iona, who ruled a network of far-flung monasteries that could not be described as a territorial system at all. [13]

Still other aspects of Irish life had the effect of insinuating aristocrats, intellectuals, and the scholarly-minded into the ranks of the church. Fosterage had long been used in Ireland to bind *túaths* together: sons of the nobility were placed at an early age in the households of persons of higher rank. The arrangement tended to create more powerful bonds than those between parent and child. Fosterling and *nutritor* (foster-parent) were bound to each other for a lifetime. As the monastic idea took hold, increasing numbers of young people were placed as foster-children in church establishments, there to be reared and educated. The monk-tutor easily came to be regarded as a *nutritor*. Add to this the circumstance that when the druids lost their grip the monasteries took over the role of the famed druidical schools as centers of learning. It was perhaps no accident that the tonsure adopted by the monks of Ireland closely copied that of the druids (instead of the accepted Christian "crown" the monks shaved the front of their heads from ear to ear, as the druids had done).

Important external influences were also in play, complementing the effect of ancient custom. Before the archaeologists were able to demonstrate the existence of trade contacts with the eastern Mediterranean, the similarities, down to the most minute details, between the practices of developed Irish monasticism and monastic forms that evolved in Egypt and Palestine were a fascinating puzzle. How could it be, for instance, that Irish monks carried their Gospel books in little tooled-leather "budgets" that were precise counterparts of the book satchels that swung so characteristically from the shoulders of monks along the Nile? [14] How did it happen that there were pegs for hanging such satchels in the beehive cells at Skellig Michael and book cupboards in the walls of the round tower at Disert Oengus (County Limerick), just as Lord Curzon observed them at the Abyssinian monastery at Souriani? What was the explanation of the early use of the interlace pattern in the borders of illuminated manuscripts prepared by monks in remote Irish scriptoria? Copts painted the same design in crosses on the walls of ancient tombs, defacing splendid images of lordly pharaohs while consecrating those dim and dusty corridors to a foreign religion. Was it only coincidence that Coptic and Irish bookbinders used the same system of stitching?[15] There is clear evidence now, based on patient classification of pottery sherds, that direct sea communications did indeed exist between Ireland and the Crimea, the Danube and the Nile, by way of Gibraltar: "Where amphorae could travel, so too could pilgrims, occasional refugees, books and ideas" (see plate 74).[16]

We must not overlook or misjudge the importance of the British mainland as a formative influence. A web of contacts spread all across the Irish Sea. The first British monastery that existed before the year 500 appears to have been the one at Tintagel, on the Cornish coast. (After completing the first draft of this chapter, I learned from A. M. Cubbon that there is a controversy among scholars about Tintagel. Charles Thomas thinks that it is medieval, whereas C. A. Ralegh Radford maintains that the early dating of the establishment is correct.) This small site perches precariously on the slope of a formidable promontory on which stand remains of an Iron Age fort. No names can be associated with this evocative place, but when we move northward to Wales, we arrive at the establishment of men known to have contributed to the spread of the monastic idea to Ireland. Hagiographers of later date have played havoc with facts and almost hopelessly snarled the lives of their heroes in their eagerness to attribute to them everything glorious, such as pilgrimages to the Holy Land, study in Rome, or acquaintance with all the other luminaries of preceding centuries. It is possible, nonetheless, to find faint suggestions of some kind of association with Lérins and Auxerre. We are on firmer ground when we come to the famed Irish monastery founder Finnian of Clonard (d. 549). His first monastery was already in being before he came into contact with Cadoc and Gildas of Wales. Following Cadoc's principles, Finnian appears to have transformed his monastery, stressing the importance of sacred scholarship and thus in due time making his Irish monasteries competent rivals of secular centers. With reference to the influence of Gildas on Finnian, John Ryan attributes to Gildas "the amazing extension of the monastic institute in Ireland and the more rigorous concept of the monastery as a place of retirement from the world." This in turn, Ryan points out, was to have an effect on the role of Irish abbots.[17]

The burgeoning of the monasteries came in the century after Patrick. Although later generations of church historians were eager to enhance the prestige of their own establishments by claiming Patrick as founder and patron, there is little to show that Patrick himself made much headway. His *paruchia* (diocese) was a small one; although some royal personages accepted the new religion, he labored all his life in a pagan land. The British mainland continued to be a source of trouble. His blistering letter to British King Cor-

Plate 74. Irneit's cross slab, Maughold, Isle of Man, late seventh–early eighth century. Detail showing an Eastern-style chi-rho with its characteristic open loop or tail at the top of the cross. This open loop is also seen on Coptic work (see plate 58). The inscription on this cross relates to a Celtic bishop named Irneit. Irneit's cross slab, Maughold, no. 47 [27]. *Courtesy of Manx Museum and National Trust.*

oticus, protesting an atrocity against a group of newly baptized converts, shows that this supposedly Christian ruler, whose home ground seems to have been in the vicinity of Strathclyde and whose stronghold was the rock of Dumbarton, had allowed his "soldiers" to go ashore in Ireland where they slaughtered innocent persons and carried women off into slavery. That happened around 459, the year of Finnian's death. If it is correct that Coroticus was a fair counterpart of his contemporary Aegidius in Gaul, maintaining a tiny enclave in the name of the empire, we can only sigh that this ruler of a Christian dominion was behaving badly, but we must concede that Coroticus was even farther removed from civilizing imperial centers than Aegidius had been.[18] Whatever success Patrick may have had in reducing the barbarity of Irish raiding on the mainland was offset by activity of this kind in the north. We shall see that in the time of Columba of Iona the Irish who had migrated to Scotland in turn had quite a problem on their hands confronting the Britons and the Picts.

It is a long jump from Patrick's day to the age of the saints as exemplified by Columba. Columcille, as he was affectionately called, was no former slave, no one-time captive swineherd with dreams of converting a wayward foreign folk for the glory of God. Columba sprang from the powerful royal line the Uí Néill. He was a direct descendant of Niall of the Nine Hostages and also—more important, perhaps—a descendant of Loarn, ruler of the Irish colony from Dalriada, established in western Scotland. He never forgot his tribal connections; his movements show a close correlation with political events.

In Columba's day monasticism had become an acknowledged and essential feature of Irish life. The principle of ascetic renunciation of the world was accepted. That a man whose credentials were such that he could reasonably aspire to the kingship of Tara should elect to become a monk might not cause popular astonishment, but that such a man should decide to banish himself required an explanation. Surviving stories are indicative of some perplexity among the people. Columba left his beloved land, it was said, in self-imposed or even church-dictated exile as penance for involvement in a bloody conflict, the famous Battle of Cúil Dreimne, which was the climax of a struggle for the kingship of Tara. It is true that Columba left Ireland for Dalriadic Scotland shortly thereafter (the battle was fought in 560, and he arrived at the stronghold of his cousin King Conall two years later). In popular estimation, a holy man would embroil himself in a battle only if it concerned church matters. Therefore, Columba was supposed to have incited the members of his *túath* because King Diarmait of Tara had ruled against him in favor of his friend Finnian in a dispute over the possession of a psalter.

A political interpretation of the event would make more sense. Diarmait of Tara had a precarious hold on the kingship, but he was reckless enough to assert his claims aggressively. His boldness in going through with the *feis* (the

Plate 75. "Columba's house" at Kells, Eire. Like the better-known "Saint Kevin's house" at Glendalough, this little building combined an oratory on the ground floor with living quarters upstairs. According to George Petrie, it can scarcely be questioned that both houses were erected for the private devotions of the founders of the respective monasteries (Petrie, *The Ecclesiastical Architecture of Ireland: The Round Towers*, p. 357).

ancient ceremony of ritual mating with Tara) must have stirred up a number of potential claimants who were only too willing to view this action as a challenge. Columba was not a claimant, in spite of his clear eligibility. He had already become a monk and had established a monastery at Derry in 545, on land given him by Ainmire, the head of a branch of the northern Uí Néill. Ainmire was one of the participants in the Battle of Cúil Dreimne. The carnage in that encounter was bloody, and Diarmait of Tara was defeated but not eliminated. He was defeated again in the following year after more aggressions on his part, but he struggled on stubbornly until 565, when he was killed. In view of his consistently poor relationship with the clergy, it is just possible that Diarmait embodied the last pagan resistance in Ireland.[19] His death initiated a period of utter confusion in which rivals for the kingship of Tara rose and fell with dizzying rapidity. The supremacy ultimately went to Áed son of Ainmire, of the Uí Néill, though Áed did not assume the rule of Tara at that point.

By this time Columba's own position had gone from strength to strength. There was nothing in his experience that could have contributed to thought processes similar to those of the continental bishops who in their sophistication could appreciate the potentials of a career in the church. All of them (men like Ambrose of Milan and Sidonius and Remigius in Gaul) had enough knowledge of the world and the workings of empire to be able to make such an assessment, grasping the power inherent in the far-flung network of the church hierarchy. In Columba we have a man innocent of the power structure of the mother church and dependent on a system adapted to tribal conditions, putting himself into a position where whatever authority he was to assert through the monastic system would be by force of persuasion or possibly of threat, but not by the brute power of the sword. Columba was a poet with the innate admiration of the Celts for eloquence and the magic power of words and spells. He must have come to his decision by this route, not through the Roman churchman's respect for administrative order.

Cutting family ties in favor of wandering (*peregrinatio*) was the approved form of "white martyrdom" among the Irish, for whom such detachment spelled bitter pain. Columba's own *peregrinatio* was surely inspired by the deepest impulses of religious devotion, yet there were political overtones that cannot be ignored. Trouble between colonizing Scotti from Dalriada and the Picts in Scotland must have had something to do with Columba's choice of Iona as the scene of his exile. About half a century before his day an invading force of Scotti under some of Columba's ancestors had taken possession of land in western Scotland, at the expense of the Picts. In Columba's young manhood the descendants of the invaders gained a firm grip on the territory around Dunadd, the stronghold of their leader, Gabrán. In 558, Gabrán was defeated by the Picts; shortly thereafter Brude mac Maelchon, king of the northern Picts, managed to reduce the new king of Scottish Dalriada (Columba's cousin

Plate 76. Lag ny Keeilley, Isle of Man. The small enclosure, which included a cell for a priest (possibly a Culdee) and an oratory (*keeill*), perches on a natural platform near the foot of the almost perpendicular precipice of Cronk ny Irree laa. The oratory is in the foreground, far left (Kermode, *The Manx Archaeological Survey*, pp. 19–29).

Conall) to vassalage. Conall's position was doubly weak because he also owed tribute to the ruler of the kingdom of Ulidia, who was overking of the Dalriada in Ireland. Conflicting stories suggest that tiny Iona, where Columba and his twelve disciples settled, was border territory. Perhaps this underlies the confusion about the granting of Iona to Columba. According to some sources he received it from King Conall; according to others the donor was Brude mac Maelchon, the Pictish king.

In any event, in the pivotal year 565, when Diarmait of Tara met his death and conflict over the succession began in earnest, Columba set off on a journey northward from Conall's fortress to confront King Brude in his stronghold near Inverness. There must have been some plan to negotiate on behalf of Conall, though all we have to go on is the adoring biography of Columba written by his successor, Abbot Adamnan of Iona. Politics were of no interest to Adamnan. He tells us entertainingly about Columba's encounter with a formidable aquatic beast (the first time that the Loch Ness monster raises its fearsome head in literature) and shows us a defiant druid at Brude's court. He also lets us hear Columba's famed singing voice drowning out a malevolent druidical choral chant. The only item of even faintly political nature that interested Adamnan concerned a churchman. In this instance Columba demanded protection for some of his monks, who were heading toward the Orkneys to establish a monastic outpost there. Brude was a powerful king: his vassals included not only Conall in the south but also the ruler of the Orkneys. Addressing Brude, Columba spoke with calm authority: "Do thou carefully instruct this chief whose hostages are in thy hand that no evil befall them within his dominions."

The main thrust of Columba's efforts was directed at the establishment of the Scottish Dalriadic kingdom on a firm, independent footing. That he was able to accomplish this after years of patient maneuvering is clear evidence of his secular power. Conall died in 574. By that time Columba had apparently gained the confidence of King Brude and also had enough authority to enforce his personal choice of Conall's successor, Áedán son of Gabrán, who was not the obvious candidate for the office. Columba consecrated him at Iona (in the first royal consecration anywhere in Britain), and thereafter he moved to promote the new king's interests both in Scotland and in Ireland. To extricate him from tribute-paying status in Ireland, Columba accompanied King Áedán to a meeting in Derry in the following year, 575. Once again a colorful narrative cluttered with miracles, magic, thunderbolts and angels obscures the nature of the event, but it is clear that Columba was able to bring about an agreement between Áedán and the powerful Áed son of Ainmire (Columba's kinsman), whereby the Dalriadic fleet would belong to the Scottish kingdom, to avoid claims on it by the new king of Tara.

At the close of his long career the serene old abbot, taking one last, fond look at domestic little Iona, its mill, its barns, and its old workhorse, which wept on his bosom, could gaze back on a series of unprecedented successes accruing to his kinsmen that were to have extraordinary consequences in the secular world—even the implanting of Goidelic or Gaelic speech and a new religion in the Highlands.

Political manipulator though he was, we must not unfairly deny Columba his sainthood. Quiet, pious contemplation of an ineffable deity did not come easily to him. He has been called vindictive, passionate, bold—a soldier and a man of strife. In other words, he was a man of his age. That age had another side to it: it was a period when intensity of religious conviction could color every wakeful act and every dream. Columba the politician was the same man who superstitiously made the protective sign of the cross over new milk that it might not sour—the same man who fasted and kept nightlong vigils and who passed his few hours of sleep lying on stone with a stone for a pillow. The same malicious demons that tormented Antony in the Egyptian desert tormented him, and were overcome by incessant prayer. It is reported—accurately, no doubt—that, as he died, his face was ruddy and suffused with the light of gladness. Like Antony, Columba knew that he was crossing the threshold to a realm of perpetual adoration, for which his being longed.[20]

Columba's Iona is disappointing today. The holy spirits and even the demons have been driven off by markers and monuments and bored guides who drone a garbled story. We can sense what Iona must have been if we travel out into the Atlantic, eight miles off the Dingle peninsula of Ireland, to that astounding remnant of the monastic age, the huge, craggy pyramidal rock Skellig Michael. The date of the tiny monastery there is unknown. Its remaining physical structures are of stone, in contrast to the flimsy wattle-and-daub of Iona that disappeared centuries ago, but the differences are not so great as to be misleading. The men who exiled themselves from the green mainland, bobbing across the frightening water in their little skin boats to disembark on the forbidding mountain in the sea must have shared Columba's vision and his courage. The stairway that they built of slabs that tilt crazily across the slanting face of the mountain tells us that these monks were no weaklings. Strong backs and strong hands they had, and also a driving belief in the rightness of their lives. The little beehive huts that they built for themselves on a minute flat patch in the saddle of the mountain are sturdy, still proof against howling wind and the spume that sweeps over the very pinnacle of the eight-hundred-foot summit in winter. Sea pinks grow in rock crevices where the monks must have cultivated vegetables to supplement the fish they caught. The graveyard plot for departed brothers has a row of simple, nameless headstones marked with rudimentary crosses. Out over the wrinkled sea below the precipices the enormous yellow-headed gannets soar, and far off in the distant haze lies Ireland. What a place for prayer and ecstasy. What a place for sheer audacity.

So far we have looked at the Picts only through Irish eyes. Let us try now to imagine how the mainland Britons saw them. It is difficult to conceive of any period following the advent of the Romans when the rude peoples in the north would not have weighed heavily on the Britons' minds, because of the drain of sustaining a huge military apparatus to keep them at bay. For more than three centuries resistance against barbarian pressure had continued practically unabated.

Our first glimpse of the tribes in Scotland is reminiscent of our view of the woebegone Vandals after their defeat at Carthage. In A.D. 84 the Roman general Agricola had pursued his quarry relentlessly to a place somewhere near Moray Firth, known as Mons Graupius, and there he inflicted a terrible defeat on a host that Tacitus numbered at thirty thousand combatants, who arrived with chariots and armed with enormous blunt swords and little shields. A third of this force was annihilated in the battle. Tacitus pictured the survivors, "men and women wailing together," as they wandered in distraction about the field of carnage, unable to form a plan. Many in their raging despair fired their own homes, and "we had proof that some of the men laid violent hands on their wives and children in a kind of pity."[21]

The Picts were not a homogeneous people.[22] There was a Mesolithic stock in Scotland that may have represented a circumpolar culture like that of the Eskimos. Animals carved on standing stones by the Picts at a later time are especially charming and lively. Some are like Chinese brushwork in their fleetness; it is with amazement that we consider that the carvers slowly worked these skimming creations by incising a line in the rude, unyielding stone, first pecking it out and then patiently honing it to a shallow groove. This Bronze Age technique was generally understood and used in Britain,[23] but representation of natural forms in this way was peculiar to the Picts. No Celt had such a perception of the world about him. The configuration of animal joints and muscles in this simple, vigorous work is oddly reminiscent of Scythian metalwork from farthest Asia. This similarity, along with the philologists' judgment that the language of the Picts contained non–Indo-European traces surviving from the speech of the Bronze Age aborigines, justifies the thought that the Picts may have descended in part from some stock that once roamed across the polar regions all the way from China.

These fisher-hunters were displaced or absorbed by two major immigrating groups. The first probably was made up of Welsh speakers, a Gaulish folk who settled in southern Scotland in the fertile regions now known as Fyfe and Angus. The second group, a pre-Belgic people who had been pushed out of southern England by incoming Celts from the continent, settled in Orkney and Shetland, in the Hebrides, and in the northwest part of the Scottish mainland. The latecomers were vaguely related to the Gauls, but they must have descended from the megalithic builders of the Mediterranean rather than from the more northerly continental peoples who occupied southern Scotland.[24]

Names changed, but we can always discern a demarcation of sorts between the two groups, with a break between them along the edge of the Highlands mountain mass. In the third century there were Mæatæ in the north and Caledones south of them. In the fourth century we read about Venturiones and Dicalydones. By Bede's time it was acceptable to write of northern and southern Picts, as though there were two defined confederations with similar cultures. Still later, medieval sources indicate that Pictland had seven provinces, each with its own king and subkings.[25] This idea is intriguing because it may offer an explanation for the enigma of the fourteen carved symbols on Pictish standing stones that remain to delight and confound us.[26] These symbols appear in various combinations that seem to follow a code. One is a crescent, for example, while two are floriated rods, a V rod and a bent Z rod. The crescent may be crossed by a V rod, but never by a Z rod. Similarly, there is a double disk "spectacles" symbol that may be crossed by a Z rod, but never by a

Plate 77. Pictish symbol stone, Inverurie, Grampian Region, Scotland. A floriated Z-rod is imposed on the "spectacles" symbol. Like many other remains from past ages, this stone narrowly escaped destruction. It had been used in construction of a dike to protect the low-lying churchyard and was about to be smashed by a mason who was making repairs when an alert antiquarian noticed it (Spalding Club, *Sculptured Stones of Scotland*, 1:35, "Inverury no. 3").

V. The rods never appear alone (see plate 77). We might be bold enough to venture a guess that in some way the rods modify the meaning of the symbol on which they are imposed and that this might signify one of the seven provincial overkings and his underlings.

Pagan carvings are found all over Pictland, heavily concentrated around Moray Firth. Southward, in Angus, we see a gradual merging of the early symbols with the Christian cross. At Meigle there is an immense, glorious cross that is entirely devoid of the mysterious rods, mirrors, serpents, "elephants," and abstract flowers found on the early standing stones. Daniel in the lions' den is the central motif, yet there are extraordinary elements (to name one, a Syrian centaur with a tree branch over his shoulder, a motif that appears on a Coptic fabric in Lyons) that show what far-flung foreign influences had trickled in by unknown routes and how uncertainly Christianity had established itself in Pictland even by the eighth century.

Northern Pictland and southern Pictland were not necessarily at war before the coming of the Romans, but there was distrust on both sides. The Picts fortified their homesteads to try to live out their lives as uneventfully as possible. Their fortifications, like the standing stones, differ in style in the north and south.

The *murus gallicus* of southeast Scotland is a fortification that is found on the Continent also. This "vitrified" fort is so called in reference to the effect of fire on timber-laced stone. When the wood burned, whether accidentally or by intention, flues formed in the walls between the stones and fusion resulted from the extreme heat. Since the walls enclosed living quarters, we might speculate that a housewife started the fire by knocking over something in her little domain, but other explanations are possible. An enemy (Roman) could have slighted the fort, or the builders could have deliberately fired it themselves to strengthen it. The idea of a domestic accident is humanly appealing, but the largest of the vitrified forts, the huge one at Burghead, on Moray Firth, had a distinctly military aspect. No housewife could have fired that threatening structure by overturning a tiny lamp.

There are puzzling souterrains in Angus and Perthshire. Their nearest counterparts are the Cornish fogous, those underground passageways built on a curve with a paved floor, heavy walls, and corbeled roof (see plate 78). Some of the souterrains in Scotland have drains in the floors and might have served as underground byres, though the thought of trying to get cattle to turn around in such constricted quarters is daunting. Not long ago it was proved that small, low-walled huts associated with the Pictish souterrains stood aboveground. These curious passages therefore may have been for storage. What we contemplate is no fortification or refuge or cattle byre but merely a Pictish pantry.[27]

In the north there is an entirely different kind of fort, and an astonishing one it is. This is the broch, a round dry-masonry tower built around a space that was once roofed over. The tower itself is a double shell, with a stairway going up through it clockwise. This part is roofed over with heavy corbels. There are various closely related classes and subclasses of brochs; all look forbidding. At the checkpoints inside the entrances an attacker fumbling about in the dark would surely meet a speedy death.[28] Euan MacKie's authoritative investigations date the brochs to a century or two before the coming of the Romans, which is disconcerting, because they look unutterably ancient. Lethbridge states categorically that brochs were invented in Scotland. MacKie's date has to be accepted because of the hard evidence that he presents, but Lethbridge's idea of local invention is bothersome. A climb to the top of the

Plate 78. Fogou at Carn Euny, Cornwall. Cornish fogous and Scottish souterrains are much alike. This subterranean retreat is sixty-six feet long and roofed with corbeled slabs.

Plate 79. The broch of Mousa, Shetland, second–first century B.C. This is the largest survival of the broch culture. Although it was clearly a fortified structure, it appears to have been utilized as living quarters. The core is hollow. There were wooden floors across the hollow so that in effect the broch was a "high-rise" apartment house. The various levels were reached by stairs enclosed in the walls. Brochs bear a startling similarity to the nuraghi of Sardinia. See color plate 12.

spectacular forty-foot broch on Mousa, a Shetland island, compared with a similar scramble up through the walls of a nuraghe in Sardinia drives home the point that if the broch was an invention there was some astonishingly close "prior art" (see plate 79 and color plate 12). The nuraghe also has hollow walls, a stairway coiling up through them, corbels, and checkpoints in its passages.[29] The nuraghe culture is dated roughly from about 1200 B.C. up to the arrival of the Carthaginians in Sardinia, about 435 B.C.

When we turn back to Roman Britain's problem of controlling the northerners, we find that Agricola's campaign ended abruptly at Mons Graupius. Emperor Domitian blundered deplorably by recalling the victorious general before he had stabilized the north. If Agricola had been allowed to complete his task, there would no doubt be a network of Roman roads and a chain of forts all the way up through Scotland, and archaeological evidence would show that that part of the world had been pacified and Romanized. As it was, the threat remained for centuries. It took a decade or two for the northern tribes to recover from Agricola's crippling blow, but with the passage of time they gradually coalesced, to form confederations poised for attack and vengeance at the propitious moment. We therefore see the erection of two barriers, the impressive system called Hadrian's Wall stretching across the border between Wallsend, near Newcastle, and Bowness, on the Solway near Carlisle, and the later Antonine Wall beyond it. The north remained wild and barbaric; the debatable land on the Scottish side of Hadrian's Wall is still numinous and strange.

Along Hadrian's Wall we can catch a sense of what it must have been like to be one of the anonymous little people caught in the toils of imperial undertakings. It would serve our purpose better not to struggle up to the Hotbank Crags, where the magnificence of the panorama might seduce us into envy. We should toil instead along the gentler stretches near Gilsland, for instance, setting our faces into driving rain mile after lonely mile in an empty countryside where there is nothing more than an occasional sodden sheep for company. Along this way trudged weary sentries, drenched through and chilled, far from home and kindred, defending a foreign land against lurking foes. Some comfort supposedly could be gained from the grim thought that it would take only twenty-five years of this to win the honor of retirement with Roman citizenship and a home in one of the *coloniae* like Colchester on the south, where there were such amenities as theaters and temples and wives. Meanwhile, there were the gaming houses and the sleazy brothels huddled in the lee of the wall. Meanwhile, also, there were the wet and the boredom.

A commander's view of the situation from the comfort of his legionary fortress with its splendid masonry would be distinctly different from that of his unfortunate sentries. His was the knowledge that his masterfully constructed stronghold interlocked with the other major forts along the wall and that response to an emergency could be executed with lightning speed. Cavalry forts stood on the east and the west, with infantry in the center. In less than an hour as many as a thousand cavalrymen could be concentrated to intercept attackers at any specified point north of the wall in a ten-mile range.

As long as the wall was efficiently manned, it was militarily successful, though it must have been a constant economic burden. Politically it had its drawbacks. The full complement in the heyday of the Roman occupation was something on the order of thirty-five thousand men.[30] A multitude like that, crowded together, could easily become fretful and restive. In Gibbon's words the legions of Britain had long been famous for "a spirit of presumption and arrogance."[31]

At times the wall was not effectively garrisoned. In 140, under Emperor Antonius Pius, a new campaign was undertaken against the northern tribes, but the Romans repeated the blunder of stopping too soon. A new, shorter wall was built farther north, again to bar any advance by the barbarians. This Antonine Wall, constructed in 141, was gradually abandoned in a pullback completed thirteen years later, with restoration of the defensive line at Hadrian's Wall. The southward retreat was a clear admission of the Romans' failure to master the ominously growing strength of their opponents.

In 196 a struggle developed over the imperial office. One of the contenders, Albinus, moved off to Gaul with the legions to attack Septimius Severus. That triggered a rampage of destruction by the southern tribal confederation beyond the wall. The great fortress of the Sixth Legion at York was demolished, and the whole northern part of the province was overrun.

Severus disposed of his adversary and sent a new governor to deal with the barbarians. Inexplicably, the attack was directed against the coalition of Caledones still farther north, who had not participated in the disorder, while the actual invaders were bought off. Time was gained at any rate for reconstruction and refurbishing of the wall, but by 206 the danger of renewed aggression must have become serious, because Emperor Severus himself appeared on the scene. He established a base on the banks of the River Tay, far in the north. This was no temporary marching camp; it was a legionary fortress large enough for thirty-five hundred men.

The wall was overrun again in 297, when once again the actions of a usurper had indirectly robbed it of its soldiery. This usurper was Carausius, the able leader who appears to have been responsible for the construction of the powerful Saxon Shore forts along the coast as protection for his overseas stronghold at Boulogne, from which he controlled northern Gaul for a few years.[32] When he was killed, in 297, his assassin withdrew to Britain, summoning the legions and auxiliaries from their wall stations to support him. The marauding tribes who swarmed southward in their wake and engaged in an orgy of pillage were now called Picts by their contemporaries, but they must have been the same troublemakers as before. They were driven back by Constantius Chlorus, who restored the wall and established a firmer command system, with a dux Britanniarum for the land forces and a *comes* in charge of the Saxon Shore.

Next came the disaster of 367. This time the wall was manned, and a coastal fleet was also at hand, but the army had become demoralized by the avarice of its commanders. The Picts in their remote fastnesses must have become aware of the general decay and made use of that knowledge in planning their attack. In a dazzling action the Picts carried the wall by direct assault, in concert with a seaborne maneuver that turned its flank. The count of the Saxon Shore was killed. The dux Britanniarum was ambushed and taken captive. The entire operation conceived by the barbarians belies any notion that they were lacking in military sophistication. The timing, thrust, and coordination of movement would do credit to any modern army.

Not too long ago exasperated scholars felt justified in grumbling that the Picts must have been nothing more than figments of the imagination of court panegyrists, because it was hard to credit the existence of any alarming mass of threatening people whose excavated homesteads suggested a quiet, pastoral life. Could Pacatus, eulogizing Emperor Theodosius I, or Claudian, Stilicho's panegyrist, have made it all up? Count Theodosius, father of Emperor Theodosius I, would not have thought so. When he was dispatched to restore order, he confronted a chaotic situation. The Picts were ranging all over the place, dragging off captives and cattle and loads of booty. The Roman troops were wandering aimlessly and had to be recalled by a proclamation of general amnesty.

The wall was rather carelessly repaired after the onslaught, but fourteen years later Maximus allowed himself to be elevated to the purple by the still volatile troops of Britain, and he took them along to Gaul for use in forcing himself on the empire as Theodosius's co-Augustus in Trier. From that time the wall was abandoned, and the Picts had little to stop them.

Something peculiar happened on the southern border of Pictland, in territory known as Manau Guotodin, around the head of the Firth of Forth. Whoever they were, the people of Manau Guotodin, under their king, Cunedda, migrated to western Wales, from which, it is said, they expelled various Irish colonies. The rulers of Manau Guotodin had Pictish names, though there is nothing to indicate that the people were actually Picts. Their migration may have occurred as early as Stilicho's time or in the days of Maximus the usurper. If so, Cunedda and his people were deliberately transplanted to Wales as federates of the Roman Empire for protection against Irish raiders. If, however, the movement occurred as late as 490, when the Dalriadic Irish were establishing a toehold in Scotland, displacing a Pictish population from that area, we might surmise that Pictish pressure elsewhere in the north displaced the people of Manau Guotodin. If it occurred at that same time as part of the struggle of the mainland Britons against both invading Irish in the west and Saxons landing in the east, we might think that the Britons had retained enough Roman sophistication to adopt the practice of making federate troops a first line of defense.[33]

This last hypothesis is tempting because it might be stretched to cover the baffling case of the British leader Vortigern. According to the sixth-century Welsh historian Gildas, a *superbus tyrannus* brought in Saxons for defense against the Picts, thus opening the way for the ultimate undoing of all of Britain. Bede and the writers after him identified Gildas's tyrant as Vortigern. Vortigern's historicity is not in question, though as the official villain of the period he has acquired a lurid reputation that would better suit a legendary character. There is a statement in conjunction with an Easter table made up for the year 447 that Vortigern ruled in the consulship of the emperors Theodosius and Valentinian (in 425) and that the Saxons arrived early in his reign, in the consulship of Felix and Taurus (in 428). The theory has long since been discarded that any one specific year can be taken for the arrival of the Saxons, as though it happened in one enormous surge, but the dates are of interest in any case. We know that there were many disturbances in Britain then and that Saint Germanus of Auxerre made his first trip across the Channel at about that time. The whole empire had been thrown into a state of turmoil by the usurpation of John, and Britain was in a period of extreme disarray. Ostensibly Germanus came to Britain as the scourge of the Pelagians. In some accounts Vortigern figures as the head of a heretical Pelagian party, and Germanus is depicted in hot pursuit of the archsinner.[34] It seems more likely that Germanus's mission had to do with military matters. The bloodless battle that he led against Picts and Saxons at some unlocated place may not have been entirely the product of an admiring hagiographer's imagination. Then, too, we wonder about the visit to the shrine of Saint Alban at Verulamium. Of all the cities of Britain Verulamium alone offers convincing archaeological evidence of a continuous fairly prosperous existence through all the upheavals of those difficult times, when most urban centers fell into decay. Was advice and assistance given for defense of the city?

It is possible that Vortigern had inherited some quasimilitary authority. His name means something like "overlord": an extant inscription indicates that he was the son-in-law of the usurper Maximus. Was his "name" in fact a title?[35] The core of his domain seems to have been east-central Wales and the main valley of the Severn. From this base he may have extended his authority to areas once occupied by the Romans, to become a "tyrant." We know that he had a council of elders, perhaps made up of representatives of the towns that had been left to their own devices by the terms of the message from Emperor Honorius. These council members would have ranked among the most Romanized of British leaders, and a proposal to call in barbarians to help against the Picts and the raiders from Ireland would not have alarmed them. Teutons had figured largely in the Roman military defense scheme as far back as anyone in Britain could remember. Besides, we must remember that in spite of our bristling image of belligerent Romans, most of them were never trained in warfare. They were incapable of responding as a militia when the regular armed forces failed them. Worse than that, rich magnates all over the empire had always been reluctant to sacrifice their private means to equip able-bodied retainers as defenders of the homeland. Feudalism was still a long way off, and the use of mercenaries was accepted as entirely normal. There seems little to justify denunciation of Vortigern as a traitor merely because he summoned the Saxons. The justification in many minds lies in the indisputable fact that the Saxons took over, and in the end England emerged as the only part of the western empire where the language and customs of the Teutons prevailed.

There was no sudden large-scale "coming of the Saxons," in spite of what Gildas wrote or Bede believed. It is impossible to say where Vortigern's original mercenaries were planted. More Saxons under their leaders Hengist and Horsa were quartered in Kent, probably in 450, in a deployment that was appropriate for countering sea raids. If it looks odd to deploy defenders so far south when the threat comes from lands north of Hadrian's Wall, we should reflect that Gildas referred to Picts and Scotti alike as *transmarini*. The Picts were intrepid seamen.

The Picts were controlled for a time, but before long the Saxon mercenaries went into revolt, to the peril of anything that remained of Roman civilization in Britain. They overran the east, though Gildas's lurid accounts of death and destruction must be discounted. Archaeologists thus far have never found a fire layer either in the towns or in the outlying villas.[36] It was a peculiarity of the battles mentioned in the chronicles that they almost invariably took place at river crossings and fords. The one known exception occurred in a later Saxon landing, when the huge Saxon Shore fort at Pevensey, in Sussex, was besieged by a new contingent of invaders under their leaders Aelle and Cissa. They "slew all the inhabitants. There was not even one Briton left there."[37]

By the time of the Pevensey slaughter the Saxon tide in Britain was at the full, because Clovis and his Franks stood as a firm barrier against any more Saxon incursions into Gaul. British failure at Pevensey, despite the protection of the frowning walls, must mean that the defense of Britain had devolved upon people who had no knowledge of the Roman art of war.

Clovis killed Syagrius, "the king of the Romans," in 486. Britain too had her "last Roman" in the person of a heroic general named Ambrosius Aurelianus. There is no question of the historicity of this man, in spite of the legends that accumulated around him that he was a magic boy without a father and that his blood was supposed to have a peculiar potency. Ambrosius came from senatorial stock. Some statements about him suggest that he and Vortigern headed rival parties. Vortigern was said to fear him. During the early years of Vortigern's period of dominance a mysterious battle took place between Ambrosius (or his father) and one of Vortigern's colleagues. It is likely that both Ambrosius and Vortigern had inherited positions of authority and that both were able military commanders struggling against a multiplicity of foes. The difference lay in their tactics. Whereas Vortigern chose to call in mercenaries, Ambrosius rallied the Britons and led them in a series of battles. Ambrosius's fortunes ebbed and flowed, but at last he won a "God-given victory" over the Saxons (thought to have occurred sometime before the year 475). "From that time forth, sometimes the Britons were victorious, sometimes the enemy, up to the year of the siege of Mount Badon, which was almost the most recent but not the least slaughter of the gallows-crew."[38] Gildas, from whom this vague statement comes, was born in 490, the accepted and probably correct date of the siege of Mount Badon. Gildas is silent about the hero of Mount Badon, though he must have known the name of the British commander of this great battle, which at least pushed back the Saxons from the upper Thames Valley and allowed the Britons in the west a chance to breathe again. Gildas's silence is strange, because the name Arthur has been a magic one through all the succeeding ages.

Arthur was not a king. In the words of a historical compendium assembled by some unknown individual in the tenth century,[39] he fought "cum regibus Brittonum sed ipse dux erat bellorum" ("along with the kings of the Britons but he himself was Duke [or leader] of battles" (Alcock's translation).[40] The title faintly echoes the lapsed Roman rank dux Brittaniarum, which had described the office of commander of the standing army along Hadrian's Wall. If indeed "dux" in reference to Arthur was a title and not just an expression that meant that he was a tremendous fighter, it must have indicated that he led some kind of mobile field force that could range along the frontiers of British-held territory. The list of twelve battles in which he is said to have fought is unreliable on two counts. It may have originated in a heroic poem, but even if it has a factual basis, identification of the sites of these encounters is practically impossible. If we take the list at face value as history and also accept some of the hotly contested identifications of the battlegrounds, we must admit that the list fits the idea of a troubleshooter who was able to throw his troops into action where the threat of the moment was maximal. We cannot, however, even be sure who the enemy was. The Battle of Coit Celidon may have been somewhere in Scotland, north of Carlisle. There the clash could have involved Strathclyde Britons or Picts or even Angles from Northumberland. In the battle of Linnuis, Arthur may have pitted his cavalry against Saxons as far southwest as Dorset, between the Piddle and the Trent. The battle of Camlann, in which he died, seems to have been a struggle involving Britons exclusively, possibly near the Roman fort at Birdoswald. As for Mons Badonis, the scene of Arthur's famous triumph over the Anglo-Saxons, a good case can be made for the outskirts of Bath.[41] All in all, we are left with the impression of a small army capable of moving with speed from one danger spot to another to fight various foes.

There remains the question of fabled Camelot. Was there such a place? Recent excavations at Cadbury-Camelot, as the site in Somerset is called, seem to provide an affirmative answer to the question, though we must sadly discard any notion of plumed knights clanking about great medieval battlements. In any case, even if it was not Camelot, it has been demonstrated that this Bronze Age hill fort was successively abandoned and reoccupied through the centuries and that in Arthur's day it was completely refurbished, the whole eighteen acres of the hilltop being enclosed to form a secure center of operations for a fair-sized military force. The Arthurian gate tower is of considerable interest because it is, in Alcock's words, a "distinctly romanized element" yet is essentially non-Roman in construction. Both the gate and the great hall that was the administrative center were the work of competent carpenters. All knowledge of the laying of masonry with mortar apparently had been lost.

If Arthur, the most famous "king" of the period, was in fact not a king at all but a military commander fighting on behalf of British kings, who were the royal personages whom he served, and from whom did they receive their authority? The Irish had kings, and so did the Picts, while the Saxons had their elected leaders like Hengist, but the Romanized Britons had had no kings for centuries. If royalty was in their tradition in the fifth century, it was a skewed Roman tradition. They had seen a succession of usurpers to the imperial office; such men they conventionally called tyrants. We remember that Gildas wrote of the *superbus tyrannus*, whom Bede identified as Vortigern. Likely candidates for such command would be the magistrates of the towns, who made use of whatever remained of military forces as instruments of power, to become "kings" in the eyes of their barbarian opponents, as the Franks in Gaul thought of Syagrius as king of the Romans. Although they became rulers by application of surviving Roman practice, they quickly became barbarian kings in the mold of an earlier heroic age.

Many of the small kingdoms of the Britons were ephemeral, little more to us than names with the look of legend. Their chances of survival were slim at best. As far as tactics were concerned, they fielded their armies with great élan but without any detectable plan. They armed themselves mentally with the thought that theirs was a Roman tradition, though whatever contact they had ever had with Rome must have been tenuous indeed. The kingdom of Dyfed, for example, appears to have been made up of descendants of an Irish war band (the Déisi) who may have been enlisted as federates by the usurper Maximus on the eve of his departure for the Continent in 383. About fifty years later the Dyfed dynasty was headed by a man whose memorial stone presents the curious inscription "Votepor Protector" (Stilicho was a *protector* at the court of Constantinople when he was a young man). By the wildest stretch of the imagination, the only *protector* among Votepor's ancestors from whom he could have inherited such a title might have been an attendant or even a hostage to the usurper Maximus.

Another important dynasty—that of the kingdom of Gwynedd—traced its line to Cunedda, who at some unknown date had led the people of Manau Guotodin down from the borders of Pictland to drive out Irish colonists and settle in their stead in Wales. The sixth-century king of Gwynedd, the renowned Maelgwn, was supposedly a grandson of Cunedda. Here again there are interesting Roman associations that were important in the eyes of later generations. Cunedda's grandfather was called Paternus of the Red Cloak. The name is Roman, and a red cloak was the distinguishing garb of a Roman general.

We should not overlook one other kingdom, Scottish Dalriada, under Saint Columba's aggressive young kinsman Áedán son of Gabrán, whom Columba consecrated. It was Áedán who challenged the forces of King Ethelfrith of Northumbria in 603 and met disaster in the Battle of Dagsastan. "From that time on, no king of the Scots durst come into Britain to make war on the English," says Bede.[42]

Even the sturdiest, most-concerted rally could not have dislodged the Anglo-Saxons, but a strong British alliance might at least have managed to enforce some kind of territorial partition. Instead, the warring Teutonic realms prevailed. British military effort might be to no avail, but unarmed men from Columba's little holy island were to help mold the developing English world.

THE ANGLO-SAXON
HEPTARCHY AND THE
CITY OF GOD

THE permanence of the Anglo-Saxon settlement is witnessed in the names of the seven major kingdoms: Kent, Essex, Wessex, Sussex, East Anglia, Mercia, and Northumbria. The names are still meaningful, though we may not be too sure of the boundaries of those realms, and our understanding of the fluctuating fortunes of all of them may be weak.

According to the Venerable Bede, the people who in 547 established a beachhead at Bamburgh under their leader, Ida, were Angles from what we would identify as South Jutland, while the Saxons on the south came from lands between the Elbe and the Weser. He believed that the settlers on and near the Isle of Wight came from northern Jutland. Archaeologists would dispute some of these statements and offer evidence that Frisian and Frankish elements were present as well, but it still can be said that the incomers brought with them the language, customs, and pagan outlook of a Germanic stock.

Archaeological recovery of early Saxon homes in England is well-nigh impossible because the settlements have been inhabited almost continuously. As Leslie Alcock says, "It is inevitable that those migration-period villages which took root and flourished are now most inaccessible,"[1] buried as they are under stratum upon stratum of dwellings right up to those of the present day. A few possibly atypical sites have been found whose excavated sunken-floored homes bear little or no evidence that the original owners engaged in agricultural pursuits. The general impression is one of disorder and squalor, but by analogy to finds on the Continent it can be assumed that the immigrants were indeed hard-working farmers.

What about the fabled royal halls, like the one in *Beowulf* with its gold-shot tapestries, in which the king played the harp and the mead flowed freely? Yeavering, in Northumbria, must have been such a place. It is here that Bede locates the famous mass conversion by Bishop Paulinus. The site was detected by aerial photography; it has been possible to trace the outlines of a complex

308

timber-aisled hall about one hundred feet long. Yeavering had little chance of survival because Cadwallon of Gwynedd destroyed it in 632, and, after a period of rebuilding, Penda of Mercia razed it in 651. It was finally abandoned in 680 after a second reconstruction.[2]

Arthur's gallantry at Badon in 490 provided at best only a temporary respite for the Britons. By 577 the people of Wessex were in motion, emerging from their original base around the Solent. According to *The Anglo-Saxon Chronicle*, in that year "Cuthwine and Ceawlin fought against the Britons and slew three kings, . . . and they captured three cities, Gloucester, Cirencester and Bath." This aggressive action served to wedge Wales and Cornwall apart.

The Saxons had their ups and downs. In 584, "Ceawlin and Cutha fought against the Britons, . . . and Cutha was slain: and Ceawlin . . . departed in anger." In 592 "There was great slaughter at Adam's Grave and Ceawlin was expelled." He died the following year. A few years later, in 597, a strong king emerged in Wessex, but the entry in the *Chronicle* still describes constant hostilities: "In this year Ceolwulf began to reign in Wessex, and ever fought and made war either against the Angles, or against the Welsh, or against the Picts, or against the Scots." The chronicler regarded this man as enough of a fixture to warrant the listing of his royal ancestors, all the way back to Bældæg (Baldar), a son of Woden.

To mention *The Anglo-Saxon Chronicle*, and to quote from it, is in itself to make an indirect comment on the changes in progress in Britain. The new-comers were true barbarians: all their knowledge of past history was limited to what they could learn from their bards. Literacy was a Roman contribution, specifically a contribution of Roman Christianity. The surviving chronicles are latter-day productions, to be sure, but they are based on earlier documents, now lost, some of which dated back to the seventh century.[3] It is worth noting that the earliest were written not in Kent, where we might expect to find the strongest Roman element, but rather in the north. It is risky to make a defini-tive judgment in a matter like this.

Christianity had had a precarious existence in Britain for centuries. In the Anglo-Saxon kingdoms, the rulers tended to apostasize when the fortunes of battle went against them. In spite of the defeats, however, Christianity con-tinued as a slender thread running through British history all the way back to the days of Saint Alban the martyr. From tiny beginnings during the Roman occupation, when worship was conducted in "hall churches" and private homes like the well-known villa at Lullingstone, in Kent, the church had grown to assume a recognizable Roman structure. British bishops attended the Council of Arles of 314, possibily representing the four provinces into which Britain was then divided. Although Saint Germanus does not appear to have met with any persons of authority in the British ecclesiastical hierarchy when he made his two trips across the Channel early in the fifth century, some such hierarchy must have been in existence; otherwise, the appeal for assistance in coping with Pelagianism would not have been sent out. Even far in the north, at Whithorn, on the Galloway coast, there seems to have been a formal episcopal seat in the fifth century, though it is difficult to determine just what Bishop Ninian was able to accomplish in that remote place. Presumably he ministered to Britons who may have taken refuge there when the Picts were routinely attacking Hadrian's Wall.[4] There was Christian activity of some kind in the vicinity of Glasgow at a somewhat later date, led by Mungo (Saint Kentigern), who may have been the bishop of the British kingdom of Strathclyde.[5] He is supposed to have had a most affecting meeting about 584 with the great abbot of Iona, in the course of which he and Columba gravely embraced and exchanged pastoral staffs.[6] The church continued actively in Wales and Cornwall, but our concern now is the church in the emergent Anglo-Saxon heptarchy.

I must digress at this point because I think that the course of Christianity in England is best explained by events in Frankish Gaul, to which Pope Gregory the Great reacted by sending Augustine to Kent. Columba was not the only Irish monk to banish himself for the sake of his soul. *Peregrinatio* was characteristic of his people. For this reason we find them wandering far north, to the Orkneys and Shetland (and even to Iceland sometime later), and across the Irish Sea into Britain.[7] The one whose self-banishment had the most significant results was Columban. Trained at the learned Irish monastic center of Bangor and ordained a priest, after many years of faithful service Columban "began to desire the pilgrimage," as his biographer Jonas puts it. With the consent of his superior Columban set out with a small train of disciples. His modern biographer G. S. M. Walker says that no particular reason can be found for the choice of France as the destination; the mere idea of distance from Ireland may have made it attractive.[8] Missionary zeal would not wholly account for the selection of Gaul, because that part of the West had been Christian for a long time.

The viewpoint of the Irish *peregrini* was poles apart from that of clerics bred in the Roman system. Even that most politically minded abbot Columba of Iona had no intention of becoming part of a vast close-knit power structure. When an Irish monk went on pilgrimage, he cut his ties with the home monastery and set to work entirely on his own, in whatever place his intuitions or his fortune led him to settle. He was indifferent to any Roman bishop who might rule the territory in question. This is in sharp contrast to the attitude of Augustine of Canterbury, who periodically sent progress reports to Pope Gregory soliciting his advice and who eagerly set about the task of putting subordinate bishops into key positions, as Patrick attempted unsuccessfully to do in Ireland.

Columban's little party came to a halt in what was then Austrasia around

590. They were received by King Childebert, who was moved to give Columban a little abandoned Roman fort at Annegray, on a wooded half-empty tract in the Vosges foothills, not far from Luxeuil. The site was a congenial one. The wall could easily be converted to a kind of Irish cashel, and familiar beehive huts could be erected inside the enclosure. An old temple to Diana lent itself to reconsecration to Saint Martin, for use as an oratory.[9]

Before long the tiny community began to burgeon, as had the monastic establishments along the Nile in an earlier epoch. Eager converts swarmed to the place. Soon it was necessary to open a second monastery, this time at Luxeuil, about eight miles away. Fontaines was established three miles from Luxeuil, but still the growing throng could hardly be contained. Small wonder that Columban felt the need for a secluded retreat in the woodlands where he could meditate in solitude. All the holy men had an affinity for caves (we think of the hermits' caves at Antioch, Paul's cave in the Egyptian wasteland, and Ninian's cave near Whithorn). Columban found one to his liking, from which he courteously evicted a bear in the pleasant tradition shared by the Eastern and the Irish monks, all of whom had a talent for forming kindly friendships with the wild creatures of desert, sea, or forest.[10] Today Columban's grotto can be reached by walking along a flat valley from Annegray and then up along a spur that leads out from Sainte-Marie-en-Chanois. In Columban's day there must have been a climax forest full of game; even now there are lovely stretches of dense, fresh-smelling pine woods and moss-covered boulders. Up there in the quiet, the saint must have been able to experience the serene detachment that old Antony Abbot knew in his retreat near the Red Sea.

Columban's meditations were undoubtedly more complex than Antony's because his was an elegantly educated mind. He wrote poetry of considerable distinction, and his sermons are admired for their clarity and crispness. Beyond his otherworldly musings, Columban must have frowned in his grotto sometimes, pondering the tiresome ways of Gallic churchmen who were becoming resentful of him, showing signs of making an issue of the differences in their practices. They calculated the date of Easter differently; wrong calculation of Easter was nothing short of heresy to the orthodox. A certain amount of irritation was justified on both sides. Columban refused to bow to the authority of the local bishops, and he was indignant about their known corruption. Simony had become commonplace in Gaul. Columban was moved at last to write to Pope Gregory about Easter, defending his right to follow the tradition of his native country. It was a shrewd move because the Gallic bishops themselves did not use the Paschal cycle approved by Rome. Columban's tone was respectful. Although Gregory is not known to have replied, we can hardly think that he would have dismissed the letter out of hand since it clearly acknowledged the primacy of Rome at a time when such supremacy was far from assured. An ally in the unstable Frankish domains would have been welcome. The only known, rather oblique, indication that Gregory was aware of Columban is a notation that he sent a copy of his work on pastoral care to "the priest Columbus" in 594. Even before Columban sent his letter (he attributed the pope's neglect of all four of his missives to poor postal service, engineered by Satan), the pope must have been having serious thoughts about the course of events at Luxeuil.

Gregory had good channels of information; word must certainly have reached him that the Irish pilgrim's monastic foundations were proliferating astonishingly.[11] The pope was a Benedictine, the first monk in history to reach the highest office in the church. What was he to think of the spread of a rival monastic population on the Continent? Might these undisciplined, self-righteous people become strong enough to undermine the carefully structured Roman hierarchy? What was going on in Britain, the homeland of these intractable missionaries? Was Gregory aware of the existence of Bangor and Iona? Although the names Columba of Iona and Columban of Bangor and of Luxeuil (and eventually of Bobbio, in Italy) never appear in Gregory's collected writings, his actions suggest that he decided that flanking tactics were required.

As an experienced Roman administrator, Gregory worked through available secular powers. By 595 he was in communication with Queen Brunhilda. The royal lady was in a seriously beleaguered position, clawing to maintain her domination over a unified Frankish realm, acting as regent for her illegitimate grandsons Theodoric II of Burgundy and Theodobert II of Austrasia (the youngsters whom Columban refused to bless, calling them the offspring of a harlot, in the very presence of the outraged queen and her court).

A monolithic Frankish kingdom would serve Gregory's purposes better than a welter of small antagonistic realms. Aside from the breakup of the Frankish domain, Gregory had the additional problem that Arles was no longer a suitable center of operations. He needed a more northerly base. In 595 he sent a new representative, to be vicar of his Gaulish patrimony, the presbyter Candidus. Gregory furnished Candidus with letters of introduction, especially to Brunhilda, whom he fondly called a brilliant light shining in a dark night of heathenism.

Brunhilda and Gregory needed each other, in the sense that their ambitions interlocked. For this reason the queen was able to extract a few concessions. She wanted her favorite, Syagrius of Autun, to be a metropolitan bishop, though there does not seem to have been much in his record that justified his elevation to high office. Without bothering to have Syagrius move through accepted channels, Brunhilda sent a letter to the pope with a direct request that he bestow the pallium on her protégé. Gregory responded evasively, pointing out that Syagrius had not approached him in the customary way and also that the queen's emissary was a schismatic. Having put forward these objections, he went on to indicate that the pallium, symbol of status as an archbishop, could indeed be transmitted to Syagrius if he made a personal application for it and the emperor approved. Next, in 599, having acceded to Brunhilda's wishes in this way, Gregory disclosed a plan whereby the queen would summon a reform synod to deal with the problem of simony (purchase of bishoprics from aristocratic landowners weakened papal control). According to his proposal Gregory's own representatives, Abbot Cyriacus and Bishop Aregius, could lead this important gathering, along with Bishop Syagrius. The trio cound function as a pro-Roman nucleus.

Gregory hammered away at the idea of a synod for several years. The bishops of Gaul were cold to it, and by 601 both Syagrius of Autun and Abbot Cyriacus had died. Brunhilda's fortunes were on the wane after the victory of Chlotair II over Austrasia in 600. Gregory wrote to the queen in a sterner tone. He likewise addressed a letter to Chlotair. The king did not call a synod until 614, when both Gregory and Brunhilda were dead; the meeting of 614 had nothing at all to do with the original plan. As Erich Caspar says, Gregory bet on the wrong card in his Frankish policy. Walker disagrees: he writes, "Gregory and Brunhilda initiated that alliance between the French court and the Papacy which was to make France the nucleus of western Christendom, and to extend the Pope's authority far further than the bounds of his modest French estates."[12]

In spite of the disappointing results in the Frankish kingdoms, Gregory had some recompense from Brunhilda for his favor. In 595, the year in which he launched his Frankish campaign, Gregory took a momentous step by directing one of his monks, Augustine, to proceed to Britain with the awesome assignment of converting the Anglo-Saxons. This reluctant missionary and his train of forty timid disciples set out on the journey with many misgivings and no practical preparations. By the time they had reached Aix-en-Provence, they were thoroughly unnerved by the bloodcurdling tales that the Gallic clergy told them about the ferocity of the Saxons. Augustine turned back to Rome, but Gregory was adamant; the missionary was dispatched again. This time he was fortified with letters of introduction and arrangements for Frankish interpreters to accompany the mission. Queen Brunhilda was one of the recipients of these papal letters: she appears to have responded appropriately. Her protégé Syagrius of Autun may have been the bishop who consecrated Augustine, not a bishop in Provence, as Bede was led to believe on the basis of what appears to be a forged document.[13] In the course of his journey across France, Augustine seems to have been in contact with churchmen who strongly disapproved of Columban and said that he was a man of uncompromising incivility. That sounds like a remark that could come from the lips of one of Queen Brunhilda's adherents.[14]

In 597, Augustine was allowed to land at Thanet, where an audience was arranged for him with King Ethelbert of Kent. We recall the stirring story of the solemn processional arrival of the Christians, singing the litany, following a silver cross and "the image of our Lord and Savior painted on a board." [15] The king had taken care to stage this meeting outdoors because he was distrustful of whatever magic spells the newcomers might contrive to cast on him, but he was won over to the extent that he accorded them the right to preach in his lands and gave them leave to settle in his royal city, Canterbury. When King Ethelbert at last was convinced of the rightness of Augustine's cause and allowed himself to be baptized, Pope Gregory admonished him to "unite yourself to him [Augustine] with all your mind and further his endeavors." [16]

The mission prospered, though Gregory could hardly have found a less winning and self-reliant person for the great enterprise. If Augustine's letter to Gregory that Bede quotes is indeed genuine, it reveals the intended organizer of a powerful hierarchy to be an obnoxious, small-minded individual taken up with such earth-shaking matters as the propriety of administering the Eucharist to a menstruating woman.

In 601, Gregory sent Augustine detailed instructions for the erection of the Roman hierarchical structure on English soil, apparently having in his mind's eye the optimistic vision of a Britain endowed with a fine system of cities. Augustine was made archbishop. He was to consecrate other bishops within his own province and establish a similar provincial bishopric at York. London would have its own episcopal see. As presiding bishop Augustine set about the westward extension of his authority. He summoned the bishops of the Welsh church to meet him, and he displayed himself as thoroughly arrogant. Seven British bishops accompanied by learned men, arrived to confront Augustine, who did not even show them the simple courtesy of rising from his chair to greet them. He did not seem to understand that he looked to the Welsh like a usurper. Permanent occupation of Britain by the Anglo-Saxons must have been far from a recognized fact in their minds. [17]

Augustine assured them that if they would amend their Easter computation to conform to that of Rome and make various other adjustments "we will readily tolerate all the other things you do." [18] He indicated that the conversion of the Anglo-Saxons should be a joint effort. When the Britons demurred, not wanting to save the souls of their detested enemies, Augustine told them "in a threatening manner" that someday they would "undergo the vengeance of death" at the hands of the English. It is saddening to see how much satisfaction Bede derived from the subsequent fulfillment of this prophecy in the slaughter of the "perfidious" monks of Bangor-on-Dee because they had the temerity to pray for a British victory when the forces of the Northumbrian king Ethelfrith attacked at Chester.

Laurentius, the next archbishop of Canterbury, learned to his chagrin that

Plate 80. Augustinian church at Canterbury. Little remains of Augustine's original churches. They have been remodeled and enlarged so often that it is difficult to determine what they looked like when the early monks and Saxon converts worshiped here.

not only the Britons but also the Irish were behaving badly about Easter. They were so stiff-necked that one of their bishops, visiting the British mainland, "not only refused to eat with us but even to take his repast in the same house where we were entertained." [19] Together with Bishop Mellitus of London and Bishop Justus of Rochester (both consecrated by Augustine), Laurentius addressed a letter of admonition to the Scotti that went unheeded.

Justus, Mellitus, and Laurentius stood on unstable ground. In 616, when King Ethelbert of Kent died, the realm reverted to heathenism, and Justus and Mellitus hurriedly left for the Continent. Laurentius also was preparing to retreat, but a menacing apparition of Saint Peter frightened him so much that he remained at his post. Mellitus and Justus were recalled. Pagan London would have nothing further to do with its former bishop, though Kent as a whole returned to the Christian fold.

Mass conversion of king, courtiers, and subjects did not necessarily spell permanent success. Paulinus, bishop of York, who had been sent north by Augustine along with the Christian queen of Northumbria, Ethelberga, performed spectacularly in the time of King Edwin. The queen received warm encouragement from Pope Boniface, who urged her to pray intensely for the conversion of her erring husband and sent peculiarly secular gifts to the royal lady—a silver mirror and a gilt-ivory comb. [20] The conversion of Northumbria marked a great advance for the cause of the Roman church, because Northumbria had become an important political force among the emerging Anglo-Saxon kingdoms.

Thanks to the Venerable Bede, we are informed about events relating to Northumbria, though his gentle eyes perhaps failed to perceive the bloodiness of the times he described. Northumbria's political power first became apparent when King Ethelfrith roundly defeated Saint Columba's protégé Áedán, son of Gabrán, the king of Dalriada in Scotland. Ethelfrith was slain in the very next year, 603, by half-Christian King Redwald of East Anglia, who sponsored Edwin of Deira as the new ruler of united Northumbria (Deira was the more southerly, older of the two constituent parts of the kingdom; the other was Bernicia).

By 626, Edwin had become formidable. He extended his authority over Britons as well as Saxons, Bede says, and he must have had a fleet in addition to his land forces, for he was able to attack and subdue the Isle of Man. He was known as bretwalda, the chief of the English kings. The high-sounding title did not indicate any formal authority, but a bretwalda nonetheless was a person whose opinions carried weight. Edwin emphasized his distinction by having a symbol of office carried before him not only in battle but wherever he walked along the streets of his cities: this *tufa* [21] evidently was intended to show his royal status in the Roman manner, though the Romans had departed more than two hundred years before Edwin's time. The bretwalda's prestige made his conversion to Christianity a matter of considerable importance. It also triggered an aggressive response from Cadwallon, ruler of the British kingdom of Gwynedd. Cadwallon was a Christian, but he had an ally in the person of the pagan Penda, king of Mercia, who must also have felt the threat of Northumbria. They defeated Edwin in the Battle of Hatfield Chase, in 632 or 633. This was the first British victory since Badon.

Cadwallon and Penda embarked on a furious campaign of destruction. The defeated kingdom of Northumbria crumbled into its two original parts. Bishop Paulinus and Queen Ethelberga fled in 633. The new kings of Deira and Bernicia were no match for violent Cadwallon, but the swift course of events soon brought a stronger man to power—Oswald, son of Ethelfrith of Bernicia, and nephew of Edwin of Deira. Oswald disposed of the British king Cadwallon in the "Battle of Heavenfield," near Hexham. The victory snuffed out any lingering hopes of British revival. Bede applauded wholeheartedly, not so much because of the political effects of the battle as because of King Oswald's attachment to Christianity. From that time on, the struggles between the nascent Anglo-Saxon kingdoms had a tinge of religious warfare. The shifting alignments frequently brought Christians into combat with pagans. In one case at least conversion of a defeated kingdom was an instrument of attempted domination and control.

The fact of Oswald's Christianity set in motion a train of complex ecclesiastical events that indirectly tilted England in the direction of the Holy See of Rome. Oswald had taken refuge at Iona during the dangerous upheavals following the defeat of his father. He returned to Bernicia an ardent believer. Shortly after his accession he invited the abbot of Columba's establishment to send missionaries so that "all his nation should receive the Christian faith whereof he had found happy experience in vanquishing the barbarians." [22] It was in response to this not precisely Christian invitation that the first missionary was sent out. He quickly retreated to Iona, reporting that he had been unable to accomplish anything because Oswald's subjects were "uncivilized men, and of a stubborn and barbarous disposition." [23] This missionary Corman was an "austere" man, commented Bede. The next missionary, Aidan, was not of such uncompromising zeal. During an anxious debate among the monks at Iona, Aidan said that Oswald's subjects should first be given "the milk of more easy doctrine." With King Oswald's assent serene Aidan and his band of disciples settled on the strange little tidal island Lindisfarne (Holy Island), [24] hard by the king's stronghold at Bamburgh. Clearly Oswald considered that Aidan was to serve as a tribal bishop for his people. Aidan was more or less an innocent as far as the rise and fall of earthly kingdoms was concerned. Oswald welcomed Aidan, because he himself was not politically astute in the Roman empire-building sense. The king could hardly be called an innocent, however, in view of his known machinations in the interests of his royal line. The resentful monks in the conquered territory of Lindsey (Lincolnshire) did not even want to receive Oswald's bones in their monastery until a heavenly light revealed to them just how holy their ruthless ruler had been. [25]

It may be that Aidan's very unworldliness accounted for his success as a missionary. Even though he must have winced more than once at the activities of his sovereign lords, Oswald and Oswald's successor, Oswy of Bernicia, [26] he was primarily concerned with the propagation of the faith among the lowly. He was certainly no organizer. He ruled a tribal church with no hint of any notion of fitting into some great, powerful scheme. He was not even interested in the acquisition of lands and gold for his monastery. Small wattled huts and a little timber church served his purposes adequately. He went about humbly on foot, preaching beside streams and creeks, where he could baptize his converts. In the words of a modern historian, "Christianity had never, since its earliest years, appeared in a more attractive guise." [27]

We should note parenthetically that Columban's mission to Gaul had also borne fruit in England. East Anglia had been weakly Christianized by the conversion of its king, but when a resentful pagan subject murdered him because he forgave his enemies too readily, the country lapsed into heathenism. A new king, Sigebert, returned from exile in Gaul, bringing along one of Columban's disciples. This man, Bishop Felix, who acknowledged the authority of the archbishop of Canterbury, was a successful missionary for about seventeen years. There was likewise an Irish monastery in East Anglia, established by the wandering visionary Fursa in the abandoned Saxon Shore fort that is known today as Burgh Castle.

King Oswald's successor, his brother King Oswy of Bernicia, seems to have been among the first to take a pragmatic view of the Christian faith and to attempt to make use of an organized religion for the furtherance of his own ends. To attain the high status of bretwalda, an ambitious man had few alternatives. Extermination of all one's collateral kin who might be claimants to the throne or permanent occupation of vanquished enemy territory was not feasible in the long run. At best a bretwalda was perforce rather like the priestly King of the Wood at ancient Nemi, constantly armed and on the alert in readiness to fight off a rival. Some of Oswy's predecessors had made a stab or two at unification by means of strategic royal marriages, but even that expedient did not help much among people whose very way of life was predicated on the congenial concept of assassination.

Oswy had ample reason to be wary of his kinsmen.[28] Although he had married the daughter of King Edwin as his second wife some time after 643 and thus had a claim on the loyalties of the reigning family of the rival kingdom of Deira, armed conflict threatened, and he felt constrained to order the murder of his cousin King Oswine in 652. Queen Eanfled was alarmed. She persuaded her royal husband to found a monastery in which continued prayers could be offered "for the eternal health of the kings" (meaning her husband, Oswy, and his victim Oswine). Oswy had another problem, embodied in Oswine's immediate successor, King Oswald's son Ethelwald, whose consistently rebellious attitude suggests that he felt himself to be the rightful king of Bernicia. One of Oswy's own sons, Alchfrith (not by Eanfled), seemed at one time to enjoy his father's favor, ruling as subking of Deira, but in subsequent years a conflict of some sort arose, and it is generally assumed that Alchfrith was either exiled or killed, like Ethelwald, who disappears from the records in 656. To be fair to King Oswy, it should be said that, in the absence of a definitive statement about his son Alchfrith, we might suppose that he died in the plague epidemic of 663 or 664.[29]

The years leading up to the famous "synod" of Scots and pro-Romans at the monastery of Whitby marked a turning point in Oswy's fortunes.[30] Up to that time he had been fairly well on the defensive, not only toward his own kindred but also toward the Mercian threat, which had increased tremendously under the heathen king Penda. To counteract that menace, Oswy put together a set of alliances with other Christian kings, some of whom were converted to Christianity on Oswy's urging. If Saint Aidan's successor, Bishop Finan of Lindisfarne, had had any empire-building impulses, he could have capitalized on King Oswy's activities to make himself much more powerful than the archbishop of Canterbury. Finan was an Iona man through and through, however, though unlike Aidan he had a hot temper.[31] The kingdoms whose bishops acknowledged the authority of Canterbury were few, and even there the Scottish influence was strong. Bishop Felix of East Anglia recognized the supremacy of the archbishop of Canterbury but was himself a disciple of Columban. In Wessex, where King Coenwalh had been converted, the first bishop was Agilbert, who had been trained in Ireland, and the second, Wini, was in communion with the Scots, not with Canterbury. Sussex was still heathen. The Midland Angles were heathen when Peada was made king there. For obscure reasons of state, this son of Penda asked for the hand of Oswy's daughter. The response to this request was the statement that such a marriage could take place only if Peada became a Christian. Oswy's son Alchfrith, who was Peada's brother-in-law, may have had some influence there. Bishop Finan of Lindisfarne baptized Peada in 653 and sent missionaries to preach in the convert's realm. Three of the missionaries, Cedd, Adda, and Betti, were English (but trained by the Scots), and the fourth was Diuma, a Scot. Unaccountably King Penda allowed them to preach in Mercia also. Why did he not feel that such infiltration might be dangerous? In Essex, King Sigebert ruled a lapsed kingdom from which Augustine's Bishop Mellitus had been expelled. Oswy prevailed upon his friend Sigebert to accept the faith. Once again Finan baptized a royal convert. Cedd, one of the missionaries to Peada's kingdom, was transferred to Essex. At a later date Finan consecrated Cedd as bishop.

That was the situation at the time of the final collision between Oswy and Penda. King Penda was the attacker, so alarmingly outbalancing Oswy's available forces that the Northumbrian felt forced to offer to pay tribute. When this was refused and the battle lines were actually drawn at Winwed in 656, Penda's support turned out to be less formidable than anyone had thought. His Deiran contingent refused to fight, and the Welsh took to their heels. With no one to block him after the death of Penda, Oswy took northern Mercia, Deira, and Lindsey. Peada was allowed to keep control of southern Mercia, but in the very next year his queen (Oswy's daughter) manipulated affairs in such a way that Peada was murdered.

On the crest of his victory Oswy pushed home his Christianizing campaign. As Bede cheerfully says, Oswy, "having cut off the wicked king's head, converted the Mercians and the adjacent provinces to the grace of the Christian faith."[32] Diuma was made bishop of Mercia, Lindisfarne, and the Midland Angles. The Iona influence continued strongly. Diuma's successor Ceollach ruled briefly and then went back to Iona, to be followed in Mercia by Trumhere, who had been taught by the Scots. Trumhere presided as abbot over the monastery that Oswy and Eanfled had established in expiation of the murder of Oswine, whose kinsman Trumhere was.

When we glance at the map of the Heptarchy, we see how predominant a position the church of Iona and Lindisfarne had attained. Patches of heathenism remained, but by and large Oswy controlled a huge triangular territory in the very heart of England, almost entirely manned by churchmen associated with Lindisfarne. Oswy must have wanted to feel that his own control was reinforced by this network, but these clerics were Scots. Although they maintained friendly, admiring relations with each other, they had no idea of cooperating for a common political goal. How often we read about one of these delightful bishops wandering off to his hermitage to pray and commune with the angels (see plate 81).

King Oswy's political authority was soon challenged. Rebellion broke out in Mercia, and Wulfhere, Penda's intelligent son, emerged as the new king, the first baptized Mercian king. Control through the clergy was further loosened when Wulfhere failed to see anything bizarre in sending his new bishop, Trumhere, to Finan of Lindisfarne for consecration.

Just about the time of Bishop Finan's death in 661, King Oswy, Queen Eanfled, and Alchfrith must have begun holding serious consultations. Alchfrith had come under the influence of his newly created abbot of Ripon, young Wilfrid, whose church career had been furthered by the queen. She had encouraged him to leave Lindisfarne and go abroad, paving the way with a letter of introduction to her kinsman the king of Kent. Wilfrid had returned from this trip full of enthusiasm for things Roman. He had spent a number of years at Lyons and in Rome, where he had absorbed Roman canon law, a system that supported the primacy of the Holy See, and had the opportunity to observe the contrast between the humble Lindisfarne bishops and the grand prelates in Gaul with their splendid retinues and impressive churches. He had also seen how closely the secular and churchly rulers cooperated in governing their lands.

Officially the bone of contention between the Scots and the Romans was the conflicting calculation of the date of Easter. In a court like Oswy's, where the king's people used one date and the queen's another, following the practices of her attendant clerics from Kent, there was inconvenience at the very least, because one group was still fasting while the other was already feasting. There was also the problem of haircuts: the Scots had tonsures that bared the scalp across the front from ear to ear, while the Romans wore coronal fringes symbolizing the Crown of Thorns. Beyond these superficial differences—on the Roman side in any case—was the understanding that the very framework and discipline of the church was at stake, to say nothing of its standing in Oswy's

Plate 81. The chimneys of Farne Island, off the coast of Northumberland, England. This rocky desert island was the ideal retreat of Saint Cuthbert, bishop of Lindisfarne, who in his later years emulated the austere monks of the Egyptian desert. He was accustomed to stand all night in the cold North Sea waters to deprive himself of sleep. His friends were the "sea otters" (seals) and the birds. Monks came over from nearby Lindisfarne (Holy Island) to comfort him in his final hours.

powerful kingdom. Eanfled and Alchfrith presented their case, their arguments being reinforced by those of Abbot Wilfrid. Oswy agreed that the subject needed to be thrashed out. He summoned clergy and laymen to the Synod of Whitby in 663 or 664. Colman, the new bishop of Lindisfarne, stated his position simply: Lindisfarne's way was traditional among his people. It was Columba's way. Wilfrid, as spokesman for the Roman party, poured forth a torrent of learned discourse, confounding his less sophisticated opponents. He referred to the "rustic simplicity but pious intentions" of Columba of Iona. There was menace in Wilfrid's words in addition to the condescension and scorn: "As for you and your companions, you certainly sin if, having heard the decrees of the Apostolic See and of the universal church you refuse to follow them." It was not Columba of Iona who had been singled out for special divine favor, he went on, but "the most blessed prince of the apostles." In the end King Oswy smiled and commented that, since Peter was keeper of the keys, he preferred not to offend him and find himself barred from heaven some day. The royal decision was inevitable: the way of Rome prevailed for the sake of a royal soul and for reasons of political expediency. Perhaps King Oswy recognized that the tribal way of life did not represent the wave of the future.

Colman and his band of monks departed, leaving at Lindisfarne evidence of the frugal simplicity and goodness of their lives on the holy island. Even Bede, who abhorred wrong Easter calculations, was moved to express deep admiration for their indifference to possessions and the trappings of authority.

Colman's departure left an opening throughout England for clergy whose outlook was more worldly, in the sense that they had the sophistication to be aware of the civilization that had grown up in the days of the empire. These men would not tramp through the heather preaching a simple gospel of love and redemption. They were prepared to negotiate on equal terms with the still rude rulers of the Anglo-Saxon world. The letter addressed to King Oswy in the following year by Pope Vitalian puts all this plainly: "We therefore desire your highness will hasten to dedicate all your island to Christ, . . . establishing there the Catholic and apostolic faith. . . . Truly your highness seeks, and shall no doubt obtain, that all your islands shall be made subject to you, as is our wish and desire." [33]

The letter in question dealt with the appointment of a new archbishop of Canterbury. Oswy, acting as a devout son of the Roman church, had joined King Egbert of Kent in selecting a candidate for that vacant office and had sent him to Rome for consecration. Unfortunately the nominee had died immediately after having presented his credentials. Pope Vitalian therefore was searching, he wrote complacently, for a suitable substitute, whom he promised to consecrate in due time for the waiting English kingdoms.

Wilfrid, meanwhile, had gone to the Continent as King Alchfrith's appointee, for consecration in a regularly canonical manner as bishop of York. He experienced the keen satisfaction of being borne in a procession in a golden chair, in an elaborate ceremony at Compiègne that involved no less than twelve bishops. Wilfrid dallied too long in France: he returned to Northumbria at the head of a gorgeous retinue to find that his patron King Alchfrith was no more and that one of Aidan's original disciples, Chad, had been made a bishop in a somewhat irregular rite conducted by Bishop Wini of Wessex and two unnamed British bishops. Chad was in control of the Northumbrian church. Wilfrid had to return to his Benedictine monastery at Ripon.

Chad was a man of unadorned holiness, an anachronism in the dawn of a more politicized era. He followed Aidan's and Finan's tradition, going about on foot to preach in the open countryside. A new force would soon uproot this survival of the early days at Lindisfarne. The new force was Pope Vitalian's archbishop of Canterbury, Theodore of Tarsus. Vitalian had selected Theodore with some misgivings because, as a Greek, he might be too much imbued with the traditions of the Eastern church (Theodore had to let his hair grow for four months before he could receive an acceptably styled Western tonsure). He went to Britain accompanied by the learned Hadrian the African, abbot of a monastery near Naples who had twice refused Vitalian's offer to consecrate him archbishop of Canterbury. Bede thought that Vitalian had sent him along to keep an eye on Theodore, lest the bishop's policies fail to hew to the Roman line. The two men, Theodore and Hadrian, brought a new form of scholarship to England. They were able to read and speak both Greek and Latin. Theirs was a deep love of learning. In their long years of service in Britain they instructed their clergy not only in Holy Writ but also in music, arithmetic, astronomy, and medicine.[34] Theodore was sixty-five years old at the time of his consecration, and his reign at Canterbury lasted for more than twenty-two years. Hadrian lived until 709. By that time he had been in England for almost four decades.

Elderly as he was, Theodore had the iron self-discipline and rugged determination needed for his task. The prospect of the journey to Britain would have daunted a man with less stamina. How many times we read of the death of a man traveling between Rome and Britain. The imperial *cursus publicus*, on which eminent personages had been trundled along paved highways on important errands, was no longer in existence. Hadrian and Theodore were able to go by sea as far as Marseilles, but the overland journey to the Channel was fraught with hardship and difficulty. They had to wait at Arles, for instance, for a passport from Ebroïn, the Neustrian mayor of the palace, and Ebroïn looked upon strangers with suspicion, and he deliberately delayed the churchmen on their journey. Winter overtook them in northern France. Theodore was welcomed by the bishop of Paris, while Hadrian spent the long, cold months at Sens and Meaux, where he had friends from previous excursions abroad. Next official permission had to be sought for the landing of Theodore's English escort. At Quentavic (Saint-Quentin), Theodore became "indisposed"; his illness entailed still another delay. Altogether the trip from Rome to Canterbury required more than a year.[35] Even then, Hadrian was detained for a time because Ebroïn had become suspicious. Could this person be carrying some hurtful message from the emperor to the rulers in England?

One of the first targets of Archbishop Theodore's campaign to pull the English church into line was unoffending Chad, the bishop of York. This humble man of Iona was "upbraided," as Bede says, for the irregularity of his consecration. Chad offered no excuses and put up no resistance. "I willingly resign the office, for I never thought myself worthy of it," he said. Even stern Theodore was disarmed. He performed whatever rite he considered necessary to regularize the consecration. Chad's notion of episcopal office was not in itself entirely regular. He lived in retirement at Lastingham, a monastic site that had once been cleared of demons by month-long prayers sent up from that "lurking place for robbers and retreat of wild beasts" by his brothers Cedd and Cynebil. Theodore removed Chad to make him bishop to the Mercians, putting Wilfrid in his place at York. Chad still went about his duties on foot. Archbishop Theodore could prevail upon him to travel in a more befitting manner only by personally hoisting him onto a horse. Even at Lichfield, where Chad then presided, he lived in a little hermitage, where he was visited by angels, who eventually conducted the good man's soul to heaven.

The more earthly archbishop set about a series of episcopal visitations and became "the first archbishop whom all the English church obeyed." By 673, Theodore was able to strike a strong blow for church unity. He convoked and presided over a synod at Hertford. Bede preserves the articles that the members of this meeting were required to sign. We can read between the lines how disorderly church affairs must have been, even after Theodore's strenuous administrative efforts. No bishop was to intrude into the diocese of another. Monks were not to move from one monastery to another without special permission. The clergy were not to forsake their bishops and wander. The attendant bishops dutifully signed the document. We should make note of William Stubbs's comment about the Synod of Hertford: "This act is one of the highest historical importance, as the first constitutional measure of the collective English race." There was no secular legislation to match it until the time of King Alfred.[36]

Seven years later, in 680, Theodore called another synod, this one in Heathfield, to consider the problems of heresy that were rocking the Eastern churches (he must have kept close ties with his homeland). The opening statement of the memorandum of the synod shows how successful Theodore had been in binding the Anglo-Saxons together. The synod took place "in the tenth year of the reign of our most pious lord Ecgfrith, king of the Northumbrians, in the sixth year of the reign of Ethelfrith, king of the Mercians, in the seventeenth year of the reign of Aldhulf, of the East Angles, in the seventh year of the reign of Lothair, king of Kent." All these kings were Christians. When we reflect that the bishops acted as ministers and counselors in these kingdoms and that the kings themselves sometimes attended Theodore's synods, we see how far England had come in one man's lifetime from the tribal stage represented by impulsive King Oswine of Deira and his kindly missionary Aidan of Iona.

Sir Winston Churchill, commenting on the strange fact that Theodore was never canonized, went on to say that "the remarkable Asiatic was the earliest of the statesmen of England, and guided her steps with fruitful wisdom."[37] No doubt Churchill was thinking of Theodore's astute move in 675 following the death of King Oswy, when his successor, King Ecgfrith, attacked Mercia by seizing Lindsey. The timing of this aggresion looked propitious because an unknown younger brother of Wulfhere had just assumed the rule of Mercia, but the new king Ethelred responded manfully to the challenge, overrunning Kent and even burning the city of Rochester. In 679 he advanced to the banks of the Trent, where a great battle ensued. Although Ethelred was the victor and therefore was poised for invasion of Northumbria, the outcome was ominous because Ecgfrith's young brother was killed. This youth was Ethelred's brother-in-law. There would be no clean-cut end to the hostilities. In the words of Bede, "There was now reason to expect a more bloody war, and most lasting enmity between those kings and their fierce nations." [38] Unexpectedly, Archbishop Theodore injected himself into the situation as a mediator. Under his guidance a blood price was accepted, and peace was established on condition that Lindsey revert to Mercia—a hard blow for Northumbria. Bede was gratified that the wholesome admonitions of the archbishop had been heeded and that there was a lasting peace, but he does not appear to have noticed that Theodore had paved the way for King Ethelred, who soon became overlord of Kent. This development Theodore could have foreseen. We might think that he would have wanted to avoid it, but his judgment was correct. Mercia was the most powerful of the English nations. Therefore, Mercia should prevail in the interests of stabilizing and centralizing the Anglo-Saxon kingdoms. [39] Theodore strengthened his own hand by establishing three new episopal sees in Mercia.

Before Theodore's time a see was coterminous with the territory of a kingdom; in the event of major conquests the diocese necessarily expanded and became unwieldy. The firm division into manageable units that ultimately cut across territorial boundaries was the keystone of Theodore's work. Most of the bishops saw the wisdom of this policy and accepted it—but not Wilfrid, bishop of York. The division of York was not handled with the adroitness that we might expect from Archbishop Theodore, who went over Wilfrid's head to King Ecgfrith and simply presented Wilfrid with the fait accompli. His great diocese was much reduced. The bishop of York knew his canon law and protested vigorously. Assembled clerics laughed derisively when Wilfrid announced that he was going to Rome to appeal to the Holy See, but off he went with great confidence and determination. He was setting a precedent: it was the first appeal from England to the authority of the pope.

A long book would hardly do justice to Bishop Wilfrid's astounding life and fortunes. Suffice it to say with reference to the quarrel over the bishopric of York that he presented his arguments before the pope on two separate occasions and that both times he was declared to be in the right. On the first appeal, in 679, Pope Agatho's decision did no more than state that it was Wilfrid, not Theodore, who should have selected bishops for his fragmented diocese. Wilfrid was instructed to return to England and expel Theodore's appointees, replacing them with men of his own choice. Ecgfrith found this judgment unacceptable and threw Wilfrid into solitary confinement for nine months.

Wilfrid had many adventures in the succeeding years and was not restored to York until 687, when Archbishop Theodore, then in his faltering eighties, became contrite and desirous of making amends. After the death of Theodore in 690, Wilfrid's clashes with Aldfrith, the new Northumbrian king, were so severe that he had to take refuge in Mercia, where he appears to have stayed for about eleven years as bishop of Leicester.

The second appeal to Rome occurred in 703, when Wilfrid's enemies banded together under Archbishop Berhtwald of Canterbury with the intention of depriving him of all his extensive holdings in both Northumbria and Mercia. Wilfrid passionately defended himself, rejecting any decision from Canterbury. This time the pope responded to Wilfrid's personal appeal by sending letters to the kings of Northumbria and Mercia with instructions to hold a council to make immediate and lasting peace among all contenders. Otherwise, he wrote, all must present themselves in Rome. Kings could still be defiant. Although Ethelred of Mercia accepted the pope's orders, King Aldfrith of Northumbria refused. It was only after Aldfrith's death that a synod was called to hear the papal letters. Abbess Elffled, King Aldfrith's sister, then rose to state that the late king had told her that it was his intention to make peace with Wilfrid. In the end Wilfrid received his glorious old Northumbrian monasteries Hexham and Ripon and became bishop of Hexham. No longer an expatriate, still extremely wealthy, the aging aristocrat lived on a few more years to savor his belated vindication.

In the furious encounter just before his second appeal to Rome, Wilfrid summed up his accomplishments. He reminded his antagonists that it was he who had brought the Northumbrians to the correct observance of Easter and that it was he who had brought the rule of Saint Benedict to the north. He had introduced antiphonal singing, he went on, and also the correct monastic tonsure. All this is true, but Wilfrid was a complex person, and he had done much more. Celts and Teutons reacted differently to Christianity: Wilfrid had responded as an Anglo-Saxon. Not for him the quiet abnegation and humble Celtic devotion to a Redeemer. His Christ was a king in majesty, a triumphant conqueror whose followers were like a nobleman's retinue, bound to him in personal allegiance. The daily life of the church, he felt, should emphasize this glory. For that reason Wilfrid built huge churches in the Roman manner, clothed their altars in purple, decked them with chalices that were masterpieces of the metalworker's art, encased his illuminated vellum Gospel books in bejeweled gold, and surrounded himself with all the pomp befitting a member of Christ's own train. Let us make no mistake. Wilfrid was not a vainglorious power seeker. He had a profound belief in the importance of visible symbols.

By nature Wilfrid was an aristocrat and a leader.[40] Born into an upper stratum of pagan society, he was a favorite at King Oswy's court, and while he

Plate 82. Chapel of Saint Patrick, Heysham, overlooking Morcambe Bay, Lancashire, England. The cable-carved arch surmounts some of the earliest known Saxon long-and-short work, in which long narrow stones are alternatingly set horizontally or vertically, to make the structure rigid by forming a tenon. The upright pieces jut out slightly, so that a decorative effect results at the corners of the building (Leclercq, "Bretagne (Grande)," *DA*, vol. 2, pt. 1, cols. 1191–92).

was still in his teens, he was sent to the monastery of Lindisfarne as attendant to one of the king's companions who was in poor health. There Wilfrid learned to read. That must have opened up immense vistas for him, because he soon expressed the wish to travel abroad, not in any way experiencing the desire for *peregrinatio* in the Irish sense. Specifically, he wanted to go to Rome. He was a privileged youth, handsome and charming. He set off armed with a letter of introduction from his Northumbrian queen to her kinsman the king of Kent. His companion on the journey was another young nobleman, Benedict Biscop, the indefatigable traveler who was to found the double monasteries Jarrow and Wearmouth, where Bede spent his scholarly life, poring over books brought by Benedict Biscop from afar. The two young men parted at Lyons, where Wilfrid settled for a year, to be guided in his studies by Archbishop Annemundus, the brother of Count Dalfinus, who ruled at Lyons. Annemundus had enough political influence in his own right to be able to propose to Wilfrid that he become governor of part of Gaul and marry Annemundus's niece, by that means becoming a member of the powerful family. Instead,

Wilfrid pressed on to Rome to study canon law. On the return journey he spent three more years at Lyons and might have tarried still longer in the pleasant company of worldly churchmen had not his friend and patron Archbishop Annemundus been killed in a revolution instigated by Ebroïn, the mayor of the palace (we remember that it was Ebroïn who had made difficulties for Theodore and Hadrian in their journey to Britain). Back in England, Wilfrid somehow became acquainted with the king of Wessex, who introduced him to King Oswy's son, King Alchfrith of Deira. Impressive gifts went hand in hand with royal favor. Wilfrid became abbot of the important establishment at Ripon, and at the age of twenty-nine was ordained a priest by the bishop of Dorchester.

The king (Alchfrith), the bishop (Agilbert), and Wilfrid were the prime movers at Whitby, where Oswy, whether through a statesman's insight or merely out of concern for his immortal soul, ruled in favor of the pro-Romans against the monks of Lindisfarne. Next King Alchfrith sent Wilfrid to Gaul to be consecrated by Agilbert, bishop of Paris. On that occasion Wilfrid rode in a golden chair in a procession so gorgeous that it must have been the realization of his most fanciful dreams. We recall that by the time he returned to assume his duties, heading a retinue of 120 men, his patron Alchfrith had disappeared, and humble holy Chad had become bishop in his stead. Later, in 669, Wilfrid received his bishopric at the hands of Archbishop Theodore. He selected York as the center of his diocese and immediately set about restoring the ruined church that Bishop Paulinus had built in the days of King Edwin. This time it became a much grander edifice, with a lead roof and glazed windows.

The consecration of his monastic church at Ripon must have been a stirring moment for Wilfrid. We can imagine him unfurling his royal charters to read them aloud in the presence of the kings of Northumbria and Deira. The land attached to the Ripon foundation was a small country in itself.

As King Ecgfrith's victories mounted, so did Wilfrid's fortunes. The enormous monastery church at Hexham was built,[41] and the diocese was extended to include Lindsey. Even more lands came to Wilfrid from King Ecgfrith's queen, Ethelthryth. How different Wilfrid's life might have been had it not been for his entanglements with formidable queens, with all their power and willfulness. King Ecgfrith had had trouble with his wife, Ethelthryth, for years. Bede checked his facts with Wilfrid when he wrote his history, because he could not quite believe what he had been told. With Wilfrid's confirmation, he was able to report that Ethelthryth was indeed a virgin after eleven years of marriage. She wanted to be a nun. Wilfrid approved of virginity, but King Ecgfrith did not. In the end Ethelthryth received the veil from Bishop Wilfrid's hands and retired to Coldingham, where an aunt of hers was abbess. She turned over her large estates for the endowment of Wilfrid's monastery at Hexham. King Ecgfrith's second wife, Iurminburh, was far from pleased; she thought that those lands rightfully were hers as queen. She complained to the king that Bishop Wilfrid's style was ostentatious, that he outshone the king. The enmity probably had nothing to do with the decision to break up Wilfrid's bishopric, but it later proved dangerous to him when he returned from Rome with the papal decision in his favor.

In the meantime there had been his extraordinary trip to Rome for the purpose of laying his case before the pope. Wilfrid had to avoid territories controlled by Ebroïn, who had caused the downfall of Archbishop Annemundus. Ruling Neustria for the boy king Theodoric III, Ebroïn wanted to extend his control to Austrasia, where, years before, the mayor of the palace in that kingdom had seized the heir to the throne, young Dagobert II, and shipped him off to an Irish monastery. When Dagobert was twenty years old, he had come under Wilfrid's protection and had been assisted by the bishop in his successful efforts to regain his throne in 676. Ebroïn nurtured a grudge and would have been only too pleased to have Wilfrid in his clutches. Wilfrid was no innocent. He sailed north for Frisia instead of straight across to the Continent, but even in Frisia, where he lingered to preach to the heathens, Ebroïn was a threat. Ebroïn offered the king of the Frisians a bushel of gold pieces if he would surrender Wilfrid to him, but the bribe was rejected haughtily. The Frisians were converted, temporarily at least, because "the catch of fish was unusually large and the year was more than usually fruitful in every kind of produce." [42] Wilfrid was free of the wicked Ebroïn, but not so the unfortunate bishop of Lichfield, who was also en route to Rome. Ebroïn's henchmen mistakenly thought that this bishop, *Winfrid*, was their man: many of his companions were killed, and "the holy bishop was left naked and in the utmost straits of misery." [43]

On then to the territory of King Dagobert II. His Majesty had not forgotten Wilfrid's generous assistance and wanted to make a fitting return. Would Wilfrid care to become his bishop, at Strasbourg? Wilfrid declined and pushed on into Italy, where he was kindly received by King Perctarit of Campania. Like Dagobert, King Perctarit had been a fugitive in his time. When some of Wilfrid's enemies from Britain appeared offering a bribe for his surrender, Perctarit scornfully refused. The explanation that the king gave to Wilfrid is interesting because it is a reminder of the continued existence of true barbarians, even in the seventh century: "I was once an exile in the days of my youth, dwelling with a certain pagan king of the Huns who entered into a covenant with me before the idol that was his god, to the effect that he would never betray me nor hand me over to my enemies." When messengers came to offer a bribe to the Hunnic king, he dismissed them, saying, "Doubtless the gods would cut off my life if I were to commit this crime." As a worshiper of the true God, Perctarit was sure that such an act would bring about the destruction of his soul. [44]

Plate 83. Episcopal throne of Wilfrid, Hexham Abbey, Northumberland, England. *Courtesy of rector of Hexham Abbey.*

After his successful hearing in Rome, Wilfrid turned back laden with relics for his beloved churches. He passed across Dagobert's territory again, but Dagobert had been assassinated in the meantime and a bishop at the head of an armed troop confronted him. This military bishop allowed Wilfrid to pass when assured that Wilfrid's assistance to Dagobert in the past had been "for your good, not your harm."

Aside from a shipwreck on the coast of Sussex, Wilfrid underwent no more trials until he arrived in Northumbria. Angry King Ecgfrith cast him into prison, where he languished for nine months. A strong royal lady was helpful at that point: Abbess Ebbe of Coldingham, the sister of Ecgfrith, interceded on his behalf. Released from prison, Wilfrid fled to Mercia, where he was well received by the king's nephew. In 681 he was given land for his monks, and the future looked promising, but unfortunately Mercia's queen, a

Plate 84. Saxon doorway at Jarrow, near South Shields, Tyne and Wear County, England. Here the Venerable Bede lived and wrote his ecclesiastical history.

sister of King Ecgfrith, took up the cause of embittered Queen Iurminburh. Wilfrid moved on to Wessex, but the situation was repeated because the king of Wessex was a brother-in-law of Iurminburh.

Thus driven from England's Christian kingdoms, Wilfrid took refuge in Sussex, a heathen place. Sussex had never been converted. There he met favor in the eyes of King Ethelwalh, who allowed him to preach. Wilfrid converted thousands and was given a huge estate in Selsey, where he established a monastery (it should be noted in passing that all of Wilfrid's foundations were Benedictine). Inexplicably, Wilfrid appears to have turned against his royal benefactor five years later, in 686, when he assisted the exiled prince Cedwalla's efforts to gain the throne. Cedwalla gave Wilfrid a quarter of the Isle of Wight in return for his help. This king was young, brutal, and impulsive. He soon abdicated and went off to Rome, where he died in holiness in 689.

At this point Archbishop Theodore began to regret his shabby treatment of Wilfrid. Wilfrid's biographer Eddius Stephanus says that Theodore wanted Wilfrid to succeed him at Canterbury. In any case, Theodore is known to have written letters on Wilfrid's behalf to King Aldfrith, to Abbess Elffled, and to King Ethelred in Mercia. Wilfrid, as we remember, recovered Hexham and Ripon and his reduced see of York, but a quarrel with King Aldfrith came to a head five years later. Wilfrid once more took refuge in Mercia, where he became bishop of Leicester.

The next convocation to deal with the problem of Wilfrid was called in 703, under Berhtwald of Canterbury. Wilfrid's lands were sequestered, his followers excommunicated.[45] We have already noted that once again Wilfrid appealed to Rome and that once more the pope found in his favor. The Synod of Nidd was assembled after the death of King Aldfrith, and a reconciliation, or at least a compromise, was reached.

Wilfrid's status as bishop of Hexham was assured (see plate 83). He was an old man by that time, astutely aware of the ways of the world. When he felt death approaching, he called in two of his abbots and eight of his monks and opened up his treasure of gold and precious stones. He divided the treasure into four equal parts: an offering for Rome, provision for the poor, a Saxon nobleman's gift to followers who had shared his exile, and a portion cannily set aside for the abbots of Hexham and Ripon "that they may be able to purchase the friendship of kings and bishops."

This giant of the church died in 709 or 710. His turbulent life was a reflection of the complex age in which he lived. The West was no longer Roman, and Europe was about to be born. Wise old Bede was describing natural phenomena, yet his words can be taken metaphorically: in Britain "the nights are light in summer, so that at midnight the beholders are often in doubt whether the evening twilight still continues, or that of the morning is coming on."

EPILOGUE
TWO STATELY CHAIRS

N EXT to Pope Gregory's bleak monastic cell in the Church of Santo Gregorio Magno in Rome stands a carved-stone chair, Gregory's own cathedra, the very one used by the "servant of the servants of God" (see color plate 16). It is a curious seat for the head of Christ's kingdom on earth. The entire back is covered with pagan images. It must have been ancient even in Gregory's day.

It is safe to assume that Wilfrid examined it attentively when he was in Rome. He must have decided that in Northumbria he too should be seated in a manner worthy of Christ's representative. Wilfrid's chair stands near the crossing in Hexham Abbey, close to the entrance to the crypt that is all that remains of his church, which was famed as the most impressive west of the Alps (see plate 83). The chair also seems oddly inappropriate for a Catholic prelate, especially for the man who led the pro-Roman party at Whitby. Carved all of one piece of stone, it has only one decoration, the characteristically Celtic triquetra in an elongated form, on the arms.[1]

Could it be that these two princes of the church, both of whom understood the value of symbols, were silently acknowledging a debt? Gregory's Catholic church would never have emerged as a formidable power had it not been built on the foundation of the empire. The church in England would not have extended its influence as it did in the eighth century had it not been that the energetic Anglo-Saxons learned well from the *peregrini*. Before the century was out, English missionaries would go to the Continent. Willibrord was trained under Wilfrid but also spent twelve years in Ireland. Boniface, who grew up in the still-Celtic southwest, carried the faith to the Frisians and organized the church there according to Roman principles. Before the century was out, the "Carolingian renaissance" would be under way, led by Alcuin, who had an Irish teacher and took the syncretic culture that had been nurtured in the famed school at York to the court of Charlemagne. The great Roman organizers were not writers, and certainly even that famous bibliophile Benedict Biscop was not a teacher. Even after Whitby, teaching remained the responsibility of the Scots.

It is just possible that the carved motifs of ancient Rome on the papal chair and the age-old Celtic triquetra on the episcopal throne of an Anglo-Saxon bishop at Hexham were the best symbols that their august occupants could find for an age of transition.

NOTES

See References Cited for list of abbreviations used in notes

PREFACE

1. C. A. Ralegh Radford, "Two Scottish Shrines: Jedburgh and Saint Andrews," *Archaeological Journal* 112 (1955): 43–47.

CHAPTER 1. TRIER

1. Edith M. Wightman, *Roman Trier and the Treveri*, pp. 37ff.; Paul MacKendrick, *Romans on the Rhine: Archaeology in Germany*, pp. 215–47.

2. Jules Toutain, *Les cultes païens dans l'Empire romain*, pt. 1, *Les provinces latines*, vol. 3, *Les cultes indigènes nationaux et locaux*, fasc. 2, *Les cultes de la Gaule romaine*, p. 306.

3. John Rhŷs, *Celtic Folklore, Welsh and Manx*, 1:354–59; Aubrey Burl, *The Stone Circles of the British Isles*, p. 125; Eleanor Hull, *Folklore of the British Isles*, pp. 108–11; R. W. Hutchinson, *Prehistoric Crete*, pp. 213–14.

4. Sulpicius Severus *Life of Martin* 12.

5. Paul Jacobsthal, *Early Celtic Art*, p. 17 [the influence of Etruscan jewelry]; René Joffroy, "Die Kunst der Kelten," in Eggers et al., *Kelten*, p. 128; Vincent Megaw, "The Shape-Changers: Art of the Iron Age Celts," *Archaeology* 31 (1978):38 [The lobed decoration may have originated in the pointed ears of satyrs in classic art].

6. Phyllis P. Bober, "Cernunnos: Origin and Transformation of a Celtic Divinity," *American Journal of Archaeology* 55 (1951):44; Ole Klindt-Jensen, "The Gundestrup Bowl: A Reassessment," *Antiquity* 33 (1959): 161–69 [Cernunnos wears the tight-fitting trousers of the Belgae. The bowl may have originated in northern Gaul]; Albert Grenier, *Les gaulois*, pp. 238–40; Garrett S. Olmsted, *The Gundestrup Cauldron: Its Archaeological Context, the Style, and Iconography of Its Portrayed Motifs, and Their Narration of a Gaulish Version of Táin Bó Cúailnge*, p. 45 [Not identified as Cernunnos: called "the crouching god"; the posture may have no significance because the Gauls commonly sat on the floor].

7. Anne Ross, *Everyday Life of the Pagan Celts*, p. 137 [plans of *Viereckschanzen* (rectangular earthworks)].

8. Robert Graves, trans., Introduction, *Lucan: Pharsalia*, p. 13.

9. Nora K. Chadwick, *The Druids*, p. ix; M. K. Hopkins, "Social Mobility in the Later Roman Empire: the Evidence of Ausonius," *Classical Antiquity*, n.s. 11 (1961):239–49 [refers to a scholarly family of druidical stock in Bordeaux].

10. Nora K. Chadwick, *The Celts*, pp. 155ff.; Ross, *Everyday Life of the Pagan Celts*, p. 126; Pierre Lambrechts, *Exaltation de la tête dans la pensée et dans l'art des celtes*; François Salviat, *Entremont antique*, pp. 19–25.

11. Marcel Pobé, *The Art of Roman Gaul*, plates 25–43.

12. Roman Ghirshman, "Persian Art in Parthian and Sassanian Times," *Larousse Encyclopedia of Byzantine and Medieval Art*, p. 55 [*Têtes coupées* were characteristic of Iranian art in the first millennium B.C.].

13. Chadwick, *The Celts*, pp. 45ff.

14. H. Dragendorff and E. Krüger, *Das Grabmal von Igel*; Ernest Will, "De l'Euphrate au Rhin: étude sur quelques motifs ornementaux," *Syria* 31 (1954):271–85; M. Rostovtzeff, *The Social and Economic History of the Roman Empire* 1:226 [The owners of the Moselle villas were not only agriculturalists but bankers as well; that is the explanation of the money-paying scenes]; Eberhard Zahn, *Die Igeler Säule bei Trier*.

15. Sidonius Apollinaris *Ep*. 2.2.2 [Sidonius teases his friend Domitius, whom he imagines "squeezed into a deep chair made of America's population"—i.e., osier]; Joachim Marquardt, *Das Privatleben der Römer*, 1:726; Hug, "Stuhl," *RE*, 2d ser., vol. 4, col. 421; G. M. Durant, *Britain: Rome's Most Northerly Province*, p. 76. Replicas of Gallo-Roman wicker chairs are scattered throughout the Musée luxembourgeois, at Arlon, Belgium. They are unexpectedly comfortable.

16. M. I. Finley, *The Ancient Economy*, pp. 112, 201.

17. E. Sadée, "Gutsherrn und Bauern im römischen Rheinland," *Bonner Jahrbücher* 128 (1923):117.

18. Karl Christ, "Ergebnisse und Probleme der keltischen Numismatik und Geldgeschichte (Bericht 1935–1955)," *Historia* 6 (1957):215–53.

19. Alfons Dopsch, *The Economic and Social Foundations of European Civilization*, p. 54, citing H. Dragendorff, *Westdeutschland zur Römerzeit* (Frankfurt, 1910); Will, "Die Kunst im römischen Gallien," in Eggers et al., *Kelten*, p. 110.

20. Salvian 4.14; Louis Bréhier, "Les colonies d'Orientaux en Occident au commencement du moyen-âge, V^e–VIIe siècle," *Byzantinische Zeitschrift* 12 (1903):14; Henri Leclercq, "Colonies d'Orientaux en Occident," *DA*, vol. 3, pt. 2, cols. 2273–75.

21. Adolf Harnack, *The Mission and Expansion of Christianity in the First Three Centuries*, pp. 173–74.

22. Rostovtzeff, *The Social and Economic History of the Roman Empire*, 2:611.

23. Albert Grenier, "Le sanctuaire de l'Altbachtal," in *Manuel d'archéologie gallo-romaine*, pt. 4, pp. 857–74; Reinhard Schindler, *Landesmuseum Trier: Führer durch die vorgeschichtliche und römische Abteilung*, pp. 31–41; Fergus Millar [Review of W. H. C. Frend, *Martyrdom and Persecution in the Early Church*], *Journal of Roman Studies* 56 (1966):235 ["The emperors, in a multitude of different ways, were given a place in the local cults of the provinces"].

24. Wightman, *Roman Trier and the Treveri*, p. 210.

25. Max Ihm, "Der Mutter- oder Matronenkultus und seine Denkmäler," *Jahrbücher des Vereins von Alterthumsfreunden im Rheinlande* 83 (1887):75 [The *matres* may have survived at Aigues-Mortes as the Three Maries]; René Magnen, *Épona, déesse gauloise des chevaux, protectrice des cavaliers*; G. Charrière, "La femme et l'équidé dans la mythologie française," *Revue de l'histoire des religions* 188 (1975):129–88.

26. Bober, "Cernunnos," p. 44.

27. Pierre Lambrechts, *Contributions à l'étude des divinités celtiques*, pp. 81–98; G. Bauchheuss, "Zur Entstehung der Jupitergigantensäuler, *Archäologisches Korrespondenzblatt* 4 (1974):359–64 [illustrated].

28. Wightman, *Roman Trier and the Treveri*, p. 211ff.

29. Hans Lehner, "Orientalische Mysterien-Kulte im römischen Rheinland," *Bonner Jahrbücher* 129 (1924):36–91; Franz Cumont, *Astrology and Religion Among the Greeks and Romans*; J. Leclant, "Osiris en Gaule," *Studia Aegyptica* 1 (1974):263–85.

30. Gaius Julius Caesar *De bello gallico* 6.

31. Tacitus *Germania* 15.

32. Sir Mortimer Wheeler, *Rome Beyond the Imperial Frontiers*, p. 89; Hans Jürgen Eggers, "Die Kunst der Germanen in der Eisenzeit," in Eggers et al., *Kelten*, pp. 22–27.

33. E. A. Thompson, *The Early Germans*, pp. 21–22.

34. Ibid., p. 57.

35. Maurice Bouvier-Ajam, *Le temps des empereurs gaulois*, pp. 137 ff.; Ernst Stein, "Esuvius. 1," *RE*, vol. 6, cols. 696–704; H. S. Versnel, *Triumphus: An Inquiry into the Origin, Development, and Meaning of the Roman Triumph*.

36. E. A. Thompson, "Peasant Revolts in Late Roman Gaul and Spain," *Past and Present* 2 (1952):11–12.

37. Otto Seeck, "Bagaudae," *RE*, vol. 2, cols. 2766–67; Mamertinus *Panegyric to Maximian* 2.4, in Moses Hadas, *A History of Rome from Its Origins to 529 A.D. as Told by the Roman Historians*, p. 176; Thompson, "Peasant Revolts," p. 23 ["For some hundreds of years editors have foisted on the Bacaudae the senseless destruction of Autun in 269–270, although the MSS of Eumenius IV 1 give *Baticavae* and not *Bacaudicae*"]; P. le Gentilhomme, "Le désastre d'Autun en 269," *Revue des études anciennes* 45 (1943):233–39 [arguments concerning the disputed texts].

38. Jacob Burckhardt, *The Age of Constantine the Great*, pp. 58–59.

39. Camille Jullian, *Histoire de la Gaule*, 7:51–52.

40. Hubert Goltzius, *Thesavrvs rei antiqvasiae hvberrimva*, pp. 117, 121 [Four coins are listed].

41. W. Fritz Volbach, *Early Decorative Textiles*, p. 22 [Diocletian set the price of raw silk at 4,000 pieces of gold per kilo]; Marquardt, *Das Privatleben der Römer*, 1:506–16.

42. Burckhardt, *The Age of Constantine the Great*, p. 39; William T. Avery, "The *Adoratio purpurae* and the Importance of the Imperial Purple in the Fourth Century of the Christian Era," *Memoirs of the American Academy in Rome* 17 (1940):66–80.

43. Wightman, *Roman Trier and the Treveri*, p. 107.

44. Émilienne Demougeot, *De l'unité à la division de l'Empire romain, 395–410: essai sur le gouvernement impérial*, p. 53; Robert Sabatino Lopez, "Silk Industry in the Byzantine Empire," *Speculum* 20 (1945):6–7.

45. Anton Kisa, *Das Glas im Altertume*, pp. 616–27; Marquardt, *Das Privatleben der Römer*, 1:754–56; Frederic Neuberg, "Glass," *Encyclopedia of World Art*, 6:370–71.

46. Theodor K. Kempf, "Katalog der frühchristliche Abteilung des Bischöflichen Museums Trier," in Reusch, *Frühchristliche Zeugnisse*, p. 222 [A model of Constantine's double church at Trier is shown].

47. Harnack, *History of Dogma*, 4:62 [Harnack observes that, if the standards of his time are applied to Athanasius, "we can discover nothing mean or ignoble in him"]; Edward Gibbon, *The Decline and Fall of the Roman Empire*, 2:698–99 ["He never lost the confidence of his friends or the esteem of his enemies"].

48. Harnack, *History of Dogma*, 3:144ff.

49. Pierre Courcelle, *Recherches sur les "Confessions" de saint Augustin*, pp. 180–81 [The Roman officer in Augustine's narrative who was suddenly converted to monasticism by his conversation with monks outside the walls of Trier must have been Saint Jerome]; J. N. D. Kelly, *Jerome: His Life, Writings, and Controversies*, p. 30 [Courcelle is in error].

CHAPTER 2. THE STEPPES OF ASIA

1. Norman H. Baynes, "Constantine's Successors to Jovian and the Struggle with Persia," *CMH*, 1:59–62.

2. Edward Gibbon, *The Decline and Fall of the Roman Empire*, 1:695; John W. Eadie, "The Development of Roman Mailed Cavalry," *Journal of Roman Studies* 57 (1967):171 [Constantius's cavalrymen at Mursa were *clibenarii*, armored in Sassanian style; Emperor Julian thought that it was the helplessness of unarmored *equites* that accounted for their defeat].

3. Ammianus Marcellinus 20.4.4.

4. Libanius *Julianic Orations* 13.34; Christopher Walter, "Raising on a Shield in Byzantine Iconography," *Revue des études byzantines* 33 (1975):133–75; Wilhelm Ensslin, "The Court and Its Ceremonial: Dress and Insignia," *CAH*, 12:361–67; Otto Treitinger, *Die oströmischen Kaiser- und Reichsidee nach ihren Gestaltung im höfischen Zeremoniell*, pp. 20–21; Julian, *Letter to the Senate and People of Athens*, in William Cave Wright, trans., *The Works of the Emperor Julian*, 2:243–91; Glen Warren Bowersock, *Julian the Apostate*, pp. 33–54.

5. A. H. M. Jones, *The Decline of the Ancient World*, p. 62.

6. E. A. Thompson, *The Visigoths in the Time of Ulfila*.

7. Franz Altheim, "Runen als Schildzeichen," *Klio* 31 (1938):51–59 [Frankish contingents (the Cornuti) who fought with Constantine the Great at the Milvian Bridge had shields marked with a rune]; Ralph W. V. Elliott, *Runes: An Introduction*, pp. 1–13; Hans Jürgen Eggers, "Die Kunst der Germanen in der Eisenzeit," in Eggers et al., *Kelten*, pp. 72–75.

8. Ammianus Marcellinus 31.3.8.

9. Ibid., 31.2.3.

10. Ibid., 31.2.10.

11. Maenchen-Helfen, p. 214.

12. Ibid., p. 330.

13. E. A. Thompson, *A History of Attila and the Huns* pp. 43–50.

14. Ibid., p. 23.

15. Maenchen-Helfen, p. 204, citing Vegetius *Epitoma rei militaris* 3.6.5 [The Hunnic horse had "a great hooked head, protruding eyes, narrow nostrils, broad jaws, and strong stiff neck"].

16. Gad Rausing, *The Bow: Some Notes on Its Origin and Development*.

17. Sidonius Apollinaris *Carm.* 2.246–54.

18. Joachim Werner, *Beiträge zur Archaeologie des Attila-Reiches*, p. 17 [Cites the work of E. V. Zirov and K. F. Smirnov].

19. Maenchen-Helfen, pp. 306–35 [photographs of Hunnic cauldrons].

20. A. G. Wenley, "The Question of the Po-Shan-Hsiang-Lu," *Archives of the Chinese Art Society of America* 3 (1948–49):9; Jerome *Ep.* 107.10 [Jerome admonishes Laeta that her young daughter should be taught to scorn silk fabrics and "Chinese fleeces"].

21. E. D. Phillips, *The Royal Hordes: Nomad Peoples of the Steppes*, pp. 112–20.

22. Maenchen-Helfen, p. 353.

23. E. Loubo-Lesnitchenko, "Imported Mirrors in the Minusinsk Basin," *Artibus Asiae* 35 (1973):28–29.

24. G. Azarpay, "Some Classical and Near Eastern Motifs in the Art of Pazyryk," *Artibus Asiae* 22 (1959):313–39; *From the Lands of the Scythians: Ancient Treasures from the Museums of the U.S.S.R. 3000 B.C.–100 B.C.*

25. Werner, *Beiträge zur Archaeologie des Attila-Reiches*, plate 61 [bows and their decorations, from Poland and Hungary—reconstructions].

26. Ibid., pp. 51–52; Édouard Salin, *La civilisation mérovingienne d'après les sépultures, les textes et le laboratoire*, 1:318.

27. Werner, *Beiträge zur Archaeologie des Attila-Reiches*, pp. 61–68.
28. Ammianus Marcellinus 31.4.9.
29. E. A. Thompson, *A History of Attila and the Huns* p. 23; Maenchen-Helfen, p. 29 ["Adrianople was won by *equitatus Gothorum* . . . a few men of other tribes with them, but these were not Huns"].
30. Thomas Hodgkin, *The Dynasty of Theodosius*, p. 117.
31. Ernst Stein, *Geschichte des spätrömischen Reiches*, p. 300.
32. Otto Seeck, *Geschichte des Untergangs der antiken Welt*, 5:38–39.
33. Wilhelm Ensslin, "Zum Heermeisteramt des spätrömischen Reiches," *Klio* 24 (1930):102–47; Karl Friedrich Stroheker, *Germanentum und Spätantike*, pp. 9–29.
34. J. Vannerus, "Nouvelle hypothèse sur le 'Long Mur' de Bitbourt," *Revue belge de philologie et d'histoire* 11 (1933):141–45 [Gratian's immense hunting park may have been near Trier].

CHAPTER 3. MILAN

1. The following works are of general interest: Jean-Rémy Palanque, *Saint Ambroise et l'Empire romain: contributions à l'histoire des rapports de l'Église et de l'État à la fin du quatrième siècle*; F. Homes Dudden, *The Life and Times of St. Ambrose;* Angelo Paredi, *Saint Ambrose: His Life and Times*.
2. Ammianus Marcellinus 30.9.5.
3. Paredi, *Saint Ambrose*, pp. 119–20.
4. Ramsay MacMullen, *Enemies of the Roman Order: Treason, Unrest, and Alienation in the Empire*, p. 178.
5. Hans-Joachim Diesner, *Kirche und Staat im spätrömischen Reich*, pp. 44–45.
6. Pierre Courcelle, *Recherches sur saint Ambroise: "vies" anciennes, culture, iconographie*, p. 15 [Ambrose appears to have proclaimed himself a Neoplatonist in the year before his election, with the intention of making himself ineligible for episcopal office]; Otto F. A. Meinardus, *Christian Egypt: Faith and Life*, pp. 100, 104, 115 [The patriarch was ritually brought to Alexandria in chains for his consecration].
7. A. Hoepffner, "La mort du 'magister militvm' Théodose," *Revue des études latines* 14 (1936):128. See also chap. 7, n. 29, below.
8. Ammianus Marcellinus 15.10.4; Otto Seeck, "Cursus publicus," *RE*, vol. 4, cols. 1846–63; A. M. Ramsay, "The Speed of the Roman Imperial Post," *Journal of Roman Studies* 15 (1925):60–74; Henri Leclercq, "Négoce," *DA*, vol. 12, pt. 1, cols. 1082–87; H.-G. Pflaum, *Essai sur le cursus publicus sous le Haut-Empire romain*; A. H. M. Jones, *The Decline of the Ancient World*, p. 313; Thomas Pékary, *Untersuchungen zu den römischen Reichsstrassen*, pp. 173–75 [bibliography].
9. Maenchen-Helfen, pp. 42–43.
10. Johannes Geffcken, *The Last Days of Greco-Roman Paganism*, p. 290; Adolf Harnack, *History of Dogma*, 4:106–107; 3:126 [Philostorgius *Historia ecclesiastica* 2.17 is quoted. Christians of the fourth century in their confusion honored the image of Constantine the Great with incense and lanterns].
11. Meinardus, *Christian Egypt*, pp. 161–62 [One of Saint George's skulls is in Attica, another is in Crete, a shoulder blade is at Lymmasol, his right hand is on the island of Euboea, and some of his blood is at Mount Athos].
12. Courcelle, *Recherches sur les "Confessions" de saint Augustin*, pp. 145–46.
13. Ambrose's own elegantly attired little skeleton lies today between those of Gervasius and Protasius in the crypt of Sant' Ambrogio in Milan.

14. Augustine *Confessions* 6.2.2; Irving Woodworth Raymond, *The Teaching of the Early Church on the Use of Wine and Strong Drink*, pp. 128–30; Augustine *Ep.* 22.6 [The problem of drunken orgies at the tombs of the martyrs in Africa was severe].

15. Peter R. L. Brown, *Augustine of Hippo*, p. 69.

16. Maria R. Alföldi, "Münzen des 4. Jahrhunderts mit christlichen Kaiserbildnissen," in Reusch, *Frühchristliche Zeugnisse*, p. 93 [From the evidence of gold coins it appears that Victoria was poised on a globe with a wreath and a palm branch in her hands and that her statue was located behind the consuls' seats in the Curia].

17. R. H. Barrow, *Prefect and Emperor: The Relationes of Symmachus*, pp. 32–33; Lellia Cracco Ruggini, "Apoteosi e politica senatoria nel IV S.D.C.: il dittico dei Symmachi al British Museum," *Rivista storica italiana* 89 (1977):441 [The attitude of Emperor Theodosius toward things pagan wavered occasionally. He no doubt welcomed the rehabilitation of his disgraced father Theodosius the Elder, who was deified by the Roman Senate shortly after the death of Emperor Gratian].

18. John Alexander McGeachy, *Quintus Aurelius Symmachus and the Senatorial Aristocracy of the West*, pp. 141, 148–51.

19. Herbert Bloch, "The Pagan Revival in the West at the End of the Fourth Century," in Arnaldo Momigliano, ed., *The Conflict Between Paganism and Christianity in the Fourth Century*, p. 211.

20. Wilhelm Ensslin, "*Carpentum* oder *Carruca?* Bemerkungen zum Fahrrecht und Amtswagen im spätrömischen Reich und zum Versuch einer Datierung der Historia Augusta," *Klio* 32 (1939):102; Arnaldo Momigliano, "Per la interpretazione di Simmaco *Relatio* 4," *Rendiconti, Accademia dei Lincei, Classe di scienze morali, storiche e filologiche*, 8th ser., 19 (1964): 225–30; André Chastagnol, *La préfecture urbaine à Rome sous le Bas-Empire*, plate 1 [The illustration of the prefect's vehicle is taken from *Notitia dignitatum*, Bibl. nat. MS latin 9661, fol. 110].

21. Richard Klein, *Symmachus: eine tragische Gestalt des ausgehenden Heidentums*, p. 164 [The one eternal verity for Symmachus was the *res publica romana*].

22. Ambrose *Ep.* 17, quoted by Paredi, *Saint Ambrose*, p. 232.

23. Philip Levine, "The Continuity and Preservation of the Latin Tradition," in Lynn White, Jr., ed., *The Transformation of the Roman World*, pp. 206–31.

24. Norman H. Baynes, "The Dynasty of Valentinian and Theodosius the Great," *CMH*, 1:245.

25. C. Baur, "Zur Ambrose-Theodosius Frage," *Theologische Quartalschrift* 90 (1908): 401–409 [The Ambrose story appears first in Zosimus in the fifth century: it may have been sheer propaganda]; Diesner, *Kirche und Staat im spätrömischen Reich*, p. 40; Dudden, *The Life and Times of St. Ambrose*, 2:391; J. N. D. Kelly, *Early Christian Doctrines*, p. 438 [on penance].

26. W. W. Tarn, *Hellenistic Civilization*, p. 318.

27. Derwas J. Chitty, *The Desert a City: An Introduction to the Study of Egyptian and Palestinian Monasticism Under the Christian Empire*, pp. 54–55.

28. Augustin Fliche and Victor Martin, *Histoire de l'Église depuis les origines jusqu'à nos jours*, 3:333.

29. Ammianus Marcellinus 22.9.11.

30. Camille Jullian, *Histoire de la Gaule*, 7:313.

31. Bloch, "The Pagan Revival in the West at the End of the Fourth Century," p. 199.

32. Otto Seeck, *Geschichte des Untergangs der antiken Welt*, 5:244.

33. G. R. Sievers, *Das Leben des Libanius*, pp. 157–58.

34. Ammianus Marcellinus 31.12.15.

35. Pierre de Labriolle, *La réaction païenne; étude sur la polémique antichrétienne du Ier au VIe siècle*, pp. 428–33.

36. Karl Friedrich Stroheker, "Zur Rolle der Heermeister fränkischen Abstammung im späten vierten Jahrhundert," *Historia* 4 (1955):314–30 [I came across Stroheker's article long after completion of this chapter. The argument is much the same].

37. Henry Melvill Gwatkin, "Constantine and His City," *CMH*, 1:3 [Crocus, an Alamannic officer, was an early barbarian emperor-maker]. See also chap. 12, n. 30, below.

38. Geffcken, *The Last Days of Greco-Roman Paganism*, p. 186.

39. Bloch, "A New Document of the Last Pagan Revival in the West, 393–394 A.D.," *Harvard Theological Review* 38 (1945):234.

40. Seeck, *Geschichte des Untergangs der antiken Welt* 5:250.

41. Palladius 25.13; Peter R. L. Brown, "The Rise and Function of the Holy Man in Late Antiquity," *Journal of Roman Studies* 61 (1971):80–101.

42. Tacitus *Germania* 3 ["They have the well-known kind of chant that they call *baritus* . . . . They hold their shields in front of their mouths, so that the sound is amplified into a deeper crescendo by the reverberation"]; Ammianus Marcellinus 16.12.43.

43. Meinardus, *Christian Egypt*, pp. 215–17, 279.

44. Bloch, "A New Document of the Last Pagan Revival in the West," pp. 235–39.

45. Otto Seeck and Georg Veith, "Die Schlacht am Frigidus," *Klio* 13 (1913):16.

46. Ronald Baker Smith, Geology and Geophysics Department, Yale University, personal communication.

47. Seeck, "Alaricus, 2," *RE*, vol. 1, col. 1286.

48. Palanque, *Saint Ambroise et l'Empire romain*, pp. 384–85 [In the funeral oration Ambrose spoke of the nail from the True Cross that Saint Helena had caused to be mounted in Emperor Constantine's diadem: "Blessed be this nail of the Roman Empire that directs the whole world and adorns the brow of princes"]; W. H. C. Frend, "Ambrose of Milan and Theodosius, 381–95," in his *The Early Church*, pp. 198–99 ["Not the Pope but he had overthrown Arianism and paganism in the West and had assured the superiority of Church over State throughout the European Middle Ages. . . . He was not a wholly attractive character, but given the need for a man who combined the qualities of bishop and statesman . . . no better could have been found"].

CHAPTER 4. CONSTANTINOPLE

1. László Várady, *Das letzte Jahrhundert Pannoniens*, 376–476, p. 526; Charles Norris Cochrane, *Christianity and Classical Culture*, pp. 318ff.

2. J. B. Bury, *History of the Later Roman Empire from the Death of Theodosius I. to the Death of Justianian*, 1:111.

3. Émilienne Demougeot, *De l'unité à la division de l'Empire romain*, 395–410 pp. 566–69.

4. Josephus 19.114–19.

5. Robert Grosse, *Römische Militärgeschichte von Gallienus bis zum Beginn der byzantinische Themenverlassung*, pp. 260–62.

6. Alan Cameron, *Claudian: Poetry and Propaganda at the Court of Honorius*.

7. J. Rosenstein, *Alarich und Stilicho: ein Beitrag zur Geschichte der germanischen Völkerwanderung*, p. 198 [Cites Reinold Pallman, *Die Völkerwanderung von der Gothenbekehrung bis zu Alarichs Tod* (Gotha, 1862)].

8. Ch. Lacombrade, "Synésios et l'énigme du loup," *Revue des études anciennes* 48 (1946): 260–66.

9. Jordanes 29.146–47; E. A. Thompson, "The Visigoths from Fritigern to Euric," *Historia* 12 (1963): 105–26.

10. Várady, *Das letzte Jahrhundert Pannoniens*, 376–476, p. 382.

11. Maenchen-Helfen, p. 51.

12. Arthur E. R. Boak, *The Master of Offices in the Later Roman and Byzantine Empire*, p. 189–223 [Boak's version of the Eutropius story appears on pp. 272–84].

13. Otto Seeck, "Arkadios. 2," *RE*, vol. 2, col. 1143 [Zosimus *Historia nova* 5.11.1 and Claudian *De consulatu Stilichonis* 1.297 are cited].

14. Rosenstein, *Alarich und Stilicho*, p. 181.

15. Ludwig Schmidt, *Geschichte der deutschen Stämme bis zum Ausgang der Völkerwanderung*, p. 199.

16. Bury, *History of the Later Roman Empire*, 1:118, citing *Codex Theodosianus* 9.14.3.

17. Albert Güldenpenning, *Geschichte des oströmischen Reiches unter den Kaisern Arcadius und Theodosius II*, p. 107.

18. Ibid., pp. 123–25.

19. Seeck, "Arkadios. 2," *RE*, vol. 2, col. 1149.

20. Güldenpenning, *Geschichte des oströmischen Reiches unter den Kaisern Arcadius und Theodosius II*, pp. 130–31.

CHAPTER 5. ROME AND RAVENNA

1. Émilienne Demougeot, *De l'unité à la division de l'Empire romain*, 395–410, pp. 130–31; Ch. Babut, "Recherches sur la garde impériale et sur le corps d'officiers de l'armée romaine aux IVᵉ et Vᵉ siècles," *Revue historique* 39 (1914):261; R. I. Frank, *Scholae Palatinae: The Palace Guards of the Later Roman Empire*, pp. 125–26; Wilhelm Ensslin, "The Court and Its Ceremonial: Dress and Insignia," *CAH*, 12:361–67; Otto Seeck, "Adoratio," *RE*, vol. 1, cols. 400–401; William T. Avery, "The *adoratio purpurae* and the Importance of the Imperial Purple in the Fourth Century of the Christian Era," *Memoirs of the American Academy in Rome* 17 (1940):66–80 [See especially p. 68, which refers to precedence: the *protectores* came last].

2. Gerda Bruns, *Der Obelisk und seine Basis auf dem Hippodrom zu Constantinopel*, p. 71; Werner Hartke, *Römische Kinderkaiser: eine Strukturanalyse römischen Denkens und Daseins*, pp. 238–40 [One figure is tentatively identified as Stilicho]; Alan Cameron, *Porphyrius the Charioteer*.

3. Grant Showerman, *The Great Mother of the Gods*; W. Warde Fowler, *The Religious Experience of the Roman People from the Earliest Times to the Age of Augustus*, p. 330; James George Frazer, *The Golden Bough: A Study in Magic and Religion*, vol. 5, *Adonis, Attis, Osiris: Studies in the History of Oriental Religion*, 1:298–301.

4. Zosimus 5.38.3; Otto Seeck, "Serena. 2," *RE*, 2d ser., vol. 2, cols. 1672–73.

5. Émilienne Demougeot, "Saint Jérôme, les oracles sibyllins et Stilicon," *Revue des études anciennes* 54 (1952):89–91.

6. E. D. Hunt, "From Dalmatia to the Holy Land: Jerome and the World of Late Antiquity" [Review of J. N. D. Kelly, *Jerome: His Life, Writings, and Controversies*], *Journal of Roman Studies* 67 (1977):168 [In discussing Jerome, one should not overlook "the *intersection* of his career with the 'magnetic fields' emanating from different cultural foci"]; Harald Fuchs, *Der geistige Widerstand gegen Rom in der antiken Welt*, p. 87.

7. Demougeot, "Saint Jérôme," pp. 88–89.

8. Thomas Hodgkin, *The Dynasty of Theodosius; or, Eighty Years' Struggle with the Barbarians*, p. 145.

9. J. Rosenstein, *Alarich und Stilicho: ein Beitrag zur Geschichte der germanischen Völkerwanderung*, pp. 189–90.

10. Maenchen-Helfen, p. 61 [Radagaisus's "army" was the armed portion of a people trekking to a new home].

11. Arthur E. R. Boak, *Manpower Shortage and the Fall of the Roman Empire*.

12. M. I. Finley, *The Ancient Economy*, pp. 36ff.; John H. D'Arms, *Romans on the Bay of Naples: A Social and Cultural Study of the Villas and Their Owners from 150 B.C. to A.D. 400*, pp. 226–28 [The references to Symmachus's holdings are particularly interesting. He had three houses in Rome, six villas on the Bay of Naples, a villa near Rome, and others at Ostia, Laurentum, Tibur, Praeneste, Cora and Formiae].

13. Tenney Frank, *Economic Survey of Ancient Rome* [The listings in the index under the heading "Slaves" are instructive]; Mima Maxey, *Occupations of the Lower Classes in Roman Society*.

14. James E. Packer, *The Insulae of Imperial Ostia*, pp. 74–79; G. Hermansen, "The Population of Imperial Rome: The Regionaries," *Historia* 27 (1978):129–68 [conflicting definitions of the term *insula*]; Thomas Ashby, *The Aqueducts of Ancient Rome*; Hans Peter Kohns, *Versorgungskrisen und Hungerrevolten im spätantiken Rom*, pp. 87–88 [reference to the urban homeless].

15. M. K. Hopkins, "Elite Mobility in the Roman Empire," *Past and Present* 32 (1965):25; F. A. Wright, "On Jerome's Correspondence with Roman Women," in *Select Letters of St. Jerome*, pp. 483–97; Peter R. L. Brown, "Aspects of the Christianization of the Roman Aristocracy," *Journal of Roman Studies* 51 (1961):7.

16. Denys Gorce, trans., *Vie de sainte Mélanie {Gerontius}: texte grec, introduction, traduction et notes*, p. 142 [A hair shirt (*cilicia*) was made of goat hair from Cilicia, in Asia Minor].

17. Alexander Demandt and Guntram Brummer, "Der Prozess gegen Serena im Jahre 408 n. Chr.," *Historia* 26 (1977):491.

18. This is the thesis of Alfons Dopsch (*The Economic and Social Foundations of European Civilization*).

19. Émilienne Demougeot, "Note sur la politique de Stilicon de 405 à 407," *Byzantion* 20 (1950):27–37.

20. W. H. C. Frend, *The Donatist Church: A Movement of Protest in Roman North Africa*, pp. 269–72; Émilienne Demougeot, "Sur les lois du 15 novembre 407," *Revue historique de droit français et étranger* 28 (1950):403–12.

21. J. C. Russell, *Late Ancient and Medieval Population*, esp. p. 33 [comments on the longevity of pillar saints in their isolation].

22. Demougeot, *De l'unité*, p. 415.

23. J. B. Bury, *History of the Later Roman Empire from the Death of Theodosius I. to the Death of Justinian*, 1:172–73; Demougeot, *De l'unité*, p. 142; Ernst Nischer-Falkenhof, *Stilicho*; John Matthews, "Olympiodorus of Thebes and the History of the West (A.D. 407–425)," *Journal of Roman Studies* 60 (1970):83–92 [comments on Olympiodorus's accuracy and on his understanding of the anti-Stilichonian climate that prevailed in the West]; John Matthews, *Western Aristocracies and Imperial Court*, A.D. 364–425, p. 282 [Stilicho's "personal tragedy was that he did not deserve to fail"].

24. Johannes Geffcken, *Der Ausgang der griechisch-römischen Heidentums*, p. 182; Stefan Weinstock, *Libri Fvlgvrales*, p. 143.

25. Zosimus 5.35; François Paschoud, *Cinq études sur Zosime*, pp. 139–47; Demandt and Brummer, "Der Prozess gegen Serena im Jahre 408 n. Chr.," pp. 496–502.

26. J. Innes Miller, *The Spice Trade of the Roman Empire*, 29 B.C.–A.D. 641, p. 25 [Pepper was stored in *horrea pipertaria* (pepper warehouses) in the Spice Quarter. Presumably 3,000 pounds of it would have been available].

27. László Várady, *Die letzte Jahrhundert Pannoniens*, 376–476, p. 394.

28. Geza Alföldy, *Noricum*, p. 214.

29. E. A. Thompson, "Olympiodorus of Thebes," *Classical Quarterly* 38 (1944):51; Frank M. Clover, "The Family and Early Career of Anicius Olybrius," *Historia* 27 (1978):169–96, esp. p. 173 [The Anicii were more enterprising than other senatorial families. Some of their

members were Christianized at an early date and were considered to be favorable to the barbarians. They forged ties outside senatorial circles, as in the marriage of Anicius Olybrius to Placidia, daughter of Valentinian III. This marriage brought the family into contact not only with a military dynasty but also with Vandal royalty. See also chap. 9, n. 31, below]; Demougeot, *De l'unité*, p. 451.

30. Hanno Helbling, *Goten und Wandalen*, pp. 9–22; Manfred Fuhrmann, "Die Romidee der Spätantike," *Historische Zeitschrift* 207 (1968): 529–61; Fuchs, *Der geistige Widerstand gegen Rom in der antiken Welt*, pp. 87–90 [Rome as the Eternal City].

31. Ludwig Schmidt, *Geschichte der deutschen Stämme bis zum Ausgang der Völkerwanderung*, p. 219 [Visigoths and Vandals did not make Rome a city of ruins; the Roman magnates and churchmen robbed the ancient structures]; Angelo Penna, "La sibilla tiburtina e le nove età del mondo," *Atti e memorie della Società tiburtina di storia e d'arte* 45 (1972):49, 69 [Translation from the Greek: "Under Arcadius and Honorius, Rome will become a single street, and a city of one street." The same expression, alluding to Alaric's sack of the city, is found in *Oracula sibyllina* 3.364, 8.165].

32. Melania the Younger and her husband, Pinianus, for instance, took refuge at her large estate at Tagaste, the birthplace of Augustine.

Chapter 6. Narbonne, Barcelona, and Arles

1. Karl Friedrich Stroheker, *Der senatorische Adel im spätrömischen Gallien*, p. 45; Bernard S. Bachrach, *A History of the Alans in the West from Their First Appearance in the Sources of Classical Antiquity Through the Early Middle Ages*, p. 60; Otto Seeck, *Geschichte des Untergangs der antiken Welt*, 7:48–50; Otto Seeck, "Iovinus. 5," *RE*, vol. 9, cols. 2012–13.

2. J. B. Bury, *History of the Later Roman Empire from the Death of Theodosius I to the Death of Justinian*, 1:194.

3. Edward Gibbon, *The Decline and Fall of the Roman Empire*, 2:182; Ammianus Marcellinus 31.2.9.

4. Stewart Irvin Oost, *Galla Placidia Augusta: A Biographical Essay*, p. 114.

5. Philostorgius compared this marriage to the union of clay and iron, drawing the analogy from the popular Book of Daniel.

6. Orosius 7.43.

7. Bachrach, *A History of the Alans*, p. 31.

8. Oost, *Galla Placidia Augusta*, pp. 290–91 [Placidia never forgot her firstborn; just before her death in 450, she appears to have had the infant's body reinterred in Rome, near her own intended resting place].

9. A. H. M. Jones, *The Later Roman Empire, 284–602: A Social, Economic, and Administrative Survey*, 2:1109.

10. Ibid., app. 2, *Notitia dignitatum*, p. 1425; Otto Seeck, *Regesten der Kaiser und Päpste für die Jahre 311 bis 476 n. Chr.*, p. 332 (*Codex Theodosianus* 14.10.4, Ravenna, December 12, 416).

11. W. H. C. Frend, *The Donatist Church: A Movement of Protest in Roman North Africa*, p. 274, citing *Codex Theodosianus* 17.2.3.

12. Otto Wermelinger, *Rom und Pelagius*, p. 202 [Most of the antiheresy laws in *Codex Theodosianus* concerned Manichaeism or the practice of magic]; Sulpicius Severus *Life of Martin* 7 [Martin's performance of a magical rite of resuscitation, in which he prostrated himself on the corpse, is described.].

13. Sulpicius Severus *Dialogues* 26 (Postumianus).

14. Oost, *Galla Placidia Augusta*, p. 148 [on secret police].

15. W. Böhne, "Brictius," *Lexikon für Theologie und Kirche*, vol. 2, col. 685.

16. Ch. Babut, *Le concile de Turin*, esp. pp. 38–42; Henry Chadwick, *Priscillian of Avila: The Occult and the Charismatic in the Early Church*, pp. 157–65.

17. Oost, *Galla Placidia Augusta*, p. 149.

18. Jager, abbé [Jean Nicolas], *Histoire de l'Église catholique en France d'après les documents les plus authentiques depuis son origine jusqu'au concordat de Pie VII*, 1:353.

19. E. A. Thompson, "Zosimus on the End of Roman Britain," *Antiquity* 30 (1956): 164–65.

20. John Morris, "Dark Ages Dates," in Michael E. Jarrett and Brian Dobson, eds., *Britain and Rome: Essays Presented to Eric Birley on His Sixtieth Birthday*, pp. 147–48.

21. E. A. Thompson, "Peasant Revolts in Late Roman Gaul and Spain," *Past and Present* 2 (1952): 11–23; Thompson, "Zosimus on the End of Roman Britain," pp. 163–67; J. M. Wallace-Hadrill, "Gothia and Romania," *Bulletin of the John Rylands Library* 44 (1961):213–37; B. Czúth, "Die Quellen der Geschichte der Bagauden (Anfänge des V. Jahrhunderts)," *Acta antiqua et archaeologica* 9 (1965):31–43; Erika Engelmann, "Zur Bewegung der Bagauden im römischen Gallien," in Helmut Kretzchmer, ed., *Von Mittelalter zur Neuzeit, zum 65. Geburtstag von Heinrich Sproemberg*, p. 384 [The sharp conflict within the church stemming from the ascetic movement provided a "good culture medium" for a coalition of Christians and Bacaudae]; J. N. L. Myres, "Pelagius and the End of Roman Rule in Britain," *Journal of Roman Studies* 50 (1960):34 ["It might be thought that a doctrine that laid stress on the universal exercise of *liberum arbitrium* . . . would have strengthened the forces of proletarian unrest and provided the Bagaudae with revolutionary slogans. . . . Yet there is little evidence that at this period Pelagian ideology had penetrated far below the upper crust of Romanized society"]; Frank M. Clover, *Flavius Merobaudes: A Translation and Historical Commentary*, pp. 47–50.

22. Georges de Plinval, *Pélage: ses écrits, sa vie, et sa réforme*, p. 351, n. [The Eastern emperors do not appear to have taken special legal measures against the Pelagians]; ibid., p. 346 [Whereas the Pelagians suffered hard times in 418 and 421, they became audacious again in 423, after Galla Placidia had fled from Ravenna. Plinval neglects to mention that by that time Emperor Constantius III had died]; Wermelinger, *Rom und Pelagius*, pp. 208–209 [Constantius never regarded the Pelagians as social agitators]; G. I. Bonner, "How Pelagian Was Pelagius? An Examination of the Contentions of Torgny Bohlin," *Studia Patristica*, vol. 9, pt. 3, pp. 350–58.

23. John Morris, "Pelagian Literature," *Journal of Theological Studies*, n.s. 16 (1965): 43–49.

24. Myres, "Pelagius and the End of Roman Rule in Britain," pp. 21–36 [The abandoned British *civitates* were congenial ground for a revitalized Christianity]; Nora K. Chadwick, "Intellectual Contacts Between Britain and Gaul in the Fifth Century," in Hector Munro Chadwick et al., *Studies in Early British History*, p. 209.

25. Jacques Fontaine, trans., *Vie de saint Martin {par} Sulpice Sévère*, 1:704–707 [comments by Fontaine].

26. Peter R. L. Brown, "Pelagius and His Supporters: Aims and Environment," *Journal of Theological Studies*, n.s. 19 (1968):98.

27. Fernand Benoit, "L'Hilarianum d'Arles et les missions en Bretagne (V^e–VIe siècles)," in *Saint Germain d'Auxerre et son temps*, p. 181.

28. Bury, *History of the Later Roman Empire*, 1:206–207 [Germanus's command extended over five provinces: "His authority ran in Sens and Auxerre"].

29. Donald A. White, *Litus Saxonicum: The British Saxon Shore in Scholarship and History*, pp. 56–105 [Fig. 2 shows locations of fortifications on the Gallic Shore]; Wallace-Hadrill, "Gothia and Romania," pp. 216–17; Stephen Johnson, *The Roman Forts of the Saxon Shore*, p. 89; Paul Grosjean, "La seconde visite de s. Germain d'Auxerre en Grande-Bretagne,"

Analecta Bollandiana 75 (1957):175 [reference to semaphore signals]; Nora K. Chadwick, *Poetry and Letters in Early Christian Gaul*, p. 263; Nora K. Chadwick, *Early Brittany*, pp. 136–42, 148–49.

30. Benoit, "L'Hilarianum d'Arles," pp. 181–83; Gabriel Le Bras, "Introduction," *Saint Germain d'Auxerre et son temps*, p. xix; Élie Griffe, *La Gaule chrétienne à l'époque romaine*, 2:298.

31. R. G. Collingwood and J. N. L. Myres, *Roman Britain and the English Settlements*, pp. 295–301.

32. Salvian 7.2.

33. E. A. Thompson, "The Settlement of the Barbarians in Southern Gaul," *Journal of Roman Studies* 46 (1956):65–75.

34. Stroheker, *Der senatorische Adel im spätrömischen Gallien*, p. 47; Jérôme Carcopino, "À propos du poème de Rutilius Namatianus," *Revue des études latines* 6 (1928):183 [Rutilius departed from Rome in 415]; Alan Cameron, "Rutilius Namatianus, St. Augustine, and the Date of *De reditu*," *Journal of Roman Studies* 57 (1967):31–39 [The poet left Rome on or about October 13, 417].

35. Joseph Zeller, "Das Concilium der septem provinciae in Arelate," *Westdeutsche Zeitschrift für Geschichte und Kunst* 24 (1905):18–19.

36. Felix Burckhardt, "Galla Placidia: eine römische Kaiserin des 5. Jahrhunderts," *Schweizerische Rundschau* 25 (1925):413.

37. Bury, *History of the Later Roman Empire*, 1:210, 222; Ernest Barker, "Italy and the West, 410–476," *CMH*, 1:406.

38. Sidonius Apollinaris *Carm.* 2.138–40.

CHAPTER 7. CARTHAGE AND THE HIGH PLAINS OF AFRICA

1. Paul Monceaux, *Histoire littéraire de l'Afrique chrétienne depuis les origines jusqu'à l'invasion arabe*, 4:390–91. [Includes an inventory of the documents of the *Gesta collationis Carthaginensis*].

2. Adolf Harnack, *The Mission and Expansion of Christianity in the First Three Centuries*, pp. 470–71.

3. Robert F. Evans, *Pelagius: Inquiries and Reappraisals*, p. 29.

4. B. H. Warmington, *The North African Provinces from Diocletian to the Vandal Conquest*, p. 92.

5. Henry Melvill Gwatkin, *Early Church History to A.D. 313*, 2:238.

6. G. L. Prestige, "Tradition: or, the Scriptural Basis of Theology," in his *Fathers and Heretics: Six Studies in Dogmatic Faith*, pp. 1–22; Hans von Campenhausen, *Tradition and Life in the Church*, pp. 7–18.

7. Edward White Benson, *Cyprian: His Life, His Times, His Work*, p. 27; Arnold A. Ehrhardt, "Cyprian, the Father of Western Christianity," *Church Quarterly Review* 113 (1943): 178–96; Arnold A. Ehrhardt, *The Apostolic Succession in the First Two Centuries of the Church*, p. 129; Hans von Campenhausen, *Ecclesiastical Authority and Spiritual Power in the Church in the First Three Centuries*, pp. 265–92; Martin Hengel, *Property and Riches in the Early Church: Aspects of a Social History of Early Christianity*, p. 79 [At times Cyprian was forced pragmatically to go against tradition: he made over his property to the church but took back his estates when their requisition was threatened].

8. John R. Knipfing, "The *libelli* of the Decian Persecution," *Harvard Theological Review* 16 (1923):352.

9. Ehrhardt, *Apostolic Succession*, pp. 98–99.

10. Gwatkin, *Early Church History*, 2:287.

11. G. Hartel, ed., *Acta Proconsularis Cypriani. Opera, cx sqq.*, pp. 23–26.

12. W. H. C. Frend, *The Donatist Church: A Movement of Protest in Roman North Africa*, p. 79 ["Such names as Donatus . . . which occur over and over again in Africa, are direct translations of Punic theophonic names. So Donatus or Adeodatus=Given of Baal or Iatanbaal. . . . They suggest a certain fatalism in outlook, and an absolute subjection of the individual to the inscrutable decrees of the god"].

13. Ibid., p. 177.

14. F. Martroye, "Une tentative de révolution sociale en Afrique," *Revue des questions historiques* 76 (1904):353–416; 77 (1905):1–53; Ernest Llewellyn Woodward, *Christianity and Nationalism in the Later Roman Empire*, pp. 41–49; Ernst Stein, *Geschichte des spätrömischen Reiches*, p. 402 [Heraclian was able to turn Donatist bitterness to account in his revolt]; Glanville Downey, "Coptic Culture in the Byzantine World: Nationalism and Religious Independence," *Greek and Byzantine Studies* 1 (1958):134–35 ["Nationalism embraces the ethnic and linguistic factors which make for divisiveness. But illiteracy represents the factors which keep nationalism alive"]; Erwan Marec, "Les ruines d'Hippone et la Numidie de saint Augustin," *Algeria* 29, n.s. 61 (1961): 10 [The Donatist schism provided means for expression of ancient Berber instincts of rebellion against all hierarchy. Ultimately it opened the way for the Vandals]; Hans-Joachim Diesner, "Die Lage der nordafrikanische Bevölkerung im Zeitpunkt der Vandaleninvasion," *Historia* 11 (1962): 110 [The major part of the population must have drawn its own conclusions from the egotistical behavior of the magnates, and therefore it no longer had any "Roman" interests]; A. H. M. Jones, "Were Ancient Heresies National or Social Movements in Disguise?" *Journal of Theological Studies*, n.s. 10 (1959):280–97; Frend, *The Donatist Church*, pp. 172–73.

15. Sister Wilfrid Parsons, trans., *Saint Augustine: Letters*, vol. 1, letter 66.2. [Parsons describes this letter as "Book Against the Schismatic Crispinus ca. 402: no salutation."]; Scholars are in disagreement about the term "Punic." The language may have been Libyan or neo-Punic. The following citations indicate the general direction of the arguments: Marec, "Les ruines," p. 10 [Most of Augustine's fellow citizens at Hippo were Berbers of pure stock with little or no intermixture of foreign blood: the language was that of the pre-Punic cave artists and dolmen builders]; T. D. Barnes, "The Family and Career of Septimius Severus," *Historia* 16 (1967):96 [It must have been customary to mock African orators for their supposed lack of familiarity with Latin. "It may attest the survival of the Punic language among the lower orders of society"]; Peter R. L. Brown, "Christianity and Local Culture in Late Roman Africa," *Journal of Roman Studies* 58 (1968):85–95 [Latin spread to the countryside, its propagation fostered by ecclesiastical controversy that was conducted exclusively in that language]; Homer F. Pfeiffer, "The Roman Library at Timgad," *Memoirs of the American Academy in Rome* 9 (1931):157–65 [The very presence of such a structure suggests that the hinterland population may not have been illiterate and that Latin culture may have penetrated to Timgad, a Donatist center]; Claude Lepelley and Brigitte Beaujard, "Du nouveau sur les villes de l'Afrique romaine au temps de saint Augustin" [Resumé of Lepelley's doctoral dissertation and a stenographic report of his defense of it at the Sorbonne], *Revue des études augustiniennes* 23 (1977):422–31 [The cities of the Eastern provinces, including Numidia, knew no external menace until the coming of the Vandals and had an active, structured urban life based on economic prosperity. The situation that Courtois described as general actually obtained only in Mauretania].

16. Adolf Harnack, *History of Dogma*, 3:334–35.

17. Augustine *City of God* 15.9 [In another age Augustine might have been a scientist].

18. William Seston, *Dioclétien et la tétrarchie*, 1:123–24, citing Lactantius *Divinarum institutionum libri septem* 7.15.19.

19. Henri Basset, "Les influences puniques chez les berbères," *Revue africaine* 62 (1921): 348–49.

20. Benson, *Cyprian*, p. xxxi.

21. M. Caudel, *Les premières invasions arabes dans l'Afrique du Nord*, p. 65.

22. Michael Grant, *The Climax of Rome*, p. 242.

23. Frend, *The Donatist Church*, p. 101.

24. Ammianus Marcellinus 28.6.1.

25. Frend, *The Donatist Church*, p. 73.

26. Ammianus Marcellinus 29.5.48.

27. Procopius 3.25.6–8.

28. Ammianus Marcellinus 29.5.54–55; Stéphane Gsell, *Histoire ancienne de l'Afrique du Nord*, 1:257–59 [Rock drawings of dromedaries are mentioned: they may or may not be prehistoric]; Franz Altheim, *Die Soldatenkaiser*, pp. 127–32 [military use of camels]; G. G. Lapèyre and A. Pellegrin, *Carthage latine et chrétienne*, p. 134 [Camels were introduced in the third century by Syrian cohorts]; Christian Courtois, *Les Vandales et l'Afrique*, pp. 98–99 [There is no Berber word for *camel*, but there is no reason to think that the camel has not been in African from earliest historic times]; E. Daumas, "The Camel," in his *The Ways of the Desert*, pp. 98–109.

29. A. Hoepffner, "La mort du 'magister militvm' Théodose," *Revue des études latines*, 14 (1936): 128; Andreas Alföldi, *A Conflict of Ideas in the Late Roman Empire: The Clash Between the Senate and Valentinian I*, pp. 91–92; André Chastagnol, *La préfecture urbaine à Rome sous le Bas-Empire*, p. 431 [A conspiracy against Valentinian I had ramifications in Africa as early as 366. The accused conspirators may have managed to drag in Theodosius, who was probably executed about 375, before the death of Valentinian]; Alexander Demandt, "Der Tod des älteren Theodosius," *Historia* 18 (1969): 598–626 [thorough investigation and comprehensive bibliography]; Frend, *The Donatist Church*, p. 199, citing Orosius *Historiarum libri adversus paganos* 7.33.

30. Courtois, *Les Vandales et l'Afrique*, p. 146; Monceaux, *Histoire littéraire de l'Afrique chrétienne*, 4:65.

31. Warmington, *The North African Provinces*, p. 87; Ch. Saumagne, "Ouvriers agricoles ou rôdeurs de celliers? Les circoncellions d'Afrique," *Annales d'histoire économique et sociale* 6 (1934): 351–64; Emil Tengström, *Donatisten und Katholiken: soziale, wirtschaftliche und politische Aspekte einer nordafrikanischen Kirchenspaltung*, pp. 168–92; Diesner, *Kirche und Staat im spätrömischen Reich*, pp. 53–77.

32. Frend, *The Donatist Church*, p. 64 [Donatists and Catholics alike tried to have their opponents appointed to the city councils, because their duties as tax collectors would spell financial ruin for them].

33. John M. Rist, "Augustine on Free Will and Predestination," in R. A. Marcus, ed., *Augustine: A Collection of Critical Essays*, pp. 244–45.

34. Monceaux, *Histoire littéraire de l'Afrique chrétienne*, 4:392.

35. Frend, *The Donatist Church*, pp. 184–85.

36. Ibid., pp. 293–94; Madeleine Moreau, *Le dossier Marcellinus dans la correspondance de saint Augustin*.

37. Frend, *The Donatist Church*, p. 297.

38. Diesner, *Kirche und Staat*, pp. 102–106.

39. René Cagnat, *L'armée romaine d'Afrique et l'occupation militaire de l'Afrique sous les empereurs*, p. 743; Warmington, *The North African Provinces*, p. 25.

40. Diesner, *Kirche und Staat*, p. 108.

41. Tacitus *Germania* 13, 14.

42. Robert Grosse, *Römische Militärgeschichte von Gallienus bis zum Beginn der byzantinischen Themenverlassung*, p. 285; Otto Seeck, "Bucellarii," *RE*, vol. 3, cols. 934–39; Theodor Mommsen, *Gesammelte Schriften*, 6:241ff.; Ernst Stein, *Geschichte des spätrömischen Reiches*, 1:364–65; P. Guilhiermoz, *Essai sur l'origine de la noblesse en France au Moyen Âge*, pp. 5–22;

E. A. Thompson, "Olympiodorus of Thebes," *Classical Quarterly* 38 (1944): 47 [Olympiodorus's *Fragment* 9 indicates that the term *bucellarii* came into being under Honorius].

43. Justinian's chief armed attendant in the San Vitale mosaic at Ravenna wears a bulla with the emperor's portrait and carries a shield adorned with the *labarum*. Four *bucellarii* are shown in attendance on Theodosius I and his family on the frequently reproduced silver *missorium* (platter or charger) in the Real Academia de la Historia, Madrid.

44. Lynn White, Jr., "The Temple of Jupiter Revisited," in his *The Transformation of the Roman World*, pp. 302–304.

45. Vito Antonio Sirago, *Galla Placidia e la trasformazione politica dell' Occidente*, pp. 271–73.

46. Augustine *Ep.* 220.7; E. A. Freeman, *Western Europe in the Fifth Century*, pp. 310–11 [The relations of Boniface and Augustine "set before us the nature of the ecclesiastical influences under which a layman of the highest rank and character and personal importance could be brought in days when Arles and Carthage were decidedly more Christian than Rome"].

47. Courtois, *Les Vandales et l'Afrique*, p. 338.

48. Ludwig Schmidt, "Bonifatius und der Uebergang der Wandalen nach Afrika," *Historische Vierteljahrsschrift* 2 (1889): 451–55; Diesner, *Kirche und Staat*, p. 112; Sirago, *Galla Placidia*, p. 269; Stewart Irvin Oost, *Galla Placidia Augusta*, p. 221.

49. Schmidt, "Bonifatius," pp. 449–62; Oost, *Galla Placidia Augusta*, pp. 224–25; Stein, *Geschichte des spätrömischen Reiches*, p. 475; Ernest Barker, "Italy and the West, 410–476," *CMH*, 1–409; Otto Seeck, *Geschichte des Untergangs der antiken Welt*, 7: 108; Diesner, *Kirche und Staat* p. 114.

50. Courtois, *Les Vandales et l'Afrique*, p. 59.

51. Lapèyre and Pellegrin, *Carthage*, p. 112.

52. Courtois, *Les Vandales et l'Afrique*, p. 161.

53. Possidius 28.

54. Frend, *The Donatist Church*, p. 305, citing Leo *Ep.* 168.18.

55. André Morazzani, "Essai sur la puissance maritime des Vandales," *Bulletin de l'Association Guillaume Budé*, 4th ser., 25 (1966): 543.

56. Ibid., p. 547.

57. Mommsen, "Aëtius," *Gesammelte Schriften* 4: 536.

58. Frank M. Clover, *Flavius Merobaudes: A Translation and Historical Commentary*, pp. 30–32 [Aëtius's second wife presumably was Pelagia, a Gothic princess, the mother of Gaudentius].

59. Isidore of Seville *Historia Gothorvm Wandalorvm Sveborvm ad a. DCXXIV* 74. [There is little agreement among historians about the extent of the territories ceded to the Vandals. Perhaps Isidore's realistic description is to be preferred: he said that they received the "partem Africae quam Wandeli possederant"].

60. Schmidt, "The Sueves, Alans and Vandals in Spain, 409–429: The Vandal Dominion in Africa, 429–533," *CMH*, 1: 307 [The independent dating of regnal years by the Vandals was unique among the barbarians. The Burgundians, for example, reckoned their reigns by Roman consular years and indictions].

Chapter 8. Vandal Africa

1. Procopius 3.3.23–25, 4.6 "He was an exceedingly discerning person"]; 4.13–14 [". . . displayed a foresight worth recounting"].

2. Jordanes 168–69.

3. Christian Courtois et al., *Tablettes Albertini: actes privées de l'époque Vandale (fin du Ve siècle)*, pp. 189–211.

4. Paulinus 30 [The Frankish princes who had questioned Arbogast understood the power of Bishop Ambrose. They exclaimed, "So you conquer because you are beloved by that man who says to the sun 'stand' and it stands!"].

5. Christian Courtois, *Victor de Vita et son œuvre*, p. 83.

6. Hans-Joachim Diesner, *Fulgentius von Ruspe als Theologe und Kirchenpolitiker*, pp. 9–29.

7. Adolf Harnack, *History of Dogma*, 5:257.

8. Merobaudes *Panegyric* 2.25–27, in Frank M. Clover, *Flavius Merobaudes: A Translation and Historical Commentary*, p. 13.

9. J. B. Bury, *History of the Later Roman Empire from the Death of Theodosius I. to the Death of Justinian*, 1:256; J. R. Moss, "The Effects of the Policies of Aëtius on the History of Western Europe," *Historia* 22 (1973):731 [With his background as a cavalryman, his friendship with the Huns, and his political links to the Gallic landowners, Aëtius may have failed to perceive the importance of the sea lanes; hence his apparent indifference to the fate of Africa].

10. Clover, *Flavius Merobaudes*, p. 54.

11. Wilhelm Ensslin, "Valentinianus. 4," *RE*, vol. 14, cols. 2239, 2244; Ernst Stein, *Geschichte des spätrömischen Reiches*, p. 502.

12. Louis Hamblen, *Attila et les Huns*, p. 77; Helene Homeyer, *Attila der Hunnenkönig von seinen Zeitgenossen dargestellt*, p. 136.

13. Franz Altheim, *Attila und die Hunnen*, pp. 132–43 [reference to Priscus *Fragment* 16].

14. Maenchen-Helfen, p. 130.

15. J. B. Bury, "Justa Grata Honoria," *Journal of Roman Studies* 9 (1919):12–13.

16. Felix Burckhardt, "Galla Placidia: eine römische Kaiserin des 5. Jahrhunderts," *Schweizerische Rundschau* 25 (1925):419.

17. Altheim, *Attila und die Hunnen*, p. 135; Maenchen-Helfen, pp. 269–70.

18. Salvian 7.9.

19. Élie Griffe, *La Gaule chrétienne à l'époque romaine*, 2:62.

20. Abbé Gand, "Deux hommes face à face: Aëtius et Attila," *Bulletin trimestriel de la Société archéologique et historique de l'Orléanais*, n.s. 3 (1963):39.

21. Thomas Hodgkin, *The Dynasty of Theodosius*, p. 201.

22. Jordanes 36.186.

23. Maenchen-Helfen, p. 141.

24. Altheim, *Attila und die Hunnen*, p. 148; Wolfram Eberhard, *Kultur und Siedlung der Randvölker Chinas*, p. 47; R. Leicher, *Die Totenklage in der deutschen Epik von der ältesten Zeit bis zur Nibelungenklage*, pp. 14–18 [A review of scholars' definitions of the term *strava*].

25. Herodotus *Persian Wars* 4.7, in A. D. Godley, trans., *Herodotus*, vol. 2.

26. Procopius 3.5.5–6.

27. Henri Leclercq, "Léon Ier," *DA*, vol. 8, pt. 2, col. 2533.

28. Christian Courtois, *Les Vandales et l'Afrique*, pp. 4–5; Enrico Besta, *La Sardegna medioevale*, pp. 4–5; Maurice Le Lannou, *Pâtres et paysans de la Sardaigne*, pp. 125–26; Raimondo Carta Raspi, *Storia della Sardegna*, pp. 259–62 [The idea of a Moorish colony is absurd; it was a deportation of troublemakers].

29. Diesner, *Der Traum des Godas: Geschichtliches Bild aus der Vandalenzeit* [a curious attempt to reconstruct the story of events in Sardinia].

30. Procopius 3.8.12–13.

31. Courtois, *Les Vandales et l'Afrique*, p. 239.

32. Ibid., p. 288.

33. Procopius 3.15.20.

34. Ibid., 4.1.9–11.

35. Ibid., 3.20.22–23.
36. Leicher, *Totenklage*, p. 21. [It was characteristic of the Vandals to become so distraught over the death of a hero, as over that of Gelimer's brother Ammatas, that the demands of the moment were forgotten]; Ari Kiev, "Psychiatric Disorders in Minority Groups," in Peter Watson, ed., *Psychology and Race*, pp. 416–31.
37. Procopius 3.25.11–18.
38. Ibid., 3.25.23–26.
39. Ibid., 4.4.1–8.
40. Ibid., 4.14.19–20.
41. W. Kaegi, "Arianism and the Byzantine Army in Africa, 533–546," *Traditio* 21 (1965):23–53.
42. Franz Görres, "Die vermeintliche germanische (vandalische) Abstammung einer überaus zahlreichen nordafrikanischer Vervölkerung," *Historisches Jahrbuch* 32 (1911):323–32 [Such people might just as well be descendants of Visigoths from Spain].
43. B. H. Warmington, *The North African Provinces from Diocletian to the Vandal Conquest*, pp. 20–26; Charles Diehl, *L'Afrique byzantine: histoire de la domination byzantine en Afrique, 533–709* [plans and drawings of fortifications].

CHAPTER 9. OSTROGOTHIC ITALY

1. John H. Ward, "The Notitia dignitatum," *Latomus* 33 (1974):431–32 [Aëtius was also wary. In 429, when Placidia's minister Felix was advanced in rank, Aëtius appears to have forced through a promotion for himself].
2. Bernard S. Bachrach, *A History of the Alans in the West from Their First Appearance in the Sources of Classical Antiquity Through the Early Middle Ages*, pp. 62–64.
3. Karl Friedrich Stroheker, *Germanentum und Spätantike*, p. 255.
4. Odet Perrin, *Les Burgondes, leur histoire des origines à la fin du 1ᵉʳ royaume (534)*, pp. 303–304.
5. Otto Seeck, *Geschichte des Untergangs der antiken Welt*, 6:48, 392; André Loyen, *Sidoine Apollinaire et l'esprit précieux en Gaule aux derniers jours de l'Empire*, pp. 78–79.
6. Otto Seeck, "Iovinus. 5," *RE*, vol. 9, 2012–13; Stroheker, *Der senatorische Adel im spätantiken Gallien*, p. 47.
7. Sidonius Apollinaris *Ep*. 5.9.1.
8. Stroheker, *Germanentum*, p. 253; Eugen Ewig, "Dans le brouillard burgonde et franc," *Annales de Bourgogne* 43 (1971):104.
9. Ernst Stein, *Geschichte des spätrömischen Reiches*, p. 505.
10. Sidonius Apollinaris *Carm*. 2.452–55.
11. Ibid., lines 557–59; Stroheker, *Der senatorische Adel*, p. 53 [It is not correct, as Camille Jullian contended, that Avitus headed a separatist movement: "The concept of the Roman Empire still lived strongly in the Gallic senators"].
12. Stroheker, *Der senatorische Adel*, pp. 48–49.
13. Sidonius Apollinaris *Carm*. 8, *Ep*. 9.16.16–24; Paul Allard, "Sidoine Apollinaire sous les règnes d'Avitus et de Majorien," *Revue des questions historiques* 42, n.s. 29 (1908):434 [Such homage occurred infrequently in Rome, where the emperor conferred it upon the request of the Senate]; Samuel Dill, *Roman Society in the Last Century of the Western Empire*, p. 39 [Not all statuary disappeared in subsequent disorders. In the time of Emperor Justinian, 3,785 statues remained in the city].
14. Loyen, *Sidoine Apollinaire*, pp. 50–51.
15. Assunta Nagl, "Odoacer," *RE*, vol. 17, cols. 1888–89 [The name is Teutonic]; Rob-

ert I. Reynolds and Robert Sabatino Lopez, "Odoacer: German or Hun?" *American Historical Review* 52 (1946–47):36–53 [He was a Hun]; J. M. Wallace-Hadrill, *The Barbarian West, A.D. 400–1000: The Early Middle Ages*, p. 33 [". . . a Hun named Odoacer; and we must assume that a part of his following was also Hun"]; Maenchen-Helfen, p. 388 [Edecon, Odovacar's father, was a Hun]; Sune Lindqvist, "Heruler och Daner," *Tor: Meddelanden från Uppsala universitets museum för nordiske fornsaker* 9 (1963):127, 130 [The runic word *erilaR* was the equivalent of the term *eorl* or *iarl*, signifying a leader. The Heruli were warriors who returned to Denmark after having seen military service as elites among the Roman mercenaries. The tribal connotation was the result of misunderstanding. If Lindqvist's theory is correct, Odovacar's title rex Herulorum would not have indicated tribal origin].

16. Ottorino Bertolini, "L'aristocrazia senatoria e il senato di Roma come forza politica sotto i regni di Odoacre e di Teodorico," in *Atti del I. Congresso nazionale di studi romani*, 1:462–75; G. B. Picotti, "Sulle relazioni fra re Odoacre e il senato e la chiesa di Roma," *Rivista storica italiana*, 5th ser., 4 (1939):363–86 [Odovacar bowed to the major forces that represented *romanitas*]; André Chastagnol, *Le sénat romain sous le règne d'Odoacre: recherches sur l'épigraphie du colisée au Ve siècle*; Wilhelm Barth, *Kaiser Zeno*, p. 52; A. H. M. Jones, "The Constitutional Position of Odoacer and Theoderic," *Journal of Roman Studies* 52 (1962):130; Johannes Sundwall, *Abhandlungen zur Geschichte des ausgehenden Römertums*, pp. 180, 195; M. A. Wes, *Das Ende des Kaisertums im Westen des römischen Reichs*, p. 156.

17. Wallace-Hadrill, *The Barbarian West*, p. 33: Barth, *Kaiser Zeno*, p. 50 ["the most attractive ruling figure of his day"]; J. B. Bury, *History of the Later Roman Empire from the Death of Theodosius I. to the Death of Justinian*, 1:409–11.

18. Wilhelm Ensslin, "Rex Theodericus inlitteratus?" *Historisches Jahrbuch* 60 (1940): 391–96 [It is not true that Theodoric had to use a stencil to initial state papers. The passage properly referred to Emperor Justin, and there was an error in transcription].

19. Heinrich Laufenberg, *Der historische Wert des Panegyricus des Bischofs Ennodius*; Maurice Dumoulin, "Le gouvernement de Théodoric et la domination des Ostrogoths en Italie d'après les oeuvres d'Ennodius," *Revue historique* 78 (January–February, 1902):1–7; (March–April, 1902):241–65; 79 (1902):1–22 [Includes a translation of Ennodius's panegyric (78:243). From the day on which an army commander was dispatched to combat the regent of Italy, Odovacar was regarded as a usurper]; Ensslin, *Theoderich der Grosse*, p. 77.

20. Thomas Hodgkin, *Theodoric the Goth: The Barbarian Champion of Civilisation*, p. 140; Wes, *Das Ende des Kaisertumas*, p. 163 [From his sojourn in the Eastern court in his youth, Theodoric knew what was expected of a ruler of the Romans].

21. Wes, *Das Ende des Kaisertums*, p. 143 [Cassiodorus *Variae* 2.35 is cited]; D. A. Bullough, "Urban Change in Early Medieval Italy: The Example of Pavia," *Papers of the British School of Rome* 34, n.s. 21 (1966):92 [Theodoric constructed a palace at Pavia].

22. Procopius 5.2.14–15.

23. Sundwall, *Abhandlungen zur Geschichte des ausgenhenden Römertums*, p. 195; Wes, *Das Ende des Kaisertums*, p. 156 [Cautions against the drawing of a sharp line between antibarbarians and pro-Byzantines. Both groups wanted to save Rome and her culture].

24. Procopius 5.3.6–7.

25. Adolf Harnack, *History of Dogma*, 4:198.

26. Walter Ullmann, "Leo I and the Theme of Papal Primacy," *Journal of Theological Studies*, n.s. 11 (1960): 25–51.

27. B. T. A. Evetts, *The Churches and Monasteries of Egypt and Some Neighboring Countries*, pp. 239–40.

28. Harnack, *History of Dogma*, 4:206.

29. Ibid., p. 210.

30. Ibid., p. 222; Gerhart B. Ladner, "The Impact of Christianity," in Lynn White, Jr., ed., *The Transformation of the Roman World*, p. 73 ["It was Cyril and not Nestorius who asserted

and saved the core of Christian religiousness"]; Patrick T. R. Gray, *The Defense of Chalcedon in the East (451–553)*.

31. Wes, *Das Ende des Kaisertums*, pp. 158–59 [Pope Felix III was elected in 483, under Odovacar. He was a member of the family of the Anicii, and his election took place in the mausoleum that was the resting place of another member of that family, Emperor Olybrius. The author says that it was not "pure irony" that the first pope from the Roman aristocracy should have been chosen there. Rather, it was an indication of a conscious readiness to exchange old political claims for the ideal of spiritual primacy]. See also chap. 5, n. 29, above.

32. Friedrich Loofs, *Das Leben und die polemischen Werke des Leontius von Byzanz*, pp. 244–61.

33. H. St. L. B. Moss, *The Birth of the Middle Ages, 395–814*, p. 71 ["He was regarded as a martyr by the Catholics, though it is truer to call him a martyr for the senatorial cause"]; William Bark, "Theodoric vs. Boethius: Vindication and Apology," *American Historical Review* 49 (1944): 410–26; Charles Henry Coster, "The Fall of Boethius: His Character," in his *Late Roman Studies*, pp. 54–103 ["It seems very difficult to consider him technically a martyr. The fate of Boethius was inextricably entwined with the conflict between the Arian Goth and the Catholics of Italy and the East"]; E. Bach, "Théodoric, romain ou barbare?" *Byzantion* 25–27 (1957): 413–20.

34. Bark, "Theodoric vs. Boethius," p. 425.

35. Procopius 5.1.35–39.

36. Ibid., 2.3–4, 4.30–31.

37. Ramsay MacMullen, "Roman Bureaucratese," *Traditio* 18 (1962): 364–78.

38. Pierre Courcelle, "Le site du monastère de Cassiodore," *Mélanges d'archéologie et d'histoire, École française de Rome* 55 (1938): 259–307.

39. F. Homes Dudden, *Gregory the Great: His Place in History and Thought*, 1:172.

40. D. J. Chapman, "Cassiodorus and the Echternach Gospels," *Revue bénédictine* 28 (1911): 283–92.

41. H. Zimmer, *Pelagius in Irland: Texte und Untersuchunger zur patristischen Literatur*, p. 15.

42. Peter Hunter Blair, *The World of Bede*, p. 128; Chapman, "Cassiodorus," pp. 290–91.

CHAPTER 10. LOMBARD ITALY

1. J. B. Bury, *History of the Later Roman Empire from the Death of Theodosius I. to the Death of Justinian*, 2:204.

2. Procopius 6.20; Gian Luigi Barni, *La conquête de l'Italie par les Lombards*, p. 29 [It is estimated that five million people died, most of them from starvation].

3. John W. Barker, *Justinian and the Later Roman Empire*, p. 87.

4. Procopius 7.1.19–22.

5. Ibid., 5.18.4–6, 12–14.

6. Charles Diehl, *Théodora, impératrice de Byzance*, p. 195.

7. Thomas Hodgkin, *Italy and Her Invaders*, vol. 4, bk. 5, p. 439.

8. Procopius 7.6.20–26; Bury, *History of the Later Roman Empire*, 2:269.

9. Procopius 3.12.9.

10. Ibid., 7.20.29–30.

11. Hodgkin, *Italy and Her Invaders*, vol. 4, bk. 5, p. 456.

12. Procopius 7.22.11–12, 15–16.

13. Ibid., 37.1–3.

14. Ibid., 8.31.17–21.

15. Bernard S. Bachrach, *A History of the Alans in the West from Their First Appearance in the*

Sources of Classical Antiquity Through the Early Middle Ages, pp. 91–93.

16. James Bryce, Viscount Bryce, *The Holy Roman Empire*, p. 48.

17. Robert Folz, *L'idée d'empire en Occident du V⁽ au XIV⁽ siècle*, pp. 21–22.

18. J. M. Wallace-Hadrill, *The Barbarian West, A.D. 400–1000: The Early Middle Ages*, pp. 46–47; Barni, *La conquête de l'Italie*, pp. 48–49; Ernesto Bernareggi, "L'imitazione della moneta d'oro di Bisanzio nell' Europa barbarica," in *Atti del Convegno di studi longobardi*, pp. 25–26 [Coins of Cunibert were original in that they presented Saint Michael, patron of the Lombards].

19. Barni, *La conquête de l'Italie*, p. 42.

20. William Dudley Foulke, trans., *History of the Lombards {by} Paul the Deacon*, p. 92 n.; F. Homes Dudden, *Gregory the Great: His Place in History and Thought*, 1:174.

21. Ludo Moritz Hartmann, *Geschichte Italiens im Mittelalter*, vol. 2, pt. 1.

22. Ernst Stein, "La disparition du Sénat de Rome à la fin du VI⁽ siècle," *Bulletin de la Classe des lettres et des sciences morales et politiques de l'Académie royale de Belgique*, 5th ser., 25 (1939):308–22.

23. Peter Llewellyn, *Rome in the Dark Ages*, p. 93.

24. Hartmann, *Geschichte Italiens*, p. 136.

25. Dudden, *Gregory the Great*, 2:14.

26. Ibid., 2:14–17.

27. Ibid., 2:26–29.

28. Gregory the Great *Ep.* 32.

29. *Leges Langobardorum, Rothari* 47, in Thomas Hodgkin, *Italy and Her Invaders*, 6:183; Katherine Fischer Drew, "The Barbarian Kings as Lawgivers and Judges," in Robert S. Hoyt, ed., *Life and Thought in the Early Middle Ages*, pp. 23–29.

30. *Leges Langobardorum, Liutprand* 56, in Hodgkin, *Italy and Her Invaders*, 6:402.

31. G. M. S. Walker, ed. and trans., *Sancti Columbani opera*, p. 41 [Letter 5.5: "Watch therefore, I beg you Pope, watch, and again I say watch: since perhaps Vigilius was not very vigilant." The quotation as given in the text is the version usually found in biographies of Columban].

CHAPTER 11. DESERTS AND HOLY ISLANDS

1. Karl Heussi, *Der Ursprung des Mönchtums*, p. 60.

2. James H. Breasted, *The Dawn of Conscience*, p. 318.

3. James Moffatt, "Therapeutae," in James Hastings, ed., *Encyclopedia of Religion and Ethics*, 12:318 [Porphyry *De abstinentia* 4.6–8 is quoted].

4. Ibid. [reference to Robertson Smith].

5. *Exodus* 19.

6. Adolf Harnack, *History of Dogma*, 1:112.

7. Erwin R. Goodenough, *The Politics of Philo Judaeus: Practice and Theory*, p. 68.

8. Ibid., quoting Philo *Legum allegoria* 2.85.

9. Marcel Simon, *Jewish Sects at the Time of Jesus*, pp. 120–30; Hans-Gottfried Schönfeld, "Zum Begriff 'Therapeutai' bei Philo von Alexandrien," *Revue de Qumrân* 3 (1961–62): 219–40; Antoine Guillaumont, "Philon et les origines du monachisme," in *Philon d'Alexandrie Lyon, 11–15 septembre 1966*, pp. 361–73; Henri Leclercq, "Cénobitisme. III. Monachisme juif. 2. thérapeutes," *DA*, vol. 2, pt. 2, cols. 3063–75.

10. *Matthew* 19–20.

11. Harnack, *The Mission and Expansion of Christianity in the First Three Centuries*, p. 118.

12. Heussi, *Der Ursprung des Mönchtums*, pp. 59, 61.

13. Ibid., pp. 64–65.

14. Alfred J. Butler, *The Ancient Coptic Churches of Egypt*, 1:292–94 [Description of the journey to Deir Macarius, at Nitria. Butler and his companions were briefly lost "in the valley of the shadow of death"].

15. Frederick Cornwallis Conybeare, "Asceticism," *Encyclopedia Britannica*, 2:717–20 ["The ascetic instinct is probably as old as humanity"]; James George Frazer, *The Golden Bough: A Study in Magic and Religion*, 7:38 [Fasting was included in the Eleusian mysteries]; A. Marx, "Les racines du célibat essenien," *Revue de Qumrân* 7 (1970):327 [In biblical times temporary celibacy was a means for the attainment of prophetic revelation]; George Wesley Buchanan, "The Role of Purity in the Structure of the Essene Sect," *Revue de Qumrân* 4 (1963):402 [Moses had to be ritually pure (that is, celibate) at all times because he never knew when the Lord might speak to him].

16. R. A. Knox, *Enthusiasm: A Chapter in the History of Religion, with Special Reference to the XVII and XVIII Centuries*, p. 2 ["The real enthusiast expects more evident results from the grace of God than we others"].

17. Peter R. L. Brown, *The Making of Late Antiquity*, pp. 82–85 [An explanation of Antony's asceticism. Egyptian villages in the third and fourth centuries were inhabited by "singularly abrasive" farmers who were moderately successful. Natural egoists were forced into humiliating, friction-laden contact and collaboration with their fellows. Tensions were heightened because some were more successful than others. Disengagement like Antony's was a reflex reaction].

18. Palladius 16 [Nathaniel].

19. Derwas J. Chitty, *The Desert a City*, p. 34.

20. Ibid., p. 4 [Athanasius *Vita Antonii* manuscript 865A is quoted].

21. Ibid., p. 16 [*Alphabetical Gerontikon* (Migne *Patrologia Graeca* 65 Antony, 10) is quoted].

22. Ibid., p. 29.

23. Palladius 18.4 [Macarius of Alexandria].

24. Hugh Gerard Evelyn White, *The Monasteries of the Wadi 'n Natrûn*, vol. 3.

25. Pierre du Bourguet, "Une découverte actuelle: l'art copte," in *L'art copte: Petit Palais Paris 17 juin 15 septembre 1964*, pp. 36–37 [The power that developed around the leaders of the monastic centers and the Patriarch recalls the power of the high priests of Amon. Imperial representatives had to take this power into account].

26. Palladius 32.9–12 [Pachomius and the Tabennesiotes].

27. Jacob Burckhardt, *The Age of Constantine the Great*, p. 320.

28. On the authenticity of the authorship of *Vita Antonii* see Chitty, *The Desert a City* [Chitty appears to accept it without question]; Owen Chadwick, *John Cassian*, pp. 3–5 [The general opinion is that it is genuinely Athanasius's work. Chadwick at least has "no doubt that the *Life* is a primitive document from the Egyptian desert"].

29. Palladius 11 [Ammonius].

30. Ibid., 1.4 [Isidore].

31. Peter R. L. Brown, "Pelagius and His Supporters: Aims and Environment," *Journal of Theological Studies*, n.s. 19 (1968):93–114; Peter R. L. Brown, "Aspects of the Christianization of the Roman Aristocracy," *Journal of Roman Studies* 51 (1961):1–11; J. N. L. Myres, "Pelagius and the End of Roman Rule in Britain," *Journal of Roman Studies* 50 (1960):21–36.

32. Palladius 61.4–6 [Melania the Younger]; Jerome *Ep.* 108.20.

33. Chitty, *The Desert a City*, p. 48 [Reference to *Codex Theodosianus* 12.1.63].

34. Charles Plummer, trans. and ed., *Irish Litanies*, no. 2 [The "seven Egyptians who lie in Disert Uilaig" are invoked]; J. N. Hillgarth, "Visigothic Spain and Early Christian Ireland," *Proceedings of the Royal Irish Academy*, vol. 62, sec. C, no. 6 (1962):190–91; Jacques Fontaine, *Isidore de Séville et la culture classique dans l'Espagne wisigothique*, pp. 852–59.

35. Owen Chadwick, *Western Asceticism* [Includes Cassian *Collationes* 9.6. A former hermit

described the advantage of cenobitic life, to which he had returned: "I am not subject to popularity nor therefore to the temptation of arrogance"].

36. Butler, *The Ancient Coptic Churches of Egypt*, p. 296.

37. Friedrich Prinz, *Frühes Mönchtum im Frankenreich*, p. 89.

38. Ibid., p. 113.

39. Gregory of Tours 7.35 [Reference to the use of camels for carrying freight. Camel's hair was not therefore an exotic material in Gaul.].

40. David Riesman, "The Ethics of 'We Happy Few,'" in his *Individualism Reconsidered and Other Essays*, p. 46.

41. Chadwick, *John Cassian*, p. 38; Peter Munz, "John Cassian," *Journal of Ecclesiastical History* 11 (1960): 1–22.

42. Chadwick, *John Cassian*, p. 52; on Cassian and Basil, pp. 60ff.

43. Ibid., pp. 105–106.

44. Erich Caspar, *Geschichte des Papsttums von den Anfängen bis zur Höhe der Weltherrschaft*, 1:439.

45. Trevor Jalland, *The Life and Times of St. Leo the Great*, p. 120.

CHAPTER 12. SUB-ROMAN AND MEROVINGIAN GAUL

1. Sidonius Apollinaris *Carm.* 5.596–98.

2. Leslie Alcock, *Arthur's Britain: History and Archaeology*, A.D. 367–634, p. 107.

3. Godefroid Kurth, *Clovis*, p. 228.

4. Adrien Blanchet, ed., *Carte archéologique de la Gaule romaine*, fasc. 6, plate 1, 2.

5. Sidonius Apollinaris *Ep.* 1.2.8.

6. Sidonius Apollinaris *Carm.* 23.71.

7. Sidonius Apollinaris *Ep.* 1.6.2.

8. Kurth, *Clovis*, p. 221.

9. G. Tamassia, "Egidio e Siagrio," *Rivista storica italiana* 3 (1886): 210.

10. Reinhold Kaiser, *Untersuchungen zur Geschichte der Civitas und Diozese Soissons in römischer und merowingischer Zeit*, p. 139.

11. Sidonius Apollinaris *Ep.* 1.5.2.

12. Ibid., 8.7.3.

13. Ibid., 2.1.4.

14. Ibid., 3.3.7.

15. Ibid., 3.3.9.

16. Ibid., 7.1.2.

17. Ibid., 7.7.3.

18. Ibid., 7.6.7.

19. J. M. Wallace-Hadrill, *The Long-haired Kings*, pp. 161–62.

20. Françoise Dumas, *Le tombeau de Childéric*.

21. E. A. Thompson, *The Visigoths in the Time of Ulfila*, pp. 44–47 [Roman writers also used the term *iudex* ("judge") as a semitechnical or official name for a certain type of Visigothic leader who was a chief with powers greater than that of other chiefs. "The Judge is the confederate leader and only appears at a time when the tribes have associated in a confederacy"].

22. Alcock, *Arthur's Britain*, p. 60 [King Arthur of England seems to have been the leader of a war band. He is described as a dux bellorum, which was not a proper Roman title].

23. Kurth, *Clovis*, p. 253 [Two generations after Clovis and Syagrius, Sigebert I challenged his brother Chilpéric in this way].

24. Bernard S. Bachrach, *Merovingian Military Organization, 481–751*, p. 5.

25. Karl Binding, *Das burgundisch-romanische Königreich von 443–532 n. Chr.*, p. 134.

26. Gregory of Tours 2.36.

27. Ibid., 3.2.

28. Sidonius Apollinaris *Ep.* 8.14, 9.8.

29. Kaiser, *Untersuchungen zur Geschichte der Civitas und Diozese Soissons*, pp. 218–19 [on the holdings of the Remigii in the vicinity of Laon].

30. M. M. Gorce, *Clovis, 465–511*, p. 145 [Even today French children are warned about a bogeyman, Croquemitaine, in shadowy memory of an Alamannic king, Crocus, who lived in the time of Constantine the Great]; see also chap. 3, n. 37, above; Bruno Behr, *Das alemannische Herzogtum bis 750*, p. 40.

31. Samuel Dill, *Roman Society in Gaul in the Merovingian Age*, p. 90.

32. J. B. Bury, *History of the Later Roman Empire from the Death of Theodosius I. to the Death of Justinian*, 1:461.

33. Gregory of Tours 2.31; Jean Hoyoux, "Le collier de Clovis," *Revue belge de philologie et d'histoire* 21 (1942): 169–74.

34. A. van der Vyver, "Le victoire contre les alemans et la conversion de Clovis," *Revue belge de philologie et d'histoire* 15 (1936): 898–914.

35. Gregory of Tours 2.37.

36. Wallace-Hadrill, *The Long-haired Kings*, p. 176.

37. Gregory of Tours 2.42.

38. Eugen Ewig, "Die fränkische Teilungen und Teilreiche (511–613): Die Reichsteilung von 511," in his *Spätantikes und fränkisches Gallien*, 1:118–20.

39. Gregory of Tours 3.14.

40. Ibid., 5.32.

41. Ibid., 7.14.

42. Ibid., 10.15–17.

43. Ibid., 6.4

44. Godefroid Kurth, "La reine Brunehaut," in *Études Franques*, 1:265–356; Christian Pfister, "Gaul Under the Merovingian Franks," *CMH*, 2:122–23.

45. Charles Lelong, *La vie quotidienne en Gaule à l'époque mérovingien*, p. 86.

CHAPTER 13. CELTIC OUTPOSTS IN BRITAIN

1. Leslie Alcock, *Arthur's Britain: History and Archaeology, A.D. 367–634*, pp. 5–9; John Morris, "Dark Ages Dates," in Michael E. Jarrett and Brian Dobson, eds., *Britain and Rome: Essays Presented to Eric Birley on His Sixtieth Birthday*, pp. 152–57; G. N. Garmonsway, ed. and trans., *The Anglo-Saxon Chronicle*, pp. xx–xxv.

2. T. C. Lethbridge, *Herdsmen and Hermits: Celtic Seafarers in the Northern Seas*, p. 71.

3. Charles Thomas, *Britain and Ireland in Early Christian Times, A.D. 400–800*, p. 66.

4. Tacitus *Agricola* 24.

5. Gearóid MacNiocaill, *Ireland Before the Vikings*, p. 5.

6. The relevant portions of the following works can be consulted for further discussion: J. B. Bury, *The Life of St. Patrick and His Place in History*; John Ryan, *Irish Monasticism: Origins and Early Development*; Máire de Paor and Liam de Paor, *Early Christian Ireland*; John T. McNeill, *The Celtic Churches: A History, A.D. 200 to 1200*; Ludwig Bieler, *St. Patrick and the Coming of Christianity*; Robert E. McNally, "St. Patrick, 461–1961," *Catholic Historical Review* 47 (1961): 305–24; James Carney, *The Problem of St. Patrick*; D. A. Binchy, "Patrick and His Biographers, Ancient and Modern," *Studia Hibernica* 2 (1962): 7–173; Richard Patrick Cresland Hanson, *Saint Patrick: His Origins and Career* [Patrick was a Briton, supported by the British. He never went to Gaul].

7. Ludwig Bieler, "The Mission of Palladius: A Comparative Study of Sources," *Traditio* 6 (1948):1–32; Nora K. Chadwick, *Early Brittany*, p. 149.

8. This statement discounts small military operations like that of Coroticus and his *milites* in Patrick's own time.

9. MacNiocaill, *Ireland Before the Vikings*, p. 22.

10. Bury, *The Life of St. Patrick*, pp. 104–13.

11. Kathleen Hughes, *The Church in Early Irish Society*, pp. 46–47.

12. We encountered tanistry once before, among the Vandal kings in Africa.

13. Hughes, *The Church in Early Irish Society*, pp. 86–87 ["The monastic *paruchia* was based on Irish ideas of overlordship. . . . The earliest ecclesiastical overlordship of which we have certain knowledge was that provided by Colomcille of the Uí Néill dynasty"]; MacNiocaill, *Ireland Before the Vikings*, fig. 17, "Rulers of Iona to 704"; William F. Skene, *Celtic Scotland: A History of Ancient Alban*, 2:66–75.

14. George Petrie, *The Ecclesiastical Architecture of Ireland: An Essay on the Origin and Uses of the Round Towers of Ireland*, pp. 332–40; Alfred J. Butler, *Ancient Coptic Churches of Egypt*, 2:246; J. J. Buckley, "Some Early Ornamental Leather Work," *Journal of the Royal Society of Antiquaries of Ireland* 45 (1915):307–309; John W. Waterer, "Irish Book-Satchels or Budgets," *Medieval Archaeology* 12 (1968):70–82, plates 4–7.

15. Berthe van Regemorter, "La reliure des manuscrits de s. Cuthbert et de s. Boniface," *Scriptorium* 3 (1949):46; P. Adam, "Über türkisch-arabisch-persisch Manuskripte und deren Einbände," *Archiv für Buchbinderei* 4 (1905):149; Theodore C. Petersen, "Early Islamic Bookbindings and Their Coptic Relations," *Ars Orientalis* 1 (1954):40–64.

16. Thomas, *Britain and Ireland*, p. 88.

17. Ryan, *Irish Monasticism*, p. 116.

18. Bury, *The Life of St. Patrick*, pp. 191, 314–15.

19. de Paor and de Paor, *Early Christian Ireland*, p. 48.

20. Adamnan 3.24.

21. Tacitus *Agricola* 38.

22. F. T. Wainwright, ed., *The Problem of the Picts*; Isabel Henderson, *The Picts*.

23. James S. Richardson, *The Medieval Stone Carver in Scotland*, pp. 3–4.

24. Aubrey Burl, *The Stone Circles of the British Isles*, pp. 98–212; Geoffrey of Monmouth 8.11 [What faint folk memory is embedded in Merlin's speech with reference to stones to be transported from Ireland for the construction of Stonehenge? "Giants of old did carry them from the furthest ends of Africa"].

25. Thomas, *Britain and Ireland*, p. 51.

26. Henderson, *The Picts*, p. 139, fig. 29; Robert B. K. Stevenson, "Pictish Art," in F. T. Wainwright, ed., *The Problem of the Picts*, pp. 97–128; Thomas, "The Animal Art of the Scottish Iron Age and Its Origins," *Archaeological Journal* 118 (1961):14–64 ["The naturalistic depiction of animals is an Euroasiatic legacy to La Tène. . . . Tattooing is by far the most likely way in which Pictish symbols were kept alive from the second to the fifth centuries A.D." Reference is made to Herodian *History* 3.14.7 and to the bodies found in the Pazyryk burials. In this connection see chap. 2, n. 24, above]; John Romilly Allen and Joseph Anderson, *The Early Christian Monuments of Scotland*; Stewart Cruden, *The Early Christian and Pictish Monuments of Scotland*; Albert Grenier, *Les gaulois*, p. 239 [Comments on the curious similarity of motifs on the Gundestrup bowl and St. Vigeans no. 7—sacrifice by suffocation in a cauldron; bull sacrifice]; J. Close-Brooks, personal communication [The supposed sacrifice by suffocation might be a birth scene].

27. Wainwright, *The Souterrains of Southern Pictland*.

28. Euan W. Mackie, "The Origin and Development of the Broch and Wheelhouse Building Cultures of the Scottish Iron Age," *Proceedings of the Prehistoric Society*, n.s. 31 (1965): 93–146; Lloyd Laing, *Orkney and Shetland: An Archaeological Guide*, pp. 99–120; Hugh Mar-

wick, *Ancient Monuments in Orkney*, pp. 40–44; Giovanni Lilliu, "The Nuraghi of Sardinia," *Antiquity* 33 (1959): 32–38 ["The term is taken from nur-aghe (hollow tower)." There are still about 6,500 nuraghi in existence. Barúmini, one of the most impressive today, accommodated about 300 individuals].

29. Petrie, *The Ecclesiastical Architecture of Ireland*, pp. 71–78.

30. David J. Breeze and Brian Dobson, *Hadrian's Wall.*

31. Edward Gibbon, *The Decline and Fall of the Roman Empire*, 2:40.

32. Donald A. White, *Litus Saxonicum.*

33. Alcock, *Arthur's Britain*, p. 128; Hector Munro Chadwick, *Early Scotland: The Picts, the Scots, and the Welsh of Southern Scotland*, p. 148 ["A new principle makes its appearance in the treatment of conquered, or rather reconquered, territories. They are divided among the successful general's sons. . . . These divisions now become permanent kingdoms"].

34. J. N. L. Myres, "Pelagius and the End of Roman Rule in Britain," *Journal of Roman Studies* 50 (1960): 35 [Vortigern planted Hengist in Kent to block possible invasion routes of Roman forces that might be called in from the Continent by his orthodox opponents].

35. Hector Munro Chadwick, "Vortigern," *Studies in Early British History*, p. 27; D. P. Kirby, "Vortigern," *Bulletin of the Board of Celtic Studies* 23 (1968): 48–49.

36. Such layers provide unmistakable evidence of the destruction wrought by Bouddica in A.D. 60 (the sack of London, Verulamium, and Colchester).

37. *The Anglo-Saxon Chronicle*, [year] 491.

38. Alcock, *Arthur's Britain*, p. 26, citing Gildas *De excidio et conquestu Britanniae* 25.

39. Ibid., p. 29 [Alcock designates this compendium as Nennius Historia Brittonum, BM Harleian MS 3859].

40. Alcock's translation, ibid., p. 60.

41. Ibid., pp. 61–71.

42. Bede *Ecclesiastical History* 1.34.

CHAPTER 14. THE ANGLO-SAXON HEPTARCHY AND THE CITY OF GOD

1. Leslie Alcock, *Arthur's Britain: History and Archaeology*, A.D. 367–634, p. 307.

2. Unsigned editorial comment, *Medieval Archaeology* 1 (1957): 148–49 [An odd quirk is the evidence that the Roman system of measurement prevailed in an essentially Anglo-British context].

3. G. N. Garmonsway, ed. and trans., *The Anglo-Saxon Chronicle*, p. xliii.

4. Charles Thomas, *Britain and Ireland in Early Christian Times*, A.D. 400–800, p. 80.

5. Ibid., p. 82.

6. William F. Skene, *Celtic Scotland: A History of Ancient Alban*, 2:194–95.

7. John Ryan, *Irish Monasticism: Origins and Early Development*, p. 214.

8. G. S. M. Walker, ed. and trans., *Sancti Columbani opera*, p. xix.

9. Today Annegray is no more than a small mound next to a roadway, but traces of a stone wall are said to have been found there.

10. Animal stories are to be found in abundance throughout the "lives" of the saints; Helen Waddell, *The Desert Fathers: Translations from the Latin.* pp. 35, 38 [Extracts from Jerome's life of Saint Paul, the first hermit]; Arthur Kingsley Porter, *The Crosses and Culture of Ireland* [The scene in which Paul and Antony share a loaf of bread brought to them by a crow was frequently depicted on sculptured stones]; Bede *The Life and Miracles of Saint Cuthbert, Bishop of Lindisfarne* 10, 21.

11. Walker, *Sancti Columbani opera*, p. xxxiii; Joseph McSorley, *An Outline History of the Church by Centuries (from St. Peter to Pius XII)*, p. 156 [Pius XI is quoted: "As scholarship throws an increasing light on the obscurity of the Middle Ages, the more clearly it is manifest that the

renaissance of all Christian science and culture in many parts of France, Germany and Italy is due to the labors and zeal of Columban"].

12. Walker, *Sancti Columbani opera*, p. xxii; Erich Caspar, *Geschichte des Papsttums von den Anfängen bis zur Höhe der Weltherrschaft*, 2:501.

13. Suso Brechter, *Die Quellen zur Angelsachsenmission Gregors des Grossen: eine historische Studie*, pp. 232–40.

14. Walker, *Sancti Columbani opera*, p. xxv.

15. Examples of holy pictures on wood dating from sixth- and seventh-century Coptic Egypt may offer some idea of the "image of Our Lord and Savior painted on a board." The Freer Gallery of Art, in Washington, D.C., has a pair of book covers with portraits of the Evangelists. For the technique see C. R. Morey, "East Christian Paintings in the Freer Collection," *University of Michigan Studies, Humanistic Series* 12 (1918):63–81.

16. Bede *Ecclesiastical History* 1.32; Peter Hunter Blair, *The World of Bede*, pp. 53–54 [Gregory sent a letter referring to the report of one John the Regionarius on what Syagrius had done for "our brother Augustine" and expressed thanks to Brunhilda for assistance to "our fellow bishop"]; ibid., p. 60 [Gregory's letters to King Ethelbert are of special interest because "they mark the beginnings of a change from barbarism to a literate civilization among the Anglo-Saxons"].

17. A. P. Forbes, ed., *Remains of the Late Arthur West Haddan*, pp. 315–16.

18. Bede *Ecclesiastical History* 2.2.

19. Ibid., 2.4.

20. Ibid., 2.11.

21. Alois Walde, *Lateinisches-etymologisches Wörterbuch*, 2:714 [This barbarian word first appeared in Joannes Lydus *De Magistratibus populi romani* 1.8. It designated a tuft or plume, usually worn on the crest of a helmet].

22. Bede *Ecclesiastical History* 3.3.

23. Ibid., 3.5.

24. Gareth W. Dunleavy, *Colum's Other Island: The Irish at Lindisfarne*; Richard Perry, *A Naturalist on Lindisfarne* (London: Drummond, 1946).

25. Bede *Ecclesiastical History* 3.11.

26. Ibid., 3.14 [Aidan seems genuinely to have loved Oswine of Deira, a warm-hearted, impulsive man who was murdered on King Oswy's order. Aidan predicted Oswine's death, weeping because "this nation is not worthy of such a ruler." We may surmise that he at least suspected Oswy's intention].

27. G. M. Trevelyan, *History of England*, 1:88.

28. D. P. Kirby, "Northumbria in the Time of Wilfrid," in *Saint Wilfrid at Hexham*, esp. pp. 17–21.

29. Margaret Deanesly, *The Pre-Conquest Church in England*, p. 90.

30. Arthur West Haddan and William Stubbs, eds., *Councils and Ecclesiastical Documents Relating to Great Britain and Ireland*, 3:106n. [The Whitby conference was entirely a Northumbrian gathering. Archbishop Deusdedit of Canterbury was absent, perhaps because of illness. There is no mention of the Whitby meeting in *The Anglo-Saxon Chronicle*]; Margaret Deanesly and Paul Grosjean, "The Canterbury Edition of the Answers of Pope Gregory I to St. Augustine," *Journal of Ecclesiastical History* 10 (1959):143 [It is doubtful that the Easter controversy became acute in the West before Columban's appeal to Gregory in 600].

31. Bede *Ecclesiastical History* 3.25.

32. Ibid., 3.24.

33. Ibid., 3.29.

34. Ibid., 5.3 [In the words of Berthun, abbot of Beverly, "I remember that Archbishop Theodore, of blessed memory, said, that bleeding at that time was very dangerous, when the light of the moon and the tide of the ocean is [*sic*] increasing"].

35. Dorothy Whitelock, *The Beginnings of English Society*, p. 175 [Reference is made to an itinerary in 990 from Rome to the Somme that gives the names of seventy-nine stages. We can assume that the journey was no less arduous in Theodore's day].

36. William Stubbs, "Theodorus. 7," in William Smith and Henry Wace, eds., *Dictionary of Christian Biography, Literature, Sects, and Doctrines*, 4:928.

37. Sir Winston Spencer Churchill, *The History of the English-speaking Peoples*, 1:82.

38. Bede *Ecclesiastical History* 4.21.

39. W. J. Corbett, "England (to c. 800) and English Institutions," *CMH*, 2:557.

40. D. H. Farmer, "Saint Wilfrid," in D. P. Kirby, ed., *Saint Wilfrid at Hexham*, pp. 35–59; Eddius Stephanus; Eleanor Shipley Duckett, "Wilfrid of York," in her *Anglo-Saxon Saints and Scholars*, pp. 101–214.

41. Edward Gilbert, "Saint Wilfrid's Church at Hexham," in Kirby, *Saint Wilfrid at Hexham*, pp. 81–113.

42. Eddius Stephanus 26.

43. Ibid., 25.

44. Ibid., 28.

45. Whitelock, *The Beginnings of English Society*, p. 32 [As Anglo-Saxons, Wilfrid's followers understood the import of the letter written to them by the bishop of Sherborne reminding them that it was their duty to share his exile. Whitelock cites this in a discussion of the Teutonic tradition of bonds existing between a chieftain and his companions].

CHAPTER 15. EPILOGUE: TWO STATELY CHAIRS

1. George Petrie, *The Ecclesiastical Architecture of Ireland: An Essay on the Origin and Uses of the Round Towers of Ireland*, pp. 323–25.

REFERENCES CITED

ABBREVIATIONS USED IN NOTES

Adamnan
    Anderson, Alan Orr, and Margaret Ogilvie Anderson, eds. and trans. *Adomnan's Life of Columba*. London: Nelson, 1961.
Ammianus Marcellinus
    Rolfe, John C. trans. *Ammianus Marcellinus*. 3 vols. Loeb Classical Library. Cambridge, Mass.: Harvard University Press, 1971–72.
The Anglo-Saxon Chronicle
    Garmonsway, G. N., ed. and trans. *The Anglo-Saxon Chronicle*. New York: Dutton, 1975.
Augustine *City of God*
    Bourke, Vernon J., ed. *Saint Augustine: The City of God: An Abridged Version from the Translation by Gerald G. Walsh et al.* 1950. Reprint. Garden City, N.Y.: Doubleday, Image Books, 1958.
Augustine *Confessions*
    Ryan, John Kenneth, trans. *The Confessions of St. Augustine*. 1960. Reprint. Garden City, N.Y.: Doubleday, Image Books, 1958.
Augustine *Ep.*
    Baxter, James Houston, trans. *St. Augustine: Select Letters*. Loeb Classical Library. London: Heinemann, 1930.
Bede *Ecclesiastical History*
    Bede's Ecclesiastical History of the English Nation. [Translated by J. Stevens, revised by J. A. Giles, notes by L. C. Jane.] Everyman's Library, no. 479. London: Dent, 1970.
CAH
    Cambridge Ancient History. 12 vols. Cambridge: At the University Press, 1923–39.
CMH
    Cambridge Medieval History. 8 vols. New York: Macmillan Co., 1911–36.
DA
    Cabrol, Fernand, and Henri Leclercq. *Dictionnaire d'archéologie chrétienne et de liturgie*. Paris: Letouzey et Ané, 1907–.
Eddius Stephanus
    Colgrave, B., ed. *The Life of Bishop Wilfrid, by Eddius Stephanus*. Cambridge: At the University Press, 1927.

363

Eggers et al., *Kelten*
    Eggers, Hans-Jürgen, et al. *Kelten und Germanen in heidnischer Zeit*. Baden-Baden: Holle, 1965.
Gaius Julius Caesar *De bello gallico*
    Warrington, John, ed. and trans. *Caesar's War Commentaries: De bello gallico and De bello civili*. Everyman's Library, Classical, no. 702. London: Dent, 1953.
Geoffrey of Monmouth
    Evans, Sebastian, trans. *History of the Kings of Britain, by Geoffrey of Monmouth*. Revised by Charles W. Dunn. New York: Dutton, 1958.
Gregory of Tours
    Dalton, O. M., trans. *The History of the Franks by Gregory of Tours*. 2 vols. Oxford: Clarendon Press, 1927.
Gregory the Great *Ep.*
    Philip Schaff and Henry Wace, eds. *A Select Library of the Nicene and Post-Nicene Fathers of the Christian Church*. 2d ser. 14 vols. New York: Christian Literature Co., 1890–1900. Vol. 12, 1895.
Herodotus *Persian Wars*
    Godley, A. D., trans. *Herodotus*. 4 vols. Loeb Classical Library. London: Heinemann, 1921–24.
Jerome *Ep.*
    Fremantle, W. H., trans. *The Principal Works of St. Jerome*. Select Library of the Nicene and Post-Nicene Fathers of the Christian Church. 2d ser., vol. 6. New York: Christian Literature Co., 1893.
Jordanes
    Mierow, Charles Christopher, trans. *The Gothic History of Jordanes*. 2d ed. 1915. Reprint. Cambridge: Speculum historiale, 1966.
Josephus *Jewish Antiquities*
    Thackeray, H. St. J., Ralph Marcus, and Louis H. Feldman, trans. *Josephus*. Vols. 4–9, *Jewish Antiquities*. 6 vols. Loeb Classical Library. London: Heinemann, 1930–65.
Libanius *Julianic Orations*
    Norman, A. F., trans. *Libanius: Selected Works*. Vol. 3, *The Julianic Orations*. Loeb Classical Library. Cambridge, Mass.: Harvard University Press, 1969.
Maenchen-Helfen
    Maenchen-Helfen, J. Otto. *The World of the Huns: Studies in Their History and Culture*. Edited by Max Knight. Berkeley and Los Angeles: University of California Press, 1973.
Orosius
    Deferrari, Roy J., trans. *Paulus Orosius: The Seven Books of History Against the Pagans*. Fathers of the Church, vol. 50. Washington, D.C.: Catholic University of America Press, 1964.
Palladius
    Meyer, Robert T., trans. *Palladius: The Lausiac History*. Ancient Christian Writers, no. 34. Westminster, Md.: Newman Press, 1965.
Paulinus
    Kaniecka, Mary Simplicia, trans. *Vita Sancti Ambrosii Mediolanensis Episcopi a Paulino eius notario ad beatum Augustinum conscripta*. Revised text. Catholic University of America Patristic Studies, vol. 26. Washington, D.C.: Catholic University of America, 1928.
Paul the Deacon
    Foulke, William Dudley, trans. *History of the Lombards {by} Paul the Deacon*. Sources of Medieval History. Philadelphia: University of Pennsylvania Press, 1974.
Possidius
    Weiskotten, Herbert T., ed. and trans. *Sancti Augustini vita scripta a Possidio episcopo*. Revised

text. Princeton, N.J.: Princeton University Press, 1919.

Procopius

Dewing, H. B., trans. *Procopius*. 7 vols. Loeb Classical Library. Cambridge, Mass.: Harvard University Press, 1953–62.

RE

Paulys Real-Encyclopädie der classischen Altertumswissenschaft. Edited by G. Wissowa. Stuttgart, 1894–.

Reusch, *Frühchristliche Zeugnisse*

Reusch, Wilhelm, ed. *Frühchristliche Zeugnisse im Einzugsgebiet von Rhein und Mosel*. Trier, 1965.

Salvian

Sanford, Eva M., trans. *On the Government of God by Salvian*. New York: Octagon Books, 1966.

Sidonius Apollinaris *Carm.*

Sidonius Apollinaris *Ep.*

Anderson, W. B., trans. *Sidonius: Poems and Letters*. 2 vols. Loeb Classical Library. Cambridge, Mass.: Harvard University Press, 1963–65.

Sulpicius Severus *Dialogues*

Sulpicius Severus *Life of Martin*

Hoare, Frederick Russell, trans. *The Western Fathers: Being the Lives of SS. Martin of Tours, Ambrose, Augustine of Hippo, Honoratus of Arles, and Germanus of Auxerre*. The Makers of Christendom. New York: Sheed and Ward, 1954.

Tacitus *Agricola*

Tacitus *Germania*

Mattingly, H., trans. *Tacitus: The Agricola and The Germania*. Revised by S. A. Hanford. Harmondsworth: Penguin Books, 1970.

Zosimus

Buchanan, James J., and Harold T. Davis, trans. *Zosimus: Historia nova: The Decline of Rome*. San Antonio, Texas: Trinity University Press, 1967.

OTHER WORKS CITED

Adam, P. "Über türkisch-arabisch-persische Manuskripte und deren Einbände." *Archiv für Buchbinderei* 4 (1905):145–52, 161–68, 177–85; 5 (1905):3–9.

Adamnan. See Alan Orr Anderson and Margaret Olgivie Anderson, eds. and trans.

Alcock, Leslie. *Arthur's Britain: History and Archaeology, A.D. 367–634*. Harmondsworth: Penguin Books, 1971.

Alföldi, Andreas. *A Conflict of Ideas in the Late Roman Empire: The Clash Between the Senate and Valentinian I*. Oxford: Clarendon Press, 1952.

Alföldi, Maria R. "Münzen des 4. Jahrhunderts mit christlichen Kaiserbildnissen." In Reusch, *Frühchristliche Zeugnisse*, pp. 83–97.

Alföldy, Géza. *Noricum*. The Provinces of the Roman Empire. London: Routledge & Kegan Paul, 1974.

Allard, Paul. "Sidoine Apollinaire sous les règnes d'Avitus et de Majorien." *Revue des questions historiques* 42, n.s. 39 (1908): 426–52.

Allen, John Romilly, and Joseph Anderson. *The Early Christian Monuments of Scotland: A Classified, Illustrated, Descriptive List of Monuments, with an Analysis of Their Symbolism and Ornamentation*. Edinburgh: Society of Antiquaries of Scotland, 1903.

Altheim, Franz. *Attila und die Hunnen*. Baden-Baden: Verlag für Kunst und Wissenschaft, 1951.

————. "Runen als Schildzeichen." *Klio* 31 (1938):51–59.

————. *Die Soldatenkaiser.* Frankfurt on the Main: Klostermann, 1939.

Ammianus Marcellinus. *Res gestarum.* See John C. Rolfe, trans.

Anderson, Alan Orr, and Margaret Ogilvie Anderson, eds. and trans. *Adomnan's Life of Columba.* London: Nelson, 1961. [Abbr. Adamnan]

Anderson, Mosa. *St. Ninian, Light of the Celtic North.* London: Faith Press, 1964.

Anderson, W. B., trans. *Sidonius: Poems and Letters.* 2 vols. Loeb Classical Library. Cambridge, Mass.: Harvard University Press, 1963–65. [Abbr. Sidonius *Carm.* and Sidonius *Ep.*]

The Anglo-Saxon Chronicle. See G. N. Garmonsway, ed. and trans.

L'art copte: Petit Palais 17 juin 15 septembre 1964. Catalog. Paris: Ministère d'État affaires culturelles, 1964.

Ashby, Thomas. *The Aqueducts of Ancient Rome.* Edited by I. A. Richmond. Oxford: Clarendon Press, 1935.

Augustine. *De civitate Dei.* See Vernon J. Bourke, ed.

————. *Confessiones.* See John Kenneth Ryan, trans.

————. *Epistolae.* See Sister Wilfrid Parsons, trans.; James Houston Baxter, trans.

Avery, William T. "The *adoratio purpurae* and the Importance of the Imperial Purple in the Fourth Century of the Christian Era." *Memoirs of the American Academy in Rome* 17 (1940):66–80.

Azarpay, G. "Some Classical and Near Eastern Motifs in the Art of Pazyryk." *Artibus Asiae* 22 (1959):313–39.

Babut, Ch. *Le concile de Turin.* Paris: Champion, 1910.

————. "Recherches sur la garde impériale et sur le corps d'officiers de l'armée romaine aux IVᵉ et Vᵉ siècles." *Revue historique* 39 (1914):225–93.

Bach, E. "Théodoric, romain ou barbare?" *Byzantion* 25–27 (1957):413–20.

Bachrach, Bernard S. *A History of the Alans in the West, from Their First Appearance in the Sources of Classical Antiquity Through the Early Middle Ages.* Minneapolis: University of Minnesota Press, 1973.

————. *Merovingian Military Organization, 481–751.* Minneapolis: University of Minnesota Press, 1972.

Bark, William. "Theodoric vs. Boethius: Vindication and Apology." *American Historical Review* 49 (1944):410–26.

Barker, Ernest. "Italy and the West, 410–476." *CMH*, 1:392–431.

Barker, John W. *Justinian and the Later Roman Empire.* Madison: University of Wisconsin Press, 1966.

Barnes, T. D. "The Family and Career of Septimius Severus." *Historia* 16 (1967):87–107.

Barni, Gian Luigi. *La conquête de l'Italie par les Lombards.* Paris: Michel, 1975.

Barrow, R. H. *Prefect and Emperor: The Relationes of Symmachus.* Oxford: Clarendon Press, 1973.

Barth, Wilhelm. *Kaiser Zeno.* Inaugural-Dissertation, Basel. Basel, 1894.

Basset, Henri. "Les influences puniques chez le berbères." *Revue africaine* 62 (1921):340–74.

Bauchheuss, G. "Zur Entstehung der Jupitergigantensäuler." *Archäologisches Korrespondenzblatt* 4 (1974):359–64.

Baur, C. "Zur Ambrose-Theodosius Frage." *Theologische Quartalschrift* 90 (1908):401–409.

Baxter, James Houston, trans. *St. Augustine: Select Letters.* Loeb Classical Library. London: Heinemann, 1930. [Abbr. Augustine *Ep.*.]

Baynes, Norman H. "Constantine's Successors to Jovian and the Struggle with Persia." *CMH*, 1:55–117.

————. "The Dynasty of Valentinian and Theodosius the Great." *CMH*, 1:218–49.

Beckwith, John. *Coptic Sculpture, 300–1300.* London: Tiranti, 1965.

Bede. *Bede's Ecclesiastical History of the English Nation.* [Translated by J. Stevens, revised by

J. A. Giles, notes by L. C. Jane.] Everyman's Library, no. 479. London: Dent, 1970. [Abbr. Bede *Ecclesiastical History*]

―――――. *The Life and Miracles of St. Cuthbert, Bishop of Lindisfarne*. Translated by J. Stevenson. In *Bede's Ecclesiasticcal History of the English Nation*, pp. 286–348. London: Dent, 1970.

Bede, Giuseppina Sommella, ed. *Le mura di Aureliano a Roma: esposizione documentaria organizzata dal Centro internazionale per lo studio delle cerchia urbane*. Quaderni del Centro internazionale per lo studio delle cerchia urbane, no. 5. Lucca, 1972.

Behr, Bruno. *Das alemannische Herzogtum bis 750*. Geist und Werk der Zeiten, no. 41. Bern: Lang, 1975.

Benoit, Fernand. "L'Hilarianum d'Arles et les missions en Bretagne (V ᵉ–VI ᵉ siècles)." In *Saint Germain d'Auxerre et son temps*, pp. 181–89.

Benson, Edward White. *Cyprian: His Life, His Times, His Work*. London, Macmillan & Co., 1897.

Bernareggi, Ernesto. "L'imitazione della moneta d'oro di Bisanzio nell' Europa barbarica." In *Atti del Convegno di studi longobardi (Udine-Cividale 15–18 maggio 1969)*, pp. 19–27. [Udine?]: Deputazione di storia patria per il Friuli, 1969.

Bertolini, Ottorino. "L'aristocrazia senatoria e il senato di Roma come forza politica sotto i regni di Odoacre e di Teodorico." In *Atti del I. Congresso nazionale di studi romani*, 1:462–75. Rome, 1929.

Besta, Enrico. *La Sardegna medioevale*. Palermo: Reber, 1908.

Bielder, Ludwig. "The Mission of Palladius: A Comparative Study of the Sources." *Traditio* 6 (1948):1–32.

―――――. *St. Patrick and the Coming of Christianity*. A History of Irish Catholicism, vol. 1, [pt.] 1. Dublin: Gill, 1967.

Binchy, D. A. "Patrick and His Biographers, Ancient and Modern." *Studia Hibernica* 2 (1962):7–173.

Binding, Karl. *Das burgundisch-romanische Königreich von 443–532 n. Chr. 1868*. Reprint. Aalen: Scientia Verlag, 1969.

Blair, Peter Hunter. *The World of Bede*. New York: St. Martin's Press, 1971.

Blanchet, Adrien, ed. *Carte archéologique de la Gaule romaine*. Institut de France, Académie des inscriptions et belles-lettres. Forma orbis romani. Paris: Leroux, 1931–.

Bloch, Herbert. "A New Document of the Last Pagan Revival in the West, 393–394 A.D." *Harvard Theological Review* 38 (1945):199–244.

―――――. "The Pagan Revival in the West at the End of the Fourth Century." In Arnaldo Momigliano, ed. *The Conflict Between Paganism and Christianity in the Fourth Century*, pp. 193–218. 1964. Reprint. Oxford: Clarendon Press, 1970.

Boak, Arthur E. R. *Manpower Shortage and the Fall of the Roman Empire*. Ann Arbor: University of Michigan Press, 1955.

―――――. *The Master of Offices in the Later Roman and Byzantine Empire*. New York: Macmillan Co., 1919.

Bober, Phyllis Pray. "Cernunnos: Origin and Transformation of a Celtic Deity." *American Journal of Archaeology* 55 (1951):13–51.

Böhne, W. "Brictius." *Lexikon für Theologie und Kirche*. 10 vols. Freiburg im Breisgau: Herder, 1930–38. Vol. 2, col. 685.

Bonner, G. I. "How Pelagian Was Pelagius? An Examination of the Contentions of Torgny Bohlin." *Studia Patristica* vol. 9, pt. 3, pp. 350–58. Texte und Untersuchungen zur Geschichte der altchristlichen Literatur, vol. 94. Berlin: Akademie Verlag, 1966.

Bourke, Vernon J., ed. *Saint Augustine: The City of God: An Abridged Version from the Translation by Gerald G. Walsh et al. 1950*. Reprint. Garden City, N.Y.: Doubleday, Image Books, 1958. [Abbr. Augustine *City of God*.]

Bouvier-Ajam, Maurice. *Le Temps des empereurs gaulois*. Paris: Le Pavillon, 1974.

Bowersock, Glen Warren. *Julian the Apostate*. Cambridge, Mass.: Harvard University Press, 1978.

Breasted, James H. *The Dawn of Conscience*. New York: Scribner, 1933.

Brechter, Suso. *Die Quellen sur Angelsachsenmission Gregors des Grossen: eine historische Studie*. Münster in Westfalen: Aschendorff, 1941.

Breeze, David J., and Brian Dobson. *Hadrian's Wall*. London: Lane, 1976.

Bréhier, Louis. "Les colonies d'Orientaux en Occident au commencement du moyen-âge. V^e–VIIIe siècle." *Byzantinische Zeitschrift* 12 (1903): 1–39.

Brown, Peter R. L. "Aspects of the Christianization of the Roman Aristocracy." *Journal of Roman Studies* 51 (1961): 1–11.

———. *Augustine of Hippo*. Berkeley and Los Angeles: University of California Press, 1970.

———. "Christianity and Local Culture in Late Roman Africa." *Journal of Roman Studies* 58 (1968): 85–95.

———. *The Making of Late Antiquity*. Cambridge, Mass.: Harvard University Press, 1978.

———. "Pelagius and His Supporters: Aims and Environment." *Journal of Theological Studies*, n.s. 19 (1968): 93–114.

———. "The Rise and Function of the Holy Man in Late Antiquity." *Journal of Roman Studies* 61 (1971): 80–101.

Bruns, Gerda. *Der Obelisk und seine Basis auf dem Hippodrom zu Constantinopel*. Istanbul, 1935.

Bryce, James, Viscount Bryce. *The Holy Roman Empire*. New ed. London: Macmillan & Co., 1950.

Buchanan, George Wesley. "The Role of Purity in the Structure of the Essene Sect." *Revue de Qumrân* 4 (1963): 397–406.

Buchanan, James J. and Harold T. Davis, trans. *Zosimus: Historia nova: The Decline of Rome*. San Antonio: Trinity University Press, 1967. [Abbr. Zosimus.]

Buckley, J. J. "Some Early Ornamental Leatherwork." *Journal of The Royal Society of Antiquaries of Ireland* 45 (1915): 300–309.

Bullough, D. A. "Urban Change in Early Medieval Italy: The Example of Pavia." *Papers of the British School at Rome* 34, n.s. 21 (1966): 82–130.

Burckhardt, Felix. "Galla Placidia: eine römische Kaiserin des 5. Jahrhunderts." *Schweizerische Rundschau* 25 (1925): 409–19; 481–89.

Burckhardt, Jacob. *The Age of Constantine the Great*. Translated by Moses Hadas. 1949. Reprint. Garden City, N.Y.: Doubleday, Anchor Books, 1956.

Burl, Aubrey. *The Stone Circles of the British Isles*. New Haven, Conn.: Yale University Press, 1976.

Bury, J. B. *History of the Later Roman Empire from the Death of Theodosius I. to the Death of Justinian*. 2 vols. 1923. Reprint. New York: Dover, 1958.

———. "Justa Grata Honoria." *Journal of Roman Studies* 9 (1919): 1–13.

———. *The Life of St. Patrick and His Place in History*. 1905. Reprint. Freeport, N.Y.: Books for Libraries Press, 1971.

Butler, Alfred J. *The Ancient Coptic Churches of Egypt*. 2 vols. 1884. Reprint. Oxford: Clarendon Press, 1970.

Cabrol, Fernand, and Henri Leclercq. *Dictionnaire d'archéologie chrétienne et de liturgie*. Paris: Letouzey et Ané, 1907–. [Abbre. *DA*].

Caesar, Gaius Julius. *De bello gallico*. See John Warrington, ed. and trans.

Cagnat, René. *L'armée romaine d'Afrique et l'occupation militaire de l'Afrique sous les empereurs*. 1913. Reprint. New York: Arno Press, 1975.

Cambridge Ancient History. 12 vols. Cambridge: At the University Press, 1923–39. [Abbr. *CAH*].

Cambridge Medieval History. 8 vols. New York: Macmillan Co., 1911–36. [Abbr. *CMH*].

Cameron, Alan. *Claudian: Poetry and Propaganda at the Court of Honorius*. Oxford: Clarendon Press, 1970.

———. *Porphyrius the Charioteer*. Oxford: Clarendon Press, 1973.

———. "Rutilius Namatianus, St. Augustine, and the Date of *De reditu*." *Journal of Roman Studies* 57 (1967): 31–39.

Campenhausen, Hans von. *Ecclesiastical Authority and Spiritual Power in the Church in the First Three Centuries*. Stanford, Calif.: Stanford University Press, 1969.

———. *Tradition and Life in the Church*. London: Collins, 1968.

Carcopino, Jérôme. "À propos du poème de Rutilius Namatianus." *Revue des études latines* 6 (1928): 180–200.

Carney, James. *The Problem of St. Patrick*. Dublin: Dublin Institute for Advanced Studies, 1961.

Caspar, Erich. *Geschichte des Papsttums von den Anfängen bis zur Höhe der Weltherrschaft*. Vol. 1, *Römische Kirche und Imperium Romanum*. Tübingen: Mohr, 1930. Vol. 2, *Das Papsttum unter byzantinischer Herrschaft*. Tübingen: Mohr, 1933.

Caudel, M. *Les premières invasions arabes dans l'Afrique du Nord: l'Afrique du Nord, les byzantins, les berbers, les arabes avant les invasions*. Paris: Leroux, 1900.

Chadwick, Hector Munro. *Early Scotland: The Picts, the Scots, and the Welsh of Southern Scotland*. 1949. Reprint. New York: Octagon Books, 1974.

———, et al. *Studies in Early British History*. Cambridge: At the University Press, 1954.

Chadwick, Henry. *Priscillian of Avila: The Occult and the Charismatic in the Early Church*. Oxford: Clarendon Press, 1976.

Chadwick, Nora K. *The Celts*. Baltimore, Md.: Penguin Books, 1970.

———. *The Druids*. Cardiff: University of Wales Press, 1966.

———. *Early Brittany*. Cardiff: University of Wales Press, 1969.

———. "Intellectual Contacts Between Britain and Gaul in the Fifth Century." In Hector Munro Chadwick et al. *Studies in Early British History*, pp. 189–263. Cambridge: At the University Press, 1954.

———. *Poetry and Letters in Early Christian Gaul*. London: Bowes & Bowes, 1955.

Chadwick, Owen. *John Cassian*. Cambridge: At the University Press, 1968.

———. *Western Asceticism*. Philadelphia: Westminster Press, 1958.

Chapman, D. J. "Cassiodorus and the Echternach Gospels." *Revue bénédictine* 28 (1911): 283–92.

Charlesworth, Dorothy. *Hardknott Roman Fort*. London: Her Majesty's Stationery Office, 1972.

Charrière, G. "La femme et l'équidé dans la mythologie française." *Revue de l'histoire des religions* 188 (1975): 129–88.

Chastagnol, André. *La préfecture urbaine à Rome sous le Bas-Empire*. Publications de la Faculté des lettres et sciences humaines d'Alger, vol. 34. Paris: Presses universitaires de France, 1960.

———. *Le sénat romain sous le règne d'Odoacre: recherches sur l'épigraphie du colisée au Ve siècle*. Bonn: Habelt, 1966.

Chitty, Derwas J. *The Desert a City: An Introduction to the Study of Egyptian and Palestinian Monasticism Under the Christian Empire*. Oxford: Blackwell, 1966.

Christ, Karl. "Ergebnisse und Probleme der keltischen Numismatik und Geldgeschichte (Bericht 1935–1955)." *Historia* 6 (1957): 215–53.

Churchill, Sir Winston Spencer. *History of the English-speaking Peoples*. Vol. 1, *The Birth of Britain*. New York: Dodd, Mead, 1956.

Clover, Frank M. "The Family and Early Career of Anicius Olybrius." *Historia* 27 (1978): 169–96.

———. *Flavius Merobaudes: A Translation and Historical Commentary*. Transactions of the

American Philosophical Society, n.s. 61, pt. 1. Philadelphia, 1971.

Cochrane, Charles Norris. *Christianity and Classical Culture: A Study of Thought and Action from Augustus to Augustine*. London: Oxford University Press, 1944.

Colgrave, B., ed. *The Life of Bishop Wilfrid, by Eddius Stephanus*. Cambridge: At the University Press, 1927. [Abbr. Eddius Stephanus].

Collingwood, R. G., and J. N. L. Myres. *Roman Britain and the English Settlements*. 2d ed. Oxford: Clarendon Press, 1937.

Columban. *Opera*. See G. S. M. Walker, ed. and trans.

Conybeare, Frederick Cornwallis. "Asceticism." *Encyclopaedia Britannica*. 29 vols. Cambridge: At the University Press, 1911. 2:717–20.

Corbet, W. J. "England (to c. 800) and English Institutions." *CMH*, 2:543–74.

Coster, Charles Henry. "The Fall of Boethius: His Character." In his *Late Roman Studies*, pp. 54–103. Cambridge, Mass.: Harvard University Press, 1968.

Courcelle, Pierre. *Recherches sur les "Confessions" de saint Augustin*. Paris: Boccard, 1968.

———. *Recherches sur saint Ambroise: "vies" anciennes, culture, iconographie*. Paris: Études augustiniennes, 1973.

———. "Le site du monastère de Cassiodore." *Mélanges d'archéologie et d'histoire, École française de Rome* 55 (1938):259–307.

Courtois, Christian, et al. *Tablettes Albertini: actes privées de l'époque vandale (fin du Ve siècle)*. Paris: Arts et métiers graphiques, 1952.

———. *Les Vandales et l'Afrique*. Paris: Arts et metiers graphiques, 1955.

———. *Victor de Vita et son œuvre: étude critique*. Algiers: Imprimerie officielle du Gouvernement général de l'Algérie, 1954.

Cracco Ruggini, Lellia. "Apoteosi e politica senatoria nel IV S.D.C.: il dittico dei Symmachi al British Museum: *Rivista storica italiana* 89 (1977):425–89.

Cruden, Stewart. *The Early Christian and Pictish Monuments of Scotland: An Illustrated Introduction, with Illustrated and Descriptive Catalogues of the Meigle and St. Vigeans Collections*. Edinburgh: Her Majesty's Stationery Office, 1964.

Cumont, Franz. *Astrology and Religion Among the Greeks and Romans*. 1912. Reprint. New York: Dover, 1960.

Cyprian. *Opera*. See G. Hartel, ed.

Czúth, B. "Die Quellen der Geschichte der Bagauden (Anfänge des V. Jahrhunderts)." *Acta antiqua et archaeologica* 9 (1965):31–43.

Dalton, O. M., trans. *The History of the Franks by Gregory of Tours*. 2 vols. Oxford: Clarendon Press, 1927. [Abbr. Gregory of Tours]

D'Arms, John H. *Romans on the Bay of Naples: A Social and Cultural Study of the Villas and Their Owners from 150 B.C. to A.D. 400*. Cambridge, Mass.: Harvard University Press, 1970.

Daumas, E. *The Ways of the Desert*. 9th ed. Translated by Sheila M. Ohlendorf. Austin: University of Texas Press, 1971.

Deanesly, Margaret. *The Pre-Conquest Church in England*. London: Black, 1964.

———, and Paul Grosjean. "The Canterbury Edition of the Answers of Pope Gregory I to St. Augustine." *Journal of Ecclesiastical History* 10 (1959):1–49.

Deferrari, Roy J., trans. *Paulus Orosius: The Seven Books of History Against the Pagans*. Fathers of the Church, vol. 50. Washington, D.C.: Catholic University of America Press, 1964. [Abbr. Orosius]

Delauney, Ferdinand. *Moines et sibylles dans l'antiquité judéo-grecque*. 2d ed. Paris: Didier, 1874.

Delbrueck, Richard. *Die Consulardiptychen und verwandte Denkmäler*. 2 vols. Studien zur spätantiken Kunstgeschichte, vol. 2. Berlin: De Gruyter, 1929.

———. *Spätantike Kaiserporträts von Constantinus Magnus bis zum Ende des Westreichs*. Berlin: De Gruyter, 1933.

Delehaye, Hippolyte. *Les saints stylites*. Subsidia hagiographica, no. 14. Brussels: Société des Bollandistes, 1923.

Demandt, Alexander. "Der Tod des älteren Theodosius." *Historia* 18 (1969): 598–626.

————, and Guntram Brummer. "Der Prozess gegen Serena im Jahre 408 n. Chr." *Historia* 26 (1977): 479–502.

Demougeot, Émilienne. *De l'unité à la division de l'Empire romain, 395–410: essai sur le gouvernement impérial*. Paris: Librairie d'Amérique et d'Orient, 1951.

————. "Note sur la politique de Stilicon de 405 à 407." *Byzantion* 20 (1950): 27–37.

————. "Saint Jérôme, les oracles sibyllins, et Stilicon." *Revue des études anciennes* 54 (1952): 89–91.

————. Sur les lois du 15 novembre 407." *Revue historique de droit français et étranger* 28 (1950): 403–12.

de Paor, Máire, and Liam de Paor. *Early Christian Ireland*. Ancient Peoples and Places. New York: Praeger, 1958.

Desjardins, Ernest. *Géographie historique et administrative de la Gaule romaine*. 4 vols. 1876. Reprint. Brussels: Culture et civilisation, 1968.

Dewing, H. B., trans. *Procopius*. 7 vols. Loeb Classical Library. Cambridge, Mass.: Harvard University Press, 1953–62. [Abbr. Procopius]

Dictionary of Christian Biography, Literature, Sects, and Doctrines. Edited by William Smith and Henry Wace. 4 vols. London: Murray, 1877–87.

Diehl, Charles. *L'Afrique byzantine: histoire de la domination byzantine en Afrique, 533–709*. Paris: Leroux, 1896.

————. *Théodora, impératrice de Byzance*. Paris: Rey, 1904.

Diesner, Hans-Joachim. *Fulgentius von Ruspe also Theologe und Kirchenpolitiker*. Stuttgart: Calwer Verlag, 1966.

————. *Kirche und Staat im spätrömischen Reich*. Berlin: Evangelische Verlagsanstalt, 1963.

————. "Die Lage der nordafrikanischen Bevölkerung im Zeitpunkt der Vandaleninvasion." *Historia* 11 (1962): 97–111.

————. *Der Traum des Godas: Geschichtliches Bild aus der Vandalenzeit*. Leipzig: Roedler & Amelang, 1969.

Dill, Samuel. *Roman Society in Gaul in the Merovingian Age*. 1926. Reprint. New York: Barnes & Noble, 1966.

————. *Roman Society in the Last Century of the Western Empire*. 2d ed., rev. New York: Meridian Books, 1958.

Dopsch, Alfons. *The Economic and Social Foundations of European Civilization*. 1937. Reprint. New York: Fertig, 1969.

Downey, Glanville. "Coptic Culture in the Byzantine World: Nationalism and Religious Independence." *Greek and Byzantine Studies* 1 (1958): 119–35.

Dragendorff, H., and E. Krüger. *Das Grabmal von Igel*. Trier: Lintz, 1924.

Drew, Katherine Fischer. "The Barbarian Kings as Lawgivers and Judges." In Robert S. Hoyt, ed. *Life and Thought in the Early Middle Ages*, pp. 7–29. Minneapolis: University of Minnesota Press, 1967.

du Bourguet, Pierre. "Une découverte actuelle: l'art copte." In *L'art copte: Petit Palais Paris 17 juin 15 septembre 1964*, pp. 25–48. Paris: Ministère d'État affaires culturelles, 1964.

Duckett, Eleanor Shipley. "Wilfrid of York." In her *Anglo-Saxon Saints and Scholars*, pp. 101–214. New York: Macmillan Co., 1947.

Dudden, F. Homes. *Gregory the Great: His Place in History and Thought*. 2 vols. 1905. Reprint. New York: Russell & Russell, 1967.

————. *The Life and Times of St. Ambrose*. Oxford: Clarendon Press, 1935.

Dumas, Françoise. *Le tombeau de Childéric*. Paris: Bibliothèque nationale, 1976.

Dumoulin, Maurice. "Le gouvernement de Théodoric et la domination des Ostrogoths en Italie d'après les œvres d'Ennodius." *Revue historique* 78 (January–February 1902): 1–7; (March–April 1902): 241–65; 79 (1902): 1–22.

Dunleavy, Gareth W. *Colum's Other Island: The Irish at Lindisfarne.* Madison: University of Wisconsin Press, 1960.

Durant, G. M. *Britain: Rome's Most Northerly Province.* New York: St. Martin's Press, 1969.

Eadie, John W. "The Development of Roman Mailed Cavalry." *Journal of Roman Studies* 57 (1967): 161–73.

Eberhard, Wolfram. *Kultur und Siedlung der Randvölker Chinas.* T'oung pao: archives concernant l'histoire, les langues, la géographie, l'ethnographie et les arts de l'Asie orientale, supplement to vol. 36. Leiden: Brill, 1942.

Eddius Stephanus. *Life of Columba.* See B. Colgrave, ed.

Eggers, Hans-Jürgen, et al. *Kelten und Germanen in heidnischer Zeit.* Baden-Baden: Holle, 1964. [Abbr. Eggers et al., *Kelten*].

————. "Die Kunst der Germanen in der Eisenzeit." In Eggers et al., *Kelten*, pp. 5–91.

Ehrhardt, Arnold A. *The Apostolic Succession in the First Two Centuries of the Church.* London: Lutterworth Press, 1953.

————. "Cyprian, the Father of Western Christianity." *Church Quarterly Review* 113 (1943): 178–96.

Elliott, Ralph W. V. *Runes: An Introduction.* Manchester: University of Manchester Press, 1963.

Encyclopedia of Religion and Ethics. See James Hastings, ed.

Engelmann, Erika. "Zur Bewegung der Bagauden im römischen Gallien." In Hellmut Kretzchmer, ed. *Von Mittelalter zur Neuzeit, zum 65. Geburtstag von Heinrich Sproemberg*, pp. 373–85. Forschungen zur mittelalterlichen Geschichte, no. 1. Berlin: Rütton & Loening, 1956.

Ensslin, Wilhelm. "*Carpentum* oder *Carruca*? Bemerkungen zum Fahrrecht und Amtswagen im spätrömischen Reich und zum Versuch einer Datierung der *Historia Augusta.*" *Klio* 32 (1939): 89–105.

————. "The Court and Its Ceremonial: Dress and Insignia." *CAH*, 12: 361–67.

————. "Rex Theodericus inlitteratus?" *Historisches Jahrbuch* 60 (1940): 391–96.

————. *Theoderich der Grosse.* Munich: Münchner Verlag, 1947.

————. "Valentinianus. 4." *RE*, vol. 14, cols. 2232–59.

————. "Zum Heermeisteramt des spätrömischen Reiches." *Klio* 23 (1929): 306–25; 24 (1930–31): 102–47, 467–502.

Espérandieu, Émile. *Recueil général des bas-reliefs de la Gaule romaine.* Collection de documents inédits sur l'histoire de France. Paris: Imprimerie nationale, 1907–

Evans, Robert F. *Pelagius: Inquiries and Reappraisals.* New York: Seabury Press, 1968.

Evans, Sebastian, trans. *History of the Kings of Britain, by Geoffrey of Monmouth.* Revised by Charles W. Dunn. New York: Dutton, 1958. [Abbr. Geoffrey of Monmouth]

Evelyn-White, Hugh Gerard. *The Monasteries of the Wadi 'n Natrûn.* 3 vols. Publications of the Metropolitan Museum of Art Egyptian Expedition [2, 7–8]. New York, 1926–33.

Evetts, B. T. A. *The Churches and Monasteries of Egypt and Some Neighboring Countries*, attributed to Abû Ṣâliḥ the Armenian, with added notes by Alfred J. Butler. 1895. Reprint. London: Butler & Tanner, 1969.

Ewig, Eugen. "Dans le brouillard bourgonde et franc." *Annales de Bourgogne* 43 (1971): 103–105.

————. *Spätantikes und fränkisches Gallien*, Vol. 1, *Die fränkische Teilungen und Teilreiche (511–613).* Munich: Artemis Verlag, 1976.

Farmer, D. H. "Saint Wilfrid." In D. P. Kirby, ed. *Saint Wilfrid at Hexham*, pp. 35–59. Newcastle upon Tyne: Oriel Press, 1974.

Ferguson, John. *Pelagius: A Historical and Theological Study.* 1956. Reprint. New York: AMS Press, 1977.

Finley, M. I. *The Ancient Economy.* Sather Classical Lectures, vol. 43. Berkeley and Los Angeles: University of California Press, 1973.

Fliche, Augustin, and Victor Martin. *Histoire de l'Église depuis les origines jusqu'à nos jours.* Paris: Blond & Gay, 1934–.

Folz, Robert. *L'idée d'empire en occident du V' au XIV' siècle.* Aubier: Montaigne, 1953.

Fontaine, Jacques. *Isidore de Séville et la culture classique dans l'Espagne wisigothique.* 2 vols. Paris: Études augustiniennes, 1959.

————. *Vie de saint Martin {par} Sulpice Sévère.* 3 vols. Série de textes monastiques d'Occident, nos. 22–24. Sources chrétiennes, 133–35. Paris: Éditions du cerf, 1967–69.

Forbes, A. P., ed. *Remains of the Late Arthur West Haddan.* Oxford: Parker, 1876.

Förster, Else. "Katalog der frühchristlichen Abteilung des Rheinisches Landesmuseums Trier." In Reusch. *Frühchristliche Zeugnisse,* pp. 17–54.

Foulke, William Dudley, trans. *History of the Lombards {by} Paul the Deacon.* Sources of medieval history. Philadelphia: University of Pennsylvania Press, 1974. [Abbr. Paul the Deacon]

Fowler, W. Warde. *The Religious Experience of the Roman People from the Earliest Times to the Age of Augustus.* London: Macmillan & Co., 1911.

Frank, R. I. *Scholae Palatinae: The Palace Guards of the Later Roman Empire.* Papers and Monographs of the American Academy in Rome, vol. 23. Rome, 1969.

Frank, Tenney. *Economic Survey of Ancient Rome.* Baltimore, Md.: Johns Hopkins University Press, 1940.

Frazer, James George. *The Golden Bough: A Study in Magic and Religion.* Vols. 5–6, *Adonis, Attis, Osiris: Studies in the History of Oriental Religion.* 3d ed. 2 vols. 1914. Reprint. London: Macmillan & Co., 1927. Vols. 7–8, *Spirits of the Corn and of the Wild.* 3d ed. 2 vols. 1912. Reprint. London: Macmillan & Co., 1925.

Freeman, E. A. *Western Europe in the Fifth Century.* London: Macmillan & Co., 1904.

Fremantle, W. H., trans. *The Principal Works of St. Jerome.* Select Library of Nicene and Post-Nicene Fathers of the Christian Church, 2d ser., vol. 6. New York, 1893. [Abbr. Jerome *Ep.*]

Frend, W. H. C. "Ambrose of Milan and Theodosius 381–95." In his *The Early Church,* pp. 190–99. Philadelphia: Lippincott, 1966.

————. *The Donatist Church: A Movement of Protest in Roman North Africa.* 1952. Reprint. Oxford: Clarendon Press, 1971.

From the Lands of the Scythians: Ancient Treasures from the Museums of the U.S.S.R., 3000 B.C.–100 B.C. Metropolitan Museum of Art Bulletin 32, no. 5 (1973–74). Reprint. New York, 1975.

Fuchs, Harald. *Der geistige Widerstand gegen Rom in der antiken Welt.* Berlin: De Gruyter, 1938.

Fuhrmann, Manfred. "Die Romidee der Spätantike." *Historische Zeitschrift* 207 (1968): 529–61.

Gand, abbé. "Deux hommes face à face: Aëtius et Attila." *Bulletin trimestriel de la Société archéologique et historique de l'Orléanais* n.s. 3 (1963): 36–39.

Garmonsway, G. N., ed. and trans. *The Anglo-Saxon Chronicle.* New York: Dutton, 1975. [Abbr. *The Anglo-Saxon Chronicle*]

Gayet, Albert Jean. *L'art copte.* Paris: Leroux, 1902.

Geffcken, Johannes. *Der Ausgang der griechisch-römischen Heidentums.* Heidelberg: Winter, 1920.

————. *The Last Days of Greco-Roman Paganism.* Translated by Sabine MacCormack. Rev. ed. 1929. Reprint. Amsterdam: North-Holland, 1978.

Geoffrey of Monmouth. *History of the Kings of England*. See Sebastian Evans, trans.

Gerontius. *Vita s. Melaniae Iunioris*. See Denys Gorce, trans.

Ghirshman, Roman. "Persian Art in Parthian and Sassanian Times." *Larousse Encyclopedia of Byzantine and Medieval Art*, pp. 47–64. Feltham: Hamlyn, 1968.

Gibbon, Edward. *The Decline and Fall of the Roman Empire*. Edited by Oliphant Smeaton. 3 vols. New York: Modern Library, n.d.

Gilbert, Edward. "Saint Wilfrid's Church at Hexham." In D. P. Kirby, ed. *Saint Wilfrid at Hexham*, pp. 81–113. Newcastle upon Tyne: Oriel Press, 1974.

Godley, A. D., trans. *Herodotus*. 4 vols. Loeb Classical Library. London: Heinemann, 1921–24.

Goltzius, Hubert. *Thesavrvs rei antiqvasiae hvberrimva*. Antwerp, 1618.

Goodenough, Erwin R. *The Politics of Philo Judaeus: Practice and Theory*. Hildesheim: Olm, 1967.

Gorce, Denys, trans. *Vie de sainte Mélanie {Gerontius}: texte grec, introduction, traduction et notes*. Sources chrétiennes, no. 90. Paris: Éditions du cerf, 1962.

Gorce, M. M. *Clovis, 465–511*. Paris: Payot, 1935.

Görres, Franz. "Die vermeintliche germanische (vandalische) Abstammung einer überaus zahlreichen nordafrikanischen Vervölkerung." *Historisches Jahrbuch* 32 (1911): 323–32.

Grant, Michael. *The Climax of Rome*. New York: New American Library, 1968.

Graves, Robert, trans. *Lucan: Pharsalia: Dramatic Episodes of the Civil Wars*. Penguin Classics, no. 166. Baltimore, Md.: Penguin Books, 1957.

Gray, Patrick T. R. *The Defense of Chalcedon in the East (451–553)*. Studies in the History of Christian Thought, vol. 20. Leiden: Brill, 1979.

Gregory of Tours. *History of the Franks*. See O. M. Dalton, trans.

Gregory the Great. *Epistolae*. In Philip Schaff and Henry Wace, ed. *A Select Library of the Nicene and Post-Nicene Fathers*. 2d ser. 14 vols. New York, Christian Literature Co., 1890–1900. Vol. 12, 1895. [Abbr. Gregory the Great *Ep.*]

Grenier, Albert. *Les gaulois*. Paris: Payot, 1970.

———. "Le sanctuaire de l'Altbachtal." In *Manuel d'archéologie gallo-romaine*, pt. 4, pp. 857–74. Paris: Picard, 1960.

Griffe, Élie. *La Gaule chrétienne à l'époque romaine. 2. L'Église des Gaules au Vᵉ siècle*. New ed., rev. Paris: Letouzey et Ané, 1966.

Grosjean, Paul. "S. Patrice à Auxerre sous S. Germain: Le témoignage des noms gaulois. Notes d'hagiographie celtique, 27." *Analecta Bollandiana* 75 (1957): 158–74.

———. "La seconde visite de S. Germain d'Auxerre en Grande-Bretagne." Notes d'hagiographie celtique, 28." *Analecta Bollandiana* 75 (1957): 174–80.

Grosse, Robert. *Römische Militärgeschichte von Gallienus bis zum Beginn der byzantinischen Themenverlassung*. Berlin: Weidmann, 1920. Reprint. New York: Arno, 1975.

Gsell, Stéphane. *Histoire ancienne de l'Afrique du Nord*. 8 vols. Pairs: Hachette, 1913–28.

Guilhiermoz, P. *Essai sur l'origine de la noblesse en France au Moyen Âge*. 1902. Reprint. New York: Franklin, 1960.

Guillaumont, Antoine. "Philon et les origines du monachisme." In *Philon d'Alexandrie, Lyon 11–15 septembre 1966*, pp. 361–73. Colloques nationaux du Centre national de la recherche scientifique. Paris: Éditions du Centre national de la recherche scientifique, 1967.

Güldenpenning, Albert. *Geschichte des oströmischen Reiches unter den Kaisern Arcadius und Theodosius II*. Halle: Niemeyer, 1885.

Gwatkin, Henry Melvill. "Constantine and His City." *CMH*, 1: 1–23.

———. *Early Church History to A.D. 313*. 2 vols. London: Macmillan & Co., 1909.

Hadas, Moses, ed. *A History of Rome from its Origins to 529 A.D. as Told by the Roman Historians*.

Garden City, N.Y.: Doubleday, Anchor Books, 1956.

Haddan, Arthur West, and William Stubbs, eds. *Councils and Ecclesiastical Documents Relating to Great Britain and Ireland.* 3 vols. 1869–78. Reprint. Oxford: Clarendon Press, 1964.

Hamblen, Louis. *Attila et les Huns.* Paris: Presses universitaires de France, 1972.

Hanson, Richard Patrick Cresland. *Saint Patrick: His Origins and Career.* Oxford: Clarendon Press, 1968.

Harnack, Adolf. *History of Dogma.* 3d ed. Translated by Neil Buchanan. 1900. 7 vols. in 4. Reprint. New York: Dover, 1961.

———. *The Mission and Expansion of Christianity in the First Three Centuries.* Translated and edited by James Moffatt. 1908. Reprint. Gloucester, Mass.: Smith, 1972.

Hartel, G., ed. *Acta Proconsularis Cypriani. Opera. cx sqq.* In *Transactions and Reprints from the Original Sources of European History,* vol. 4. 1897. Reprint. New York: AMS Press, 1971.

Hartke, Werner. *Römische Kinderkaiser: eine Strukturanalyse römischen Denkens und Daseins.* Berlin: Akademie-Verlag, 1951.

Hartmann, Ludo Moritz. *Geschichte Italiens im Mittelalter,* Vol. 2, pt. 1, *Römer und Langobarden bis zum Teilung Italiens.* 1900. Reprint. Hildesheim, Olm: 1969.

Hastings, James, ed. *Encyclopedia of Religion and Ethics.* 13 vols. New York: Scribner, 1924–27.

Hatt, Jean-Jacques. *Kelten und Galloromanen.* Translated by G. Schecher. Munich: Nagel, 1970.

Helbing, Hanno. *Goten und Wandalen.* Zurich: Fretz & Wasmuth, 1954.

Henderson, Isabel. *The Picts.* Ancient Peoples and Places, vol. 54. New York: Praeger, 1967.

Hengel, Martin. *Property and Riches in the Early Church: Aspects of a Social History of Early Christianity.* Translated by John Bowden. Philadelphia: Fortress Press, 1974.

Hermansen, G. "The Population of Imperial Rome: The Regionaries." *Historia* 27 (1978): 129–68.

Herodotus. *History.* See A. D. Godley, trans.

Heussi, Karl. *Der Ursprung des Mönchtums.* Tübingen: Mohr, 1936.

Hillgarth, J. N. "Visigothic Spain and Early Christian Ireland." *Proceedings of the Royal Irish Academy,* vol. 62, sec. C, no. 6 (1962): 167–94.

Hoare, Frederick Russell, trans. *The Western Fathers: Being the Lives of SS. Martin of Tours, Ambrose, Augustine of Hippo, Honoratus of Arles, and Germanus of Auxerre.* The Makers of Christendom. New York: Sheed and Ward, 1954. [Abbr. Sulpicius Severus *Dialogues*; Sulpicius Severus, *Life of Martin*]

Hodgkin, Thomas. *The Dynasty of Theodosius; or, Eighty Years' Struggle With the Barbarians.* Oxford: Clarendon Press, 1889.

———. *Italy and Her Invaders.* Vol. 4, bk. 5, *The Imperial Restoration.* Reprint. New York: Russell & Russell, 1967. Vol. 6, *The Lombard Kingdom, 600–744.* Oxford: Clarendon Press, 1895.

———. *Theodoric the Goth: The Barbarian Champion of Civilisation.* New York: Putnam, 1897.

Hoepffner, A. "La mort du 'magister militvm' Théodose." *Revue des études latines* 14 (1936): 119–29.

Homeyer, Helene. *Attila der Hunnenkönig von seinen Zeitgenossen dargestellt.* Berlin: De Gruyter, 1951.

Hopkins, M. K. "Elite Mobility in the Roman Empire." *Past and Present* 32 (1965): 12–26.

———. "Social Mobility in the Later Roman Empire: The Evidence of Ausonius." *Classical Quarterly,* n.s. 11 (1961): 239–49.

Hoyoux, Jean. "Le collier de Clovis." *Revue belge de philologie et d'histoire* 21 (1942): 169–74.

Hug. "Stuhl." *RE,* 2d ser., vol. 4, cols. 398–422.

Hughes, Kathleen. *The Church in Early Irish Society.* Ithaca, N.Y.: Cornell University Press, 1966.

Hull, Eleanor. *Folklore of the British Isles*. London: Methuen, 1928.

Hunt, E. D. "From Dalmatia to the Holy Land: Jerome and the World of Late Antiquity" [Review of J. N. D. Kelly. *Jerome: His Life, Writings, and Controversies*. London: Duckworth, 1975]. *Journal of Roman Studies* 67 (1977): 166–71.

Hutchinson, R. W. *Prehistoric Crete*. Baltimore, Md.: Penguin Books, 1963.

Ihm, Max. "Der Mutter- oder Matronenkultus und seine Denkmäler." *Jahrbücher des Vereins von Alterthumsfreunden im Rheinlande* 83 (1887): 8–200.

Irish Litanies. See Charles Plummer, trans. and ed.

Isidore of Seville. *Historia Gothorvm Wandalorvm Sveborvm ad a. DCXXIV*. In Monumenta Germaniae historica inde ab anno Christo quintesimo usque ad annum millesimum et quingentisimum. Auctorum antiquissimorum, vol. 11, pt. 2. Berlin: Weidmann, 1894.

Jacobsthal, Paul. *Early Etruscan Art*. Oxford: Clarendon Press, 1944.

Jager, abbé [Jean Nicolas]. *Histoire de l'Église catholique en France d'après les documents les plus authentiques depuis son origine jusqu'au concordat de Pie VII*. 21 vols. Paris: Le Clere, 1862–76.

Jalland, Trevor. *The Life and Times of St. Leo the Great*. London: Society for the Promotion of Christian Knowledge, 1941.

Jerome. *Opera*. See W. H. Fremantle, trans.

Joffroy, René. "Die Kunst der Kelten." In Eggers et al., *Kelten*, pp. 125–48.

Johnson, Stephen. *The Roman Forts of the Saxon Shore*. London: Elek, 1976.

Jones, A. H. M. "The Constitutional Position of Odoacer and Theoderic." *Journal of Roman Studies* 52 (1962): 126–30.

———. *The Decline of the Ancient World*. A General History of Europe. New York: Holt, Rinehart and Winston, 1966.

———. *The Later Roman Empire, 284–602: A Social, Economic, and Administrative Survey*. 2 vols. Norman: University of Oklahoma Press, 1964.

———. "Were Ancient Heresies National or Social Movements in Disguise?" *Journal of Theological Studies*, n.s. 10 (1959): 280–97.

———, et al. *The Prosopography of the Later Roman Empire*. Cambridge: At the University Press, 1971–.

Jordanes. *Getica*. See Charles Christopher Mierow, trans.

Josephus, Flavius. *Jewish Antiquities*. See H. St. J. Thackeray et al., trans.

Julian. *Opera*. See Wilmer Cave Wright, trans.

Jullian, Camille. *Histoire de la Gaule*. Vol. 7, *Les empereurs de Trèves*. Paris: Hachette, 1926.

Kaegi, W. "Arianism and the Byzantine Army in Africa, 533–546." *Traditio* 21 (1965): 23–53.

Kaiser, Reinhold. *Untersuchungen zur Geschichte der Civitas und Diozese Soissons in römischer und merowingischer Zeit*. Rheinischer Archiv, no. 89. Bonn: Röhrscheid, 1973.

Kaniecka, Mary Simplicia, trans. *Vita Sancti Ambrosii Mediolanensis Episcopi a Paulino eius notario ad beatum Augustinum conscripta*. Rev. text. Catholic University of America Patristic Studies, vol. 26. Washington, D.C.: Catholic University of America, 1928. [Abbr. Paulinus]

Kelly, J. N. D. *Early Christian Doctrines*. 2d ed. New York: Harper & Row, 1960.

———. *Jerome: His Life, Writings, and Controversies*. London: Duckworth, 1975.

Kempf, Theodor K. "Katalog der frühchristlichen Abteilung des Bischöflichen Museums Trier." In Reusch, *Frühchristliche Zeugnisse*, pp. 175–235.

Kermode, P. M. C. *The Manx Archaeological Survey*. Douglas, Isle of Man: Manx Museum and National Trust, 1968.

Kiev, Ari. "Psychiatric Disorders in Minority Groups." In Peter Watson, ed. *Psychology and Race*, pp. 416–31.

Kirby, D. P., ed. *Saint Wilfrid at Hexham*. Newcastle upon Tyne: Oriel Press, 1974.

———. "Vortigern." *Bulletin of the Board of Celtic Studies* 23 (1968): 37–59.

Kisa, Anton. *Das Glas im Altertume*. Leipzig: Hiersemann, 1908.

Klaeber, F. "Attila's and Beowulf's Funeral." *PMLA* 42 (1927): 255–67.

Klein, Richard. *Symmachus: eine tragische Gestalt des ausgehenden Heidentums*. Impulse der Forschung, vol. 2. Darmstadt: Wissenschaftliche Buchgesellschaft, 1971.

Klindt-Jensen, Ole. "The Gundestrup Bowl: A Reassessment." *Antiquity* 33 (1959): 161–69.

Knipfing, John R. "The *Libelli* of the Decian Persecution." *Harvard Theological Review* 16 (1923): 345–90.

Knox, R. A. *Enthusiasm: A Chapter in the Hisotry of Religion, with Special Reference to the XVII and XVIII Centuries*. New York: Oxford University Press, 1950.

Kohns, Hans Peter. *Versorgungskrisen und Hungerrevolten im spätantiken Rom*. Antiquitas, 1st ser., vol. 6. Bonn: Habelt, 1961.

Kurth, Godefroid. *Clovis*. Tours: Mame, 1897.

———. "La reine Brunehaut." In *Études franques*. 2 vols. Vol. 1, pp. 265–356. Paris: Champion, 1919.

Labriolle, Pierre de. *La réaction païenne: étude sur le polémique antichrétienne du Ier au VIe siècle*. Paris: Artisan du livre, 1941.

Lacombrade, Ch. "Synésios et l'énigme du loup." *Revue des études anciennes* 48 (1946): 260–66.

Ladner, Gerhart B. "The Impact of Christianity." In Lynn White, Jr., ed. *The Transformation of the Roman World: Gibbon's Problem After Two Centuries*, pp. 59–91. Berkeley and Los Angeles: University of California Press, 1973.

Laing, Lloyd. *Orkney and Shetland: An Archaeological Guide*. London: David & Charles, 1974.

Lambrechts, Pierre. *Contributions à l'étude des divinités celtiques*. Rijksuniversiteit te Gent. Werken uitgegeven door de Faculteit van de wijsbegeerte en letteren, no. 93. Bruges: De Tempel, 1942.

———. *Exaltation de la tête dans la pensée et dans l'art des celtes*. Dissertationes archaeologicae Gandenses, vol. 2. Bruges: De Tempel, 1954.

Lapèyre, G. G. and A. Pellegrin. *Carthage latine et chrétienne*. Paris: Payot, 1950.

Laufenberg, Heinrich. *Der historische Wert des Panegyricus des Bischofs Ennodius*. Inaugural-Dissertation Rostock. Rostock, 1902.

Le Bras, Gabriel. "Introduction." In *Saint Germain d'Auxerre et son temps*, pp. xiii–xxv. Auxerre: L'Universel, 1950.

Leclant, J. "Osiris en Gaule." *Studia Aegyptica* 1 (1974): 263–85.

Leclerq, Henri. "Bretagne (Grande)." *DA*, vol. 2, pt. 1, cols. 1191–92.

———. "Cénobitisme. III. Monachisme juif. 2. Thérapeutes." *DA*, vol. 2, pt. 2, cols. 3063–75.

———. "Colonies d'Orientaux en Occident." *DA*, vol. 3, pt. 2, cols. 2266–77.

———. "Léon Ier." *DA*, vol. 8, pt. 2, cols. 2532–38.

———. "Négoce." *DA*, vol. 12, pt. 1, cols. 1082–87.

Le Gentilhomme, P. "Le désastre d'Autun en 269." *Revue des études anciennes* 45 (1943): 233–39.

Lehner, Hans. "Orientalische Mysterien-Kulte im römischen Rheinland." *Bonner Jahrbücher* 129 (1924): 36–91.

Leicher, R. *Die Totenklage in der deutschen Epik von der ältesten Zeit bis zur Nibelungenklage*. Germanistische Abhandlungen, vol. 58. Breslau: Marcus, 1927.

Le Lannou, Maurice. *Pâtres et paysans de la Sardaigne*. Tours: Arrault, 1941.

Lelong, Charles. *La vie quotidienne en Gaule à l'époque mérovingien*. Paris: Hachette, 1963.

Lepelley, Claude, and Brigitte Beaujard. "Du nouveau sur les villes de l'Afrique romaine au temps de saint Augustin." *Revue des études augustiniennes* 23 (1977): 422–31.

Lethbridge, T. C. *Herdsmen and Hermits: Celtic Seafarers in the Northern Seas*. Cambridge: Bowes & Bowes, 1950.

Levine, Philip. "The Continuity and Preservation of the Latin Traditon." In Lynn White, Jr., ed. The *Transformation of the Roman World: Gibbon's Problem after Two Centuries*, pp. 206–31. Berkeley and Los Angeles: University of California Press, 1973.

Lexikon für Theologie und Kirche. 2d ed. 10 vols. Freiburg im Breisgau: Herder, 1930–38.

Libanius. *Julianic Orations*. See A. F. Norman, trans.

Life of Saint Melania. See Denys Gorce, trans.

Lilliu, Giovanni. "The Nuraghi of Sardinia." *Antiquity* 33 (1959): 32–38.

Lindqvist, Sune. "Heruler och Daner." *Tor: Meddelanden från Uppsala universitets museum för nordiske fornsaker* 9 (1963): 123–39.

Llewellyn, Peter. *Rome in the Dark Ages*. London: Faber and Faber, 1971.

Loofs, Friedrich. *Das Leben und die polemischen Werke des Leontius von Byzanz*. Leipzig: Hinrich, 1887.

Lopez, Robert Sabatino. "Silk Industry in the Byzantine Empire." *Speculum* 20 (1945): 1–42.

L'Orange, Hans Peter. *Romerske kaiser in marmor og bronse*. Oslo: Dreyer, 1967.

Loubo-Lesnitchenko, E. "Imported Mirrors in the Minusinsk Basin." *Artibus Asiae* 35 (1973): 25–61.

Loyen, André. *Sidoine Apollinaire et l'esprit précieux en Gaule aux derniers jours de l'Empire*. Paris: Société des études latines, 1943.

Lucan. *Pharsalia*. See Robert Graves, trans.

McGeachy, John Alexander. "Quintus Aurelius Symmachus and the Senatorial Aristocracy of the West." Ph.D. dissertation, University of Chicago, 1942.

MacKendrick, Paul. *The North African Stones Speak*. Chapel Hill: University of North Carolina Press, 1979.

———. *Romans on the Rhine: Archaeology in Germany*. New York: Funk and Wagnalls, 1970.

Mackie, Euan. "The Origin and Development of the Broch and Wheelhouse Building Cultures of the Scottish Iron Age." *Proceedings of the Prehistoric Society*, n.s. 31 (1965): 93–146.

MacMullen, Ramsay. *Enemies of the Roman Order: Treason, Unrest, and Alienation in the Empire*. Cambridge, Mass.: Harvard University Press, 1966.

———. "Roman Bureaucratese." *Traditio* 18 (1962): 364–78.

McNally, Robert E. "St. Patrick, 461–1961." *Catholic Historical Review* 47 (1961): 305–24.

McNeill, John T. *The Celtic Churches: A History, A.D. 200 to 1200*. Chicago: University of Chicago Press, 1974.

MacNeill, William Hardy. *Plagues and Peoples*. Chicago: University of Chicago Press, 1976.

MacNiocaill, Gearóid. *Ireland Before the Vikings*. Gill History of Ireland, vol. 1. Dublin: Gill and MacMillan, 1972.

McSorley, Joseph. *An Outline History of the Church by Centuries (from St. Peter to Pius XII)*. St. Louis, Mo.: Herder, 1946.

Maenchen-Helfen, J. Otto. *The World of the Huns: Studies in Their History and Culture*. Edited by Max Knight. Berkeley and Los Angeles: University of California Press, 1973. [Abbr. Maenchen-Helfen]

Magnen, René. *Épona, déesse gauloise des chevaux, protectrice des cavaliers*. Bordeaux: Delmas, 1953.

Mamertinus. *Panegyric to Maximian*. [Extract] In Moses Hadas, ed., *A History of Rome from Its Origins to 529 A.D. as Told by the Roman Historians*. Garden City, N.Y.: Doubleday, Anchor Books, 1956, p. 176.

Marec, Erwan. "Les ruines d'Hippone et la Numidie de saint Augustin." *Algeria* 29, n.s. 61 (1961): 5–10.

Marquardt, Joachim. *Das Privatleben der Römer.* Edited by A. Mau. 2d ed. 2 vols. Leipzig: Hirzel, 1886.

Martroye, F. "Une tentative de révolution sociale en Afrique." *Revue des questions historiques* 76 (1904): 353–416; 77 (1905): 1–53.

Marwick, Hugh. *Ancient Monuments in Orkney.* Edinburgh: H.M. Stationery Office, 1952.

Marx, A. "Les racines du célibat essenien." *Revue de Qumrân* 7 (1970): 323–42.

Matthews, John. "Olympiodorus of Thebes and the History of the West (A.D. 407–425)." *Journal of Roman Studies* 60 (1970): 83–92.

———. *Western Aristocracies and Imperial Court, A.D. 364–425.* Oxford: Clarendon Press, 1975.

Mattingly, H[arold], trans. *Tacitus: The Agricola and the Germania.* Revised by S. A. Hanford. Harmondsworth: Penguin Books, 1970. [Abbr. Tacitus *Agricola*; Tacitus *Germania*]

———. C. H. V. Sutherland, and R. A. G. Carson, eds. *The Roman Imperial Coinage.* Vol. 9. J. W. E. Pearce. *Valentinian I–Theodosius I.* London: Spink & Sons, 1933. Reprint, 1972.

Maxey, Mima. *Occupations of the Lower Classes in Roman Society.* Chicago: University of Chicago Press, 1938.

Megaw, Vincent. "The Shape-Changers: Art of the Iron Age Celts." *Archaeology* 31 (1978): 30–43.

Meinardus, Otto F. A. *Christian Egypt: Faith and Life.* Cairo: American University in Cairo Press, 1970.

Merobaudes, Fl. *Panegyrics.* See Frank M. Clover, trans.

Meyer, Robert T., trans. *Palladius: The Lausiac History.* Ancient Christian Writers, no. 34. Westminster, Md.: Newman Press, 1965. [Abbr. Palladius]

Mierow, Charles Christopher, trans. *The Gothic History of Jordanes.* 2d ed. 1915. Reprint. Cambridge: Speculum historiale, 1966. [Abbr. Jordanes]

Millar, Fergus. [Review of W. H. C. Frend. *Martyrdom and Persecution in the Early Church.* Oxford: Blackwell, 1965]. *Journal of Roman Studies* 56 (1966): 231–36.

Miller, J. Innes. *The Spice Trade of the Roman Empire, 29 B.C.–A.D. 641.* Oxford: Clarendon Press, 1969.

Moffatt, James. "Therapeutae." In James Hastings, ed. *Encyclopedia of Religion and Ethics.* 13 vols. New York: Scribner, 1924–27, 12:315–19.

Momigliano, Arnaldo. "Per la interpretatazione di Simmaco *Relatio* 4." In *Rendiconti, Accademia dei Lincei, Classe di scienze morali, storiche e filologiche*, 8th ser., 19 (1964): 225–30.

Mommsen, Theodor. "Aëtius." In *Historische Schriften.* 3 vols. *Gesammelte Schriften*, vols. 4–6. Berlin: Weidmann, 1906–10. 1:531–60.

———. *Gesammelte Schriften.* 8 vols. Berlin: Weidmann, 1905–13.

Monceaux, Paul. *Histoire littéraire de l'Afrique chrétienne depuis les origines jusqu'à l'invasion arabe*, Vol. 4, *Le Donatisme.* Paris: Leroux, 1912.

Morazzani, André. "Essai sur la puissance maritime des Vandales." *Bulletin de l'Association Guillaume Budé*, 4th ser., 25 (1966): 539–61.

Moreau, Madeleine. *Le dossier Marcellinus dans la correspondance to saint Augustin.* Paris: Études augustiniennes, 1973.

Morey, C. R. "East Christian Paintings in the Freer Collection." *University of Michigan Studies, Humanistic Series* 12 (1918): 63–81.

Morris, John. "Dark Ages Dates." In Michael E. Jarrett and Brian Dobson, eds. *Britain and Rome: Essays Presented to Eric Birley on His Sixtieth Birthday*, pp. 145–85. Kendal: Wilson, 1966.

———. "Pelagian Literature." *Journal of Theological Studies*, n.s. 16 (1965): 26–60.

Moss, H. St. L. B. *The Birth of the Middle Ages, 395–814.* Oxford: Clarendon Press, 1935.

Moss, J. R. "The Effects of the Policies of Aëtius on the History of Western Europe." *Historia*

22 (1973):711–31.

Munz, Peter. "John Cassian." *Journal of Ecclesiastical History* 11 (1960):1–22.

Myres, J. N. L. "Pelagius and the End of Roman Rule in Britain." *Journal of Roman Studies* 50 (1960):21–36.

Nagl, Assunta. "Odoacer." *RE*, vol. 17, cols. 1888–96.

Neuberg, Frederic. "Glass." In *Encyclopedia of World Art*. 15 vols. New York, McGraw-Hill, 1959–68. 6:370–71.

Nischer-Falkenhof, Ernst. *Stilicho*. Vienna: Seidel, 1947.

Norman, A. F. *Libanius: Selected Works*. Vol. 3, *The Julianic Orations*. Loeb Classical Library. Cambridge, Mass.: Harvard University Press, 1969. [Abbr. Libanius *Julianic Orations*]

Olmsted, Garrett S. *The Gundestrup Cauldron: Its Archaeological Context, the Style, and Iconography of Its Portrayed Motifs, and Their Narration of a Gaulish Version of Táin Bó Cúailnge.* Collection Latomus, vol. 162. Brussels: Revue d'études latines, 1979.

Oost, Stewart Irvin. *Galla Placidia Augusta: A Biographical Essay.* Chicago: University of Chicago Press, 1968.

Orosius. *Hisoriarum libri adversus Paganos*. See Roy J. Deferrari, trans.

Packer, James E. *The Insulae of Imperial Rome*. Memoirs of the American Academy in Rome, vol. 31. Rome, 1971.

Palanque, Jean-Rémy. *Saint Ambroise et l'Empire romain: contributions à l'histoire des rapports de l'Église et de l'État à la fin du quatrième siècle*. Paris: Boccard, 1933.

Palladius. *Historia Lausiaca*. See Robert T. Meyer, trans.

Paredi, Angelo. Saint Ambrose: His Life and Times. Notre Dame, Ind.: University of Notre Dame Press, 1964.

Parsons, Sister Wilfrid, trans. *Saint Augustine: Letters.* 5 vols. Writings of Saint Augustine, vols. 9–13. Fathers of the Church, vols. 12, 18, 20, 30, 32. Washington, D.C.: Catholic University of America Press, 1951–56.

Paschoud, François. *Cinq études sur Zosime*. Paris: Les belles lettres, 1975.

Paul the Deacon. *De gestis Langobardorum*. See William Dudley Foulke, trans.

Paulinus. *Vita sancti Ambrosii Mediolanensis episcopi*. See Mary Simplicia Kaniecka, trans.

Paulys Real-Encyclopädie der classischen Altertumswissenschaft. Edited by G. Wissowa. Stuttgart, 1894–. [Abbr. *RE*]

Pékary, Thomas. *Untersuchungen zu den römischen Reichsstrassen*. Bonn: Habelt, 1968.

Penna, Angelo. "La sibilla tiburtina e le nove età del mondo." *Atti e memorie della società tiburtina di storia e d'arte* 45 (1972):7–95.

Perkins, J. B. Ward. "The Sculpture of Visigothic France." *Archaeologia* 87 (1936):79–128.

Perrin, Odet. *Les Burgondes, leur histoire des origines à la fin du 1ᵉʳ royaume (534): Contribution à l'histoire des invasions*. Neuchâtel: Éditions de la Baconière, 1968.

Petersen, Theodore C. "Early Islamic Bookbindings and Their Coptic Relations." *Ars Orientalis* 1 (1954):40–64.

Petrie, George. *The Ecclesiastical Architecture of Ireland: An Essay on the Origin and Uses of the Round Towers of Ireland.* 2d ed. 1845. Shannon: Irish University Press, 1970.

Pfeiffer, Homer F. "The Roman Library at Timgad." *Memoirs of the American Academy in Rome* 9 (1931):157–65.

Pfister, Christian. "Gaul under the Merovingian Franks." *CMH*, 2:109–58.

Pflaum, H.-G. *Essai sur le cursus publicus sous le Haut-Empire romain*. Mémoires présentés par divers savants à l'Académie des inscriptions et belles-lettres de l'Institut de France, vol. 14, pt. 1. Paris, 1940.

Phillips, E. D. *The Royal Hordes: Nomad Peoples of the Steppes*. New York: McGraw-Hill, 1965.

Picotti, G. B. "Sulle relazioni fra re Odoacre e il senato e la chiesa di Roma." *Rivista storica italiana*, 5th ser., 4 (1939):363–86.

Plinval, Georges de. *Pélage: ses écrits, sa vie, et sa réforme.* Lausanne: Payot, 1943.

Plummer, Charles, trans. and ed. *Irish Litanies.* Henry Bradshaw Society [Publications], vol. 62. London, 1925.

Pobé, Marcel. *The Art of Roman Gaul: A Thousand Years of Celtic Art and Culture.* Photography by Jean Roubier. Toronto: University of Toronto Press, 1961.

Porter, Arthur Kingsley. *The Crosses and Culture of Ireland.* New Haven, Conn.: Yale University Press, 1931.

Possidius. *Sancti Augustini vita.* See Herbert T. Weiskotten, trans.

Prestige, G. L. *Fathers and Heretics: Six Studies in Dogmatic Faith, with Prologue and Epilogue.* Bampton Lectures for 1940. London: Society for the Promotion of Christian Knowledge, 1968.

Prinz, Friedrich. *Frühes Mönchtum im Frankenreich.* Munich: Oldenbourg, 1965.

Procopius of Caesarea. *History of the Wars.* See H. B. Dewing, trans.

Puig i Cadafalch, J. *L'art wisigothique et ses survivances.* Paris: De Nobele, 1961.

Ralegh Radford, C. A. "The Early Church in Strathclyde and Galloway." *Medieval Archaeology* 11 (1967): 105-26.

————. "Two Scottish Shrines: Jedburgh and Saint Andrews." *Archaeological Journal* 112 (1955): 43-60.

Ramsay, A. M. "The Speed of the Roman Imperial Post." *Journal of Roman Studies* 15 (1925): 60-74.

Raspi, Raimondo Carta. *Storia della Sardegna.* Milan: Mursia, 1971.

Rausing, Gad. *The Bow: Some Notes on Its Origin and Development.* Acta archaeologica lundense, ser. in 8°, no. 6. Lund, 1967.

Raymond, Irving Woodworth. *The Teaching of the Early Church on the Use of Wine and Strong Drink.* 1927. Reprint. New York: AMS Press, 1970.

Regemorter, Berthe van. "La reliure des manuscrits de s. Cuthbert et de s. Boniface." *Scriptorium* 3 (1949): 45-51.

Reusch, Wilhelm, ed. *Frühchristliche Zeugnisse im Einzugsgebiet von Rhein und Mosel.* Trier, 1965. [Abbr. Reusch, *Frühchristliche Zeugnisse*]

Reynolds, Robert I., and Robert Sabatino Lopez. "Odoacer: German or Hun?" *American Historical Review* 52 (1946-47): 36-53.

Rhŷs, John. *Celtic Folklore, Welsh and Manx.* 2 vols. Oxford: Clarendon Press, 1901.

Rice, David Talbot. *A Concise History of Painting from Prehistory to the Thirteenth Century.* Praeger World of Art Series. New York: 1968.

Richardson, James S. *The Medieval Stone Carver in Scotland.* Edinburgh: University Press, 1964.

Riesman, David. "The Ethics of 'We Happy Few.'" In his *Individualism Reconsidered and Other Essays.* New York: Free Press, 1954.

Rist, John M. "Augustine on Free Will and Predestination." In R. A. Markus, ed. *Augustine: A Collection of Critical Essays,* pp. 218-52. Modern Studies in Philosophy. Garden City, N.Y.: Doubleday, Anchor Books, 1972.

Rolfe, John C., trans. *Ammianus Marcellinus.* 3 vols. Loeb Classical Library. Cambridge, Mass.: Harvard University Press, 1971-72. [Abbr. Ammianus Marcellinus]

Rosenstein, J. *Alarich und Stilicho: ein Beitrag zur Geschichte der germanischen Völkerwanderung.* Forschungen zur deutschen Geschichte, vol. 3. 1863. Reprint. Osnabruck: Zeller, 1968.

Ross, Anne. *Everyday Life of the Pagan Celts.* London: Batsford, 1970.

Rostovtzeff, M. *The Social and Economic History of the Roman Empire.* 2d ed., Revised by P. M. Fraser. 2 vols. Oxford: Clarendon Press, 1957.

Russell, J. C. *Late Ancient and Medieval Population.* Transactions of the American Philosophical Society, n.s. 48, pt. 3. Philadelphia, 1958.

Ryan, John. "Irish Learning in the Seventh Century: Being a Review of Some Aspects of F. Masai, *Essai sur les origines de la minature dite irlandaise.* Brussels, 1947." *Journal of the Royal Society of Antiquaries in Ireland* 80 (1950): 164–71.

―――. Ryan, John. *Irish Monasticism: Origins and Early Development.* 1931. Reprint. Ithaca, N.Y.: Cornell University Press, 1972.

Ryan, John Kenneth, trans. *The Confessions of St. Augustine.* 1960. Reprint. Garden City, N.Y.: Doubleday, Image Books, 1958. [Abbr. Augustine *Confessions*]

Sadée, E. "Gutsherrn und Bauern im römischen Rheinland." *Bonner Jahrbücher* 128 (1923): 109–17.

Saint Germain d'Auxerre et son temps: Communications presentées à l'occasion du XIXe congrès réuni à Auxerre pour commémorer le XVe centenaire de la mort de saint Germain d'Auxerre et le centenaire de la Société des sciences historiques et naturelles de l'Yonne. Auxerre: L'Universel, 1950.

Salin, Édouard. *La civilisation mérovingienne d'après les sépultures, les textes et le laboratoire.* 4 vols. Paris: Picard, 1949–59.

Salvian. *De gubernatione Dei.* See Eva M. Sanford, trans.

Salviat, François. *Entremont antique.* Aix-en-Provence, 1973.

Sanford, Eva M., trans. *On the Government of God . . . by Salvian.* New York: Octagon Books, 1966. [Abbr. Salvian]

Saumagne, Ch. "Ouvriers agricoles ou rôdeurs de celliers? Les circoncellions d'Afrique." *Annales d'histoire économique et sociale* 6 (1934): 351–64.

Schindler, Reinhard. *Landesmuseum Trier: Führer durch die vorgeschichtliche und römische Abteilung.* 2d ed. Trier, 1972.

Schmidt, Ludwig. "Bonifatius und der Uebergang der Wandalen nach Afrika." *Historische Vierteljahrsschrift* 2 (1889): 449–62.

―――. *Geschichte der deutschen Stämme bis zum Ausgang der Völkerwanderung.* 8 vols. in 2. Quellen und Forschungen zur alten Geschichte und Geographie, vols. 7, 10, 12, 22, 24, 27, 29–30. Berlin: Weidmann, 1904–18.

―――. "The Sueves, Alans, and Vandals in Spain, 409–429: The Vandal Dominion in Africa, 429–533." *CMH*, 1:304–22.

Schönfeld, Hans-Gottfried. "Zum Begriff 'Therapeutai' bei Philo von Alexandrien." *Revue de Qumrân* 3 (1961–62): 219–40.

Seeck, Otto. "Adoratio." *RE*, vol. 1, cols. 400–401.

―――. "Alaricus. 2." *RE*, vol. 1, cols. 1286–91.

―――. "Arkadios. 2." *RE*, vol. 2, cols. 1137–53.

―――. "Bagaudae." *RE*, vol. 2, cols. 2766–67.

―――. "Bucellarii." *RE*, vol. 3, cols. 934–39.

―――. "Cursus publicus." *RE*, vol. 4, cols. 1846–63.

―――. *Geschichte des Untergangs der antiken Welt.* 6 vols. in 8. Berlin: Siemenroth & Troschel, 1897–1920.

―――. "Iovinus. 5." *RE*, vol. 9, cols. 2012–13.

―――. *Regesten der Kaiser und Päpste für die Jahre 311 bis 476 n. Chr. Vorarbeit zu einer Prosopographie der christlichen Kaiserzeit.* Stuttgart: Metzler, 1919.

―――. "Serena. 2." *RE*, 2d ser., vol. 2, cols. 1672–73.

―――, and George Veith. "Die Schlacht am Frigidus." *Klio* 13 (1913): 451–67.

Seston, William. *Dioclétian et la tétrarchie.* Vol. 1, *Guerres et réformes (284–300).* Bibliothèque des écoles françaises d'Athènes et de Rome, fasc. 162. Paris: Boccard, 1946.

Severus, Sulpicius. See Frederick Russell Hoare, trans.

Showerman, Grant. *The Great Mother of the Gods.* Bulletin of the University of Wisconsin, vol. 43. Madison, 1901.

Sidonius Apollinaris. *Poems and Letters.* See W. B. Anderson, trans.

Sievers, G. R. *Das Leben des Libanius*. 1868. Reprint. Amsterdam: Rodopi, 1969.

Simon, Marcel. *Jewish Sects at the Time of Jesus*. Translated by J. H. Farley. Philadelphia: Fortress Press, 1967.

Sirago, Vito Antonio. *Galla Placidia e la trasformazione politica dell'Occidente*. Université de Louvain, Recueil de travaux d'histoire et de philologie, 4th ser., fasc. 25. Louvain, 1961.

Skene, William F. *Celtic Scotland: A History of Ancient Alban*. Vol. 2, *Church and Culture*. 1877. Reprint. Freeport, N.Y.: Books for Libraries Press, 1971.

Spalding Club. *Sculptured Stones of Scotland*. Aberdeen, 1856–67.

Stein, Ernst. "La disparition du Sénat de Rome à la fin du VIᵉ siècle." *Bulletin de la Classe des lettres et des sciences morales et politiques de l'Académie royale de Belgique*, 5th ser., 25 (1939): 308–22.

———. "Esuvius. 1." *RE*, vol. 6, cols. 696–704.

———. *Geschichte des spätrömischen Reiches*. Vol. 1. Vienna: Seidel, 1928.

Stevenson, Robert B. K. "Pictish Art." In F. T. Wainwright, ed. *The Problem of the Picts*, pp. 97–128. Edinburgh: Nelson, 1955.

Stroheker, Karl Friedrich. *Germanentum und Spätantike*. Edited by Olof Gigon. Bibliothek der alten Welt, Reihe Forschung und Deutung. Zurich: Artemis Verlag, 1965.

———. *Der senatorische Adel im spätantiken Gallien*. Enlarged edition of Habilitationsschrift (Tübingen, 1944). Tübingen, 1948. Reprint. Darmstadt: Wissenschaftliche Buchgesellschaft, 1970.

———. "Zur Rolle der Heermeister fränkischen Abstammung im späten vierten Jahrhundert." *Historia* 4 (1955): 314–30.

Stubbs, William. "Theodorus (7)." William Smith and Henry Wace, eds. *Dictionary of Christian Biography, Literature, Sects, and Doctrines*. 4 vols. London: Murray, 1877–87. 4:926–32.

Sulpicius Severus. *Dialogues*. See Frederick Russell Hoare, trans.

———. *Vita S. Martini*. See Frederick Russell Hoare, trans.; Jacques Fontaine, trans.

Sundwall, Johannes. *Abhandlungen zur Geschichte des ausgehenden Römertums*. 1919. Reprint. New York: Arno Press, 1975.

Tacitus. *The Agricola and the Germania*. See H. Mattingly, trans.

Tamassia, G. "Egidio e Siagrio. *Rivista storica italiana* 3 (1886): 193–234.

Tarn, W. W. *Hellenistic Civilisation*. 3d ed. Revised by W. W. Tarn and G. T. Griffith. Cleveland: World Publishing Co., 1969.

Tengström, Emin. *Donatisten und Katholiken: sociale, wirtschaftliche, und politische Aspekte einer nordafrikanischen Kirchenspaltung*. Acta Universitatis Gothoburgensis, Studia Graeca et Latina Gothoburgensia, vol. 18. Göteborg, 1964.

Thackeray, H. St. J., Ralph Marcus, and Louis H. Feldman, trans. *Josephus*. Vols. 4–9, *Jewish Antiquities*. 6 vols. Loeb Classical Library. London: Heinemann, 1930–65. [Abbr. Josephus *Jewish Antiquities*]

Theil, Edmund. *St. Prokulus bei Naturns*. 2d ed. Laurin Kunst-Führer, vol. 1. Bolzano: Verlagsanstalt Athesia, 1972.

Thomas, Charles. "The Animal Art of the Scottish Iron Age and Its Origins. *Archaeological Journal* 118 (1961): 14–64.

———. *Britain and Ireland in Early Christian Times*, A.D. 400–800. New York: McGraw-Hill, 1971.

Thompson, E. A. *The Early Germans*. Oxford: Clarendon Press, 1965.

———. *A History of Attila and the Huns*. Oxford: Clarendon Press, 1948.

———. "Olympiodorus of Thebes." *Classical Quarterly* 38 (1944): 43–52.

———. "Peasant Revolts in Late Roman Gaul and Spain." *Past and Present* 2 (1952): 11–23.

———. "The Settlement of the Barbarians in Southern Gaul." *Journal of Roman Studies* 46

(1956): 65–75.

———. "The Visigoths from Fritigern to Euric." *Historia* 12 (1963): 105–26.

———. *The Visigoths in the Time of Ulfila*. Oxford: Clarendon Press, 1966.

———. "Zosimus on the end of Roman Britain." *Antiquity* 30 (1956): 163–67.

Toutain, Jules. *Les cultes païens dans l'Empire romain*. Pt. 1, *Les provinces latines*, vols. 1–3. Bibliothèque de l'École des hautes études, Sciences religieuses, vols. 20, 25, 31. Paris: Leroux, 1907–20.

Treitinger, Otto. *Die oströmischen Kaiser- und Reichidee nach ihren Gestaltung im höfischen Zeremoniell*. Bad Homburg vor der Höhe: Gentner, 1969.

Trevelyan, G. M. *History of England*. Vol. 1, *From the Earliest Times to the Reformation*. 1926. Reprint. Garden City, N.Y.: Doubleday, Anchor Books, 1953.

Twyman, Briggs L. "Aëtius and the Aristocracy." *Historia* 19 (1970): 480–503.

Ullmann, Walter. "Leo I and the Theme of Papal Primacy." *Journal of Theological Studies*, n.s. 11 (1960): 25–51.

Vannerus, J. "Nouvelle hypothèse sur le 'Long Mur' de Bitbourt." *Revue belge de philologie et d'histoire* 11 (1933): 141–45.

Várady, László. *Die Auflösung des Altertums: Beiträge zu einer Umdeutung der alten Geschichte*. Budapest: Akadémiai Kiadó, 1978.

———. *Das letzte Jahrhundert Pannoniens*, 376–476. Amsterdam: Hakkert, 1969.

Versnel, H. S. *Triumphus: An Inquiry into the Origin, Development, and Meaning of the Roman Triumph*. Leiden: Brill, 1970.

Volbach, W. Fritz. *Early Decorative Textiles*. London: Hamlyn, 1969.

Vyver, A. van de. "Le victoire contre les alemans et la conversion de Clovis." *Revue belge de philologie et d'histoire* 15 (1936): 898–914.

Waddell, Helen. *The Desert Fathers: Translations from the Latin*. Ann Arbor: University of Michigan Press, 1972.

Wainwright, F. T., ed. *The Problem of the Picts*. Edinburgh: Nelson, 1955.

———. *The Souterrains of Southern Pictland*. London: Routledge & Kegan Paul, 1963.

Walde, Alois. *Lateinisches etymologisches Wörterbuch*. 4th ed. Reprint of 3d ed. Edited by J. B. Hofmann. 3 vols. Heidelberg: Winter, 1965.

Walker, G. S. M., ed. and trans. *Sancti Columbani Opera*. Dublin: Dublin Institute for Advanced Studies, 1957.

Wallace-Hadrill, J. M. *The Barbarian West, A.D. 400–1000: The Early Middle Ages*. New York: Harper & Row, Torchbooks, 1962.

———. "Gothia and Romania." *Bulletin of the John Rylands Library* 44 (1961): 213–37.

———. *The Long-haired Kings*. New York: Barnes & Noble, 1962.

Walter, Christopher. "Raising on a Shield in Byzantine Iconography." *Revue des études byzantines* 33 (1975): 133–75.

Ward, John H. "The Notitia Dignitatum." *Latomus* 33 (1974): 397–434.

Warmington, B. H. *Carthage*. Baltimore, Md.: Penguin Books, 1960.

———. *The North African Provinces from Diocletian to the Vandal Conquest*. Cambridge: At the University Press, 1954.

Warrington, John, ed. and trans. *Caesar's War Commentaries: De bello gallico and De bello civili*. Everyman's Library, Classical, no. 702. London: Dent, 1953. [Abbr. Gaius Julius Caesar, *De bello gallico*]

Waterer, John W. "Irish Book-Satchels or Budgets." *Medieval Archaeology* 12 (1968): 70–82.

Weinstock, Stefan. *Libri Fvlgvrales*. Papers of the British School at Rome, vol. 19, n.s. 6. Rome, 1951.

Weiskotten, Herbert T., ed. and trans. *Sancti Augustini vita scripta a Possidio episcopo*. Revised text. Princeton, N.J.: Princeton University Press, 1919. [Abbr. Possidius]

Wenley, A. G. "The Question of the Po-Shan-Hsiang-Lu." *Archives of the Chinese Art Society of America* 3 (1948–49): 5–12.

Wermelinger, Otto. *Rom und Pelagius*. Stuttgart: Hiersemann, 1975.

Werner, Joachim. *Beiträge zur Archaeologie des Attila-Reiches: Vorgetragen am 4. März 1955: Bayerische Akademie der Wissenschaften, Philosophisch-historische Klasse, Abhandlungen n.f. 38 A/B*. Munich: Verlag der Bayerischen Akademie der Wissenschaften, 1956.

Wes, M. A. *Das Ende des Kaisertums im Westen des römischen Reichs*. Archaeologische Studien van het Nederlands Historisch Instituut te Rome, pt. 2. The Hague: Staatsdruckerei, 1967.

Wheeler, Sir Mortimer. *Rome Beyond the Imperial Frontiers*. 1954. Reprint. Harmondsworth: Pelican Books, 1955.

White, Donald A. *Litus Saxonicum: The British Saxon Shore in Scholarship and History*. Madison: State Historical Society of Wisconsin for Department of History, University of Wisconsin, 1961.

White, Lynn, Jr., ed. *The Transformation of the Roman World: Gibbon's Problem After Two Centuries*. UCLA Center for Medieval and Renaissance Studies, Contributions, no. 3. 1966. Reprint. Berkeley and Los Angeles: University of California Press, 1973.

Whitelock, Dorothy. *The Beginnings of English Society*. 2d ed. 1965. Reprint. Pelican History of England, vol. 2. Harmondsworth: Pelican Books, 1971.

Wightman, Edith M. *Roman Trier and the Treveri*. London: Hart-Davis, 1970.

Will, Ernest, "De l'Euphrate au Rhin: étude sur quelques motifs ornementaux." *Syria* 31 (1954): 271–85.

———. "Die Kunst im römischen Gallien." In Eggers et al., *Kelten*, pp. 91–125.

Wolfson, Harry Austryn. *Philo: Foundations of Religious Philosophy in Judaism, Christianity, and Islam*. 2 vols. Cambridge, Mass.: Harvard University Press, 1947.

Woodward, Llewellyn. *Christianity and Nationalism in the Later Roman Empire*. London: Longmans, Green, 1916.

Wright, F. A. "On Jerome's Correspondence with Roman Women." In F. A. Wright, trans. *Select Letters of St. Jerome*, pp. 483–97. Loeb Classical Library. London: Heinemann, 1933.

Wright, Wilmer Cave, trans. *The Works of the Emperor Julian*. 3 vols. Loeb Classical Library. London: Heinemann, 1913.

Zahn, Eberhard. *Die Igeler Säule bei Trier*. Cologne: Rheinischer Verein für Denkmalpflege und Heimatschutz, 1970.

Zeller, Joseph. "Das Concilium der septem provinciae in Arelate." *Westdeutsche Zeitschrift für Geschichte und Kunst* (1905): 1–19.

Zimmer, H. *Pelagius in Irland: Texte und Untersuchungen zur patristischen Literatur*. Berlin: Weidmann, 1901.

Zosimus. *Historia nova*. See James J. Buchanan and Harold T. Davis, trans.

INDEX